OXFORD MONOGRAPHS ON MUSIC

HAYDN'S KEYBOARD MUSIC

Haydn's Keyboard Music
Studies in Performance Practice

BERNARD HARRISON

CLARENDON PRESS · OXFORD
1997

Oxford University Press, Great Clarendon Street, Oxford OX2 6DP
Oxford New York
Athens Auckland Bangkok Bombay Bogota
Buenos Aires Calcutta Cape Town Dar es Salaam Delhi
Florence Hong Kong Istanbul Karachi
Kuala Lumpur Madras Madrid Melbourne
Mexico City Nairobi Paris Singapore
Taipei Tokyo Toronto
and associated companies in
Berlin Ibadan

Oxford is a trade mark of Oxford University Press

Published in the United States
by Oxford University Press Inc., New York

British Library Cataloguing in Publication Data
Data available

Library of Congress Cataloging in Publication Data
Harrison, Bernard.
Haydn's keyboard music : studies in performance practice / Bernard Harrison
p.   cm.—(Oxford monographs on music)
includes bibliographical references (p.   ).
1. Haydn, Joseph 1732–1809. Piano music. 2. Performance
practice (Music)—18th century. I. Title. II. Series.
Ml410.H4H315   1997   95–49505   786'. 143—dc20
ISBN 0–19–816325–8

1 3 5 7 9 10 8 6 4 2

Typeset by Hope Services (Abingdon) Ltd.
Printed in Great Britain
on acid-free paper by
Biddles Ltd.
Guildford and King's Lynn

Dedicated to the memory of
Bob Harrison (1958–1996)

PREFACE

◊

A BASIC premiss implicit in the title of this book is that performance practices vary not only from one era to another, but from one composer to another, and that characteristic notational conventions and related performance practices may be associated with different periods in the career of one composer. Although it is possible to recognize facets of performance practice associated with music from the second half of the eighteenth century which are quite distinct from performance practices appropriate in the music of J. S. Bach or Beethoven, it is no more possible to speak of a single common practice in the performance of Classical music than it is to reduce the diversity of Baroque performance practice to a single, common practice. Hence, in this book, I concentrate on the music of a single composer, who has, moreover, been rather neglected in the performance practice literature by comparison with the numerous studies devoted to the performance of J. S. Bach's, Mozart's, and Beethoven's music.

The study of performance practice is closely associated with the study of compositional style and is inseparable from questions of chronology. Articulation, ornaments, and other facets of performance practice are not appendages to the composition but crucial aspects of the style and expression of that work and it is for this reason, rather than for any particular concern with the ideology of authenticity, that it seems to me important to devote extensive chapters to minutiae of performance. Haydn's notation of performance directions is not constant throughout his career and important phases of notational revision may be identified in the mid-1760s and again in the early 1780s. From the mid-1760s Haydn controlled facets of performance practice as part of the compositional process rather than leaving such matters solely in the domain of the performer. Consequently the manner in which we interpret performance directions must take account of the conventions operating in a particular work. A symbol may have a different meaning in an early Haydn

work to what it has in a later work and the degree to which the crucial refinements of performance are represented in Haydn's notation
is very different in an early minuet and an Adagio movement from
the 1790s. In the concentration of this book on Haydn's keyboard
music the view is also implicit that performance practices and notational conventions vary from one genre to another. Thus, for
instance, notational conventions regarding appoggiaturas in vocal
music should not be regarded as holding any particular force in
Haydn's keyboard music and evidence concerning the tempos of
minuets in Haydn's 'London' Symphonies do not inform us about
appropriate tempos for Tempo di Menuet movements in Haydn's
keyboard compositions. The suggestions regarding performance
practice put forward in this book cannot be assumed, therefore, to
apply to other genres in the Haydn canon, nor to the keyboard music
of other composers.

It should be understood that however strongly I argue in this study
for or against a particular interpretation, the views I express are interpretations, based, not infrequently, on my reading of problematic
evidence. There are rarely in the study of performance practice
clearly established historical truths. I highlight throughout the views
of others which conflict with my own and, while it is important to
recognize the validity of contrary opinions, the acceptance that there
are few questions in performance practice which do not allow a wide
variety of interpretations should be balanced by the recognition that
the flexible performance practice, which arises from ambiguous or
scanty evidence, contains problematic interpretations which are
injurious to our perception of Haydn's compositions. It is possible to
find some evidence to support any interpretation, yet this evidence
must be constantly challenged if inappropriate tempos, anachronistic
ornamentation or pedalling, or impoverished improvisation, which
are as damaging to a work as wrong notes, are to be avoided.

Eighteenth-century treatises on performance practice provide a
primary source of information for this study. The large corpus of
eighteenth-century writings on performance gives the impression of
immense diversity in practice, but its evidence of a mixed practice in
relation to many problems of performance practice, while representative of the era as a whole, is problematic in relation to the performance practice of a specific composer. Famously, both theorists and
composers differed on their understandings of the term *andantino* and
while C. P. E. Bach argued strongly for the performance of *Vorschläge*

beginning on the beat he acknowledged that this was not a universal practice. Obviously in some areas of performance practice (teachings on accentuation, for instance) there is a general consensus among eighteenth-century writers which can be assumed to be of relevance to Haydn's performance practice. Yet, on many more controversial subjects, every eighteenth-century treatise and every view on performance expressed by the writers of these treatises cannot apply equally to the keyboard music of Haydn. Such conflicting views must be assessed in relation to Haydn's music, especially in relation to the evidence of Haydn's notational habits as established from the study of his autograph manuscripts and other good sources. This evidence is often more specific than the general comments of theorists (as for instance in relation to questions of articulation) but correlations between the evidence of the music and certain treatises also suggest the special relevance of a particular body of theoretical writings. This book has benefited immensely from the research of the late Frederick Neumann over the past thirty years, in particular, from his emphasis on the true diversity of eighteenth-century theory and from his concern to deduce evidence about performance practice from the music itself. Yet as regards the performance of Haydn's music my conclusions are often in conflict with Neumann's stated views. While Neumann argued against the overreliance of some earlier scholars on the evidence of C. P. E. Bach's writings on performance, I argue that C. P. E. Bach's teachings have an important place in the study of Haydn's performance practice.

The keyboard music by Haydn addressed in this study is, in the first instance, those works which, as far as can be established, are genuine Haydn compositions. The genres addressed are the solo sonatas (Hoboken *Werkgruppe* XVI), solo *Klavierstücke* and variation sets (Hoboken *Werkgruppe* XVII), keyboard trios (Hoboken *Werkgruppe* XV), accompanied divertimenti (Hoboken *Werkgruppe* XIV), and concertos (Hoboken *Werkgruppe* XVIII). Greater emphasis is placed on those works which may be attributed to Haydn with confidence, and arguments concerning performance practice are not based on evidence adduced from works which are problematic as regards attribution. For certain subjects addressed, the evidence of those works which are transmitted in reliable sources is emphasized above those works which have a poor source history. In adducing evidence of performance practice from the music, the extant autograph manuscripts are of crucial importance, since they provide the clearest picture of the composer's notational practices. Other sources can be shown to be highly reliable in their presentation of Haydn's detailed performance indications (the English editions of the late sonatas and trios for instance) but to varying degrees Haydn's often very precise notation, of ornaments and articulation especially, suffered in the process of transmission. The performer of Haydn's keyboard music is today particularly well served by modern editors and publishers. Late nineteenth- and early twentieth-century editions of Haydn's keyboard works, frequently characterized by readings based on poor sources, by the alteration of Haydn's notation, and by editorial intervention which is strongly influenced by contemporary pianistic technique, have been replaced by an exemplary *Gesamtausgabe* (*Joseph Haydn Werke*) and by an array of practical editions, which are intended, to varying degrees, to be more 'performer friendly' than *JHW*. Yet the sources on which these editions are based are of variable quality and in performance and the study of performance practice it is well to remember that even the best edition of a work with a poor source history requires a degree of informed emendation beyond that which may be appropriate for a work surviving in an autograph source.

In the following study published translations are acknowledged in footnotes; where a translation is not acknowledged it is my own. I have retained German and sometimes French terminology in preference to an English translation when the latter is problematic or less precise. Thus the German term *Anschlag* is used because there is no precise standard English equivalent; the term appoggiatura is used in Chapter 7 when discussing a performance of the ornament on the beat, but the more flexible term *Vorschlag* is employed when referring to a pre-beat performance or to instances in which the metrical placement is ambiguous. Problems of terminology which have a direct bearing on an argument are discussed in the course of the book. I am particularly grateful to Dr Mary O'Neill for her generous advice on matters of translation.

I am grateful to the staff of the following libraries for help given in the preparation of this book and for supplying microfilms and photocopies of source materials: Music Faculty Library, Oxford; Bodleian Library, Oxford; Cambridge University Library; Music Faculty Library, Cambridge; Rowe Music Library, King's College, Cambridge; Fitzwilliam Museum, Cambridge; British Library, London; Royal College of Music, London; Queen Mother Library, Aberdeen; Universitäts-Bibliothek, Basel; Musikwissenschaftliches

Institut, Basel; Staatsbibliothek Preußischer Kulturbesitz, Berlin; Bibliothèque Nationale, Paris; Hessische Landes- und Hochschulbibliothek, Darmstadt; Niederösterreichisches Landesarchiv, Vienna; Gesellschaft der Musikfreunde, Vienna; Stadtbibliothek, Vienna; Library of Congress, Washington DC; New York Public Library.

Permission has generously been granted by Henle Verlag to use the text of *Joseph Haydn Werke, XXI: Stücke für das Laufwerk (Flötenuhrstücke)* (Munich: Henle, 1984) for examples 6.30–31, 8.5 and 8.16. I am also grateful to the University of Nebraska Press, Faber & Faber, and Indiana University Press for permission to reproduce material from Raymond Haggh's translation of Türk's *Klavierschule*, William J. Mitchell's translation of C. P. E. Bach's *Versuch über die wahre Art das Clavier zu spielen* and A. Peter Brown's *Joseph Haydn's Keyboard Music: Sources and Style*.

I have benefited from the comments and criticisms of many friends and colleagues in the preparation of this book. I am especially indebted to Dr. Susan Wollenberg who supervised my doctoral dissertation at Oxford and who subsequently commented on drafts of new material, particularly Chapter 5. I am also grateful to Dr. Harry Johnstone for his careful reading of my doctoral dissertation, to Professor Denis McCaldin for his comments on a later draft, and to an anonymous OUP reader who made numerous helpful criticisms and many suggestions regarding important details. It is a also a pleasure to acknowledge the professionalism and courtesy of Bruce Philipps and the OUP editorial staff, in particular, Helen Foster and Janet Moth. Finally, I owe many debts, too numerous to specify, to my family.

CONTENTS

◊

LIST OF MUSIC EXAMPLES

◊

LIST OF TABLES

◊

ABBREVIATIONS

◇

AM	*Acta Musicologica*
AMz	*Allgemeine musikalische Zeitung*
BJb	*Bach Jahrbuch*
CCLN	H. C. Robbins Landon, ed., *The Collected Correspondence and London Notebooks of Joseph Haydn*
EK	*Entwurf-Katalog*
EM	*Early Music*
GSJ	*Galpin Society Journal*
H.	E. E. Helm, *Thematic Catalogue of the Works of Carl Philipp Emanuel Bach*
Hob.	A. van Hoboken, *Joseph Haydn: Thematisch-bibliographisches Werkverzeichnis*
H-St	*Haydn-Studien*
HYb	*Haydn Yearbook*
HV	*Haydn Verzeichnis*
JAMS	*Journal of the American Musicological Society*
JHW	*Joseph Haydn Werke*
JRMA	*Journal of the Royal Musical Association*
Mf	*Die Musikforschung*
MJb	*Mozart Jahrbuch*
ML	*Music and Letters*
MQ	*Musical Quarterly*
MR	*Music Review*
MT	*Musical Times*
NMA	*W. A. Mozart: Neue Ausgabe sämtliche Werke*
ÖMz	*Österreichische Musikzeitschrift*
PRMA	*Proceedings of the Royal Musical Association*
RISM	*Répertoire international des sources musicales*
Wq.	A. Wotquenne, *Catalogue thématique des œuvres de Charles Philippe Emmanuel Bach*
ZfM	*Zeitschrift für Musik*
ZfMw	*Zeitschrift für Musikwissenschaft*

KEY

◊

Anh. = Anhang

Publications

A. P. Brown, *Joseph Haydn's Keyboard Music: Sources and Style* (Bloomington, Ind.: Indiana University Press, 1986).

F. Eibner and G. Jarecki, eds., *Joseph Haydn: Klavierstücke* (Vienna: Universal, 1975).

S. Gerlach, ed., *Haydn: Klavierstücke, Klaviervariationen* (2nd edn., Munich: Henle, 1981).

A. van Hoboken, *Joseph Haydn: Thematisch-bibliographisches Werkverzeichnis*, 3 vols. (Mainz: Schott, 1957–78).

JHW XV/2: *Konzerte für Klavier (Cembalo) und Orchester*, ed. H. Walter and B. Wackernagel (Munich: Henle, 1983).

JHW XVI: *Concertini und Divertimenti*, ed. H. Walter and H. Nakano (Munich: Henle, 1987).

JHW XVII/1–3: *Klaviertrios*, ed. W. Stockmeier (XVII/1–2) and S. Gerlach (XVII/3) (Munich: Henle, 1970–86).

JHW XVIII/1–3: *Klaviersonaten*, ed. G. Feder (Munich: Henle, 1966–70).

C. Landon, *Joseph Haydn: Sämtliche Klaviersonaten*, 3 vols. (Vienna: Universal, 1964–6; 3rd edn., Vienna: Universal, 1972). *Kritische Anmerkungen* (Vienna: Universal, 1982).

H. C. Robbins Landon, *The Piano Trios of Joseph Haydn: Foreword to the First Critical Complete Edition* (Vienna: Doblinger, 1970).

J. P. Larsen and G. Feder, *The New Grove Haydn* (London: Macmillan, 1982).

K. Päsler, *Joseph Haydn: Klavierwerke*, *JHW* XVI/1–3 (Leipzig: Breitkopf & Härtel, 1918).

On questions of authenticity and chronology see esp. the worklist in *The New Grove Haydn*; Brown, *Joseph Haydn's Keyboard Music: Sources and Style*; and S. Fruehwald, *Authenticity Problems in Joseph Haydn's Early Instrumental Works: A Stylistic Investigation* (Monographs in

Musicology, 8; New York: Pendragon, 1988). See also my reviews of Brown and Fruehwald in *ML* 68/3 (July 1987): 276–8 and 71/1 (Feb. 1990): 98–100.

Musical key signatures are given in abbreviated form with an upper-case letter indicating a major key, and a lower-case letter a minor one.

Table I. *Sonatas*

Key	Numbering				Chronology			Extant autograph	Remarks
	Hob.	C. Landon	JHW XVIII	Päsler	New Grove	C. Landon	A.P. Brown		
C	1	10	1	1	[?c.1750–5]	pre-1766	1750s		
Bb	2	11	1	2	[pre-?1760]	pre-1766	c.1760		
	2.a	21	1/Anh	–	[?c.1765–70]	–	–		lost
	2.b	22	1/Anh	–	[?c.1765–70]	–	–		lost
	2.c	23	1/Anh	–	[?c.1765–70]	–	–		lost
	2.d	24	1/Anh	–	[?c.1765–70]	–	–		lost
	2.e	25	1/Anh	–	[?c.1765–70]	–	–		lost
	2.g	26	1/Anh	–	[?c.1765–70]	–	–		lost
	2.h	27	1/Anh	–	[?c.1765–70]	–	–		lost
C	3	14	1	3	[?c.1765]	pre-1766	c.1761/2– c.1767		
D	4	9	1	4	[?c.1765]	pre-1766	c.1761/2– c.1767		
A	5	8	1	5	[?c.1750–5]	pre-1766	1750–5	x (i–iii)	
G	6	13	1	6	[pre-?1760]	pre-1766	c.1760		
C	7	2	1	7	[pre-?1760]	ore-1766	1750s		
G	8	1	1	8	[pre-?1760]	pre-1766	c.1760		
F	9	3	1	9	[pre-?1760]	pre-1766	1750s		
C	10	6	1	10	[pre-?1760]	pre-1766	1750s		
G	11	5	ii–iii 1/Anh	11	–	pre-1766	–		
A	12	12	1	12	[?c.1750–5]	pre-1766	1750s		
E	13	15	1	13	[pre-?1760]	pre-1766	c.1760		

Key	Numbering				Chronology			Extant autograph	Remarks
	Hob.	C. Landon	JHW XVIII	Päsler	New Grove	C. Landon	A. P. Brown		
D	14	16	1	14	[pre-?1760]	pre-1766	c.1761/2– c.1767		
C	15	–	–	15	(Spurious)	–	–		spurious
Eb	16	–	1	16	[c.1750–5]	–	1750–5		
Bb	17	–	–	17	(Spurious)	–	–		spurious (by Schwanenberger)
D	XVII: D1	7	1	–	–	pre-1766	1750s		
G	XVI: G1	4	1	–	[pre-?1760]	pre-1766	1750s		
Eb	Es2	17	1	–	[?c.1755]	–	1750–5		
Eb	Es3	18	1	–	[?c.1764]	c.1765–6	1750–5		
D	XIV: 5	28	1	–	[c.1767–70]	pre-1766	c.1767–8	x (fragment)	
c/E	47	19	1	47	[?c.1765]		c.1765		
F/f	47	57	–	47	pre-1788	pub.1788	–		
Eb	45	29	1	45	1766	1766	1766	x	
D	19	30	1	19	1767	1767	1767	x	
Ab	46	31	1	46	[c.1767–70]	c.1767–8	c.1767–8		
Bb	18	20	1	18	[c.1771–3]	c.1766–7	c.1767–8	x (fragment)	
g	44	32	1	44	[c.1771–3]	c.1768–70	c.1770		
c	20	33	2	20	1771	1771	begun 1771; completed by 1780	x (incomplete)	pub. with xvi: 35–9; Artaria, op. 30
C	21	36	2	21	1773	1773	1773	x (incomplete)	Hob. xvi: 21–6, Kurzböck
E	22	37	2	22	1773	1773	1773	x	

Key									
F	23	38	2	23	1773	1773	1773		
D	24	39	2	24	?1773	1773	1773		
E♭	25	40	2	25	?1773	1773	1773		
A	26	41	2	26	1773	1773	1773	x (incomplete)	
G	27	42	2	27	pre-1776	1776	late 1760s–1776	x	Hob. xvi: 27–32
E♭	28	43	2	28	pre-1776	1776	possibly before 1774; by 1776		*EK* Sechs Sonaten von [1]776 Hummel, op. 14
F	29	44	2	29	1774	1774[–6]	1774	x (fragment)	
A	30	45	2	30	pre-1776	1776	possibly before 1774; by 1776		
E	31	46	2	31	pre-1776	1776	possibly before 1774; by 1776		
b	32	47	2	32	pre-1776	1776	possibly before 1774; by 1776		
D	33	34	3	33	pre-1778	c.1771–3	mid-1770s		Hob. xvi: 33–4, 43, Beardmore & Birchall
e	34	53	3	34	pre-1784	c.1781–2	c.1780–3		
A♭	43	35	3	43	pre-1783	c.1771–3	mid-1770s		
C	35	48	2	35	pre-1780	c.1777–9	late 1770s–1780		Hob. xvi: 35–9, and 20; Artaria, op. 30
c♯	36	49	2	36	[?c.1770–5]	c.1777–9	mid-1770s		
D	37	50	2	37	pre-1780	c.1777–9	late 1770s–1780		

Key	Numbering				Chronology			Extant autograph	Remarks
	Hob.	C. Landon	JHW XVIII	Päsler	New Grove	C. Landon	A. P. Brown		
Eb	38	51	2	38	[?1770–5]	c.1777–9	mid-1770s		
G	39	52	2	39	pre-1780	1780	late 1770s–1780		
G	40	54	3	40	pre-1784	c.1782–4	1784		Hob. XVI: 40–2; Bossler, op. 37
Bb	41	55	3	41	pre-1784	c.1782–4	1784		
D	42	56	3	42	pre-1784	c.1782–4	1784		
C	48	58	3	48	pre-5 Apr 1789 1789	1789	1789		Breitkopf
Eb	49	59	3	49	1789–90	1789–90	1789–90	x	Artaria, op. 66; Bland, op. 66
C	50	60	3	50	[c.1794–5]	1794–5?	50/ii: 1794 (1793?) 50/i & iii: 1795	x	Caulfield, op. 79
D	51	61	3	51	[?c.1794–5]	1794–5?	1791–6		Breitkopf & Härtel, op. 93
Eb	52	62	3	52	1794	1794	1794	x	Longman, Clementi, op. 78; Artaria, op. 82

Note: The attribution to Haydn of many of the early sonatas listed here remains notoriously problematic. XVI: 15 and 17 are now unanimously regarded as spurious; Es2 and Es3 continue to be a matter of dispute but seem to me also to be spurious; the attribution to Haydn of Hob. XVI: 16 (printed in *JHW* XVIII/1), Hob. XVI: 5, and the F major/f minor version of Hob. XVI: 47 (C. Landon, no. 57) is very doubtful; the authenticity of Hob. XVI: 11 remains questionable; and although printed in the three major complete editions listed above, the authenticity of Hob. XVI: 12/i should also be regarded as questionable. Of the sonatas listed in the first twenty-eight entries of the above table, perhaps no more than fifteen of those extant are authentic Haydn sonatas.

TABLE II. *Klavierstücke, Variations*

Key	Numbering			Chronology	Extant autograph	Remarks
	Hob.	Henle	Universal	New Grove	A. P. Brown	
G	XVII: 1	1	p. 1	1765	1765	x
A	XVII: 2	2	p. 22 (in G)	[?c.1765]	c.1765	
			p. 41			
Eb	XVII: 3	3	p. 33	[c.1770–4]	c.1770–4	
C	XVII: 4	4	p. 12	1789	1789	
C	XVII: 5	5	p. 48	?Nov. 1790	1790	
f	XVII: 6	6	p. 53	1793	1793	x
D	XVII: 7	Anh. 1	–	pre-1766 [?c.1750–5]	1750s (–1766)	doubtful
F	XVII: 9	Anh. 2	p. 69	pre-1786	c.1785–6	x (sketch)

Notes: The Universal edition of Haydn's *Klavierstücke* also includes the authentic keyboard duet 'Il maestro e lo scolare', Hob. XVIIa: 1; the authentic keyboard arrangement of the variations on 'Gott erhalte den Kaiser', Hob. III: 77/ii; an authentic version for solo keyboard of Hob. XV: 22/ii (printed in *JHW* XVII/3 Anh.); an authentic arrangement of Hob. III: 41/iv; and a questionable arrangement for keyboard of Hob. XIX: 27 (Hob. XVII: 10).

Tables

TABLE III. *Concertos*

Key	Hob. no.	Chronology		Extant autograph
		New Grove	A. P. Brown	
Authentic				
C	XVIII: 1	?1756	1756(?)	x
D	XVIII: 2	pre-1767	?1756 or earlier	
F	XVIII: 3	pre-1771	1762–7	
G	XVIII: 4	pre-1781 [?*c.*1770]	?mid-1770s– 1781	
F	XVIII: 6	pre-1766	?1756–66	
D	XVIII: 11	pre-1784	mid-1770s–1784 (1780?)	
Probably authentic				
C	XVIII: 5	pre-1763	mid-1750s	
C	XVIII: 8	pre-1766	mid-1750s	
C	XVIII: 10	pre-1771	*c.*1760–2	
Doubtful				
F	XVIII: 7	pre-1766		
G	XVIII: 9	pre-1767		

TABLE IV. *Accompanied Divertimentos and Concertinos*

Numbering		Chronology		Remarks
Hob.	*JHW*	New Grove	A. P. Brown	
XIV: 1	XVII/1	pre-1766	*c.*1765–6	
XIV: 3	XVI	pre-1771 [pre *c.*1767]	*c.*1770	
XIV: 4	XVI	1764	1764	extant autograph
XIV: 7	XVI	pre-*c.*1767	1762–*c.*1770	
XIV: 8	XVI	*c.*1768–72	pre-1787	
XIV: 9	XVI	pre-*c.* 1767	1772	
XIV: 10	XVI	*c.*1764–7	*c.* pre-1782	
XIV: 11	XVI	1760	1760	
XIV: 12	XVI	pre-1772 [pre *c.*1767]	*c.*1760	
XIV: 13	XVI	pre-*c.*1767	*c.*1760	
XVIII: F2	XVI	pre-*c.*1767	*c.*1760	
XIV: C1	XVI Anh.	pre-1772 [pre *c.*1767]		questionable
XIV: C2	XVI Anh.	pre-*c.*1767	after 1762	doubtful

TABLE V. *Trios*

Numbering		Chronology			Autograph	Remarks
Hob. xv	JHW	H.C.R. Landon	New Grove	A. P. Brown		
1	XVII/1	5	pre-1766 [?c.1760–2]			Forster, op. 42
2	XVII/1	17	?c.1767–71			
34	XVII/1	11	pre-1771 [pre-?1760]			
35	XVII/1	10	pre-1771 [?c.1764–5]			
36	XVII/1	12	pre-1774 [pre-?1760]			
37	XVII/1	1	pre-1766 [pre-?1760]			
38	XVII/1	13	pre-1769 [pre-?1760]			
40	XVII/1	6	[?c.1760]			
41	XVII/1	7	pre-1767 [pre-?1760]			
f1	XVII/1	14	pre-?1760			
C1	XVII/1	2	pre-1766 [pre-?1760]			
33	XVII/1/Anh.	8	pre-1771 [pre-?1760]			lost
D1	XVII/1/Anh.	9	pre-1771			lost
5	XVII/2	18	pre-25 Oct 1784	Sept.–Oct. 1784	x (incomplete)	Forster, op. 40
6	XVII/2	19	1784	late 1784–early 1785	x (lost fragment)	xv: 6–8
7	XVII/2	20	1785	no later than autumn 1785	x	Artaria, op. 40
8	XVII/2	21	pre-26 Nov. 1785	no later than autumn 1785		
9	XVII/2	22	1785	late summer or early autumn 1785	x	xv: 9–10, 2 Forster, op. 42

Numbering			Chronology		Autograph	Remarks
Hob. xv	JHW	HCR. Landon	New Grove	A. P. Brown		
10	XVII/2	23	pre-28 Oct. 1785	late summer or early autumn 1785		
11	XVII/2	24	pre-8 Mar. 1789 [pre-16 Nov. 1788]	Aug.–16 Nov. 1788		xv: 11–13
12	XVII/2	25	pre-8 Mar. 1789 [1788–9]	pre-mid-Mar. 1789		Artaria, op. 57
13	XVII/2	26	[pre-29 Mar.] 1789	pre-29 Mar. 1789		
14	XVII/2	27	pre-[?11 Jan.] 1790	pre-11 Jan. 1790		Artaria, op. 61; L&B, op. 68
15	XVII/2	29	[pre-28 June] 1790	pre-19(?) Apr. 1790		Artaria, op. 62; Bland, op. 59
16	XVII/2	28	[pre-28 June] 1790	pre-12 Apr. 1790		Artaria, op. 63; Bland, op. 59
17	XVII/2	30	pre-?20 June 1790	pre-20 June 1790		Artaria, op. 68; Bland, op. 59
18	XVII/3	32	pre-15 Nov. 1794	pre-autumn 1794		Hob. xv: 18–20; L&B, op. 70
19	XVII/3	33	pre-15 Nov. 1794	pre-autumn 1794		
20	XVII/3	34	pre-15 Nov. 1794	pre-autumn 1794		

21	35	XVII/3	pre-23 May 1795	late 1794–early 1795		xv: 21–3 Preston, op. 71
22	36	XVII/3	pre-23 May 1795	late 1794–early 1795		
23	37	XVII/3	pre-23 May 1795	late 1794–early 1795		
24	38	XVII/3	pre-9 Oct. 1795	spring–summer 1795		xv: 24–6 L&B, op. 73
25	39	XVII/3	pre-9 Oct. 1795	spring–summer 1795		
26	40	XVII/3	pre-9 Oct. 1795 [?1794]	spring–summer 1795		
27	43	XVII/3	pre-20 Apr. 1797 [pre-? Aug. 1795]	1794–5		xv: 27–9 L&B, op. 75
28	44	XVII/3	pre-20 Apr. 1797 [pre-? Aug. 1795]	1794–5		
29	45	XVII/3	pre-20 Apr. 1797 [pre-? Aug. 1795]	1794–5		
30	42	XVII/3	pre-7 Oct. 1797 [?16 Apr.–9 Nov. 1796]	pre-9 Nov. 1796	x (fragment)	Artaria, op. 79
31	41	XVII/3	1795	1794–early 1795	x	Traeg
32	31	XVII/3	pre-14 June 1794	1791–early 1792		Artaria, op. 70; Preston

Notes: Nos. 3–4, 15–16 in H. C. R. Landon's chronological list of trios are arrangements and/or compilations of dubious authenticity.
Hob. xv: 3–4 (*JHW* XVII/2 Anh.) are very probably by Pleyel.
L&B=Longman & Broderip.

I

Instruments and Keyboard Idiom

◊

Haydn's keyboard music spans the period from the 1750s, when it is assumed he wrote his first solo keyboard works, to 1797, when he produced the keyboard version of the slow movement from the 'Emperor' String Quartet. Quite apart from changes in compositional style, this period saw many changes in the music profession, among which we may count the gradual acceptance, by composers, performers, and the musical public, of the fortepiano as the main keyboard instrument and the gradual displacement of the harpsichord and clavichord. Although it is now accepted that Cristofori had invented the *gravicembalo col piano e forte* by *c.*1700 (possibly a few years before the advent of the eighteenth century) and had solved most of the mechanical problems of construction,[1] the rise in popularity of the new instrument and the consequent, gradual decline in the use of the harpsichord occurred principally in the years 1760 to 1790.

The transfer in allegiance from one instrument to another occurred at a different pace in various countries and even within a specific geographical region composers embraced the 'new' instrument at remarkably divergent dates. In Italy, notwithstanding the early example of Giustini's *Sonate da cimbalo di piano, e forte detto volgarmente di martelletti*, published in Florence in 1732, the fortepiano seems, paradoxically, to have become dominant at a relatively late date: for example, Galuppi's *Passatempo al cembalo* of 1785 is still perfectly compatible with performance on a harpsichord.[2] Although

---

[1] H. Schott, 'From Harpsichord to Pianoforte: A Chronology and Commentary', *EM* 13/1 (Feb. 1985): 28–38.

[2] This is, of course, not to say that fortepianos or fortepiano music were unknown in Italy between Cristofori and the end of the 18th cent. Recent research by John A. Rice describes a local tradition of fortepiano manufacture and a repertoire of fortepiano music in Tuscany in the 1780s (see J. Rice, 'The Tuscan Piano in the 1780s', *EM* 21/1 (Feb. 1993): 5–26).

writers on the early history of the fortepiano frequently mention references to the use of the fortepiano in Paris in the 1750s and 1760s, including the relatively early appearance of the fortepiano in the Parisian Concerts spirituels in 1768,[3] it is not generally recognized that even in the 1780s the fortepiano was by no means accepted uncritically by the Parisian public. In the 1780s although a tradition of fortepiano virtuosos appearing at the Parisian Concert spirituel grew, as late as 1788 a reviewer in the *Mercure de France* had reservations about the instrument used in the Concert spirituel of 24 December 1787, which featured a performance by Mlle Davion of a *Concerto de piano-forte*: 'This instrument in general is not made for big concerts, and the bad sound quality of the one on which she [Mlle Davion] played detracted from her success.'[4] Indeed the survival of the harpsichord in Paris, even on the platforms of the Concerts spirituels, can be documented to 15 April 1787 when M. Ambroise l'Étendard, a pupil of Balbastre, 'played two concertos, one on the *clavecin* and the other on the *piano-forte*'.[5]

The displacement of the harpsichord by the fortepiano was, however, virtually completed by the early 1790s (Broadwoods made their last harpsichord in 1793),[6] and although research continues to document ever earlier dates for the use of the fortepiano in public concerts,[7] it is predominantly in the 1770s and 1780s that fortepianos of various types became widely available and that composers began consistently to write keyboard music which cannot be performed on a harpsichord without serious compromise.

[3] M. Brenet, *Les Concerts en France sous l'ancien régime* (Paris, 1900; repr., New York: Da Capo, 1970), 292–3; see also Schott, 'From Harpsichord to Pianoforte', 30–1, 33; R. Maunder, 'Mozart's Keyboard Instruments', *EM* 20/2 (May 1992): 212, 214.

[4] *Mercure de France*, 5 Jan. 1788, p. 38.   [5] *Mercure de France*, 28 Apr. 1787, p. 174.

[6] See D. Wainwright, *Broadwood by Appointment: A History* (London: Quiller Press, 1982), 79.

[7] It would appear that in England the public concerts by Charles Dibdin (1767), J. C. Bach (1768), and James Hook (1768) were not the first in which a fortepiano was used. Roger Fiske has documented the performance of a 'Piano e Forte Concerto' at the Little Theatre in the Haymarket on 3 February 1752: see H. D. Johnstone and R. Fiske (eds.), *Music in Britain: The Eighteenth Century* (Blackwell History of Music in Britain; Oxford: Blackwell, 1990), 217 (I am grateful to Dr Johnstone for bringing this reference to my attention). On the performance 'auf dem Fortipiano' [*sic*] by Johann Babtist Schmid [*sic*] at the Burgtheater, Vienna on 13 March [*recte* May?] 1763 see E. Badura-Skoda, 'Prolegomena to a History of the Viennese Fortepiano', *Israel Studies in Musicology*, 2 (1980): 77–99; and ead., 'Zur Frühgeschichte des Hammerklaviers', in C.-H. Mahling (ed.), *Florilegium Musicologicum: Hellmut Federhofer zum 75. Geburtstag* (Mainzer Studien zur Musikwissenschaft, 21; Tutzing: Schneider, 1988), 37–44. On the suggestion that J. S. Bach performed concertos on a fortepiano in Leipzig, see E. Badura-Skoda, 'Komponierte J. S. Bach "Hammerklavier-Konzerte"?', *BJb* (1991): 159–71.

Occasionally individuals expressed a negative attitude to one or other instrument, but for much of the eighteenth century a clear-cut distinction between harpsichord and fortepiano music did not exist, as the two instruments enjoyed an easy cohabitation. In this regard the ubiquitous designation 'per il fortepiano o cembalo' on printed title-pages in the 1780s is in fact an accurate reflection of general practice, even if for individual composers or works it may not have specified the ideal, or the composer's preferred, manner of performance. Edwin Ripin is undoubtedly correct in stating that the musically minded bourgeoisie of the eighteenth century played the latest keyboard music on harpsichord, clavichord, or fortepiano depending on availability, 'whether the composer really wanted this or not'.[8] Flexibility in this regard also applied, to some extent, to the composer-performer: Mozart is known to have played the harpsichord at least until the early 1780s and used a clavichord until the end of his career; that is, long after he had committed himself to writing principally for the fortepiano;[9] and although it is generally accepted that Haydn was writing for the fortepiano at least by 1788, it is well known that by some accounts he is reported to have used a harpsichord to direct concerts during his first London visit.[10] Similarly, although C. P. E. Bach's *Probestücke* (H.70–5) are best performed on the clavichord because of the detailed dynamic shadings and indications of *Bebung* (vibrato), he accepted as quite natural that they would be played on other instruments by the general public. In his treatise *Versuch über die wahre Art das Clavier zu spielen* C. P. E. Bach commented as follows on the performance of the *Probestücke*:

If the Lessons [*Probestücke*] are played on a harpsichord with two manuals, only one manual should be used to play detailed changes of forte and piano. It is only when entire passages are differentiated by contrasting shades that a transfer may be made. This problem does not exist at the clavichord, for

[8] 'Haydn and the Keyboard Instruments of His Time', in, J. P. Larsen, H. Serwer, and J. Webster (eds.), *Haydn Studies: Proceedings of the International Haydn Conference, Washington, 1975* (New York: Norton, 1981), 305.

[9] See e.g. Mozart's letter of 31 Oct. 1783 and L. Mozart's letter of 20 Apr. 1778; E. Anderson, ed., *The Letters of Mozart and his Family* (rev. 3rd edn., London: Macmillan, 1985), 529, 859. See also Maunder, 'Mozart's Keyboard Instruments', 207–19.

[10] Advertisements for the Haydn–Salomon concerts from Jan. to June 1791 frequently refer to Haydn presiding 'at the Harpsichord' (see H. C. R. Landon, *Haydn: Chronicle and Works*, iii (London: Thames & Hudson, 1976), 43–83). Advertisements for later concerts mention the fortepiano (see e.g. the advertisements for concerts in Jan. and Feb. 1792, ibid. 131).

on it all varieties of loud and soft can be expressed with an almost unrivaled clarity and purity.[11]

It is in this sense historically valid to perform much of Haydn's keyboard music on any keyboard instrument, or the best available instrument, but the flexibility of eighteenth-century general practice may, depending on the date of the music in question, either accord with the intention of the composer at the time of composition or produce a performance which seriously misrepresents the composer's intention. The question addressed in this chapter is: at what stage or stages of his career was Haydn writing for a specific keyboard instrument or instruments rather than in a generalized keyboard idiom?

Modern discussions on the subject of Haydn's keyboard writing and keyboard instruments have concentrated on the question of when Haydn first encountered the fortepiano. Some authors claim that this occurred as early as the 1760s, while others suggest the 1780s. Central to the question is the documentary evidence, which, although not ideally complete and at times ambiguous enough to allow more than one interpretation, is none the less the most objective source of information. Horst Walter's meticulous study of the documentary sources remains the most authoritative discussion of the subject.[12] Since Walter's study in 1970 only a small number of documentary references have come to light which add to our knowledge of the subject, most of the more recent literature being concerned to a large extent with a more speculative approach, or with matters of documentation not directly related to Haydn.[13]

No inventory of the Esterházy musical instruments was made during Haydn's lifetime, or at least none survives, and links between surviving keyboard instruments and the Esterházy establishment are tenuous. In the *Acta Musicalia* and various other documents there are various references to the keyboard instruments used at Eisenstadt and

---

[11] (Berlin, 1753, 1762); trans. W. J. Mitchell as *Essay on the True Art of Playing Keyboard Instruments* (New York: Norton, 1949), 164.

[12] 'Haydns Klaviere', *H-St* 2/4 (Dec. 1970): 256–88. A brief summary of the same is to be found in Larsen *et al.* (eds.), *Haydn Studies*, 213–16.

[13] See esp. E. Badura-Skoda, 'Prolegomena'; H. C. R. Landon, *Haydn: Chronicle and Works*, ii (London: Thames & Hudson, 1978), 343; A. P. Brown, 'The Question of Keyboard Idiom', in *Joseph Haydn's Keyboard Music: Sources and Style* (Bloomington, Ind., Indiana University Press, 1986), 134–71; S. Kleindienst, 'Haydns Clavier-Werke: Kriterien der Instrumentenwahl', in E. Badura-Skoda (ed.), *Joseph Haydn: Bericht über den Internationalen Joseph Haydn Kongress, Wien, 1982* (Munich: Henle, 1986), 53–64.

Eszterháza.[14] Most of the references concern the upkeep of various instruments referred to as 'Cembalo', 'Spinett', or generically as 'Flügel' (and its variant forms 'Flüg', 'Flig', 'Flich'), 'Clavier', or simply as 'Instrument'.[15] There is in 1764 a specific reference to the repair of the 'fürstlichen Klavikordi' ('princely clavichords').[16] The first specific reference to a fortepiano comes not from the Esterházy documents but from Haydn's own correspondence. In the much-quoted letter to Artaria of 26 October 1788, Haydn asked that '31 gold ducats' be paid to Wenzel Schanz for a 'new fortepiano'.[17] In letters to Frau von Genzinger dated 20 June 1790, 27 June 1790, and 4 July 1790 Haydn makes it quite clear that a fortepiano is necessary for the performance of the Sonata in E flat, Hob. XVI: 49, and he is increasingly insistent that Frau von Genzinger abandons her 'Flügel' (in this instance the term clearly means a wing-shaped harpsichord) and acquires a fortepiano.[18] The first categorical reference to a fortepiano in the Esterházy documents occurs as late as 1796 when Anton Walter tuned two 'fürstliche Pianofortes'.[19] It is clear that while generic terms for keyboard instruments, and specific terms for clavichords and harpsichords dominate the earlier documentary references, no unambiguous reference to the fortepiano occurs before 1788 (in Haydn's correspondence) and 1796 (in the Esterházy documents).

Various references from before 1788 have, however, been interpreted as implying an earlier date for Haydn's adoption of the fortepiano as his preferred instrument. A receipt dated 3 March 1781 noted that Anton Walter spent twelve days at Eszterháza repairing 'Clavier und Flügel Instrumenten'.[20] In this reference Walter is described as an 'Orgl [sic] und Instrument Macher', but by the early 1780s he was already gaining a growing reputation specifically as a fortepiano maker (it was in the early 1780s, certainly before 1785, that Mozart purchased a fortepiano from Walter's workshop).[21] In 1788 Haydn certainly knew enough about Walter's fortepianos to be able

---

[14] References from the *Acta Musicalia*, the documentary research of Valkó and Harich, are derived from Walter, 'Haydns Klaviere'.

[15] Walter, 'Haydns Klaviere', 257–60.   [16] Ibid. 257.

[17] *CCLN*, 79.   [18] Ibid. 104–7.

[19] Walter, 'Haydns Klaviere', 259.

[20] Ibid. 258; and H. C. R. Landon, *Haydn: Chronicle and Works*, ii. 89.

[21] See U. Rück, 'Mozarts Hammerflügel erbaute Anton Walter, Wien', *MJb* (1955): 246–62; and Maunder, 'Mozart's Keyboard Instruments', 207–19.

to compare them in some detail, and not at all favourably,[22] with those of Schanz, but if Haydn or the Esterházy establishment purchased a Walter instrument in 1781, or earlier, is not definitely established. Concerning the 1781 receipt Robbins Landon surely overinterprets the evidence when commenting that the bill of 1781 'clearly makes a precise difference between pianos (*Clavier*) and harpsichords (*Flügel*)':[23] the distinction could equally be between, for instance, a clavichord and a large wing-shaped harpsichord, and indeed this appears more likely since the existence of clavichords and harpsichords at the Esterházy residences is not a matter of debate, but the presence of a fortepiano is not otherwise established by the *Acta Musicalia* at this date.

One documentary reference cited by Robbins Landon, and unknown to Horst Walter in 1970, suggests a remarkably early date for the use of a fortepiano at Eszterháza by comparison with the evidence of the *Acta Musicalia* or Haydn's correspondence. It is reported by G. F. von R[otenstein] in Bernouilli's *Sammlung kurzer Reisebeschreibung*, that during the visit of the Empress Maria Theresa to Eszterháza in 1773 a concert was given in which music 'auf einem *Piano-forte*' was heard. Robbins Landon suggests that this instrument was a British square piano.[24] Also suggestive of an early date for Haydn's acquisition of a fortepiano, and again it is an English square piano which is probably in question, is the Guttenbrunn portrait of Haydn at the keyboard. This portrait may date from the early 1770s and depicts Haydn sitting at what appears to be a square piano.[25] Just as one cannot be entirely confident of Rotenstein's evidence on the presence of a fortepiano at Eszterháza in the 1770s when weighed against the silence of the *Acta Musicalia* and Haydn's correspondence, it cannot be known whether the representation of the keyboard instrument in Guttenbrunn's portrait is realistic or merely conventional, nor apparently can the portrait be dated precisely. Concerning both of these references to the fortepiano in the 1770s it should also

---

[22] According to Haydn 'sometimes there is not more than one instrument in ten [of Walter's] which you could really describe as good, and apart from that they are very expensive' (*CCLN*, 107).

[23] *Haydn: Chronicle and Works*, ii. 89.   [24] Ibid. 343.

[25] Ibid.; see also Brown, *Keyboard Music*, 139–40. There are two versions of this portrait; the first is less detailed than the second, which was a model for the famous engraving of Schiavonetti. Only in the second portrait and the engraving is it clear (because of the [added?] stops inside the instrument) that a square piano is represented. See L. Somfai, *Joseph Haydn: His Life in Contemporary Pictures* (London: Faber & Faber, 1969), 124–5, 213–14.

be stated that (*pace* Robbins Landon) few English square pianos dating from the 1770s have survived and there is little reason to believe that there were 'copies all over the Continent by the early 1770s'.[26]

While it is problematic to accept the evidence of Rotenstein and of the Guttenbrunn portrait as proof of the existence of a fortepiano in Eszterháza in the 1770s, equally the absence of unambiguous references to a fortepiano in Haydn's correspondence and the *Acta Musicalia* before 1788, although suggestive, is not in itself conclusive. The terminology employed in documents to refer to keyboard instruments is notoriously problematic, particularly before the 1780s. The term *cembalo*, although used to refer specifically to a harpsichord, was also sometimes employed generically in referring to keyboard instruments; similarly *Flügel* could be used to describe any keyboard instrument of a grand or wing shape, and although in certain usages, predominantly but not exclusively in North Germany, the term *Clavier* could mean clavichord, this term was also used in a generic sense. Precision should therefore not necessarily be expected from any contemporary terminology and indeed Eva Badura-Skoda has argued that one should not expect to find specific references to the fortepiano in contemporary documents since the term fortepiano (or its equivalent) 'was not in use in Italy before 1790. . . . and in south Germany and Austria it was hardly known during the 1750s and seldom used in the third quarter of the century'.[27] None the less, the terminology employed by Haydn in the extant autograph manuscripts and in the entries in the *Entwurf Katalog* would seem to confirm the evidence of Haydn's correspondence and the *Acta Musicalia*.[28] While all references in the autograph manuscripts and *EK*, apart from the organ concerto Hob. XVIII: 1,[29] are to *Cembalo* or

---

[26] H. C. R. Landon, *Haydn: Chronicle and Works*, ii. 343. While there is some evidence that English square pianos were exported to Paris in the 1760s, the assumption that they were distributed more widely is problematic. In his various travels in the 1760s, Mozart may have heard fortepianos in Paris, but the first record of Mozart performing on a fortepiano dates from 1774. See N. Broder, 'Mozart and the Clavier', *MQ* 27 (1941): 422; O. E. Deutsch, *Mozart: A Documentary Biography* (rev. edn., London: Simon & Schuster, 1990), 153; Maunder, 'Mozart's Keyboard Instruments', 212–19.

[27] 'Prolegomena', 82; see also Rice, 'The Tuscan Piano in the 1780s', 9.

[28] For a survey of Haydn's terminology see Brown, *Keyboard Music*, 144–7.

[29] Georg Feder has pointed out that a number of concertos apart from Hob. XVIII: 1 may have been intended for organ rather than harpsichord because of their restricted keyboard range. The distinction between harpsichord and organ concertos is, however, functional rather than stylistic: stylistically, none of Haydn's organ concertos is reliant on the organ and they transfer to the harpsichord and the secular context of the concert platform without falsification (see G. Feder, 'Wieviel Orgelkonzerte hat Haydn geschrieben?', *Mf* 23/4

Clavicembalo until 1790, in that year Haydn wrote 'Sonata per il Forte-piano' on the autograph of the Sonata, Hob. XVI: 49, which he wrote specifically for the fortepiano. In Haydn's correspondence from the 1780s the ambiguous term *Clavier* predominates and 'fortepiano' occurs for the first time in the aforementioned letter of 26 October 1788, in connection with the Trios, Hob. XV: 11–13, works which were also written with a fortepiano rather than any other keyboard instrument in mind.[30] In general, Haydn's terminology confirms the impression gained from documentary information relating to the availability of instruments, i.e. that it was not until the second half of the 1780s that the fortepiano is specified by Haydn, or any documentary source closely related to Haydn, in connection with any of his keyboard works. The description 'per il fortepiano o cembalo' was not used by Haydn, but it occurs constantly in printed editions of the 1780s. Sometimes this description is anachronistic: the Sonata, Hob. XVI: 18 is so described in the Artaria print of 1788 (op. 53) but the work actually dates from *c.*1766 when the alternative of performing it on a fortepiano was unlikely. Similarly, the Artaria edition of Hob. XVI: 52 (op. 82, plate no. 792) has the label 'pour le Clavecin ou Piano-Forte' when the work was obviously written for fortepiano and was thus described in the London first edition (Longman, Clementi & Co., Op. 78); moreover, the sonata is dedicated to the pianist, Clementi's pupil, Therese Jansen Bartolozzi. However, as is suggested below, significance can be attached to this label in the early 1780s when commercial motives may be seen as an influence on both Haydn's, and his publishers', view of keyboard idiom.

After 1788 Haydn's interest in and association with fortepianos of various types is well documented. There are conflicting reports as to whether Haydn directed concerts during his first London visit from the harpsichord or fortepiano, but he certainly knew the latest instruments of Broadwood, Clagget, and Stodart;[31] wrote a number of works (Hob. XVI: 50, 52, XV: 27–9, 31/ii, and possibly others) for Therese Jansen Bartolozzi;[32] and directed concerts from a fortepiano during his second London visit, if not earlier. Although the frequent claims regarding the influence of the English piano on Haydn's later

(Oct.–Dec. 1970): 440–4; and J. Mertin, 'Zu den Orgelinstrumenten Joseph Haydns', in E. Badura-Skoda (ed.), *Haydn Kongress, Wien, 1982*, 72–5).

[30] *CCLN*, 79.   [31] See Walter, 'Haydns Klaviere', 268–73.
[32] Brown, *Keyboard Music*, 46–55.

keyboard works have been overstated, Haydn was clearly interested in English instruments and wrote a number of works specifically for them and/or English performers. We also know in some detail, through his will, *Nachlassverzeichnis*, and other documents, about some of the instruments which Haydn owned from the late 1780s. Of these, only a clavichord by Johann Bohak (1755–1805) dating from 1794, is extant. Apart from this, Haydn had, according to Horst Walter, four instruments in his house in Vienna: a fortepiano by Schanz (presumably the instrument acquired in 1788); two grand pianos, one by Erard and one by Longman & Broderip; and a smaller instrument which might have been a square piano (*Tafelklavier*) or a clavichord.[33]

The Wenzel Schanz fortepiano which Haydn purchased in 1788 is mentioned in his first will, dated 5 May 1801, as item number 59, and was to be bequeathed to the daughter of Herr Kandler.[34] It is probably the same instrument which was in Haydn's house in Vienna and which he described as his 'schönes Fortepiano' when he sold it shortly before his death for 200 ducats.[35] The instrument does not therefore appear in Haydn's *Nachlassverzeichnis*. No instrument by Wenzel Schanz is extant, although a number of instruments by Johann Schanz have survived. Haydn's Schanz instrument of 1788 probably had the standard range of five octaves ($F,-f''''$) and two knee-levers (damper and moderator).

The only extant instrument linked by documentary evidence with Haydn is the Johann Bohak clavichord now in the Donaldson Collection of the Royal College of Music, London. The instrument dates from 1794, but, as Horst Walter has pointed out, Haydn could not have acquired it before 1795.[36] The Bohak instrument has a five-octave range, $F,-f'''$, and is unfretted.

According to Vincent Novello, Haydn brought a grand piano by Longman & Broderip to Vienna on his return from England.[37] The

---

[33] Walter, 'Haydns Klaviere', 273–84.

[34] H. C. R. Landon, *Haydn: Chronicle and Works*, v (London: Thames & Hudson, 1977), 53.

[35] See Walter, 'Haydns Klaviere', 265–8, 280–1; a facsimile reproduction of the document, in Haydn's own hand, recording the sale of the instrument, is reproduced in Brown, *Keyboard Music*, p. 9, plate 1.

[36] See P. James, 'Haydn's Clavichord and a Sonata Manuscript', *MT* 71 (1930): 314; Walter, 'Haydns Klaviere', 273–8.

[37] Walter, 'Haydns Klaviere', 283–4; H. C. R. Landon, *Haydn: Chronicle and Works*, iii. 415.

instrument may have been a present: between 1794 and 1797 Longman & Broderip had close ties with Haydn in their predominant commercial capacity as publishers. A grand piano by Longman & Broderip, undoubtedly the same instrument, is listed in Haydn's *Nachlassverzeichnis* where it is mentioned as having the same range (five and a half octaves: F_i-c'''') as Haydn's Erard pianoforte.[38] It is likely that such an instrument would have had two pedals, damper and *una corda*, in the English tradition, as opposed to the wider range of pedals on early nineteenth-century continental instruments. According to Novello, Haydn's instrument was in the possession of Maximilian Stadler in 1829. It is not now known to be extant, although Robbins Landon claims (without supporting documentation) that Haydn's 'Longman & Broderip piano (or an identical one) survives in private possession in Vienna'.[39]

In 1801 Erard sent Haydn a grand piano which was described in the *Nachlassverzeichnis* as being five and a half octaves in range (F_i-c''''), with the 'usual pedals' and was valued at 200 gulden. The usual pedals would probably have been four in number: bassoon, damper, moderator, and *una corda*.[40]

These instruments represent very different traditions which co-existed in the latter part of Haydn's career.[41] The Schanz fortepiano belongs to a Viennese tradition which brought a distinctive style of fortepiano manufacture to perfection in the 1780s. Such fortepianos, although by no means standardized,[42] are characterized by an extremely shallow key dip and light touch, thin strings and hammers,

---

[38] H. C. R. Landon, *Haydn: Chronicle and Works*, v. 383; Walter, 'Haydns Klaviere', 280.

[39] H. C. R. Landon, *Haydn: Chronicle and Works*, iii. 415, repeated in ibid. v. 56, n. 1. A photograph of a Longman & Broderip grand piano is included in H. C. R. Landon, *Haydn: A Documentary Study* (London: Thames & Hudson, 1981), plate 32, p. 116; the instrument is here described as 'similar to the instrument which Longman & Broderip presented to Haydn in 1794'.

[40] See H. C. R. Landon, *Haydn: Chronicle and Works*, v. 55–6, 383, 393; Walter, 'Haydns Klaviere', 280, 282–3.

[41] On the history of the piano, R. Harding, *The Pianoforte: Its History Traced to the Great Exhibition of 1851* (Cambridge: CUP, 1933; repr., New York: Da Capo, 1973) remains essential reading; see also E. M. Good, *Giraffes, Black Dragons and Other Pianos: A Technological History from Cristofori to the Modern Concert Grand* (Stanford: Stanford University Press, 1982); Wainwright, *Broadwood by Appointment*; C. Ehrlich, *The Piano: A History* (rev. edn., Oxford: Clarendon Press, 1990); R. Winter, 'Keyboards' in H. Mayer Brown and S. Sadie (eds.), *Performance Practice: Music after 1600* (New Grove Handbooks in Music; London: Macmillan, 1989), 346–73 and the articles by E. Badura-Skoda cited in n. 7, above.

[42] On the specious uniformity of Viennese fortepianos see M. Latcham, 'The Check in Some Early Pianos and the Development of Piano Technique around the Turn of the 18th Century', *EM* 21/1 (Feb. 1993): 28–42.

the latter covered with leather. In this instrument the five-octave range *F,–f'''* was standard, as was the presence of a knee-lever which lifted the dampers and a second lever (moderator) which interposed leather tabs between strings and hammers when the lever was operated. Such instruments did not, generally, have an *una corda* mechanism. Most of Haydn's fortepiano music would have been composed with such an instrument in mind. Evidently among the Viennese instruments Haydn preferred those with the lightest action: his favoured instrument, the Schanz fortepiano, was 'particularly light in touch and the mechanism very agreeable'.[43]

By contrast the Longman & Broderip instrument represents an English tradition of manufacture which is closely associated with the instruments of John Broadwood. Such instruments, in contrast to those of Viennese manufacture, have a characteristic English action, a noticeably heavier and deeper touch, a more resonant sound, and less efficient damping: two pedals, a damper pedal and an *una corda* pedal, were standard on English pianos. Broadwood extended the range of his instruments to five and a half octaves (*F,–c''''*) and later (as in Beethoven's Broadwood) to six octaves (*C,–c''''*). Performances of Haydn's keyboard music during his London trips would presumably have been on instruments of the Broadwood and Longman & Broderip type; one late sonata, Hob. XVI: 50 has a range *F,–a'''* which is otherwise not found in his keyboard music. The marked difference between the Viennese and English instruments was noted by contemporary writers. Hummel commented that the German piano 'may be played upon with ease by the weakest hand. It allows the performer to impart to his execution every possible degree of light and shade, speaks clearly and promptly.' On the other hand he noted that on the English instrument 'the touch is much heavier, the keys sink much deeper, and consequently, the return of the hammer upon the repetition of a note, cannot take place so quickly'.[44] Kalkbrenner elaborated on this contrast:

The instruments of Vienna and those of London have given rise to two different styles of playing. The performers of Vienna are remarkable for the precision, clearness, and rapidity of their execution: the instruments made in that city are also very easy to play upon, and in order to avoid a

[43] *CCLN*, 107.

[44] *Ausführliche theoretisch-praktische Anweisung zum Piano-Forte-Spiel*, 3 vols. (Vienna, 1828); trans. as *A Complete Theoretical and Practical Course of Instructions on the Art of Playing the Piano Forte* (London, 1829), pt. III, p. 64.

confusion of sound, they have dampers as far as the highest F, which occasions a great dryness of tone, particularly in passages of flowing melody. In Germany the use of the pedal is hardly known.

The English instruments have a fuller tone, and a touch somewhat heavier; which have given to the performers of that country, that fine style of playing, and that delightful manner of making their notes flow into each other, for which they are so distinguished.

For the acquisition of this style, the damper pedal is indespensably necessary, as it corrects that dryness of sound which otherwise belongs to all Piano Fortes.[45]

The Erard instrument combines a heavier action related to the English type with an array of pedals which became customary on Continental instruments in the early years of the nineteenth century. Since Haydn acquired this instrument only in 1801, after he had composed his last keyboard works, its particular characteristics cannot be considered relevant to Haydn's keyboard music.

It is clear from the terminology employed by Haydn after 1788 and from our knowledge of instruments which Haydn owned later in his career that he was writing for fortepiano from 1788 onwards if not earlier, and that in the 1790s he was familiar with both Viennese and English traditions of fortepiano making. It is also of interest that long after the fortepiano had replaced the harpsichord, Haydn continued to own and to use a clavichord. Thus we know that Haydn owned clavichords throughout his career: in his youth in Vienna, when he owned a 'worm-eaten Clavier'; at Eszterháza, where the *Acta Musicalia* testify to the presence of clavichords; and late in his career, when he purchased the Bohak instrument.[46] Notwithstanding Eva Badura-Skoda's arguments to the contrary, there is no compelling evidence that Haydn owned a fortepiano before 1788. Yet it is extremely unlikely that Haydn was unaware of Viennese fortepianos until 1788 and the more important question is not when does the documentary evidence suggest that Haydn first owned a fortepiano, but when did he begin to write keyboard music in such a way that the music requires a fortepiano rather than a harpsichord?

[45] *A Complete Course of Instruction for the Piano Forte* (London [1835]), 8.

[46] As a youth in Vienna Haydn owned a 'worm-eaten Clavier' (see Griesinger, *Biographische Notizen über Joseph Haydn*, trans. V. Gotwals, in Gotwals, *Haydn: Two Contemporary Portraits* (Madison: University of Wisconsin Press, 1968), 12); the *Acta Musicalia* testifies to the presence of clavichords in the Esterházy establishments, while as late as 1795 Haydn bought a clavichord, the extant Bohak instrument (see Walter, 'Haydns Klaviere', 256, 257, 273–8).

GENERALIZED KEYBOARD IDIOM 1750S–C.1780

Various attempts have been made to assign Haydn's keyboard music to either harpsichord, clavichord, or fortepiano based on the premiss that particular compositional figurations or performance indications are more idiomatic on one or other instrument.[47] In many instances the resultant suggestions are untenable: *Trommelbässe* (drum-basses) occur in late as well as early music and are not, as has been suggested, especially suited to the harpsichord; similarly, although Alberti basses occur in many works written for harpsichord (notably in the works of Alberti and Galuppi), in Haydn's music, where the Alberti bass is in any case not very common, it is as likely to occur in late works (cf. Hob. XVI: 45/i, 1765, and XVI: 49/i, 1790); rapid note repetitions are not more characteristic of harpsichord music than early fortepiano music and are played without any difficulty on instruments with a Viennese action. Similar comments regarding the idiomatic nature of arpeggios, syncopations, *tenuto*, *portato*, and other compositional figurations or performance indications, on a particular instrument cannot withstand scrutiny.[48]

[47] Categorizations of keyboard works based on keyboard figuration are found in Kleindienst, 'Haydns Clavier-Werke', 53–63; and L. Tung, 'Indicators of Early Piano Writing in Haydn's Sonatas', in Larsen *et al.*, (eds.), *Haydn Studies*, 323–6. For a critical response to Kleindienst's paper by van der Meer see E. Badura-Skoda (ed.), *Haydn Kongress, Wien, 1982*, 63.

[48] Howard Pollack's use of criteria such as texture, the occurrence of octave passages, appoggiaturas, *cantabile* melodic lines, and *adagio* interruptions to characterize music suitable for one or other instrument is particularly suspect (H. Pollack, 'Some Thoughts on the "Clavier" in Haydn's Solo *Claviersonaten*', *Journal of Musicology*, 9/1 (Winter 1991): 84–6). It is claimed, notably by Kleindienst ('Haydns Clavier-Werke', 58), Brown (*Keyboard Music*, 135, 159–60), and Pollack ('Clavier', 84), that the *portato* or *Tragen der Töne* indication can be realized idiomatically only on touch-sensitive instruments (i.e. clavichord and fortepiano). In North German treatises *Tragen der Töne* is closely associated with the *Bebung* and in this meaning of the term the clavichord is the only instrument on which the effect can be achieved (see Bach, *Versuch*, trans. Mitchell, 156–7). Brown, Kleindienst, and others have suggested that the effect can be imitated on a fortepiano but not on a harpsichord and thus that the presence of a *portato* indication in Haydn's keyboard music indicates that the appropriate instrument is clavichord or fortepiano, but not harpsichord. This argument assumes that the indication in Haydn's music has a similar meaning to that appropriate in North German clavichord music and is not intended purely as an indication of articulation which can be realized idiomatically on harpsichord as well as on touch-sensitive instruments. If the premiss advocated in Ch. 2 is accepted, i.e. that the *Punkt* and *portato* indications are synonymous in Haydn's music, then the association of the *Tragen der Töne* indication with Haydn's later keyboard music, and thus implicitly with music more likely to have been written for fortepiano, is weakened, since the *Punkt* occurs in early works (e.g. Hob. XVI: 19—

The performance indications which are most suggestive in an endeavour to distinguish works written for specific instruments are dynamics. Dynamic markings occur only in three pre-1780 keyboard works by Haydn preserved in autograph manuscripts, Hob. XVI: 18, 20, and 22, and of these the only extensive occurrence is in Hob. XVI: 20. Concerning Hob. XVI: 18 (*c.*1766) the various dynamic markings which Brown considers require a touch-sensitive instrument[49] derive, with only one exception, from manuscript copies and printed editions of the 1780s. The only dynamic marking found in the autograph fragment (see Ex. 5.6) occurs in connection with a change in texture and register, a type of 'fade-out' on the last phrase such as occurs in other works without dynamic indications. Here the dynamic marking is descriptive in effect and is attainable on a two-manual harpsichord or on a clavichord, but the compositional effect is obvious whether one underlines it with a change in dynamics or not.

A single dynamic marking occurs in the autograph manuscript of Hob. XVI: 22 one bar before the recapitulation (see Ex. 1.1). This *f* indication is unproblematic on a clavichord and possible (although with some difficulty) on a two-manual harpsichord, but this single dynamic marking scarcely precludes performance of the work on a single-manual harpsichord. The purpose of this single indication is not obvious, but it appears to serve a primarily structural function in emphasizing the structural 'up-beat' to the recapitulation. A single *f* indication is also found in Hob. XVI: 46. Again, this seems to mark a structural up-beat, the beginning of a sequence in the retransition which leads from the submediant to the recapitulation in the tonic. Although contextually similar to Hob. XVI: 22/i, the dynamic marking in XVI: 46/i is, however, transmitted only in secondary sources.

The only extensive use of dynamics which can be documented by an early autograph manuscript occurs in the Sonata in C minor, Hob. XVI: 20 (1771). Although certain of the dynamic indications in the autograph may be achieved individually on a harpsichord, famously, the alternation of *f* and *p* on successive notes in bars 13–14, and, for instance, the changes from *f* to *p* in bars 26–31 (Ex. 1.2) undoubtedly require a touch-sensitive instrument. In the autograph only *f*

dated autograph 1767) which were almost certainly not written exclusively for touch-sensitive instruments.

[49] Brown, *Keyboard Music*, 148–9.

Ex. 1.1. Hob. XVI: 22/i

Ex. 1.2. Hob. XVI: 20/i

and *p* markings are employed, but the frequency, close proximity, and the contexts in which they occur mean that much of the dramatic expression of the work, in particular in the first movement, is lost if a performance is attempted on a harpsichord. The first edition of this work contains more elaborate dynamic markings than those found in the autograph fragment: as well as *f* and *p*, *ff*, *pp* and *cresc* indications are used. This Artaria publication will be discussed further below, but the important point is that although the published dynamics are more numerous and contain more dynamic shadings, the indications of both the autograph and the first edition require touch-sensitive instruments. In this regard, as indeed in many others, this work is unique in Haydn's output before *c*.1780.

The perennial question regarding the C minor Sonata is which touch-sensitive instrument, clavichord or fortepiano, it was written for. Eva Badura-Skoda has commented on 'the symphonic scope' of the work and concludes that it must have been written for the fortepiano:[50] Christa Landon remarked on the crescendo marking (only in the first edition) and suggested that this 'would point to the use of a *Hammerklavier*'.[51] Similarly, H. C. Robbins Landon suggests that 'Perhaps the Sonata in C minor is Haydn's first attempt to write down music especially for this new instrument [i.e. the forte-piano]'.[52] However, Horst Walter doubts, in view of the documen-tary evidence, that Haydn was writing for a fortepiano as early as 1771 rather than specifically for the clavichord, an instrument which was available to Haydn at the time.[53] Resistance to Walter's argument, whether directly stated or implied, rests on the by-now traditional assertion that the dramatic nature of the C minor Sonata requires a fortepiano rather than a clavichord and on the frequently stated opin-ion that only in North Germany was the clavichord a performing instrument, while in Austria it was used only for practice and for composition.[54] The former can be seen to be based, at least in part, on a failure to appreciate the capabilities of good, large clavichords

[50] In Larsen *et al.* (eds.), *Haydn Studies*, 216.
[51] Pref. to *Joseph Haydn: Sämtliche Klaviersonaten* (3rd edn., Vienna: Universal, 1972), vol. i, p. xvii.
[52] *Haydn: Chronicle and Works*, ii. 343. Somewhat inconsistently, and contrary to all avail-able evidence, Robbins Landon also advocates an earlier date for Haydn's use of the forte-piano: 'We cannot believe that even Haydn's *Capriccio* of 1765 [Hob. XVII: 1] was intended for a harpsichord; it is definitely piano music' (ibid.).
[53] 'Haydn's Keyboard Instruments', in Larsen *et al.* (eds.), *Haydn Studies*, 215.
[54] See e.g. *Haydn Studies*, 302–3, n. 1.

from the second half of the eighteenth century,[55] while the latter ignores well-known matters of documentation. It is certainly true that the clavichord was most revered in North Germany and that much North German music was written expressly for it, but there is evidence that also in South Germany and Austria the clavichord was more than merely a compositional aid and practice instrument. As pointed out above, Haydn owned clavichords throughout his career and there are references to his performance of such late works as the keyboard version of the 'Kaiser' Variations on the clavichord.[56] It seems that even after the fortepiano had replaced the harpsichord, the clavichord retained its role, certainly as an instrument suitable for practice and as a compositional aid, but also, given the appropriate intimate social circumstances, as an instrument suitable for performance. Mozart too is known to have performed and practised on a clavichord throughout most of his career: he enthused about both a Stein clavichord and a Stein fortepiano in 1777 and performed on a clavichord in Linz in 1783.[57]

Given the available evidence and an understanding of the potential of a good, large contemporary clavichord the most logical conclusion is that the C minor Sonata was written expressly for the clavichord. A number of incidental, but perhaps not unrelated, matters help to explain why a single sonata with such detailed dynamic markings and apparently written for clavichord should appear in Haydn's *œuvre* in 1771. From *c*.1766 a number of Haydn's sonatas depart significantly from his earlier works in matters of style, orthography, and performance practice. Details of orthography and performance practice which appear in these works, and which derive from Haydn's encounter with C. P. E. Bach's music and with his *Versuch*, will be considered in detail in Chapter 5: they also have a bearing on the question of the instrument intended in Hob. XVI: 20. The unusual dynamic markings of the C minor Sonata can be seen in the same light as these other performance indications; that is, as the overt influence of the North German aesthetic. The dynamic indications,

[55] On this point see Ripin, 'Keyboard Instruments', 305.

[56] The references regarding Haydn's performances on a clavichord are quoted in Brown, *Keyboard Music*, 3–9.

[57] See Anderson, ed., *Mozart Letters* (3rd edn.), letters of 14 Oct. 1777 and 31 Oct. 1783, pp. 315, 859. A report in the *Musikalische Real-Zeitung* from Dresden, dated 17 June 1789, also probably refers to Mozart's clavichord playing: the report commented that Mozart's 'agility on the clavier [*Klavier*] and on the fortepiano is inexpressible' (quoted in Deutsch, *Mozart*, 347; see also Maunder, 'Mozart's Keyboard Instruments', 211–12).

especially, suggest Haydn's experimentation with an important facet of the North German style, namely the exploitation of the subtleties of performance on a clavichord. They have arguably more in common with C. P. E. Bach's use of dynamics that with Haydn's own characteristic use of dynamics adopted in the late 1780s. In particular, the immediate alternation of *f* and *p* found in bars 13–14 of the first movement in Haydn's C minor Sonata is characteristic of, for instance, Bach's *Probestücke* and the *Sonaten mit veränderten Reprisen*, both available in Vienna by mid-1760s.

It is generally and correctly acknowledged that the C minor Sonata is an exceptional work, stylistically and because of its uniquely detailed dynamic indications. There are, however, close stylistic counterparts to the C minor Sonata in works such as the Sonatas, Hob. XVI: 44, 46, 18, and 19, which are equally experimental and expressive although lacking the detailed dynamic indications of Hob. XVI: 20. It is arguably more reasonable to regard Haydn's use of dynamics in the C minor Sonata as another facet of the radical stylistic experimentation which is characteristic of this set of sonatas, than to regard the dynamic indications in isolation as Haydn's response to the challenge of writing for the first time for a fortepiano, particularly when there is no credible evidence to suggest that Haydn owned or had access to a fortepiano in 1771.

The C minor Sonata is, however, the only work of which it can be argued that the clavichord, rather than the harpsichord or fortepiano, is the instrument for which it was specifically conceived. Haydn's expressive sonatas from the mid-1760s undoubtedly lend themselves particularly well to performance on a clavichord, but unlike Hob. XVI: 20, the performance of these works on a harpsichord is in no sense problematic.[58] For most of Haydn's other keyboard works before 1780 the harpsichord and clavichord must be seen as equally appropriate, the choice of instrument being contingent more on the social context of the performance than on any inherent qualities in the music. There are, however, certain cate-

---

[58] Howard Pollack argues in a speculative article that Haydn's keyboard sonatas may be divided into three periods: 'one in which no particular instrument is designated, though the harpsichord seems a felicitous choice (1755–1765); one in which the clavichord is intended (1765–1780); and one in which the fortepiano is the instrument of preference (1780–1795)' (Pollack, 'Clavier', 86). Although attractive in certain regards and less problematic from the point of view of documentation than the notion that Haydn was writing for the fortepiano from the early 1770s, Pollack's thesis is none the less, for the reasons outlined below, too inflexible to be accepted.

gories of work for which the harpsichord is either the automatic choice, excluding the clavichord, or for which the harpsichord may have been foremost in Haydn's mind, although this need not have excluded performance on a clavichord. In the first category are, of course, the concertos and keyboard trios, which because they are ensemble pieces preclude the use of clavichord: the harpsichord, or for the concertos possibly the organ, is the instrument intended. In the second category are a number of works which may have been written with particular harpsichords in mind, but the nature of which does not actually preclude performance on either another type of harpsichord or indeed on a clavichord. This second category includes works apparently written for a harpsichord with 'short octave' tuning and works possibly written for a double-manual harpsichord.

Various authors have commented on the chords involving large stretches found in three of Haydn's keyboard works, Hob. XVII: 1, XVII: 2, and XVI: 47. They appear at first sight to require short-octave tuning of a harpsichord, but an examination of the particular pitches and intervals involved reveals that the conventional short-octave tunings C/E and G/B do not individually solve the problems of the large stretches in these works. In Hob. XVII: 1 and XVII: 2 the interval of a tenth occurs at two different pitches, some of which cannot, even individually, be performed using conventional short-octave tuning. Various explanations of these unusual chords, none of them unproblematic, have been offered.[59] The most likely explanation

---

[59] Eibner's suggestions (in the pref. to id. and G. Jarecki, eds., *Joseph Haydn: Klavierstücke* (Vienna: Universal, 1975), p. xv) that the large chords in Hob. XVII: 1 and XVII: 2 imply the use of a pedal and prove that Haydn was writing at this date for the *Hammerklavier* are unconvincing. It is extremely unlikely that a fortepiano was available to Haydn as early as 1765, but even if Haydn had a square piano at this date, as suggested by Robbins Landon, the damper mechanism would have been controlled by a hand stop which could not have produced the performance of these chords, aided by the 'pedal', desired by Eibner. Robbins Landon has suggested that 'a simplistic, but not impossible, explanation is that one of Haydn's pupils (or Haydn himself) had a left hand capable of stretching a tenth' (H. C. R. Landon, *Haydn: Chronicle and Works*, i (London: Thames & Hudson, 1980), 549). Notwithstanding the shorter octave span of eighteenth-century instruments, this seems an unlikely explanation; while some of the stretches indeed involve only a tenth, others involve playing a tenth and holding a note in between (and at an extremely awkward angle) and in Hob. XVII: 2, bar 146 the performer would be required to stretch a twelfth. David Rowland has suggested that Haydn may have intended a performance of these works on a pedal clavichord (D. Rowland, 'Early Piano Pedalling: 1750–1850', Ph.D. diss., Cambridge University, 1986, p. 102). Only a pedal clavichord which extended the range of the keyboard and thus one with a separate set of strings for the pedal board would, even hypothetically, solve the problem. There is no evidence that Haydn ever owned or had access to such an instrument, nor is there a tradition of such instruments in Vienna or at Eszterháza.

remains, however, that some unusual manipulation of short-octave tuning was intended. It is also possible that Haydn's original short-octave notation may have been corrupted in the process of transmission, accounting for at least some of the unplayable chords. Horst Walter has offered hypothetical short-octave tunings for a harpsichord which, although unconventional, render all the chords in question performable.[60] Walter's first solution is that of a double-manual harpsichord with both C/E and G/B short-octaves. The second solution mentioned by Walter involves an extremely unusual and elaborate short-octave with multiple split keys. There is no documentary evidence to link such an instrument with Haydn, but it seems that Haydn may have experimented briefly, in the mid-1760s, with an instrument with unusual short-octave tuning or with two different short-octaves on a double-manual harpsichord.

Although the extant instruments are few, it is generally accepted that the typical Austrian harpsichord of the eighteenth century was a one-manual instrument, modelled on Italian harpsichords.[61] Such an instrument may have been the norm but there is some reason for believing that Haydn may have had access to a double-manual harpsichord at certain times in his career. Although no documentary evidence is available to establish that there was a double-manual instrument at Eszterháza, nevertheless, the general point has been made that the importance of French taste in Vienna and at Eszterháza admits at least the possibility that French double-manual harpsichords may have been available.[62] Some suggestion that Haydn occasionally wrote with a double-manual harpsichord in mind is supported by internal evidence in some of his sonatas from the 1770s.

The 'Esterházy' Sonatas, Hob. XVI: 21–6, and the six sonatas of 'anno 1776', Hob. XVI: 27–32, in particular, contain occasional passages which, while certainly not proving that a double-manual instrument was intended, are undoubtedly easier to play on a double-manual instrument. One such passage in Hob. XVI: 25/ii has been cited by Kleindienst[63] and is illustrated in Ex. 1.3(*a*). The part-writing in bars 18–21 is undoubtedly possible on a single-manual

---

[60] 'Das Tasteninstrument beim jungen Haydn', in V. Schwarz (ed.), *Der junge Haydn. Bericht der Internationalen Arbeitstagung des Instituts für Aufführungspraxis der Hochschule für darstellende Kunst, Graz, 1970* (Beiträge zur Aufführungspraxis, i; Graz: Akademische Druck-und Verlagsanstalt, 1972), 237–48.

[61] See H. C. R. Landon, *Haydn: Chronicle and Works*, i. 262 and F. Hubbard, *Three Centuries of Harpsichord Making* (Cambridge, Mass.: Harvard University Press, 1965), 28.

[62] See Brown, *Keyboard Music*, 134–5.   [63] 'Haydns Clavier-Werke', 64.

Ex. 1.3. Hob. XVI: 25/ii

instrument, but the near-unisons are probably more effective on two manuals: more suggestive is the overlapping which occurs in bars 29–30 (Ex. 1.3*b*), where the execution of the trill is considerably easier on a double-manual harpsichord. It should, of course, be allowed that the near-unisons and overlapping of right and left hand which make this movement more comfortable to play on a double-manual harpsichord are an incidental product of the strict compositional discipline to which Haydn submits himself in this movement (i.e. fairly strict canonic imitation), and not necessarily the conscious product of idiomatic writing for a double-manual harpsichord. Nevertheless, the sonatas from the 1770s contain sufficient passages which gain from the separation of right and left hands on different manuals to convince me that Haydn often calculated the effect of writing for right and left hand on two manuals within a restricted register. In bar 6 of Hob. XVI: 23/ii (Ex. 1.4) the unison strongly suggests a two-manual instrument: if, as seems appropriate, the left-hand arpeggios are played with 'over-legato' it is impossible to play the right-hand *ab′* staccato unless two manuals are available. Similarly, in bars 67–77 and 106–10 of Hob. XVI: 28/i Haydn seems to deliberately exploit the interlocking of right and left hands in textures of restricted register such as do not occur in his earlier keyboard writing.

While certain works may therefore benefit from particular types of harpsichord (with short-octave, or with two manuals) it remains none the less possible to play the works in question on a

Ex. 1.4. Hob. xvi: 23/ii

single-manual harpsichord without short-octave, or indeed on a clavichord. The slight adjustments necessary to the layout of the large chords in Hob. xvii: 1, xvii: 2, and xvi: 47, or the sleight of hand necessary in connection with Ex. 1.3 and 1.4, are not sufficient reason to assign these works solely to the repertoire of two-manual harpsichord music or harpsichord with a short-octave tuning, however useful these instruments might be in these cases.

HAYDN'S KEYBOARD MUSIC FROM THE 1780S

For documentary and stylistic reasons it is difficult to sustain the argument that Haydn was writing for the fortepiano in the sonatas up to and including the Esterházy set (Hob. xvi: 21–6, published by Kurzböck in 1773) and the sonatas of 'anno 1776' (Hob. xvi: 27–32). Although there is no conclusive documentation to establish that Haydn owned a fortepiano before 1788 there are increasingly in the 1780s suggestions in the music itself that the fortepiano was exerting an influence on Haydn's published *œuvre* for keyboard, if not immediately on his compositional style. Central to the question of when Haydn committed himself to writing for the fortepiano are the Auenbrugger Sonatas, Hob. xvi: 35–9 and xvi: 20, published as op. 30 in 1780 by Artaria, in which dynamic indications feature more prominently than heretofore.

Brown has observed that stylistically the Auenbrugger set of sonatas is 'a publisher's ideal . . . With regard to their overall style and form, . . . the published set contained two difficult sonatas (Hob. xvi: 36 and 20) of an intellectual bent, two up-to-date ones of universal popular appeal (Hob. xvi: 35 and 37), one slightly old-fashioned sonata (Hob. xvi: 38), and a work of mixed character (Hob. xvi:

39).'[64] An important factor to be considered in connection with much of Haydn's keyboard music of the 1770s and 1780s is the composer's awareness of the large market for which his authentic editions were intended. Perhaps more than any other set the Auenbrugger Sonatas are the perfect *Kenner und Liebhaber* set with regard, as Brown has pointed out, to their stylistic diversity, but also in connection with the question of keyboard idiom there is a diversity which makes the designation of the title-page 'per il clavicembalo o fortepiano' particularly apt. Brown has also commented on the latter:

Of the Auenbrugger Sonatas Hob. XVI: 35–39, 20 published in 1780, all except Hob. XVI: 37 contain dynamic markings. Viewed as a set, however, these sonatas 'per il Clavicembalo o Forte Piano' must have represented in their use of dynamics a publisher's ideal: some are more suitable for the harpsichord, some more suitable for the *fortepiano*. But few of the latter depend so heavily on their dynamic markings for the total effect as to exclude the set from the sizable market of harpsichord owners as, for example, the late works for London very well might have done.[65]

Viewed as a set, therefore, these sonatas might well be regarded as transitional with regard to style and to keyboard idiom. Brown does not, however, pursue the relationship between compositional style and keyboard idiom in these works. The most striking feature of the set is that those sonatas which might well be regarded as being progressive stylistically seem to be less reliant on a touch-sensitive instrument than those sonatas which were either written earlier or which stylistically seem to be closer to Haydn's keyboard style of the 1760s and early 1770s than to the style of the 1780s. There is no direct correlation between the stylistically progressive and the use of dynamics which might suggest the development of an idiomatic fortepiano style; the idea of transition and the evolution of an idiomatic forte-piano style in association with a progressive compositional style is untenable for individual works, although as a whole the set may well be regarded as transitional in relation to the Kurzböck (1773) and Bossler (1784) sets.

The most extensive use of dynamics is to be found in the Sonata in C minor, Hob. XVI: 20, written in 1771 (and which, as suggested above, may well be a clavichord work), in the Sonata in C sharp

---

[64] *Keyboard Music*, 326. Based in part on this reasoning Brown has posited the following internal chronology for the set: Hob. XVI: 20—begun 1771 (finished by 1780); Hob. XVI: 36, 38—mid-1770s; Hob. XVI: 35, 37, 39—late 1770s to 1780 (ibid. 123).

[65] Ibid. 152.

minor, Hob. XVI: 36, which is the closest stylistic companion of the C minor work, and in the conservative E flat major Sonata, Hob. XVI: 38. In these works the dynamics sometimes emphasize details which are inherent in the composition itself. In the opening of the C sharp minor Sonata, for instance, there is an implicit contrast of *f* and *p* dynamic levels in the first two bars which emphasizes the change in texture and range. On clavichord or fortepiano the effect can be emphasized by appropriate dynamics; on a double-manual harpsichord it is possible to switch from coupled 8′ sets of strings to a single 8′ set. The compositional effect is, however, still apparent on a single-manual instrument. Similarly, in bar 20 of Hob. XVI: 36/iii the *fz* marking on the diminished seventh merely emphasizes an accent which is inherent in the passage: the accent is present because of the sudden expansion to a six-note chord and the addition of a *Vorschlag* (see Ex. 1.5). Neither does the diminished seventh in bar 20 of Hob. XVI: 36/ii rely solely on the dynamic marking *ff* for emphasis: it is already emphatic because of a pitch accent and the textural expansion to a five-note chord from the three- and four-note chords earlier in the phrase. There are, however, in these three sonatas a number of passages in which dynamics do not simply emphasize what is apparent; nor are these passages possible on a double-manual harpsichord. In Hob. XVI: 36/i bars 24–6 the change from *p* to *f* to *ff* is indicated in a passage in which the pitch descends and the texture is thin (Ex. 1.6*a*); the crescendo from *p* to *f* in Hob. XVI: 38/i, bars 14–16 must be achieved in a passage in which the texture does not change (see Ex. 1.6*b*). The performance of passages such as these on a harpsichord involves a compromise, and a touch-sensitive instrument does seem to be required.

Ex. 1.5. Hob. XVI: 36/iii, Menuet Moderato

Although it cannot be claimed that Hob. XVI: 36 and 38 were written exclusively for the clavichord, the stylistic association of these works with Hob. XVI: 20 suggests that the use of dynamics owes more

Ex. 1.6(*a*) Hob. XVI: 36/i, (*b*) Hob. XVI: 38/i

to the past, i.e. to Haydn's previous experimentation with dynamics in Hob. XVI: 20, than to a new attempt at an idiomatic fortepiano style. One passage in particular in Hob. XVI: 38/i is pointedly reminiscent of the unusual use of dynamics in Hob. XVI: 20 (see Ex. 1.7, and cf. Ex. 1.2). The division between stylistic progression and the exploitation of dynamics is most marked in Hob. XVI: 37 and 39, which contain few stylistic references to Haydn's style of the mid-1760s and early 1770s but which are the most conservative of the Auenbrugger set as regards the use of dynamics. There are no dynamic markings in the first movement of Hob. XVI: 37 and the few dynamic indications in the second and third movements of this work are perfectly compatible with performance on a harpsichord. In Ex. 1.8 the *pp* repetition of a subphrase at bars 14–15 allows sufficient time to change manual, or even to operate a stop on a harpsichord, while the *fz* accent in bar 16 is 'written into' the music. In the third movement of Hob. XVI: 37 and in Hob. XVI: 39 the dynamic indications are generally either echo effects, or merely underline textural

Ex. 1.7. Hob. XVI: 38/i

Ex. 1.8. Hob. XVI: 37/ii

effects (see, for instance, bars 38–43 of Hob. XVI: 39/iii where the textural 'fade-out' is reminiscent of Hob. XVI: 18). Only in one instance in these two sonatas (bars 52–3 of Hob. XVI: 39/ii) does the use of dynamics seem to require a touch-sensitive instrument. As regards the use of dynamics Hob. XVI: 35 lies somewhere between the practice of Hob. XVI: 20, 36, 38 and Hob. XVI: 37, 39. The range of dynamics in Hob. XVI: 35 is greater than in Hob. XVI: 37 and 39 and contains indications for *pp*, *p*, *f* and *ff* as well as a *cresc* indication. In most instances, however, the dynamics underline changes of texture or emphasize accents inherent in the music, though two passages in particular are less effective if performed on a harpsichord rather than on a touch-sensitive instrument (Ex. 1.9).

In the Auenbrugger Sonatas as a whole the use of dynamics is inconsistent. Individual movements contain no dynamic indications; in some sonatas the use of dynamics is reminiscent of the earliest of

Ex. 1.9. Hob. XVI: 35/i

the sonatas, Hob. XVI: 20 (Haydn's clavichord style); in many instances the dynamics are conservative in that they merely emphasize accents or changes of texture. The overall impression is not of Haydn developing an idiomatic fortepiano style, since, as pointed out, the stylistically progressive sonatas are most conservative in the use of dynamics, but rather of Haydn responding to the challenge of publishing a set of works for a large commercial market by including, in a rather haphazard manner, dynamic indications which in the 1780s were increasingly topical. It is possible that Haydn's use of dynamics in keyboard music may have originally been informed by his experience with clavichords and harpsichords rather than from any deliberate attempt at developing a fortepiano idiom, and that the use of dynamics in the Auenbrugger Sonatas is a response to matters of commerce rather than inspired by access to a fortepiano.

Dynamics were becoming increasingly frequent in keyboard music published in Vienna and elsewhere in the 1770s and 1780s. In the upsurge of music publishing in Vienna in the 1780s the inclusion of dynamics may have been a prerequisite, or at least a desirable feature, in a marketable opus; thus, sonatas written much earlier were published in the 1780s in updated versions with dynamics added and secondary sources sometimes contain dynamic markings that are lacking in extant autograph manuscripts. In the case of Haydn's Hob. XVI: 20 the additional dynamics of the first edition by comparison with the autograph manuscript are probably authentic, since the edition is authentic. This sonata is therefore Janus-faced, probably written as a clavichord sonata in 1771 but when published in 1780 it is representative of the new impulse, a tendency to update earlier sonatas intended for wider public distribution. The same tendency is witnessed in other works. While the autograph fragment of Hob. XVI: 18, dating from *c.*1766, contains only one dynamic marking, the Artaria publication and manuscript copies from the 1780s contain many details of dynamics, articulation, and ornamentation which are very probably not authentic. Because the autograph manuscript is incomplete these sources are of primary importance in establishing the text for much of the work, but they are none the less problematic textually. One of the main sources for this work, apart from the autograph fragment, is a manuscript copy in the hand of a Viennese copyist known from other sources to have prepared his texts from secondary material, often printed editions.[66] If the authenticity of the

---

[66] See C. Landon, Pref. to *Haydn: Sämtliche Klaviersonaten*, vol. i, pp. xxi–xxiii.

dynamic markings in the first movement of this work is open to question (since the autograph of the first movement is not extant), so too
is their date: they cannot be dated in any source to before the 1780s
and probably represent a later revision of the work. The single
dynamic marking in the Sonata, Hob. XVI: 46 may also be a product
of scribal updating. This sonata has a very similar history of transmission to Hob. XVI: 18, i.e. manuscript copies, including one from
the same Viennese scribe mentioned in connection with Hob. XVI:
18, dating from the 1780s, and printed editions from the late 1780s.[67]
The work itself dates from *c.*1767/8. A particularly early and striking
instance of updating is witnessed in the dynamic markings of Hob.
XVI: 29/i. These quite elaborate markings derive from manuscript
copies and are not present in the corresponding places in the extant
autograph fragment. This sonata dates from 1774 and was dissemi-
nated in authentic manuscript copies with the other sonatas of 'anno
1776'. It appears to represent an early instance of the process of
updating, whether by Haydn or the scribe, which became more
commonplace in the 1780s.[68]

    It is interesting that in three sonatas, Hob. XVI: 43, 33, and 34, pub-
lished in 1783 but possibly written around the same time as the
Auenbrugger set,[69] dynamics are noticeably less frequent than in the
Auenbrugger Sonatas. In Hob. XVI: 33 there are no dynamic indications whatsoever; in Hob. XVI: 34 a change from *p* to *f* twice in the
first movement, a change from *f* to *p* once in the second movement,
and a single *fz* accent on a syncopation in the third movement are
compatible with performance on any keyboard instrument. Only in
Hob. XVI: 43, although dynamics are still relatively infrequent, is
there a suggestion that a touch-sensitive instrument is more appropriate, since from bar 35 to 55 of the first movement the dynamic
level changes from *f* to *p* to *pp*. Although the chronology of these
sonatas may be connected with the paucity of dynamics by comparison with the Auenbrugger set, it is more likely that the explanation
lies in the fact that Hob. XVI: 33, 34, and 43 were not apparently written or compiled by Haydn as a set with a view to publication in the

[67] *Sämtliche Klaviersonaten*, vol. i, pp. xxii–xxiii.

[68] Interestingly Rice has also noted a process of updating in connection with published
fortepiano music in Tuscany in the 1780s. See Rice, 'The Tuscan Piano in the 1780s', 13–
15.

[69] C. Landon suggests that Hob. XVI: 33 and 43 date from the early 1770s and Hob. XVI:
34 from 'after 1780'. See C. Landon, preface to *Haydn: Sämtliche Klaviersonaten*, vol. i, p. xvii
and vol. iii, p. xviii. See also Brown, *Keyboard Music*, 121, 123.

manner of the Artaria op. 30; no authentic edition of these works is extant and the Beardmore & Birchall edition of 1783 is probably a pirated edition not connected with the composer.[70] The relative infrequency of dynamics and the lack of an authentic edition for the sonatas Hob. XVI: 33, 34, and 43 contrast noticeably with the Auenbrugger set, but in one regard at least the two sets are similar; in neither the Beardmore & Birchall set nor the Artaria op. 30 can dynamics be considered an indicator of stylistic modernity. The Sonata in E minor, Hob. XVI: 34 is undoubtedly the most progressive of the three sonatas as regards style and, largely because of this, it has been argued that chronologically it is the latest work. However, the only sonata in this set in which dynamics feature with any prominence is the Sonata in E flat, Hob. XVI: 43 which is either stylistically retrospective or actually written much earlier than the E minor Sonata.

It seems to me significant that inauthentic editions, such as the Beardmore & Birchall edition of Hob. XVI: 33, 34, and 43, contain few dynamics, whereas authentic editions contain more, and that there is no association between Haydn's more recent compositional style and the use of dynamics: this suggests that Haydn was not at this stage writing exclusively for the fortepiano and that the dynamics of the authentic editions of the period were inspired in the first instance by commercial motives. For these reasons it is understandable that it is mainly in authentic printed editions of the 1780s, in particular the Bossler print of the 'Esterházy' Sonatas, Hob. XVI: 40–2 (published in 1784) and the series of trios written for London and Viennese publishers from the mid-1780s, that Haydn's increasing use of dynamics, and, to the extent that the two are synonymous, the development of a fortepiano style can be traced.

Brown has observed that the 'Esterházy' Sonatas, Hob. XVI: 40–2 'mark another important turning point in Haydn's writing for the touch-sensitive instruments'[71] and indeed the opening pages of Hob. XVI: 40 are full of passages which cannot effectively be performed on a harpsichord, as, for instance, the accents on metrically weak beats

---

[70] See C. Landon, *Haydn: Sämtliche Klaviersonaten*, vol. iii, p. xviii. The coincidence of a poor source history and the lack of dynamic indications is also apparent in Haydn's Concerto in D major, Hob. XVIII: 11. Concerning the dating of this work see Brown, *Keyboard Music*, 132 and *JHW* xv/2, ed. H. Walter, p. vii and concerning the question of which instrument it was written for see *JHW* xv/2, p. ix.

[71] *Keyboard Music*, 152.

Ex. 1.10. Hob. XVI: 40/i

and the changes from *p* to *pp* to *f* to *p* in the essentially unchanging texture of Hob. XVI: 40/i, bars 9–17 (Ex. 1.10). The decisive feature is the consistency with which such dynamic effects are employed in these sonatas by comparison with earlier works. Although the 'Esterházy' Sonatas, Hob. XVI: 40–2, can undoubtedly be performed on a clavichord, it is unlikely that they were intended for a market of clavichord players and it is significant that the title-page mentions only the pianoforte. Initially the trios seem, as Brown has pointed out, conservative in the use of dynamics by comparison with the Sonatas, Hob. XVI: 40–2;[72] the dynamic indications in Hob. XV: 5 are infrequent and often support changes in texture or emphasize compositional effect, especially accents. In the Trios, Hob. XV: 9, 2, and 10 (published by Forster in 1785), Hob. XV: 6–8 (published by Artaria in 1785), and Hob. XV: 11–13 (published by Artaria in 1789) the dynamic effects are still less frequent than in the 'Esterházy' Sonatas, Hob. XVI: 40–2, but, *pace* Brown,[73] increasingly the use of dynamics is independent of textural effect and cannot effectively be performed on a harpsichord (see Ex. 1.11). The Trios, Hob. XV: 11–13, which Haydn wrote with his 'new fortepiano' in mind, represent no dramatic departure in the use of dynamics, as the 'Esterházy' Sonatas did, but a continuation of the gradual process in which dynamic effects

---

[72] *Keyboard Music*, 154.
[73] Brown finds in Hob. XV: 6–8 'the same ambivalence of idiom' as in Hob. XV: 5 (Brown, *Keyboard Music*, 154).

Ex. 1.11. Hob. xv: 10/ii

which are not possible on the harpsichord become part of the composer's style.

It is clear from Haydn's letters that in 1789 he was committed to writing keyboard music specifically for the fortepiano; stylistically the music published in that year, Hob. xv: 11–13 and xvi: 48, confirms that a harpsichord is no longer a viable alternative. While documentation does not establish precisely when Haydn began to conceive keyboard music specifically for the fortepiano it seems likely that the crucial years in Haydn's change from a generalized keyboard idiom towards a committed orientation to the fortepiano are 1780–8. In these years the pace of the change in Haydn's writing as witnessed by the increasing use of dynamic indications would appear to be quite different in the composer's solo sonatas than in the trios. The Sonatas, Hob. xvi: 35–9, 33–4, and 43 do not seem to require exclusively a performance on the fortepiano and the ubiquitous description 'per il clavicembalo o fortepiano', supplemented with the option of performance on a clavichord, would seem to be perfectly apt and, as far as can be ascertained from the existing evidence, in accord with the composer's intention. However, in the next set of sonatas, Hob. xvi: 40–2, the choice of instrument seems to be suddenly narrowed, since a performance of these works on a harpsichord involves a considerable compromise with respect to the profuse dynamic indications. On the other hand, the series of trios which began to appear in 1785 display a more gradual process by which the dynamic effects which make performance on a harpsichord problematic appear with increasing frequency after Hob. xv: 5.

Notwithstanding recent research which documents early performances on the fortepiano in Vienna and elsewhere, it seems unlikely that, even if Haydn had access to a fortepiano before the 1780s, his keyboard music can be viewed as being exclusively conceived for the fortepiano before *c.*1784. It may be no less than 'the heretical truth' that, by comparison with some of his contemporaries (notably Mozart and Steffan), Haydn was in this regard not an innovator but a 'dedicated follower of fashion'.

2

Articulation

◊

The eighteenth-century theorists who deal with the subject of articulation in keyboard music describe four different types of touch,
namely staccato, legato, the 'ordinary' touch,[1] and *portato* or *Tragen
der Töne*. While there is a considerable degree of uniformity in these
eighteenth-century theoretical descriptions of each type of touch,
important distinctions need to be made between eighteenth- and
nineteenth-century discussions of this subject, and not a few problematic interpretations of this evidence in the modern literature
require re-evaluation.

Staccato

Staccato is, according to C. P. E. Bach, indicated by either a *Strich* or
a *Punkt*[2] and the duration of the notes so marked is 'a little less than
half of their notated length', although Bach indicates that the extent
of the staccato is dependent on the value of the note, the tempo and
the dynamic level. Staccato occurs 'in general' in 'leaping passages
and rapid tempos'.[3] Marpurg's description in the *Anleitung zum
Clavierspielen* is similar to Bach's, but he recommends that the staccato note be held 'for half' its value.[4] In *Principes du clavecin*, Marpurg

---

[1] Although many authors describe this type of touch, Marpurg and Türk are among the
few authors who actually use the terms *ordentliche* and *gewöhnliche*.

[2] Bach makes no functional distinction between *Punkt* and *Strich* and prefers the former
in his 'Lessons' (i.e. the *Probestücke*) only to avoid the confusion which might arise between
the *Strich* and fingering numerals.

[3] C. P. E. Bach, *Versuch*, trans. Mitchell, 154.

[4] 'Dem Schleissen ist das Abstossen entgegen gesetzet, welches darinnen besteht, daß man
eine Note nicht nach ihrem Wehrte, sondern sie nur etwann bis zur hälfte aushält. Dieses

gives the realization of the staccato note as exactly half the notated value (table II, figs. 8.a–c) and adds that the staccato *Strich* is sometimes used instead of the *Punkt*.[5] Türk's comments at the end of the eighteenth century on the notation of staccato are an elaboration on those of Bach, but in one respect (the question of whether the distinction between *Strich* and *Punkt* is functional) they are prophetic of nineteenth-century descriptions: 'The signs at *a* [i.e. *Strich*] and *b* [i.e. *Punkt*] have the same meaning, but some would like to indicate by the stroke (*a*) that a shorter staccato be played than that indicated by the dot (*b*).'[6] Regarding the duration of the staccato note Türk agrees with the description of Marpurg,[7] although he explains, like Bach, that adjustments must be made according to the character of the piece, the tempo, and the dynamic level:

If the character of a composition is serious, tender, sad, etc., then the detached tones must not be as short as they would be in pieces of a lively, humorous, and the like, nature. Occasional detached tones in a songful Adagio are not to be as short as they would be in an Allegro. For forte one can play detached notes a little shorter than for piano. The tones of skips in general have a more pronounced staccato than the tones in intervals progressing by step, etc.[8]

In the nineteenth century theorists made a clear distinction between the *Punkt* and *Strich* in the notation of staccato: Clementi, writing in 1801, commented that staccato indicated by a *Strich* entails 'lifting the finger up, as soon as it has struck the key', but if a *Punkt* is used, this, 'when composers are EXACT in their writing, means LESS staccato than the preceding mark; the finger, therefore, is kept down somewhat longer'.[9] Clementi, in common with most theorists, adds the stereotyped cautionary comment that the degree of staccato depends on the character of the piece.

wird durch Puncte über oder unter den Noten die abgestossen werden sollen, angezeiget'. *Anleitung zum Clavierspielen* (Berlin, 1755), 28.

[5] 'En place des points on se sert quelquefois de petites lignes'. *Principes du clavecin* (Berlin, 1756), 34 and table II, figs. 8.a–c.

[6] *Klavierschule, oder Anweisung zum Klavierspielen für Lehrer und Lernende* (Leipzig & Halle, 1789), trans. R. Haggh (Lincoln, Nebr.: University of Nebraska Press, 1982), 342.

[7] 'In playing detached tones one lifts the finger from the key when half the value of the note is past and pauses for the remaining period.' Ibid. 343.

[8] Ibid.

[9] *Introduction to the Art of Playing on the Pianoforte* (London, 1801), ed. S. Rosenblum (facsimile repr., New York: Da Capo Press, 1974), 8. Clementi continues to comment that a 'still less' degree of staccato is indicated by the combination of dots and slur, ⌢ . The changing significance of this notation is discussed below.

The theoretical descriptions of staccato are therefore relatively straightforward, with the apparent synonymity of the *Strich* and *Punkt* in the eighteenth century being as well documented, at least in sources devoted to keyboard music, as the durational distinction between the two is in the nineteenth century. In practice, the situation is far more complex. Notwithstanding the reservations of some scholars, Mozart undoubtedly distinguished between the *Strich* and *Punkt* in his autograph manuscripts, although not always consistently, and the *Strich* appears to serve a number of functions: it often seems to imply a durational distinction from the staccato *Punkt* (that is, a shorter staccato than implied by the dot), but sometimes seems to bear the connotation of added dynamic emphasis, which is particularly apparent when a *Strich* appears over a long note or over the first of two tied notes.[10] Confusion is increased by the presence of the ubiquitous *Keil* or wedge symbol in eighteenth-century printed editions, and it still needs to be emphasized that the *Keil* is purely a product of engraved music, it does not appear in eighteenth-century autographs and has no independent musical significance. Suggested interpretations of the *Strich* and *Punkt* in Mozart's music remain, to some extent, problematic because of palaeographic problems in distinguishing the two signs in Mozart's autographs, the undoubted inconsistencies which sometimes occur in these manuscripts (Neumann's 'grey area of casualness' between clearly identifiable strokes and dots), and because of the corruption of Mozart's notation in the process of transmission. Beethoven also appears to have distinguished between *Strich* and *Punkt*, as is clear from the well-known correction to the second movement of his Seventh Symphony, and from a letter from Beethoven to Karl Holz, dated 1825:[11] again, however, the precise meaning of each symbol in Beethoven's music is unclear and, even more than in the case of Mozart, the situation is complicated by palaeographic and text-critical problems.

From Haydn's autographs it is clear that his normal indication for

[10] For a discussion of this subject see esp. H. Albrecht (ed.), *Die Bedeutung der Zeichen Keil, Strich und Punkt bei Mozart* (Kassel: Bärenreiter, 1957); and F. Neumann, 'Dots and Strokes in Mozart', *EM* 21/3 (Aug. 1993), 429–35.

[11] See Rothschild, *Musical Performance in the Times of Mozart and Beethoven* (Lost Tradition in Music, 2; London: A. & C. Black, 1961), 48–9, 99–101 (facsimile of Beethoven's letter to Holz on p. 100); a full trans. of the letter may be found in E. Anderson, *The Letters of Beethoven*, iii (London: Macmillan, 1961), 1241–2. See also G. Nottebohm, *Beethoveniana* (Leipzig: Peters, 1872), 107–25; and W. S. Newman, *Beethoven on Beethoven: Playing His Piano Music His Way* (New York: Norton, 1988), 139–46.

staccato is the *Strich* and that only on a few occasions, and in very specific contexts, is the *Punkt* used. Moreover, in Haydn's autographs, unlike those of Mozart and Beethoven, there are fewer palaeographical problems with regard to the two indications: on the relatively rare occasions on which the *Punkt* occurs, it is readily distinguishable from the *Strich*. The situation is certainly more complicated with regard to the printed sources of Haydn's music, but it is possible to establish Haydn's practices concerning the notation of staccato with a degree of precision impossible in the works of Mozart and Beethoven. Haydn's orthographic habits and the relationship between the *Punkt* and *portato* in Haydn's music are discussed in detail below.

Legato

The legato touch is indicated by the presence of a slur and the notes under such a slur must be, according to C. P. E. Bach, 'held for their full length'.[12] Marpurg and Türk both mention that it is necessary to indicate legato by a slur when this manner of touch is required and their descriptions of the duration of notes encompassed by the slur are similar to Bach's.[13] It is important to note that legato touch was generally required to be notated by a slur in the second half of the eighteenth century and was not understood as the normal touch. In practice, however, slurs were not always indicated where legato is appropriate. C. P. E. Bach mentions that 'It is a convenient custom to indicate by appropriate marks only the first few of prolonged successions of detached or legato notes, it being self-evident that all of the tones are to be played similarly until another kind of mark intervenes.'[14] In practice it is required of the performer (although not necessarily of the editor) to supply additional slurs in far more instances than the simple practice of continuation mentioned by Bach. In the early works of Haydn and Mozart few articulation marks are found. Even in the much more precisely notated late works, the performer must supplement the composer's markings on many occasions.

[12] *Versuch*, trans. Mitchell, 154.
[13] '*Couler* c'est ne relever le doigt de la note précédente que l'on n'ait touché la suivante'. Marpurg, *Principes du clavecin*, 34. 'For tones which are to be slurred, the finger should be allowed to remain on the key until the duration of the given note is completely past, so that not the slighest separation (rest) results'. Türk, *Klavierschule*, trans. Haggh, 344.
[14] *Versuch*, trans. Mitchell, 154–5.

The slurs in eighteenth-century music are in general short slurs, frequently encompassing only the notes of one beat, sometimes the notes of a group of beats and rarely, in keyboard music, being longer than a bar in length. Characteristically slurs conform to the metre of a piece of music, grouping together the notes which encompass a beat, or group of beats, and rarely crossing the bar line. Only when all the notes of a bar of music are covered by one slur is the legato touch implied for the whole bar. When, however, the characteristic pattern of shorter slurs occurs (as, for instance, in 4/4 time when a pattern of sixteen semiquavers is grouped into four slurs each encompassing four semiquavers) a general legato touch is not intended since a *silence d'articulation* is required between each slur. This seemingly obvious point is emphasized since the majority of modern writers on the subject of articulation have difficulty in accepting literally the implications of this characteristic grouping of short slurs. Herman Keller suggests that:

We must therefore try to distinguish between the instances in which such slurs were drawn simply as a matter of convenience, especially of the engraver (as in the distinction between the wedge and the dot), and those in which the composer demanded a change of bow from the string players and carried over this designation to the keyboard instruments as well.[15]

It is not altogether clear in what way short slurs are a convenient way of indicating longer slurs; certainly, autograph manuscripts contain enough longer slurs to suggest that when a composer required them he notated them literally, without apparent inconvenience. Although slurs were problematic in engraving, long slurs drawn with a graver, as they frequently were, were no more problematic than short slurs. Moreover, when engravers used a combination of punches to indicate a long slur the overlapping of shorter slurs was easily effected (see Ex. 2.21*f*). It should also be mentioned that if short slurs were a mere conventional method of indicating longer slurs, no eighteenth-century treatise records this convention. While Keller advocates the elision of many short slurs, which should be 'understood as a continuous legato', he adds the cautionary comment that 'it is not true . . . that one should simply lengthen every slur that appears peculiar or illogical at first sight'.[16]

---

[15] *Phrasierung und Artikulation* (1955), trans. L. Gerdine as *Phrasing and Articulation* (London: Barrie & Rockliff, 1966), 58–9.

[16] Ibid. 59.

P. and E. Badura-Skoda maintain a distinction, not found in eighteenth-century treatises, between 'legato' and 'articulation' slurs:

Examining Mozart's own slurs (that is to say, slurs which occur in his manuscripts and which have definitely not been added by editors), one can distinguish legato slurs from articulating slurs by the fact that they extend over several notes and often end at the bar-line or before the last note. This is disconcerting at first, but it is easily explained by the fact that in classical music the use of slurs originated in violin bowing.[17]

The characteristic classical pattern of groups of short slurs, whether it derives from bowing or not, is disconcerting only if one's concept of touch is that of a continuous legato. This would sometimes seem to be the case: 'In almost every cantabile theme it is necessary to link the notes by playing legato; even when a literal interpretation of articulating slurs would lead one to lift the hand from the keys, one should not do so.'[18] In a recent study Robin Stowell perpetuates this tradition. Like Keller and P. and E. Badura-Skoda, he maintains that short slurs should be treated in a cumulative manner, elided into a long legato line: 'typically for the period, he [Mozart] usually indicated a continuous legato by slurring each bar separately, but with no break intended between.'[19]

Two passages from eighteenth- and nineteenth-century theory have been cited to support this concept of elision. This 'evidence' is worth quoting and re-evaluating. The first passage is from Czerny's *Piano Forte School, Op. 500*: 'although the slurs are not continuous, but are broken into several lines, they are considered as forming but one, and no perceptible separation must take place'.[20] By the time Czerny

[17] *Mozart-Interpretation* (1957), trans. L. Black as *Interpreting Mozart on the Keyboard* (London: Barrie & Rockliff, 1962), 55.

[18] Ibid. 56.

[19] 'Leopold Mozart Revised: Articulation in Violin Playing during the Second Half of the Eighteenth Century', in R. L. Todd and P. Williams (eds.), *Perspectives on Mozart Performance* (Cambridge Studies in Performance Practice; Cambridge: CUP, 1991), 138. Badura-Skoda's suggestion that the performer must distinguish between 'articulation' and 'legato' slurs is also followed closely in G. Jenkins, 'The Legato Touch and the "Ordinary" Manner of Keyboard Playing from 1750 to 1850', Ph.D. diss., Cambridge University, 1976, i. 69–70. Sandra Rosenblum, although for the most part respecting the composer's notation, lists various exceptional instances in which she suggests that slurs might be elided; see S. Rosenblum, *Performance Practices in Classic Piano Music: Their Principles and Application* (Bloomington, Ind.: Indiana University Press, 1988), 175–83.

[20] *Vollständige theoretisch-praktische Pianoforte-Schule . . . Op. 500*, 3 vols. (Vienna, 1839), trans. J. H. Hamilton as *Complete Theoretical and Practical Piano Forte School . . . Op. 500*, 3 vols. (London, 1839), i. 187.

was writing, a fundamental change had taken place in performance practices; Czerny and other nineteenth-century theorists advocate a continuous legato touch and thus for them the notation of a succession of short slurs was anachronistic; consequently, in their practice these slurs were elided into a seamless legato. The change in style is best observed in Clementi's approach to articulation, since his career overlaps with that of Haydn, Mozart, Beethoven, and the 'new' style of the 'London Pianoforte School'. In Clementi's *Introduction to the Art of Playing on the Pianoforte* of 1801, legato is advocated as the normal touch:

N.B. When the composer leaves the LEGATO, and STACCATO to the performer's taste; the best rule is, to adhere chiefly to the LEGATO; reserving the STACCATO to give SPIRIT occasionally to certain passages, and to set off the HIGHER BEAUTIES of the LEGATO.[21]

Yet Clementi did not always play in this manner, which is evidently characteristic of his later performances: interestingly, the continuous legato is associated by Clementi with developments in piano construction, in particular the English piano. Contemporary reports state that his later manner of performance resulted from 'the gradual perfecting of the *English* concert grand fortepiano in particular, the earlier faulty construction of which had practically excluded the possibility of a more singing, more legato style of playing'.[22] The contrast between the legato style advocated by Czerny and Clementi on the one hand and both eighteenth-century descriptions of articulation and the characteristic notation of slurs in eighteenth-century music on the other hand, is as marked as the considerable differences between the Viennese and English pianos of the period.[23]

A passage from Türk has also been cited as evidence for the elision of slurs into a continuous legato. Türk says of the passage quoted in Ex. 2.1*a* that he has indicated the 'incorrect kind of division . . . by rests' and later that this particular extract should be executed in the manner of Ex. 2.1*b*.[24] It has been concluded from this that Türk

[21] p. 9. [22] Quoted in Deutsch, *Mozart*, 542.

[23] Many writers in the early 19th cent. describe the differences between Viennese and English piano and associate the heavier action of the latter with a legato touch. The performance style of Mozart and the 'Mozart school' are regarded as decidedly old-fashioned by these writers by comparison with a new generation of pianists who employed a legato style. See Kalkbrenner, *A Complete Course of Instruction for the Piano Forte*, 8; Czerny, *Pianoforte School, Op. 500*, iii. 100; Czerny, *On the Proper Performance of all Beethoven's Works for the Piano*, ed. Badura-Skoda (Vienna: Universal, 1970), 5.

[24] *Klavierschule*, trans. Haggh, 329–30.

Ex. 2.1. Türk, *Klavierschule*, trans. Haggh, (*a*) p. 329, (*b*) p. 330

implied the elision of the short slurs into a continuous legato.[25] Yet
this passage from Türk's *Klavierschule* is concerned with the analogy
between rhetoric to music; in particular, the practice of separating the
Einschnitte in a composition. The incorrect passage is a caution not to
separate 'by rests' except at the end of an *Einschnitt*. Türk's point is
simply that the degree of separation implied by the slurs is less than
that appropriate at the end of an *Einschnitt*. Nowhere does he imply
that one should ignore the smaller *silence d'articulation* required by the
slurs of Ex. 2.1*b*.

It is significant that, apart from the above-quoted, controvertible
passage from Türk, no eighteenth-century theoretical reference supports the idea that slurs should be elided into a continuous legato.
The nineteenth-century interpretation of patterns of short slurs as a
conventional way of notating continuous legato has no basis in
eighteenth-century theory, and it seems to me to be particularly suspect to ignore one of the most characteristic features of eighteenth-
century notation on the basis of later concepts of articulation. The
disconcerting nature of short slurs to some modern commentators
can be seen to derive from the influence of nineteenth-century practices and especially from the sonority of the nineteenth-century
piano. In the music of Haydn and Mozart the groupings of short slurs
are intended to be interpreted literally and the *silence d'articulation*, of
flexible duration, between the slurs is an essential part of the style.
Articulation of this type will be seen to be an integral part of Classical
metrical and rhetorical accentuation.

'Ordinary' Touch

The third type of touch, sometimes referred to as the 'ordinary'
touch, is described by C. P. E. Bach as follows:

[25] Jenkins, 'Keyboard Playing', 69. Stowell ('Leopold Mozart Revised', 131) also maintains, incorrectly, that Türk distinguished between 'legato' and 'articulation' slurs.

Tones which are neither detached, connected, nor fully held are sounded for half their value, unless the abbreviation *Ten.* (hold) is written over them, in which case they must be held fully. Quarters and eighths in moderate and slow tempos are usually performed in this semidetached manner. They must not be played weakly, but with fire and a slight accentuation.[26]

Although the existence of this type of touch is well documented, at least in German theory, no consensus exists on the extent of the separation involved in the ordinary touch. Marpurg comments as follows in his *Anleitung zum Clavierspielen*:

In contrast to the legato and staccato there is the ordinary manner of playing in which the finger is lifted from the key just before the following note is played. The ordinary manner of playing, since it is always taken for granted, is never marked.[27]

Türk also recommends a lesser degree of separation than Bach, suggesting that in the ordinary style of playing, 'the finger is lifted a little earlier from the key than is required by the duration of the note'. He recommends that a crotchet may be played in this manner as ♪ꞎ or ♪.ꞎ 'depending on the circumstances' and specifically objects to Bach's recommended 'half-value' for the following reasons:

(1) the character of a composition necessitates a variety of restrictions in this respect; (2) the distinction between the tone which is actually detached and that which is to be played in the customary manner is practically abolished; and (3) the execution would probably become too short (choppy) if every note not slurred was held for only half of its value, and consequently the second half would be a rest.[28]

The disagreements concerning the actual extent of the detachment involved in the ordinary touch are understandable since this will vary depending not only upon the musical context, but also on the instrument used, the acoustic in which the performance is taking place, and on personal taste. The three accounts quoted above do, however, agree on a number of important points: first, that a manner of touch existed which involved a degree of separation less than that implied

---

[26] *Versuch*, trans. Mitchell, 157.

[27] 'Sowohl dem Schleifen als Abstossen ist das ordentliche fortgehen entgegen gesetzet, welches darinnen besteht, daß man ganz hurtig kurz vorher, ehe man die folgende Note berühret, den Finger von der vorhergehenden Takte aufhebet. Dieses ordentliche Fortgehen wird, weil es allezeit vorausgesetzet wird, niemahls angezeiget' (p. 29).

[28] Türk, *Klavierschule*, trans. Haggh, 345–6.

by staccato indications and secondly, that this manner of touch did not have a special notation, but applied to notes not bearing any other indication of touch. This latter point is problematic and exemplifies the considerable gap between contemporary theory and practice. In theory, notes to be played in the ordinary style are recognizable since they are unmarked and are distinct from the other common manners of touch which require specific notation.[29] In practice, composers did not supply the appropriate indications for legato, staccato, and *Tragen der Töne* on every occasion they were required and thus any unmarked note may, on the one hand, indicate the ordinary touch or, on the other, simply be an instance of neglect in specifying another, intended touch. In the early works of Haydn, for instance, very few indications of articulation are found: it is obvious therefore that this does not imply that every unmarked note is played in the ordinary manner. In this respect the term ordinary touch is misleading since it should not be assumed that this form of touch was necessarily the most widely used: the idea that any one general manner of articulation was prevalent in eighteenth-century music is untenable. A cursory glance at any work bearing detailed instructions as regards articulation (e.g. Hob. XVI: 23) will clearly reveal a great diversity in articulation, with no one touch dominating. The ordinary touch is an important aspect of articulation in much eighteenth-century music, but it cannot be regarded as the dominant mode of articulation: it cannot be assumed for every unmarked note but only in connection with those for which another mode of touch cannot be assumed. C. P. E. Bach's comment that the ordinary touch usually applied to crotchets and quavers in a slow or moderate tempo is helpful as a general guideline and confirms the impression that, for instance, continuous movement in semiquavers is, in general, divided into metrical patterns of slurs and is not played in the ordinary manner.

---

[29] Darbellay points out that general rules in Bach's *Versuch* are formulated as a priori propositions designed to cover all possible cases. The propositions are, however, only true in practice if the codified notational system on which the proposition relies is observed in all cases. This is clearly not always true in practice, even (*pace* Darbellay) in the notation practice of C. P. E. Bach. See Darbellay, 'C. P. E. Bach's Aesthetic as Reflected in his Notation', in S. Clark (ed.), *C. P. E. Bach Studies* (Oxford: Clarendon Press, 1988), 43–63.

Tragen der Töne

Tragen der Töne is described by C. P. E. Bach thus:

The notes of Figure 169 [Ex. 2.2] are played legato, but each tone is noticeably accented. The term which refers to the performance of notes that are
both slurred and dotted is *portato* [*Tragen der Töne*].
 A long, affettuoso tone is performed with a vibrato [*Bebung*]. The finger
that depresses and holds the key is gently shaken. The sign of a vibrato
appears in Example *a* [see Ex. 2.2]. The best effect is achieved when the
finger withholds its shake until half the value of the note has passed.[30]

Ex. 2.2. C. P. E. Bach, *Versuch*, trans. Mitchell, p. 156, fig. 169

Elsewhere Bach clarified that 'the *portato* and vibrato of Figure 169
apply only to the clavichord'.[31] Taken literally, this statement implies
that *Tragen der Töne*, like *Bebung*, involves a fluctuation in the pitch
of the notes marked ⌢ . Marpurg's description in *Principes du
clavecin* also contains the dual instruction that the notes marked by
both slur and dot should be held for their full length and accented a
little.[32] Marpurg mentions that this type of touch is not possible on
'clavecins ordinaires', and again, like C. P. E. Bach, his example consists of quavers moving in conjunct motion (see Ex. 2.3).[33] Türk's
description of *Tragen der Töne* in his *Klavierschule* is consistent with
those of Bach and Marpurg:

The playing of notes which are slurred and yet detached [*Tragen der Töne*]
is signified either as shown in *a* or by the word *appoggiato* [see Ex. 2.4] The

Ex. 2.3. Marpurg, *Principes du clavecin*, table II, fig. 9

---

[30] *Versuch*, trans. Mitchell, 156.   [31] Ibid. 157.
[32] 'Quand le signe du détaché & du coulé se trouvent reünis sur deux ou plusieurs notes
de suite, cela signifie qu'il faut *soutenir également les notes jusqu'à leur valeur expirée, en y
appuyant un peu*' (p. 34).
[33] 'Mais cette manière de rendre le son n'est pas praticable sur les clavecins ordinaires.'
Ibid. and table II, fig. 9.

Ex. 2.4. Türk, *Klavierschule*, trans. Haggh, p. 343

dot indicates the pressure which every key must receive and by the curved
line the player is reminded to hold the tone out until the duration of the
given note has been completed. One should guard against the overexag-
geration of a tone . . . which some call howling.[34]

It is clear from the reference to howling, an exaggerated variation in
pitch through excessive finger pressure, that Türk also understood
the term *Tragen der Töne* specifically in connection with the clavichord. A further reference to the term in the *Klavierschule* reaffirms
the basic North German understanding of the term *Tragen der Töne*
as a feature of performance on the clavichord:

A sustained playing of tones [*Tragen der Töne*] means that when one tone
progresses to another, there will be no interruption of the sound. On the
clavichord, this so called sustaining is very easily attained, because pressure
may be exerted on the key after the attack has been made.[35]

The performance of *Tragen der Töne* on the clavichord involves the
sustaining of the individual notes, the accentuation of each note, and
an expressive emphasis on each note by a slight variation of pitch
(achieved by slowly increasing and decreasing the pressure on the key
after the initial attack). This manner of performance is pertinent to
the interpretation of *Tragen der Töne* indications in Haydn's keyboard
works when they are performed on a clavichord.

Tragen der Töne cannot, however, be regarded as exclusively a
feature of performance on the clavichord: its indication occurs
commonly in violin music, in keyboard music written in a general
keyboard idiom (i.e. not exclusively for any particular keyboard
instrument), and also in music written specifically for the fortepiano
(as for instance in Haydn's Sonata in E flat, Hob. XVI: 49, a fortepiano
sonata written specifically with an instrument of Wenzel Schanz in
mind). While fluctuation in the pitch of a note is, of course, impossible in the performance of *Tragen der Töne* on keyboard instruments
other than the clavichord, the other elements involved in the performance of *Tragen der Töne*, i.e. the sustaining and the slight accentuation of each note (and perhaps an expressive accent on each note

[34] Türk, *Klavierschule*, Trans. Haggh, 343.   [35] Ibid. 421 n. 69.

equivalent to the fluctuation of pitch on a clavichord), are feasible and likely interpretations of the *Tragen der Töne* indications in harpsichord and fortepiano music. It is of interest in this regard that descriptions of *portato* bowing in the eighteenth century do not mention the fluctuation in pitch characteristic of the clavichord, but are in other respects similar to the descriptions of *Tragen der Töne* in German sources quoted above. L. Mozart describes *portato* thus:

It happens also that under the circle [i.e. slur] or, if the circle be under the notes, over the same, dots are written under or over the notes. This signifies that the notes lying within the slur are not only to be played in one bow-stroke, but must be separated from each other by a slight pressure of the bow.[36]

The apparent difference between L. Mozart's wording 'separated from' and the phrases 'sustained playing of tones', 'to hold the tone out' (in Türk and Marpurg), and the term 'legato' in Bach's *Versuch* is illusory. L. Mozart describes the separation as taking place in the same bow-stroke. Considering that the most common context in which *Tragen der Töne* occurs is in connection with the repetition of the same pitch, a slight separation is inevitable (on a violin the momentary stopping of the bow and on a fortepiano the momentary release of the key to allow the hammer to be thrown again at the string). What appears to be the aim in all of these descriptions is a performance involving the minimum amount of separation between each note, and the expressive accentuation of each note.[37]

Explanations of the meaning of the indication ⌢ specifically in connection with fortepiano music do not apparently survive before the nineteenth century. Hummel's description is of interest since it retains something of the character of the eighteenth-century descriptions quoted above:

When a curved line is drawn over the dots ⌢ , which generally takes place in passages of a singing character, the notes must, as it were, be gently detached by the fingers, and each, for itself, receive a certain increasing degree of emphasis.[38]

---

[36] *Versuch einer gründlichen Violinschule* (Augsburg, 1756), trans. E. Knocker as *A Treatise on the Fundamental Principles of Violin Playing* (Oxford: OUP, 1948), 45.

[37] Concerning *portato* bowing see R. Stowell, *Violin Technique and Performance Practice in the Late Eighteenth and Early Nineteenth Centuries* (Cambridge: CUP, 1985), 176.

[38] *Instructions*, pt. I, p. 66.

Other nineteenth-century accounts belong to a new tradition, reflecting the considerable change in practices of articulation and, within the context of an increasing emphasis on a legato manner of performance, the *Tragen der Töne* indication was categorized as a type of staccato touch, rather than, as previously, a touch requiring the sustaining or holding out of notes. Czerny, in volume i of his *Piano Forte School, Op. 500*, describes the indication ⌢ as a '*lingering stac-cato* touch, which is as it were, a medium between the *legato* and the *staccato*'.[39] In volume iii of the same opus we find, perhaps, the origin of the modern understanding of the indication ⌢ , which Czerny describes as a 'mezzo-staccato touch' and which entails holding the requisite notes for 'only somewhat more than half their usual value, say for about 2 thirds of it'.[40] Underlying Czerny's comment on articulation is a clear understanding of legato as the predominant touch. Clementi's advocacy of legato, mentioned above, is confirmed by Czerny's description of the general manner of articulation:

When nothing is placed over the notes, and they are not separated by rests; they are, in compliance with a general rule, always to be played in a smoothly connected manner; for the *Legato* style is the rule, and the *Staccato* the exception.[41]

Both Clementi and Czerny describe two basic types of touch; legato, the prevailing touch, and staccato. The latter was variable, the *Strich*, *Punkt*, and ⌢ indicating progressively lesser degrees of staccato. This new codification of manners of touch is confirmed in Kalkbrenner's remarks on staccato, in which the degree of staccato is progressively indicated by the slur and dot combination, the *Punkt*, and the *Strich*:

Commas ⅠⅠⅠⅠⅠ over notes, mean that they are to be played short, or *staccato*. The dot .... means that the finger should be raised, but that the notes should not be played quite so short as those with the mark of the comma. The lines and dots together, mean that the notes should be played as if with the same finger.[42]

A number of points emerge from these quotations: a general legato style ('the Higher Beauties of the Legato') is taken for granted in the nineteenth century, while the ordinary touch of the eighteenth century has disappeared as a common usage which did not require a

[39] p. 186.   [40] Ibid. iii. 24.   [41] Ibid. i. 189.
[42] *Complete Course of Instruction for the Piano Forte*, 6.

specific notation. The variable degree of separation previously understood, without notation, as the ordinary touch, is in the nineteenth
century specifically indicated by the *Punkt* and by the combination of
Punkt and slur. The eighteenth-century indication for *Tragen der Töne*
therefore survived into the nineteenth century, but indicated a type
of touch equivalent to the eighteenth-century ordinary touch. The
special expressive meaning of *Tragen der Töne* in the eighteenth century seems to have disappeared in nineteenth-century theory. The
two very different traditions of articulation represented by mid-
eighteenth century German writers and general nineteenth-century
descriptions are summarized in Tables 2.1 and 2.2.

The concept of a 'general touch' is tenable for nineteenth-century
keyboard music. A legato touch is to be assumed, unless some sort of
staccato touch is specified. Legato is the norm, whether specified or
not; staccato is the exception, which should be specified. As suggested above, the explanation for the nineteenth-century emphasis
on the legato touch must be connected, at least in part, with changes
in piano construction, in particular with the deeper and heavier
touch of the English piano.

The concept of a general touch in keyboard performance in the
second half of the eighteenth century is much more problematic. As
has been pointed out above, the ordinary touch in the eighteenth
century was not indicated by any particular notation, but unlike
legato in the nineteenth century, it cannot be considered as a predominant manner of articulation. Some eighteenth-century sources

TABLE 2.1 *Eighteenth-Century German descriptions of touch*

Type	Indication	Description
staccato	ı or ·	$\frac{1}{2}$ or $< \frac{1}{2}$ value of note
'ordinary'	no indication	$\frac{1}{2}$ or $> \frac{1}{2}$ value of note
Tragen der Töne	⌒··	'sustained' and 'accented'
legato	⌒	generally patterns of short slurs: notes under slurs joined, but slurs separated by *silence d'articulation*

TABLE 2.2 *Nineteenth-Century descriptions of touch*

Type	Indication	Description
staccato	❘ and · and ⌢̇	varying degrees of staccato: 'short', 'less sharp', 'lingering staccato', or 'mezzo-staccato'
legato	slurs, or no indication	predominant touch whether indicated or not

advocate legato as a general touch in keyboard performance.[43] Miller commented that the 'best Masters . . . generally use the Legato [as the common touch]';[44] Pasquali stated that 'The Legato is the touch that this treatise endeavours to teach, being a general touch fit for almost all kinds of passages';[45] and Manfredini advocated legato as appropriate 'on almost any occasion'.[46] It is quite possible that legato was the common touch in certain regional styles in the second half of the eighteenth century (which may be associated, on the scant evidence available, with Italy and, not surprisingly perhaps, England, where an Italian influence might be expected). A general legato touch is, however, incompatible with commentaries on articulation in German treatises from the second half of the eighteenth century and with the notation (in particular the characteristic slur patterns) of Haydn's keyboard music, and indeed, with the notation of German and Austrian keyboard music generally in the second half of the eighteenth century. Even in cantabile slow movements, commonly associated with the legato touch, detailed indications of articulation in Haydn's music contradict the notion that a general legato style is appropriate. It is clear that nineteenth-century articulation differed radically from that of the eighteenth century, the pervasive legato of the former contrasting with the latter style which involved legato slurs over small groups of notes and an ordinary detached touch which mediated between the legato and the staccato; in addition,

---

[43] Legato articulation played an important part in certain styles in the earlier part of the eighteenth century, as seems clear from Rameau's pref. 'De la mechanique des doigts sur le clavessin', in his *Pièces de Clavecin* of 1724 and from the large number of slurs that appear in e.g. F. Couperin's preludes published as part of his treatise *L'Art de toucher le clavecin* (Paris, 1716).

[44] *Institutes of Music, or Easy Instructions for the Harpsichord* (London, [1771]), 15.

[45] *The Art of Fingering the Harpsichord* (Edinburgh, 1757), 26.

[46] *Regole armoniche* (Venice, 1775), 28.

Tragen der Töne indications in the eighteenth century represented a special expressive effect rather than a mezzo-staccato articulation. Beyond the clarification of this change in style, theoretical writings are of limited use. Since articulation markings in Viennese keyboard music suggest that a sophisticated, heterogeneous interaction of a variety of touches rather than a single pervasive touch was the norm, more precise information on articulation in this music is best sought by examining the notational practices of individual composers.

HAYDN'S NOTATION

Strich and *Punkt*

Haydn's normal, or perhaps only, indication of staccato is the *Strich*. Unlike the autograph manuscripts of Mozart and Beethoven, there are remarkably few instances in Haydn's autographs of keyboard works where the *Strich* is not clearly written and recognizable as such. The *Punkt* also occurs in autograph manuscripts of keyboard works, rarely in early autographs but relatively frequently in the 1780s and 1790s, and apart from a few occasions (mostly in hastily written autographs) it is clearly identifiable and easily distinguishable from the *Strich*. The situation is more complex with regard to printed editions where the engraver's own practices frequently take precedence over the composer's careful notation. This is immediately apparent when a comparison is made between autograph manuscripts and printed editions. In the autograph manuscript of the Sonata in E flat, Hob. XVI: 52 Haydn clearly distinguishes between *Strich* and *Punkt*, but in Artaria's edition of this work (op. 82, plate no. 792) the *Punkt* is employed exclusively by the engraver, obliterating the distinction found in Haydn's notation.[47]

In many of Artaria's publications of Haydn's music in the late 1780s and the 1790s the *Punkt* is employed as the predominant, if not exclusive, indication of staccato (e.g. op. 57, plate no. 239; op. 75, plate no. 624) and although autograph manuscripts are rarely extant for comparison, there can be no doubt that this feature of orthography derives from the engravers and not the composer. This is clear

---

[47] The reverse is also true, though less frequently. In bar 21 of Hob. XVI: 29/i where the *Punkt* is used in the surviving autograph fragment the 1st edn. of Hummel (op. 14, plate no. 390) has a staccato *Strich*.

because in those autographs that have survived the *Strich* is used as the norm, with the *Punkt* representing an occasional qualification, while in many Artaria editions this balance is reversed. Frequently these Artaria editions are not first editions, especially in the case of the late Trios, and the fact that the editions of Forster, Longman & Broderip, and Preston generally use the *Strich* where the Artaria editions employ a *Punkt* is further evidence of the unreliable nature of this aspect of notation in many Artaria editions.

In the Artaria edition of Hob. xv: 24/ii (op. 75, plate no. 624) the *Punkt* is used in bar 1 of the keyboard part, while a *Keil* is used for the same context in the violin part: it is probable in this case that the keyboard and violin parts were prepared by different engravers, a further indication that in many printed editions the choice of *Strich* or *Punkt* is dependent on the whim of the engraver, or the availability of specific punches, rather than on the notation of the sources from which the edition was prepared. Here and elsewhere in prints of Haydn's keyboard music, no special meaning can be attached to the use of the *Keil*. Its occurrence in printed sources is simply a matter of the engraver's convenience and can normally be regarded as being synonymous with the *Strich*, although a few instances occur in which it can be demonstrated that the *Keil* is used where Haydn wrote a *Punkt* in the autograph manuscript.

In attempting to establish the respective meanings of *Strich* and *Punkt* in Haydn's music the notation of the autographs is the prime source of information, although examples are also selected from secondary sources in which the *Strich* is the predominant notation but in which the *Punkt* also occurs occasionally in contexts similar to its occurrence in autograph manuscripts.

The meaning of the *Strich* is not in question: it is used to indicate normal staccato, as is clear from, for instance, the autograph of Hob. xv: 31/ii, where the notes marked with a *Strich* are accompanied by the verbal instruction 'staccato'. It is also interesting that while in bar 2 of Hob. xvi: 45/iii the left-hand notation of the autograph reads ♪₇ , at the parallel passage in bar 51 the notation is ♪ : this seems to reflect the standard theoretical descriptions of staccato, but should not be regarded as other than a general guideline, since the duration of a staccato note will depend on context, acoustic, and the instrument used. The basic question concerns the meaning or meanings that can be attributed to the *Punkt* when it occurs in reliable sources and when it is differentiated from the staccato *Strich*.

In the keyboard music the earliest autograph instance of differentiation between *Strich* and *Punkt* occurs in Hob. XVI: 19, dated 1767. For perhaps a decade from 1767 the *Punkt* occurs in autograph manuscripts infrequently, but the clarity with which Haydn distinguishes between *Strich* and *Punkt* suggests that the notational distinction is functional. In the second movement of Hob. XVI: 19 (see Ex. 4.1, bar 1) Haydn makes a clear distinction between the *Punkt*, which marks repeated quaver notes in the right hand, and the left-hand staccato crotchets are indicated by the *Strich*: similarly in Hob. XVI: 26/i (1773) the *Punkt* is used in bar 6 in a similar context over repeated quaver notes (Ex. 2.5), and is clearly distinguished in the autograph manuscript from the use of the *Strich* in bar 5.[48] The notational precision of these examples is typical of the composer: equally characteristic is the context in which the *Punkt* occurs. In the 1760s and 1770s the *Punkt* occurs almost exclusively in autograph manuscripts over repeated-note patterns, usually quavers in moderate tempos, or semiquavers in slow tempos. From the 1780s, when the *Punkt* occurs more frequently in Haydn's keyboard music, this context remains a *locus classicus*, but increasingly the *Punkt* is also associated with conjunct movement in semiquavers or demisemiquavers, both ascending and descending, at moderate or slow tempos (or with longer note values in faster tempos). In the autograph fragment of Hob. XVI: 29 the *Punkt* again occurs in the context of repeated-note patterns (first movement, bars 1, 21 ff.), but this work also contains an early instance of conjunct demisemiquavers at a slow tempo marked by a *Punkt* (see Ex. 2.6). Although this passage does not survive in the autograph fragment, it is derived from reliable sources and, moreover, is typical of Haydn's use of the *Punkt* in later works which do survive in autograph sources (cf. Ex. 2.9). Haydn's use of the *Punkt*

Ex. 2.5. Hob. XVI: 26/i

---

[48] The earliest surviving autographs in which distinctions are to be found between *Strich* and *Punkt* are those for the sonatas Hob. XVI: 19 (1767), 22 (1773), 26 (1773), and 29 (1774).

Ex. 2.6. Hob. XVI: 29/ii

in later works is more liberal and somewhat more diversified than in the works of the 1760s and 1770s, but its association with the two contexts illustrated in Ex. 2.5–6 remains strong. It is notable that these contexts are strikingly similar to the contexts associated with *portato* or *Tragen der Töne* in eighteenth-century treatises (cf. Ex. 2.2–4), the music of C. P. E. Bach and others, and, as will be seen, the notation of *portato* in Haydn's autograph manuscripts.

It is informative to examine two autograph manuscripts (those of the Sonatas in E flat, Hob. XVI: 49 and 52) in which both the *portato* indication ⌣ and the *Punkt* occur. In the first movement of Hob. XVI: 49 the characteristic motif, consisting of repeated notes in the rhythm ⁷♩♩♩ , occurs for the first time at bars 53 ff. and is marked *portato* in bars 53–4 (see Ex. 2.7*a*): in the continuation of this pattern in bars 55–6, the *portato* indication is absent (in the first editions as well as in the autograph), but it is appropriate to continue this manner of touch. In bars 108–31, a 'retransition' which prepares for the return to the tonic key, this motif is used extensively but the articulation in bars 108–10 is indicated only by the *Punkt*, without a slur (Ex. 2.7*b*). The composer reverts to the *portato* indication in bar 111, but the remainder of the passage lacks any indication of articulation for this repeated-note motif (except for the recurrence of the *Punkt* indication once in bar 127). It is logical in this context to assume that one articulation is appropriate for this motif, that *portato* should be understood as the appropriate articulation where no indication is found, and that the *Punkt* has the same meaning in this instance as *portato*.

In bar 14 of Hob. XVI: 52/ii the main double-dotted motif of the movement occurs in the left hand accompanied by repeated notes in the right hand, each of the latter being marked by a *Punkt* (Ex. 2.8*a*): when this passage recurs in bar 46, the notation of the repeated notes is the same. Considering the context of note repetition, *portato* touch

Ex. 2.7. Hob. XVI: 49/i

would seem to be the intention, a suspicion which is perhaps confirmed by the notation of bar 25: this bar, while certainly not directly parallel to bars 14 and 46, contains the same texture (i.e. the left-hand dotted-note motif and repeated notes in right hand) and, interestingly, the repeated notes are marked *portato* on the first beat, an indication which should presumably be continued for the following two beats (Ex. 2.8*b*). The interchangeability of *Punkt* and *portato* indications in Haydn's autographs is not confined to repeated-note patterns, but also occurs in other contexts. *Portato* is often specified by its normal indication in conjunct passages (see Ex. 2.9*a* and *b*), but it is equally characteristic that similar contexts are notated elsewhere with the *Punkt* (cf. Ex. 2.9*c* and *d*).

It could be argued that, for instance, in Ex. 2.7*b* Haydn is merely careless in omitting the slurs of the normal *portato* indication, but since he is consistently 'careless' in this regard, we must assume that he was less concerned to differentiate between *Punkt* and *portato* indications than he was to distinguish between *Punkt* and *Strich*. The impression is gained from the autograph manuscripts that in his

Ex. 2.8. Hob. XVI: 52/ii

(*a*)

(*b*)

Ex. 2.9(*a*) Hob. XVI: 52/i, (*b*) Hob. XVI: 49/ii, (*c*) Hob. XVI: 49/ii, (*d*) Hob. XVI: 49/ii

(*a*)

(*b*)

(*c*)

(d)

distinction between *Punkt* and *Strich* Haydn intended to indicate different articulation, but that he regarded the *Punkt* and *portato* indications as synonymous, or at least as serving very similar functions.

It is of interest that some eighteenth-century engravers appear to have regarded Haydn's *Punkt* and *portato* indications as being synonymous. In the autograph of Hob. xv: 7 Haydn uses the *Punkt* in a characteristic passage of conjunct semiquavers in bar 46 of the first movement, while the contemporary editions of Artaria and Longman & Broderip employ a *portato* indication in the same passage.[49] The close association of *Punkt* and *portato* indications is also occasionally apparent in works surviving only in poor secondary sources: a comparison of the readings for bars 14 and 17 of the E minor and F minor versions of Hob. xvi: 47 suggests that both indications served the same function (Ex. 2.10*a*–*b*): it is significant that in a very similar context in Hob. xv: 18/ii, bar 53 (Ex. 2.10*c*) the *Punkt* is used in the keyboard part, but *portato* is indicated in the violin part, which has the same notes.

It may therefore be suggested that the *Punkt*, as it is found in Haydn's autograph manuscripts and in reliable secondary sources, is associated with the contexts characteristic of *portato* and that Haydn regarded both notations as synonymous. Elsewhere it is likely that the occurrence of the *Punkt* is a corruption of the *Strich*, Haydn's normal staccato indication (even when the *Punkt* survives in the most authoritative source and consequently is reproduced in modern Urtext editions). There is little evidence from the autograph manuscripts of Haydn's keyboard music to allow the various interpretations of the *Punkt* associated with the works of Mozart and Beethoven: in

---

[49] Similarly, while the *Punkt* occurs in the autograph manuscript of Hob. xvi: 52/ii, bar 50, the Artaria edn. has at this point a *portato* indication. In Hob. xvi: 19 the Artaria edn. does not employ separate punches to achieve Haydn's distinction between *Strich* and *Punkt*, but interestingly, although the *Keil* is used throughout this edn., on some occurrences of the theme illustrated in Ex. 4.1 the engraver adds a slur to the *Keil* indications where Haydn's autograph has a *Punkt*: clearly the engraver interpreted Haydn's *Punkt* as indicating *portato*.

Ex. 2.10(*a*) Hob. XVI: 47 (E minor version)/i Adagio, bars 14, 17, (*b*) Hob. XVI: 47 (F minor version)/ii, Larghetto, (*c*) Hob. XV: 18/ii

particular, the idea that the *Punkt* represents a 'lighter staccato',[50] or 'mezzo-staccato', is misleading for the keyboard works of Haydn, since *portato* (as indicated by ⌢ and by the *Punkt*, if the above argument is accepted) is closer in type to legato than to the normal staccato. A particularly Haydnesque use of *portato* in the F minor Variations, Hob. XVII: 6, bars 50–1 illustrates that the difference between mezzo-staccato and *portato* interpretations is not simply a matter of theoretical definition (see Ex. 2.11*a*). Since the *portato* semiquavers in this passage are separated by rests one should not 'hold the tone out' until the next semiquaver is played, as in normal *portato* playing, and thus ignore the rests. Yet if the sense of *portato* or *Tragen der Töne* is sought, one should arguably 'hold out' the semiquavers for their full value (that is, sustain them until the rests), rather than short-

[50] Stanley Sadie writes regarding Mozart's music that 'Repeated short, light staccato notes are nearly always given dots, and notes demanding accentuation or standing at the end of a phrase more often carry wedges (or dashes).' See pref. to *Mozart: Sonatas for Piano* (London: Associated Board of the Royal Schools of Music, 1981), i. 8.

ening them in any way (as implied by the understanding 'mezzo-staccato'). The *portato* indication is, in this context, closer in meaning to *tenuto* than staccato. It is not surprising given Haydn's notational habits that the Haydnesque *portato* of the F minor Variations occurs in other works (as in Hob. xv: 20/ii, Ex. 2.11*b*) with the *Punkt* used in place of the *portato* indication.

Ex. 2.11(*a*) Hob. xvii: 6, (*b*) Hob. xv: 20/ii

Incomplete Notation: Accentuation and Analogy

However detailed Haydn's notation of articulation may be, it is clear that it is not intended to be comprehensive. Performers were and are required to add articulation markings by completing Haydn's guidelines or by following eighteenth-century conventions. It is no more possible here to give comprehensive instructions for the completion of Haydn's articulation markings than it is advisable for modern editors to clutter up a text with suggestions regarding articulation. General guidelines are provided by the eighteenth-century treatises which deal with articulation (as discussed above).[51] Thus, staccato may primarily be associated with faster tempos and disjunct melodies, the ordinary touch primarily with crotchets and quavers, and *Tragen der Töne* or *portato* with repeated-note patterns and conjunct motion in slow or moderate tempos. Theoretical discussions of legato are generally vague, but it is clear from discussions on ornamentation that

---

[51] See also Rosenblum, *Performance Practices*, 144–58.

the notes which form an ornament are played legato. Thus not only is an appoggiatura joined legato to its note of resolution, whether a slur is indicated or not, but the notes of other *Spielmanieren*, the *Schleifer* and arpeggio for instance, should generally be joined in a legato slur when the ornament is indicated by a symbol. It is also clear from the notation of extant Haydn autographs that subdivisions of a bar are grouped in patterns of short slurs which encompass a beat, or group of beats, but which characteristically do not cross the bar line. When such slurs are not indicated by the composer, conventional patterns of short slurs should be added by the performer, bearing in mind the close relationship between articulation and the conventional accentuation.

Many German treatises consider in some detail the topic of accentuation and in so doing often have recourse to analogies between musical performance and the art of the orator:

Whoever would read a poem and the like in such a way that it becomes comprehensible to the listener must place a marked emphasis on certain words or syllables. The very same resource is also at the disposal of the practicing musician.[52]

The analogy is sometimes pursued in the terminology used to distinguish between accents which derive from their strong metrical positions (sometimes referred to as 'grammatical' accents) and expressive accents which are not defined solely by metre (sometimes referred to as 'rhetorical' or 'pathetic' accents).[53] In discussions of metrical accents, authors devote considerable attention to the conventional hierarchies of strong and weak beats characteristic of different metres (referred to commonly as 'good' and 'bad' notes, or 'long' and 'short'). Marpurg's description of the conventional accentuation in binary and ternary metres is representative of the literature:

Every first and every third beat is good; the second and fourth are bad. Subdividing each beat into two lesser parts, the first is always good and the second bad. Therefore in dividing the 4/2 measure into eight crotchets, or the 4/4 measure into eight quavers, each first, third, fifth, and seventh note

---

[52] Türk, *Klavierschule*, trans. Haggh, 324.

[53] The term rhetorical accent is probably borrowed by Koch and Sulzer from Rousseau's *Dictionnaire de musique* (Paris, 1768), although both Koch and Sulzer use the term in the more general sense of an expressive accent which is quite different to Rousseau's usage in the context of text–music relationships. The most comprehensive discussion of the contexts associated with the rhetorical or expressive accent in instrumental music is found in Türk, *Klavierschule*, trans. Haggh, 326–9.

will be good; and every second, fourth, sixth and eighth note will be bad. The good notes are also called long, and the bad short, on account of their internal value. . . .

All first beats of this ternary metre [i.e. in 3/2, 3/4, and 3/8] are good, and the second and third are bad. In subdividing each beat into two other notes, each first is good in comparison with the following.[54]

Sulzer adapted the conventional symbols of poetic scansion to convey the same message (see Ex. 2.12).

Ex. 2.12. Sulzer, *Allgemeine Theorie*, s.v. 'Tact'

Rhetorical accents are, on the other hand, less subject to prescription. They derive from the imagination of the composer and the intuition of the performer, may occur on any beat of the bar, and are more emphatic than metrical accents.[55] Türk, attempting to define some of the contexts associated with such accents, mentioned the following: appoggiaturas, tied notes, syncopated notes, dissonant intervals and chromatic notes of various types, and notes which are

[54] 'Chaque premier & chaque troisième tems est *bon*; le second & le quatrième est *mauvais*. En subdivisant chaque tems en deux moindres parties, la première en est toûjours bonne, & la seconde mauvaise. Donc en divisant la mesure de quatre blanches en huit noires, ou la mesure de quatre noires en huit croches, toute *première, troisième, cinquième, & septième note* sera *bonne*; & toute *seconde, quatrième, sixième & huitième* note sera *mauvaise*. Les bonnes notes se nomment aussi *longues* & les mauvaises *brèves*, par rapport à leur quantité intrinsèque. . . . Tout *premier tems* de cette mesure ternaire est *bon* & le *second & troisième* sont *faux*. En subdivisant chaque tems en deux autres notes, toute première est bonne en comparaison de la suivante.' (Marpurg, *Principes du clavecin*, 23, 25). Further detailed discussions of accentuation are to be found in id., *Anleitung*, 19–25; id.,'Vom den verschiedenen Taktarten', in *Kritische Briefe über die Tonkunst*, 3 vols. (Berlin, [1759–64]), i. 98–104; J. G. Sulzer, *Allgemeine Theorie der Schönen Kunste* (2nd edn., Leipzig, 1792–4), s.v. 'Takt', 'Accent', 'Vortrag'; H. C. Koch, *Musikalisches Lexikon* (Frankfurt, 1802), s.v. 'Accent'; Türk, *Klavierschule*, trans. Haggh, 89–91, 324–36. See also G. Houle, *Metre in Music, 1600–1800: Performance, Perception and Notation* (Bloomington, Ind.: Indiana University Press, 1987) and C. Hogwood, 'A Supplement to C. P. E. Bach's *Versuch*: E. W. Wolf's *Anleitung* of 1785', in Clark (ed.), *C. P. E. Bach Studies*, 133–57.

[55] Koch, *Lexikon*, s.v. 'Accent'.

'distinguished by their length, highness, and lowness' (from his examples Türk seems to have especially in mind high and low notes which are approached by large intervalic leaps).[56] This list merely provides guidelines since what seems to be implied is that any note which might be regarded as particularly expressive, for whatever reason, requires a rhetorical accent.

It is equally problematic to state precisely how accents, be they grammatical or rhetorical, are conveyed in performance. This is clearly a matter of immense subtlety, not easily described, and it is of importance that accentuation, particularly the regularly recurring patterns of metrical accents, is not interpreted in a rigid or mechanical way. Accents may be implicit in the music, requiring little added emphasis from the performer, as, for instance, when a composer places changes of harmony and a thicker texture on strong beats, making the metre of a passage obvious. Compositional conventions therefore feature in some theoretical discussions of accentuation. Many of Marpurg's comments on metrical accentuation seem to be concerned primarily with what Neumann calls 'musical prosody' and are addressed in the first instance to the composer rather than the performer: thus Marpurg is concerned that caesuras, dissonances, and the long syllables of a text are placed on good notes.[57] Other metrical and rhetorical accents require emphasis in performance, to a greater or lesser extent depending on context, and the emphasis may be conveyed by dynamics, agogics, articulation, or a combination of some or all of these.

Terminology used in describing accentuation is often suggestive of a temporal distinction between accented and unaccented notes, but F. Neumann has pointed out that the terms 'long' and 'short' in such discussions commonly relate to emphasis or quantity as in metrics and not to a pervasive system of inequality.[58] Nevertheless, agogic accentuation is an important facet of performance in eighteenth-century music. It is not employed on every good or long note and thus is not the normal means of conveying the metrical accentuation of a work, but is associated particularly with expressive or rhetorical accents

---

[56] *Klavierschule*, trans. Haggh, 326.

[57] See Marpurg, *Principes du clavecin*, 20; F. Neumann, 'The French *Inégales*, Quantz, and Bach', *JAMS* 18/3 (Fall 1965): 335–43.

[58] See 'French *Inégales*', 313–58. Accented and unaccented notes were in the 18th cent. referred to variously as 'bon et mauvais tems', 'gute und schlechte Note', 'buona & cativa', 'long and short', 'longues et brèves', 'Arsis et Thesis', 'anschlagende und nachschlagende', 'innerlich lange und innerlich kurze'.

which occur less frequently and less regularly. Türk's comments on the practice of 'lingering on certain tones' (his equivalent to the relatively modern term agogic accent, which derives from Riemann) in the following passage:

Another means of accent, which is to be used much less often and with great care, is lingering on certain tones. The orator not only lays more emphasis on important syllables and the like, but he also lingers upon them a little. But this kind of lingering, when it occurs in music, cannot, of course, always be of the same duration, for it appears to me to depend primarily upon (1) the greater or lesser importance of the note, (2) its length and relationship to other notes, and (3) the harmony which is basic to them.

  Because it is recognized by everyone, I do not have to provide evidence for the possibility of lingering somewhat longer on a very important note than on one less important.[59]

Agogic emphasis may coincide with metrical accentuation, since rhetorical accents often occur on metrically strong beats, but in general the metrical accentuation is conveyed consistently by means other than agogics, if the latter is to be employed 'much less often and with great care'. Obviously, on the clavichord and fortepiano dynamics may be utilized subtly to convey metrical accentuation, but unrelenting dynamic emphasis on every good note is clearly as inappropriate as lingering on every good note. Metrical accentuation is a complex phenomenon: it may be inherent in the music, or may be conveyed by a combination of occasional agogic and dynamic emphasis. Another, and perhaps the most common, factor in conveying metrical accentuation in performance is articulation and therein lies the explanation for the ubiquitous short slur patterns in music from the second half of the eighteenth century. These short slur patterns are not directly derivative of violin-bowings; nor does the characteristic beaming of notes in keyboard music of this period inform us directly about articulation.[60] Beaming, bowing, and keyboard slur patterns are, however, related in that each reflects the metrical accentuation of the music. The fact that slurs infrequently cross the bar line in Haydn's keyboard music is not simply a matter of

[59] *Klavierschule*, trans. Haggh, 327–8.

[60] *Pace* P. and E. Badura-Skoda who state that 'in classical music the use of slurs originated in violin bowing' (Badura-Skoda, *Interpreting Mozart*, 55): A. P. Brown suggests that 'The notation of rhythmic braces with regard to values of eighth, sixteenth, and thirty-second notes affects the articulatory rendition' (Brown, *Performing Haydn's 'The Creation': Reconstructing the Earliest Renditions* (Bloomington, Ind.: Indiana University Press, 1986), 67).

notational convention, but reflects the primacy of the accent on the first beat of the bar, a *silence d'articulation* before the first beat being a primary means of conveying this accent (especially on the harpsichord, but also on the clavichord and fortepiano), although it may be reinforced by other (compositional, agogic, or dynamic) means. Similarly, whether a passage of continuous semiquavers in common time is grouped into four slurs of four notes or two slurs of eight notes is a consequence of the accentuation and tempo of a piece; a *silence d'articulation* after a slur imparts, as required, accents on the first and third, or the first, second, third, and fourth beats of the bar depending on the appropriate accentuation. In completing the articulation markings in sparsely notated music 'standard' articulation which reflects the metre and tempo of the piece should be employed as the norm. Many of Haydn's most detailed indications of articulation may thus be understood as more specific characterizations of a theme, or as contradictions of standard metrical articulation. A cross-bar slur may in this way be read as a deliberate compositional play with convention, in the same way as a syncopation is a deliberate disruption of conventional accentuation. The problem of incomplete notation becomes a matter of observing an unnotated norm when more specific indications are lacking.

The opening of the Sonata, Hob. XVI: 23 is a good example of Haydn's incomplete notation: indications of articulation are relatively sparse but nevertheless provide sufficiently detailed guidelines to the performer once the general necessity for a *silence d'articulation* before the first and third quaver beats is understood (see Ex. 2.13, where commas are used to indicate *silences d'articulation* and crossed slurs are my completions). In the first nine bars the observation of metrical accents, by preceding the accents with a *silence d'articulation*, is all that is generally required to complete the notation. For instance, in the demisemiquaver four-note groups of bars 2, 4, 5, 6, 7, and 8 the staccato note or slur which precedes each group and the assumed *silence d'articulation* after each group (appropriate since each group precedes a primary accent) indicates that four-note slurs are appropriate. Haydn does not specify the articulation for the dotted-note motif of the opening, but the performer's options are limited to and

 if the accents on the first and third beats of the bar are to be con-

veyed by the articulation (the 'ungrammatical' articulation

Ex. 2.13. Hob. XVI: 23/i

Ex. 2.13. *cont.*

would, for me, only be justifiable here if indicated by the composer).
Likewise in the first half of bar 6, the staccato markings and an
assumed *silence d'articulation* before the second crotchet beat define

the performer's options as ♪♪♪♪ or ♪♪♪♪ . Haydn's slur indi-

cations in bars 2, 4, 7, and 8 may thus be understood as qualifications
of the normal 'metrical articulation', weakening the accent on the
third quaver beat in each case. These slurs also, of course, help to clarify the articulation of the notes preceding and following those
marked with a slur. The separation of f' in bar 2 from the preceding
and following notes is implicit since a *silence d'articulation* precedes a
slur (otherwise Haydn would have written a slur over the first three
notes of the bar) and a bar line. In the left-hand quaver movement of
bars 3–4, 6, and 9 the omission of any indications of articulation is
probably a positive instruction: the quavers are most characteristically
performed with the ordinary touch, although occasional slurred quavers are not impossible.

In bars 13 to 20 the right-hand articulation markings are to a great
extent specified by the composer and the occasional missing details
are self-evident: slurs are implicit on the demisemiquaver four-note
up-beats to bars 12, 14, and 16 (i.e. with a *silence d'articulation* following a staccato indication and before the first beat of a bar), and a slur
is also implicit on the first two quaver beats of bar 19 since the $b\natural'$ is
an appoggiatura (both metrical accentuation and the preceding and

following staccato indications confirm that the first two beats form a unit). The left-hand semiquavers in bars 13–20 may be performed with the ordinary touch, two slurs of four notes or one eight-note slur per bar, but with a *silence d'articulation* before the bar line articulating the metre and changes of harmony. In bars 21 ff. Haydn indicates the articulation for the left hand, but, in omitting slurs in the demisemiquaver right-hand part, conventional metrical slurring is presumably implied: thus in bars 21–5 the demisemiquavers may, depending on taste, be played with slurs articulating each quaver beat, each crotchet beat, or each bar, but it is very probably less characteristic to play them in a continuous legato without a *silence d'articulation* before each bar line. It should perhaps be noted that articulation is the primary means of conveying the metrical accentuation of the opening of this movement in performance: emphatic agogic accents are inappropriate on the first and third quaver beats of bar 1 since these beats are already inherently long because they are harmonized while the metrically short second and fourth quaver beats are accompanied by left-hand rests.

The extent of the *silence d'articulation* (and of the accent thus imparted) should be, of course, greatly variable. In Ex. 2.14, for instance, the paired slurring establishes the first, third, fifth, and seventh semiquavers as good in relation to the second, fourth, sixth, and eighth semiquavers. However, by allowing a slightly longer *silence d'articulation* before the first and fifth semiquavers the importance of the first and third quaver beats can be suggested in relation to the second and fourth beats. In this instance the first and fifth semiquavers are also appoggiaturas requiring a rhetorical accent and the exaggerated *silence d'articulation* may be supplemented appropriately by an agogic accent. Articulation may also contribute to the rhetorical accentuation of notes not metrically prominent. In Ex. 2.15, for instance, the second quaver beat of bar 27 is not a good note, but the extraordinarily expressive chromaticism (approached by a leap of a diminished seventh, the ab'' is harmonized by the flat submediant of F major which by sleight of hand becomes an augmented sixth) requires a rhetorical emphasis by whatever means possible. A *silence d'articulation* (which may in this case be quite exaggerated) is implicit before the ab'' (because of the following slur), but the accent on ab'' may be reinforced by an agogic accent, on a fortepiano and clavichord by a dynamic accent, and on a clavichord perhaps even by *Bebung*.

Ex. 2.14. Hob. XVI: 2/i

In adding articulation markings to passages lacking specific indications the accentuation of the passage is therefore a principal consideration. Other considerations, in particular the existence of detailed
articulation markings elsewhere in the same movement, may also be
of relevance in deciding on appropriate articulation for a given passage. The most unproblematic instance in which the appropriate
articulation for a passage may be derived from articulation markings
elsewhere is the practice of continuation referred to by C. P. E. Bach
(quoted above). It should be understood from Bach's comment that
the continuation of an appropriate manner of articulation in immediate repetition is in question and that the comment in no way provides a wider justification for supplying articulation markings based
on remote parallel passages. Instances in Haydn's keyboard music in
which 'missing' articulation indications may be supplied by the
process of continuation are common (see e.g. Ex. 2.7*a*, discussed
above), and it is also appropriate that immediate repetitions which
contain some, but less specific, articulation markings than initial statements be completed by a similar process of continuing the more
detailed indication. In a brief commentary on bowing in sources for
the *Creation* A. P. Brown makes a similar observation: 'The initial
articulation for a repeated passage generally establishes the
bowing/articulation for the entire group of repetitions, even if a

Ex. 2.15. Hob. XVI: 2/i

more general marking follows, but it is superseded by a more detailed indication.'[61]

Continuation of an indicated manner of articulation is, however, quite different to the practice of supplying articulation on the basis of parallel passages. The latter has been a common practice among some editors and performers of Haydn's music and while it may be justifiable at times it has also been much abused, leading to a uniformity in articulation which is at variance with the evidence of the sources.[62] When the repetition of a passage lacks articulation completely, or such indications are less specific, then completion by analogy may well be justified. However, when repetitions bear different indications which are as, or more, specific than those which characterize the initial statement, uniform articulation for initial and subsequent statements of a passage is undesirable: at best in such instances a dubious uniformity replaces variety and at worst an important stylistic feature of the composition is obliterated.

No objection can be made in principle to the practice of supplementing sparse indications of articulation by the comparison of parallel passages: it is unproblematic, for instance, for the performer (although not necessarily the editor) to complete the less detailed articulation of Hob. xvi: 49/iii, 41–3 by analogy with Hob. xvi: 49/iii, 25–7, since the articulation in the former, although less specific, is of the same type; i.e. there is no suggestion that a contrast in articulation is intended. In the Fantasia in C major, Hob. xvii: 4, the music of bars 70–85 recurs twice, at bars 195 ff., where the articulation markings are less complete by comparison with the original statement, and again at bars 305 ff., where the articulation markings are almost totally lacking (see Ex. 2.16). It is justifiable in this instance to supply the articulation markings for the repetitions of the passage by analogy with the more detailed notation of the parallel passage. Yet this example also highlights Haydn's common practice of varying articulation in repetitions. Within bars 70–85, the music of 72–3 is repeated twice, at the same pitch or sequentially, with subtle changes in articulation (cf. bars 72–3, 76–7, 78–9). In completing the articulation marking of bars 195–213 and 305–23, bar 307 should, for

[61] *The Creation*, 63.

[62] See J. Webster, 'The Significance of Haydn's Quartet Autographs for Performance Practice', in C. Wolff (ed.), *The String Quartets of Haydn, Mozart and Beethoven: Studies of the Autograph Manuscripts* (Isham Library Papers, 3; Cambridge, Mass.: Harvard University Press, 1980), 80–4.

Ex. 2.16. Hob. XVII: 4

instance, be played with three staccato notes, by analogy with bar 72, and not with the articulation of bars 76 or 78. In this example the 'remote' analogy is a good adviser and preserves local variations in articulation, but elsewhere it is frequently the case that Haydn varies the articulation in passages of structurally important thematic recurrence: in such instances the completion of articulation markings by remote analogies between parallel passages is ill-advised.

Articulation and Variation

Haydn's notation of details of performance practice underwent a striking change in the mid-1760s. His more specific notation from this time affected aspects of ornamentation, embellishment, and occasionally dynamics, and not surprisingly one also finds increasingly specific indications of articulation from the mid-1760s. The more precise notation is symptomatic of the composer's concern to exploit in the compositional process details of performance practice traditionally left to the discretion of the performer. The most characteristic way in which Haydn exploits performance practice is as a means of variation and in this regard his use of contrasting articulation in areas of local (the variation of immediate repetition, sequential or otherwise) or remote (variation in areas of thematic recurrence of structural significance) repetition closely parallels the exploitation of embellishment for similar purposes in his keyboard music from the mid-1760s to the 1790s.

In Haydn's autograph manuscripts from 1766 one frequently finds two or more different patterns of articulation for various appearances of a theme which must be regarded as conscious variation rather than accidental error. In many instances the recognition of the changing articulation as variation is unproblematic since it is cast in sections of a composition which are clearly variations on previously stated material, and the 'new' articulation is recognizable as a contributing element to that variation. Changes in articulation in conjunction with other elements of variation are apparent, for instance, in the Finale of the Sonata in C minor, Hob. XVI: 20, where the main theme recurs in a varied form at bars 79 ff. (cf. Ex. 2.17*a* and *b*). Here Haydn

Ex. 2.17. Hob. XVI: 20/iii

embellishes the melody slightly and also introduces subtle alterations in the articulation of the theme: legato replaces staccato in the left hand of bars 79 and 80 and in the right hand on the second and third beats of the same bars; in bar 81 an increased degree of separation between the beats is made explicit by the 'new' notation ♪.

Divergent articulation is not always quite so easily recognizable as deliberate variation, particularly when variation is confined to the articulation and the thematic recurrence is in other respects exact. The autograph manuscript of the finale from the Trio in D major, Hob. XV: 7 contains few articulation marks, yet these are sufficient to indicate the intended variation in the final occurrence of the rondo refrain. Haydn does not write any slurs in the keyboard part over the various appearances of the refrain until bars 152–5 (cf. Ex. 2.18*a* and *b*). Here, however, on its last appearance, the refrain is characterized by slurs which cross the beat and the bar line. This atypical slurring clearly represents a variation on the articulation of the refrain as it previously appears. In the first statement of the refrain articulation markings are almost entirely lacking except for two staccato marks, but these staccato indications are sufficient to indicate a contrast between typical metrical articulation for the refrain throughout most of the movement (clearly, because of the second staccato indication of bar 1, there is a *silence d'articulation* before bar 2) and the atypical slurring of bars 152 ff. It is, of course, necessary to complete details in the articulation of the rondo refrain, but this should be done in such a way as to preserve the implied contrast in articulation. Semiquaver groups in the refrain should probably be slurred in four-note groups, or in any case in a manner consistent with the metrical accentuation implied by the staccato notes: on the other hand, in the last occurrence of the refrain, one might justifiably play cross-beat and cross-bar slurs in bars 159–63 and 175–7 (where Haydn does not indicate the articulation), by analogy with bars 152–5, rather than with the initial statement of the refrain.

The third movement of the Sonata in G major, Hob. XVI: 27 is in many respects similar to the movement just described: like Hob. XV: 7/iii it is a finale in 2/4 time with similar rhythmic, melodic, and textural organization and problems of articulation. Unlike the finale of Hob. XV: 7, Hob. XVI: 27/iii survives only in non-autograph sources,[63] and variation in articulation take place within the frame-

[63] See C. Landon, *Kritische Anmerkungen* (Vienna: Universal, 1982) for *Haydn: Sämtliche Klaviersonaten*, 58. Inconsistent articulation is sometimes a matter of dispute among editors

Ex. 2.18. Hob. xv: 7/iii

work of a variation form. The sources of this movement diverge on many details regarding articulation and consequently the editions of Landon and Feder frequently present different readings. Yet, whatever their differences as regards detail, the sources agree in one respect, namely the paucity of articulation marks throughout the movement with the exception of the 'third variation' (bars 73–104). This section is quasi-developmental and interrupts the additive strophic variation structure of the movement. Unlike the figurative variations of bars 25 to 72, this section returns to the melodic and rhythmic patterning of the theme but has an autonomous phrase structure with written-out reprises and harmonic digressions in minor keys not found in the theme itself. Significantly the thematic material is characterized by the addition of new details of articulation: the quaver movement in this section is grouped into slurred patterns of mostly three and four notes, where the theme has no indications. It is reasonable to believe that this graphic difference represents a real distinction in performance, that is, variation in the articulation.

even when an autograph manuscript is extant for the work in question. An interesting instance occurs in Hob. XVI: 45, 2nd movement, where in the sequential repetitions of a motif in bars 23–4 and the parallel passage at bars 68–9 the articulation in the autograph is different on each of its four occurrences. In the edn. of *JHW* the articulation is transcribed fairly literally preserving the inconsistencies of the autograph, while C. Landon's edn. tends to 'iron out' the inconsistencies and produces a more uniform articulation for the motif. It seems clear to me that Haydn's diverse articulation is intentional, not least because in bar 23 Haydn emended his first thoughts in a subsequent revision: clearly he gave the articulation some thought.

Undoubtedly one must add some slurs in performing the theme itself (for instance, between the appoggiaturas and their notes of resolution in bars 22 and 23, which are not indicated in the sources), but the notation of the theme should arguably be, in general, interpreted quite literally with a predominance of 'ordinary', detached, quavers here contrasting with the slurred note-groups of bars 73–104. To add slurs profusely by analogy in playing the theme at the beginning of the movement, when no convincing model for this analogy exists, would weaken the implied contrast of the central section.

Some of Haydn's most systematic and imaginative exploitations of articulation are found in his so-called monothematic sonata-form movements. In such movements identical or similar themes appear in the tonic and dominant (or the equivalent) keys, but in many cases the theme is characterized differently in each tonal area by alterations to one or more parameter of style. In the string quartets or symphonies, texture and orchestration are commonly altered for the version of the theme in the dominant: in the keyboard music, ornamentation and, especially, articulation are frequently utilized to characterize the dominant version of the theme anew.

The autograph manuscript for the Finale of the Sonata in F major, Hob. XVI: 23, although extant only for the first fifty-six bars, is a fair copy and contains remarkably precise instructions as regards articulation: consequently the editions of this sonata by Landon and Feder agree in almost all respects. However specific the notation of the manuscript, it is clearly not complete in every detail: thus, for instance, the appoggiaturas in bars 18 and 20 must be slurred to their notes of resolution, although there are no slurs in the autograph (the slurs in Landon's edition are editorial). Similarly, the semiquaver passages, notably bars 28–31, 77–82, but also 22–3 and elsewhere, contain no indications of articulation and should presumably be performed with appropriate slur patterns as discussed above. The main thematic material of the movement is, however, notable for the meticulous notation of articulation. The theme which occurs in the dominant at bar 33 is closely related to the first theme but is characterized by strikingly contrasting articulation (cf. Ex. 2.19a and b). Within this dominant area, the articulation is also exploited as a means of local variation: compare, for instance, the staccato of bar 33 and the two-note slurs of bar 35. Similarly in the embellished repeat of bars 33–40 in bars 41–8 a significant change in the repetition is the variation in articulation. In the tonic version of the theme the

Ex. 2.19. Hob. XVI: 23/iii

(*a*)

(*b*)

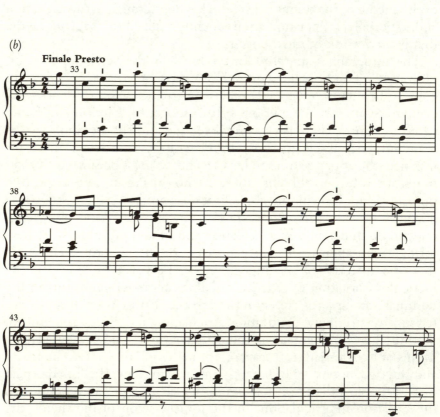

mixture of two-note slurs and unmarked notes (the latter, given the precision of the notation, must be assumed to indicate the ordinary touch) requires no completion or emendation by analogy: the addition of slurs, or staccato to unmarked notes would, in particular, blur intentional contrasts. As within the dominant area, the tonic theme also has local contrasts. The similar patterns of notes in bars 1, 3, and 9 have distinctive articulation if the unmarked notes of bars 1 and 9 are read literally and detached in the ordinary manner.[64]

Haydn's subtlest exploitation of this type of variation is perhaps found in the monothematic first movement of the Sonata in C, Hob. XVI: 50 and in a number of the late piano trios. Unlike Hob. XVI: 23, XVI: 52, and many of the string quartets where variation in the articulation is found in extant autograph manuscripts and may confidently be attributed to Haydn, in Hob. XVI: 50 and the late piano trios the best sources are almost exclusively non-autograph sources. In these cases discrepancies in articulation between parallel passages may be deliberate and derived from Haydn, but the possibility that they are the accidental result of errors in the process of transmission cannot be ruled out. The first edition of Caulfield is the principal source for Hob. XVI: 50 and although C. Landon has commented on 'the inaccurately placed dynamic markings' in this edition,[65] it seems to me to be in other regards a reliable source: in particular, the 'inconsistent' articulation is so systematically exploited as an integral part of the compositional style that it is difficult to believe that the variant details of articulation could but derive from the composer. The theme which begins this movement (Ex. 2.20a) is characterized by the contrast between detached initial arpeggio and descending fifths and the cross-beat slurs for the descending sevenths of bars 2–3. The transformed and embellished counterstatement of this theme (beginning at bar 7) retains the characteristic articulation, with detached arpeggio and fifths, and slurred descending sevenths. The same is true of the variant of this theme which appears in the dominant at bar 20. However, the variant beginning at bar 30 contains a significant alteration in articulation with the staccato descending-fifth intervals of previous themes slurred in the same manner as the descending sevenths (Ex. 2.20b). The differences between these versions of the 'same' theme are exploited in the development section and in the ,

---

[64] Similar contrasting articulation between the tonic and dominant versions of a theme occur in the autograph manuscript of Hob. XVI: 52/i (cf. bars 1–5 and 33–6).

[65] *Haydn: Sämtliche Klaviersonaten*, vol. iii, p. xx.

Ex. 2.20. Hob. XVI: 50/i

recapitulation: distinctions in articulation are systematically exploited and invested with structural significance.

In the development section, as Haydn 'analyses' his material tonally and motivically, the articulation is also transformed. At the opening of the development section, bars 54 and 55 contain the thematic variant of bar 20 but the articulation is that of bar 30 with slurred descending fifths, and in bars 60–1 the arpeggio figure is for the first time written as crotchets and not as quavers followed by quaver rests. More obviously, the further variation in articulation at bars 73 ff. underlines the most dramatic point in the development, where the 'flattest' key of the movement, A flat major, is reached. This point is characterized by an imaginative transformation of the main theme, as staccato quavers and rests are replaced by legato crotchets in bar 73 and the descending fifths and sevenths are, for the first time, both slurred (bars 73–5). The addition of the open–pedal indication emphasizes the structural importance of the passage (Ex. 2.20*c*). A similar co-ordination between tonal effect and articulation is seen in the recapitulation, where a synthesis of previously conflicting elements is found. The most overt reference to the development in the recapitulation is also underlined by, and, indeed, primarily recognizably because of, the articulation, when the colouring that characterized the A flat major section in the development returns at bars 120 ff. with legato articulation and an even more extensive use of the open–pedal effect. The transformation of articulation here is not a matter of dispute, since the effect is not reliant simply on the placement of slurs in the sources but is confirmed by other aspects of the notation. Therefore one should not easily dismiss another change in articulation at the beginning of the recapitulation, where slurred descending fifths and sevenths characterize the opening theme in a slightly different way than at the beginning of the exposition (Ex. 2.20*d*). The slurred descending fifths may be an engraver's error, but given the manifold transformations in the articulation of this theme, the version of bars 102 ff. arguably represents a conscious synthesis of the articulation of bars 1 ff. and 30 ff. In a work such as this one should not expect the first theme to be restated exactly in the recapitulation, as the slight embellishments of bars 104–7 and 109 by comparison with the exposition confirm. The divergent articulation between bars 1–2 and 102–3 should not therefore be regarded as problematic.

Variation in articulation of the type discussed in connection with

Hob. XVI: 50/i is not an isolated phenomenon and is particularly characteristic of Haydn's late piano trios. Since in these works the divergent articulation is not confined to the piano part, important questions also arise concerning ensemble playing, especially the notion that co-ordination among ensemble players should extend to uniformity in articulation. The first movement of Hob. XV: 18 poses some of the most interesting and complex problems of articulation in the Haydn canon. In this movement the articulation of the principal theme of the movement is, even for Haydn, unusually diverse, in the piano and the string parts. As in the case of Hob. XVI: 50, and indeed, virtually all of Haydn's late piano trios, no autograph manuscript is extant for Hob. XV: 18. The possibility that the articulation of the principal source (Longman & Broderip, op. 70) is, at least in part, due to error cannot be discounted, but it is possible to see in the apparent chaos a systematic exploitation of articulation which suggests that the diversity is not accidental and militates against the imposition of uniformity by extensive alteration of articulation on the basis of parallel passages.

The variety of articulation is immediately apparent in bars 3–4, where three different articulations characterize the three appearances of the main five-note motif: thus the right- and left-hand statements in the piano part have distinctive articulation and the left-hand articulation differs from the violin articulation, although the violin and piano left-hand part are in unison. The repetition of the opening motif at bars 7–8 brings further changes in the articulation: the articulation of the right- and left-hand piano parts is an inversion of that in bars 3–4 and violin articulation is again different to the piano statement (on this occasion the right hand) heard simultaneously (see Ex. 2.21*a*). When the five-note motif occurs in the dominant key (bars 45–9, Ex. 2.21*b*) the piano articulation is different from that of both bars 3–4 and 7–8, while in the development section the same motif is characterized by ever-changing combinations of articulatory patterns found in the exposition: for instance, in bars 82–8 three different patterns of articulation are heard simultaneously (violin and piano left hand) and in succession (piano right- and left-hand parts), and in bars 125–6 while the articulation of the piano part is the same as bars 3–4, the violin articulation at bar 126 differs from that in bar 4. There are also notable differences in articulation between the recapitulation at bars 151–4 (see Ex. 2.21*c*) and the initial statement of the motif at bars 3–6, and while the articulation in the unison statement by violin

Ex. 2.21. Hob. xv: 18/i

(b)

(c)

(d)

(e)

Ex. 2.21. *cont.*

and keyboard right hand agree here, the cello statement has a unique
five-note slur, heard simultaneously with a different articulation in
the keyboard left-hand part.

It is clear from the diversity of articulation for this five-note motif
that no single pattern of articulation can stand as the basis for a uniform interpretation of this five-note motif.[66] It is also clear that imi-
tative statements of this motif in the right- and left-hand piano parts
consistently employ different successive articulations and that unison
statements of the motif by violin and piano, consistently, although

---

[66] The edns. of *JHW* and H. C. R. Landon differ considerably in details of articulation,
despite the fact that the same principal source is used for both editions. Although Landon's
edn. by no means reduces the articulation of the principal motif of the movement to a
single interpretation, nevertheless there is more uniformity in his edition than in the
diplomatic transcription of *JHW*. The basis for some of Landon's readings is not clear, but
would appear to be the result of subjective editorial emendation.

not invariably, employ contrasting articulation. To a performer or editor expecting uniform articulation for a theme, the articulation in this movement might appear random. However, far from being chaotic, the movement can be seen to exploit, in ever-changing vertical and horizontal combinations, two basic patterns of articulation for the five-note motif which are strongly contrasting in character (Ex. 2.21*d*) and a third pattern, similar in character to the first in that it emphasizes the metre, of which there are three slightly different versions (Ex. 2.21*e*). Only the three-note slur of bar 46 (piano left hand) and the five-note slur of bar 152 (cello) are discordant with the three basic patterns of articulation employed consistently throughout the movement. While the performer might be tempted to reconcile these bars with one of the three basic types, even such slight emendations are difficult to justify, since the contexts in which the three- and five-note slurs occur (the 'dominant' version of a theme in a monothematic sonata-form movement, and the recapitulation) are frequently, in Haydn, points where the prevailing articulation, and other elements of performance practice, are altered.

The hypothesis that there are three basic patterns of articulation for the five-note motif and that they are deliberate rather than accidental characteristics of the movement is supported by the articulation of the counterstatement of the first theme occurring at bars 11 ff., where the same three basic patterns are preserved although the five-note motif is transformed (Ex. 2.21*f*). It is arguable that this passage, more than any other, demonstrates the deliberate use of articulation as a functional stylistic component in the movement. Repetitions of the five-note motif throughout the movement are characterized by variable combinations of three patterns of articulation, but on the only occasion when the five-note motif is transformed, the articulation is used as an element of recognition, the articulation of bars 11–12 being the same as in the initial statement at bars 3–4.

The articulation of Hob. xv: 18/i is complex, but it is problematic only if approached with modern preconceptions which demand uniformity of articulation in simultaneous and successive appearances of a theme. Non-uniformity in articulation may, of course, be a result of scribal error;[67] completion and considered emendation remain

---

[67] The apparent inconsistencies or non-uniformity described in this chapter should in no way be taken as support for the chaotic non-uniformity, largely a consequence of an uncritical approach to the source material, advocated by D. Barnett ('Non-Uniform Slurring in 18th-Century Music: Accident or Design?', *HYb* 10 (1978): 179–99). For a critical assessment of Barnett's article see Webster, 'Haydn's Quartet Autographs', 82–3, 96–7.

essential tasks for the performer. The utilization of parallel passages in the task of completing articulation is, however, justifiable only when a convincing analogy supplements less detailed, similar articulation or supplies the articulation in a passage where no indications are given. Contrasting or more detailed indications of articulation should not in principle be obliterated by an analogy to a previous, different articulation for the sake of uniformity. On the evidence of the notation in autographs and other good sources, diversity in articulation may generally be seen, not as an accident of transmission, but rather as a stylistic feature of Haydn's music which is most apparent when it is exploited as a means of variation. The increasing compositional control over details of performance practice is a notable feature of Haydn's late keyboard works. It cannot, however, be regarded as a product of a Classical style of the 1780s, but is well established in the keyboard sonatas of the late 1760s and the 1770s.

3

Questions of Rhythmic Interpretation and Tempo

◊

RHYTHM

The notated rhythms in Haydn's music, and generally in music from the second half of the eighteenth century, do not require a systematic alteration in performance. There is no convention of *notes inégales*, as is applicable to certain French music, by which notated rhythms are altered in performance according to well-documented conventions governed by the metre of the music;[1] nor is there in Haydn's music any convention requiring the systematic double-dotting of rhythms as has traditionally been claimed for the 'French overture style'.[2] This is not to say that Haydn's rhythmic notation conveys the rhythmic subtleties requisite in performance, nor that the notation is by comparison with modern notation always accurate. The notated rhythm of Haydn's music is of course subject to manifold subtle alterations in performance for accentual and expressive reasons, chief among which is the agogic accentuation discussed in Chapter 2. It is also true that certain features of modern rhythmic notation were not available to Haydn, or were only adopted by him later in his career, and that features of conventional Baroque notation which are imprecise and require modification in performance continue to occur in Haydn's

---

[1] See F. Neumann, 'French *Inégales*', 313–58.

[2] The traditional view of the 'French Overture' is summarized in R. Donington, *The Interpretation of Early Music* (1963; rev. edn., London: Faber & Faber, 1989), 448–51. Neumann's first article challenging the tradition appeared in 1965 ('La Note pointée et la soi-disant "manière française"', *Revue de Musicologie*, 51 (1965): 66–92) and was expanded upon in a number of subsequent papers, including a number of responses to his critics. These are reproduced in Neumann, *Essays in Performance Practice* (Studies in Musicology, 58; Ann Arbor: UMI, 1982). On the critical response to Neumann see esp. M. Collins, 'A Reconsideration of French Over-Dotting', *ML* 50/1 (Jan. 1969): 111–23.

music, primarily in his early music but also, to some degree, in his late music. The concern of the present chapter is with such problems of notation, with the duality of literal and implied readings of Haydn's notation. However frequently occurring, these problems are essentially matters of reading Haydn's notation and not with the application in any pervading rhythmic style or systematic inequality.

The Assimilation of Binary Patterns to Ternary Rhythms

It is well known that in Baroque music the writing of ternary subdivisions of the beat in 2/4, 3/4, 4/4, or similar metres gave rise to certain notational difficulties, primarily because the notation ♩♪ (or its equivalent) was not employed by composers. Thus, the apparent juxtaposition or superimposition of binary and ternary patterns, or of triplet and dotted notes, are commonalities in Baroque notation which require modification in performance. The need to assimilate binary rhythms to ternary divisions of the beat in Baroque music is well established in theoretical writings and by internal evidence in the music. C. P. E. Bach explained the practice succinctly:

Since the frequent use of triplets in so-called common or 4/4 time, as well as in 2/4 or 3/4 time, one finds many pieces which, instead of in these metres, would often be better written with the signatures 12/8, 9/8, or 6/8. One divides the notes found in Figure XII [Ex. 3.1] against the other voice in such a way as we see there.[3]

Here both duplet quavers and dotted quaver–semiquaver rhythms are assimilated to the pervading triplet rhythm, as is clear from Bach's description and from the alignment in his musical illustration. Again, as has frequently been demonstrated, notational evidence in Baroque music confirms this practice. Particularly convincing is the occurrence of the notation in ♪♪♪ J. S. Bach's Toccata in G minor, BWV

---

[3] 'Seit dem häuffigen Gebrauche der Triolen bey dem so genannten schlechten oder Vier Viertheil-Takte, ingleichen bey dem Zwei oder Dreyviertheil-Takte findet man viele Stücke, die statt dieser Takt-Arten offt bequemer mit dem Zwölff, Neun oder Sechs Achttheil-Takte vorgezeichnet würden. Man theilt alsdann die bey Fig. XII befindlichen Noten wegen der andern Stimme so ein, wie wir alda sehen'. (C. P. E. Bach, *Versuch über die wahre Art das Clavier zu spielen* (facsimile repr., Leipzig: Breitkopf & Härtel, 1969), pt. 1, pp. 128–9). The equivalent passage in Mitchell's trans. is on p. 160, where the text is somewhat garbled and the musical illustration is mistranscribed.

Ex. 3.1. C. P. E. Bach, *Versuch*, table VI, fig. xii

915 where the shared note-head clearly establishes that the dotted rhythm is assimilated to a triplet pattern.[4] The frequently careful alignment of semiquaver (or the equivalent) in a dotted rhythm with the third element in a triplet (as in Ex. 3.1) in good sources also supports the practice of assimilation. Such notational inexactitudes continue to occur in later eighteenth-century music and unproblematic instances where assimilation of binary to ternary rhythms is required have been cited by various authors in the music of Mozart and others.[5]

Not surprisingly, the same notational problem occurs in Haydn's music and is well illustrated by the notation in two parallel cadences in the early sonata Hob. xvi: 2/iii (Ex. 3.2). It is unlikely that Haydn intended two different rhythms in these cadences and since the notation ♩♪ was not available to Haydn, both dotted rhythm and duplet quavers may logically be regarded as approximations to this rhythm. The assimilation of binary to ternary here makes complete sense harmonically, with the synchronization of right and left hand on the last triplet quaver of the bar producing appropriate part-writing on the passing 6–3 chords. Similarly, in bars 6 and 11 of Hob. xv: c1/i the dotted rhythms in the violin part need to be synchronized with the last note of the sextuplet in the keyboard part (see Ex. 3.3). Again the notation as given is an approximation; the obviously cumbersome notation required to notate a ternary subdivision of the beat accurately in this context occurs nowhere in Haydn's music. These two bars as written by Haydn are clearly unsatisfactory, especially in bar 11 where the note *b* in the violin part, if performed on the fourth quaver beat, is poor harmonically, producing octaves with the keyboard right-hand part and rather unusual doubling: the strident major second between violin and the keyboard left hand, produced by the crossing of these parts and emphasized by the apparent doubling is improved (somewhat) by being delayed. That such common-sense

[4] See M. Collins, 'The Performance of Triplets in the 17th and 18th Centuries', *JAMS* 19/3 (Fall 1966): 281–328, esp. 304–7.

[5] A famous instance occurs in Mozart's Piano Concerto, K.450/i, bars 76, 201. See also Rosenblum, *Performance Practices*, 296–8.

Ex. 3.2. Hob. XVI: 2/iii

Ex. 3.3. Hob. XV: C1/i

assimilation of binary to ternary and consequent synchronization is often intended by Haydn is suggested by the comparison of bars 34 and 100 in Hob. XVI: 51/i, where the dotted quaver rest of bar 34 is replaced in bar 100 by two triplet quaver rests, indicating that the synchronization of right and left hands on the third triplet quaver of the second beat in both bars is appropriate (Ex. 3.4).

Ex. 3.4. Hob. XVI: 51/i

Table 3.1 presents a comparison between the modern notation used for various rhythms involving ternary subdivisions of the quaver or crotchet beat and Haydn's equivalent notation. For the first two patterns the notation is the same (whether as subdivisions of the crotchet or quaver beat): the modern notation for the third pattern is used by Haydn for subdivisions of a quaver beat, but not, apparently, for subdivisions of a crotchet beat: for the fourth pattern Haydn very rarely (as in Ex. 3.4) employs the modern notation, but usually writes a binary rhythm, dotted or equal notes: for the fifth pattern the mod- ern notation is nowhere employed by Haydn (either for subdivisions of crotchet or quaver beats) and is always represented by a binary rhythm, whether equal notes, dotted, or, perhaps, double-dotted.

TABLE 3.1 *Haydn's notation of Ternary divisions of the beat*

Modern notation	Haydn's equivalent

In Exx. 3.2–4 the need to synchronize different parts highlights the notational ambiguity and the desired assimilation of binary rhythms to the prevailing ternary pattern. Frequently, however, binary rhythms are intermixed melodically with prevailing ternary subdivisions of the beat in such a way that although no synchronization of parts is necessary the binary rhythms should often none the less be assimilated to the prevailing ternary movement. In the slow movement of Hob. XVI: 22 ternary subdivisions of the quaver beat are used throughout the movement, so that the movement might easily have been notated in 9/16. In bar 4, and elsewhere where this cadence occurs, the ternary movement is terminated by a duplet dotted figure which should very probably be read as a triplet rhythm in all parts. The dotted rhythm in bar 68 should also probably be read in the same way, the notation of the similar cadence in 27 being a clear indication that the three-part dominant seventh chord should occur on the last triplet semiquaver of the bar. Given that by the date of this work (1773) Haydn employed 'real notation' in his notation of appoggiaturas (see Ch. 7), the writing of the appoggiatura *d'* as a small quaver note in bar 8 is logical when one assumes a ternary division of the beat and, thus, a resolution of the appoggiatura on the third semiquaver triplet of the bar (see Ex. 3.5). Similarly in bar 120 of Hob. XVI: 43/i the triplet division of the beat might well be continued (see Ex. 3.6), while in the many passages of triplets or sextuplets in Haydn's music

Ex. 3.5. Hob. XVI: 22/ii

Ex. 3.6. Hob. XVI: 43/i

Ex. 3.7. Hob. XVI: 46/i

which begin with a single-note upbeat, the upbeat should also often be rendered as the last element of a triplet (as in Ex. 3.7).

The case for assimilation in these examples and many others is strong and derives from a simple notational problem, from the use of a less accurate binary notation to represent a ternary rhythm for which no accurate standard notation was available. In these examples the implied rather than the literal reading of the notation makes perfect sense. Yet it should also be allowed that when Haydn writes a dotted rhythm against a triplet, or two quavers against a triplet quaver rhythm, that he sometimes intends the literal meaning of that notation rather than the assimilation of the binary notation to ternary. Concerning the superimposition of dotted rhythms and triplets Quantz, unlike C. P. E. Bach, did not advocate assimilation:

This rule [the lengthening of a dotted note] likewise must be observed when there are triplets in one part and dotted notes against them in the other part (see (i) [Ex. 3.8*a*]). Hence you must not strike the short note after the dot with the third note of the triplet, but *after* it. Otherwise it will sound like the six-eight or twelve-eight time, as in (k) [Ex. 3.8*b*]. . . . . If you were to play all the dotted notes found beneath the triplets in accordance with their ordinary value, the expression would be very lame and insipid, rather than brilliant and majestic.[6]

[6] *Versuch einer Anweisung die Flöte traversiere zu spielen* (Berlin, 1752), trans. E. Reilly as *On Playing the Flute* (London: Faber & Faber, 1966), 68.

Ex. 3.8. Quantz, *Versuch*, trans. Reilly, p. 68

(*a*)   (*b*)

In Baroque music there may be some instances where it is not desirable to assimilate a dotted rhythm to a ternary rhythm, but the internal evidence in most Baroque music often seems to contradict Quantz. It seems in any case to be well established that in Baroque music counter-rhythms of three against two and four against three were not in use, so that apparent instances of counter-rhythms were assimilated (as in the second illustration in Ex. 3.1).[7] In the second half of the eighteenth century the situation is quite different because of the principal stylistic change in the mid-eighteenth century; that is, the slowing of harmonic rhythm. It is noticeable in the C. P. E. Bach illustration of Ex. 3.1 that the assimilation of binary rhythms to ternary is necessary to co-ordinate melody and bass in a passage with a fast rate of harmonic change (in the second illustration movement from an implied 6–3 to an implied 6–3 or 6–4–3 on the third quaver triplet, to a 6–3 on the next beat). It is perhaps significant that in the Quantz illustration where assimilation is not advocated, the part-writing is rather different and the harmonic rhythm slower, with a moving bass against a static upper part. Türk, who in general supports the practice of assimilating binary rhythms to ternary, also illustrates passages with counter-rhythms of two against three and three against four.[8] It is significant that the left-hand parts in these illustrations all employ Alberti basses or similar arpeggiated accompaniment figures which articulate a slow harmonic rhythm and give rise to these counter-rhythms (see Ex. 3.9).

From Haydn's earliest keyboard works counter-rhythms occur in a way which is quite different to Baroque music and which do not seem to allow the possibility of assimilating binary rhythms to ternary. Significantly, these counter-rhythms most frequently arise in passages with a relatively slow harmonic rhythm in which formulaic arpeggio or repeated-note figures in the left hand conflict with the metre of

---

[7] On the suggestion (not applicable to the music under consideration here) that ternary patterns should sometimes be assimilated to binary rhythms and not *vice versa*, see Collins, 'Performance of Triplets in the 17th and 18th Centuries'.

[8] *Klavierschule*, trans. Haggh, 100–1.

Ex. 3.9. Türk, *Klavierschule*, trans. Haggh, p. 100

the melody. In Hob. XVI: 35/i the four-against-three counter-
rhythm of bar 10 results from an embellishment of the melody which
conflicts with the new triplet accompaniment figure of the counterstatement (cf. bar 2). The four against three is undoubtedly intended
as a counter-rhythm—the semiquavers certainly do not easily or convincingly lend themselves to assimilation to the prevailing triplet
movement, nor can the well-established triplet figuration of the
accompaniment be altered without threatening the rhythmic coher-
ence of the passage (see Ex. 3.10). Counter-rhythms of this type are
commonplace in Haydn's keyboard music and, indeed, in much

Ex. 3.10. Hob. XVI: 35/i

keyboard music from the second half of the eighteenth century. There is here clearly not the same need for the assimilation of conflicting rhythms when one of these rhythms is a stock arpeggio figure, unlike in Baroque music where the assimilation of conflicting rhythms primarily served the purpose of co-ordinating different strands of a more contrapuntal texture, with a faster harmonic rhythm.

Given this crucial distinction in style and the undoubted existence of true (not just apparent) counter-rhythms in post-Baroque music, one must also ask the question if the same obligation exists to assimilate dotted rhythms consistently to prevailing triplet accompaniments. In Ex. 3.10, for instance, it is undoubtedly possible to play the dotted rhythm of bar 8 with the semiquaver synchronized with the third element in the left-hand triplet, but there is no harmonic reason why this is actually necessary: moreover, the rhythm of this theme on its first appearance (bars 1–8) is unambiguous (exclusively binary subdivisions of the beat with prominent use of dotted rhythms). Should one therefore necessarily alter the dotted rhythms of bar 8 simply because Haydn activates the accompaniment without altering the harmonic rhythm? It is in general true that in Haydn's keyboard music the initial themes in fast movements are not accompanied by Alberti basses or triplet arpeggio accompaniment figures. Subsequent restatements of these themes are often varied in a number of ways; the melodies may be embellished, the articulation may be altered, or, equally characteristically, the texture may be varied, particularly by introducing a more active accompaniment. When, as is frequently the case, rhythmic conflicts arise as a consequence of textural change, it seems to me to be frequently inappropriate to remove the rhythmic conflicts by accommodating the rhythm of the existing melody to a new accompaniment figure. In xv: 19/iii (Ex. 3.11) we should, perhaps, be wary of systematically altering the double-dotted rhythms of bars 2, 4, 5, and 9 in the reprise of bars 29 ff. to accommodate the new sextuplet accompaniment: likewise, the semiquavers of bar 1 should probably be performed as genuine counter-rhythms in bar 29, rather than being assimilated to the ternary rhythm of the left hand.[9]

───────────

[9] For further examples of conflicting binary and ternary rhythms arising from the process of variation, see e.g. Hob. xvi: 6/i, bars 29–30 (cf. 28–9) and Hob. xvi: 14/i, bar 11 (cf. bar 9), where embellishments in melodic restatements generate counter-rhythms of six against four. See also Hob. xvi: 49/iii where the dotted rhythms of the first phrase (bars 1–8) should

Ex. 3.11. Hob. xv: 19/iii

It is arguable that while there are many instances in Haydn's music where assimilation is either necessary or desirable there is not the same compunction on the performer to assimilate conflicting rhythms when, as is often the case in Haydn's music, the conflicting dotted or duplet rhythms against ternary rhythms arise from variation in texture and the introduction of stock accompaniment figures. The assimilation of conflicting rhythms should be less automatic in this style than in Baroque music and a more flexible approach seems to be required. Frequently within the same movement there are passages in which assimilation may be possible but more and less desirable in different places. There are, for instance, good musical reasons for not assimilating rhythms in Hob. XVI: 29/iii, bar 50 (Ex. 3.12). Here bar 50 is part of a variation and the syncopations of the theme in bar 5 are weakened if in the variation the right-hand part of bar 50 is altered to accommodate the expansion of the left hand to triplet quavers: the passage needs to be performed with counter-rhythms if the syncopations of the right-hand part are to retain their identity. While assimilating binary rhythms to ternary is very probably ill-advised here, on the other hand, in the same movement at bar 56 assimilation is undoubtedly intended for the reasons given in connection with Exx. 3.2–3.4.

Ex. 3.12. Hob. XVI: 29/iii

Slow movements in which triplet or sextuplet arpeggio accompaniment figures are present from the beginning and virtually throughout the movement are special cases in which dotted rhythms in the melody frequently suggest assimilation. Yet even in movements like XV: 25/ii, where assimilation is always an obvious possibility, a flexible approach is advisable. The dotted rhythms in the right hand of

not be altered in bars 61–8 and 102–10 where Haydn uses a new triplet accompaniment; similarly the three-against-two counter-rhythm of bars 2–3 should be performed as written, notwithstanding the fact that Haydn removes the rhythmic conflict in bars 62–3 and 104–5.

bars 1–3 may be co-ordinated with the third triplet quaver of the left hand, but in this particularly expressive Adagio it is valid for expressive reasons to avoid the consistently regular co-ordination of dotted rhythm and triplet. Similarly, in bar 30 the dotted rhythm in the violin part might well be assimilated to the pervading triplet rhythm of the piano accompaniment, but in bars 28 and 32 the *b♯'* might be played as written or in any case played longer (and thus earlier) than a triplet quaver, for expressive reasons, thus emphasizing the dissonant augmented fifth (Ex. 3.13).[10]

The flexible practice advocated here is subjective but it is not without historical foundation. While it is clear that notational problems characteristic of Baroque music survive in all of Haydn's music and that the practice of assimilating binary to ternary is applicable to his music, it is also true that genuine counter-rhythms which do not require alteration are commonplace. It is also suggestive that performing dotted rhythms literally instead of assimilating them to accompanying triplet rhythms is advocated by theorists apparently for the first time in the 1750s. Particularly striking is the fact that most instances in Haydn's music in which assimilation is possible, occur in connection with accompaniment formulas and a slow harmonic rhythm so that the same necessity for assimilation does not arise as in Baroque music. The performer must decide from case to case within each movement whether the literal meaning of the notation is intended or whether some manner of rhythmic alteration is necessary or desirable. However, one might frequently have recourse in this music to the expedient 'if it ain't broke, don't fix it'.

Dotted Rhythms

Although most eighteenth-century theorists explain the literal meaning of a dot following a note (prolonging the value of that note by half its notated value), many also stress that in performance the value of the dot varies according to context. Türk commented that 'dotted notes especially . . . require a very varied treatment according to the context in which they occur'.[11] It is as well to remember in this

---

[10] In the Adagio of Hob. XVI: 23 Rosenblum suggests assimilating the dotted rhythm and written-out slide of the melody (bar 1) to the sextuplet accompaniment (Rosenblum, *Performance Practices*, p. 303 and n. 20, p. 467). Although this is the obvious solution, there is also a strong case for a freer performance of the melody, with less regular co-ordination of right- and left-hand parts.

[11] *Klavierschule*, trans. Haggh, 350.

Ex. 3.13. Hob. XV: 25/ii

regard that 'over-dotting' is but one of the various non-literal ways in which a dotted rhythm may be interpreted. As in the notation of ternary subdivisions of the beat, a number of notational anomalies in Baroque notational practices survive in the second half of the eighteenth century, giving rise to various legitimate choices in rhythmic interpretation, quite apart from the subjective matter of matching dotted rhythms to the expressive character of the piece. The point may be illustrated by the notation ♪♫ which frequently occurs in Haydn's music. As it stands this rhythm is mathematically inaccurate and the most obvious, and frequently the most appropriate, interpretation, which editors often suggest in an editorial completion, is the performance of the fast notes as triplet demisemiquavers (♪♫): the dot in this interpretation represents its conventional value of half the duration of the preceding note. It has, however, been pointed out that in Baroque music the dot in this rhythm is frequently shorthand for a tied note (♪♫): in this interpretation the rhythm is 'under-dotted' in performance, the dot representing one quarter of the preceding note's value.[12] Over-dotting may also be an appropriate interpretation of the notation in certain contexts, as advocated by Türk and others.

It is customary, for the most part, to dwell on dotted notes longer (and therefore to play the following shorter notes even more quickly) than the notation indicates. For example: The realization of dotted notes as shown

Ex. 3.14. Türk, *Klavierschule*, trans. Haggh, p. 350

in *b* is generally chosen when the character of the composition is serious, solemn, exalted, etc., thus not only for an actual grave but also for overtures or compositions which are marked sostenuto, and the like.[13]

In many instances it is likely that when three quick notes follow a dot or double dot a triplet indication is simply missing: in Hob. XVI:

---

[12] See F. Neumann, 'External Evidence and Uneven Notes', *MQ* 52/4 (Oct. 1966): 448–64, esp. 463 and n. 26 (repr. in *Essays in Performance Practice*, 59–72).

[13] Türk, *Klavierschule*, trans. Haggh, 350. See also C. P. E. Bach, *Versuch*, trans. Mitchell, 157–8.

49/ii, for instance, the rhythm of bar 68 is ambiguous, but the parallel reading in bar 70 establishes that a double-dotted interpretation, with the demisemiquavers performed as a triplet, is intended (Ex. 3.15).[14] A triplet interpretation although often correct (as in Ex. 3.15), is not always the only, or necessarily the best, interpretation. In bar 6 of Hob. xv: 41/iii (Ex. 3.16*a*) the three hemidemisemiquavers may be played as a triplet as suggested by the editor of *JHW*, but here the dot quite possibly indicates a tie, as is appropriate in this particular trill preparation (see Ch. 6). Similarly in Hob. xvi: 35/ii the demisemiquavers of bar 24 may be read as a triplet, again as suggested by the editor of *JHW*, but it is also a viable, if not preferable, alternative to under-dot; that is, to interpret the dot as a tie (Ex. 3.16*b*). The second movement of Hob. xvi: 37 presents a particularly wide range of possibilities for the interpretation of the dotted rhythms, particularly the dotted quaver and three demisemiquaver pattern. Given that the tempo is *Largo e sostenuto*, 'under-dotting' with the dot interpreted as a tied demisemiquaver is perhaps least likely; the obvious dotted rhythm with triplet demisemiquavers is feasible, as is a double-dotted rhythm with triplet hemidemisemiquavers, or an over-dotted rhythm (with a tied hemidemisemiquaver) which is akin

Ex. 3.15. Hob. xvi: 49/ii

---

[14] Similarly, in Hob. xvi: 52/i the notation of bar 104 is ambiguous (again the triplet indication is lacking in the autograph manuscript). However, the more precise notation in the parallel passage of bar 33 clarifies that a double-dotted rhythm with triplet demisemiquavers is the correct reading.

Ex. 3.16(*a*) Hob. xv: 41/iii, (*b*) Hob. xvi: 35/ii

to Türk's illustration for 'serious, solemn, [and] exalted' pieces (Ex. 3.17).

Other notational ambiguities arise from the absence of a dot or double dot, which are particularly apparent when synchronization of two or more parts seems desirable, when the notation of an upbeat is inconsistent, or simply when the rhythms do not add up. In xv: f1/i bar 10 it would appear to be obvious that the bass note *c′* should be double-dotted, the resultant demisemiquaver thus being co-ordinated with the violin and keyboard right-hand part at the beginning of a unison cadence figure (Ex. 3.18). That double-dotted rhythms are intended is sometimes apparent from inaccurately written rhythms: such is the case in bar 3 of Hob. xvi: 39/ii where the dotted rhythm of the first beat requires a second dot to make mathematical sense (see below, Ex. 3.20). Similarly in xvi: 19/i the demisemiquaver upbeat to bar 1, which is a distinctive characteristic of the theme, is subsequently preceded by a dotted quaver rest, rather than a double-dotted quaver rest (see Ex. 4.5): the requisite second dot is added editorially in *JHW* at bars 8, 42, and 102, but at the recapitulation in bar 68, where the anacrusis is a semiquaver preceded

Ex. 3.17. Hob. XVI: 37/ii

by a dotted-quaver rest, a strong case can also be made for double-dotting the rest and playing the semiquaver as a demisemiquaver.[15]

Double-dotted rhythms are indicated occasionally by the use of ties or rests,[16] but such occurrences are erratic, and it must be assumed that at least until the 1780s Haydn does not distinguish dotted and double-dotted rhythms notationally with any consistency. Sometimes notational inaccuracies or inconsistencies, or the need for synchronization suggests the appropriateness of a double-dotted interpretation, but there are many more cases where double-dotting may be a valid interpretation although notational evidence is lacking. The opening of Hob. XVI: 2/iii, for instance, has a rhythm which is

---

[15] Similar inconsistencies in the notation of upbeats are apparent in Hob. XVI: 18/i: it is perhaps arguable that the notational distinction between the upbeat to bar 1 and the upbeat to bar 5 is intentional, but at the recapitulation the upbeat to bar 75 should very probably be emended to agree with bars 4 and 78.

[16] See e.g. *JHW* XI/1 (Munich: Henle, 1986), pp. ix, 28, 30.

Ex. 3.18. Hob. xv: f1/i

very uncharacteristic of Haydn's minuets and it seems to me that here a double-dotted crotchet is very probably intended by the composer (Ex. 3.19). The opening themes of Hob. XVI: 26/i also seems to benefit from double-dotted rhythms which match the staccato articulation and the generally quirky nature of the thematic material (see Ex. 4.7*c*).

Ex. 3.19. Hob. XVI: 2/iii

Haydn does not, however, regularly notate such rhythms using a double dot until the 1780s, when this notational expedient first occurs in the Op. 33 String Quartets and in the Auenbrugger Sonatas (XVI: 20, 35–9). (An uncharacteristic earlier occurrence is found in Hob. XVI: 33/iii, published in 1783, but quite possibly composed in the mid-1770s.) It is also from the 1780s that Haydn indicates a double-dotted interpretation of the ubiquitous pattern ♪ by adopting the more precise notation ♪ (see Ch. 8). The occurrence of the double dot remains occasional, especially in the early 1780s, and it would be unwise to assume that because some double-dotted rhythms are specifically notated, all other dotted rhythms should not

Ex. 3.20. Hob. XVI: 39/ii

be double-dotted in performance. In its early occurrence in the
keyboard sonatas, in Hob. XVI: 39/ii, a double dot is used in bar 31
but not in the parallel passage in bar 8, and, as mentioned above, a
second dot clearly required in bar 3 is lacking (see Ex. 3.20). In this
work it is indeed arguable that, paradoxically, the presence of two
dots in bar 31 does not necessarily indicate a sharply double-dotted
rhythm. The inconsistency in notation between bars 8 and 31 suggests, perhaps, that both notations are approximations to a ternary
division of the beat and that both the dotted and double-dotted
rhythms may be assimilated to the sextuplet accompaniment figure of
the left hand, as discussed above. By the mid-1780s, however,
Haydn's notation of double-dotted rhythms became more consistent:
notational inaccuracies and inconsistent notation of upbeat
demisemiquavers are much less in evidence. Flexibility is still
required of the performer in interpreting dotted rhythms in Haydn's
late works since it cannot be assumed that Haydn's more frequent use
of the double dot disallows the use of double-dotted rhythms elsewhere where only a single dot is notated. It is none the less striking
that Haydn appears to be quite careful about the notation of double-
dotted rhythms in the thematic material of his sonatas and trios from

1785 especially in connection with the first theme of the movement. The more precise notation is, for instance, reflected in the number of incipits to slow or relatively slow movements in the late piano trios which have double-dotted rhythms. Haydn's revision of his manner of notating ornaments, embellishments, and articulation, which took place from the mid-1760s, seems not to have immediately affected his notation of rhythm. It was not until a second phase of notational revision in the 1780s that many of the anomalies of Baroque rhythmic notation were resolved (chief among which is the use of the double dot, a feature which was used by other composers, such as L. Mozart and W. A. Mozart, at a much earlier date). However, like his contemporaries Haydn retained throughout his career the convenient Baroque expedient of notating some ternary subdivisions of the beat in a binary notation.

TEMPO

No single performance decision has as radical an effect on a performance as the choice of tempo. Türk commented that 'the most excellent composition has little or no effect, when it is performed in a noticeably wrong tempo', in which case 'The desired effect of the best and most forceful composition becomes confused'.[17] He does not imply that each piece has a single workable tempo: eighteenth-century theorists admit that the choice of tempo is subject to manifold practical expedients, such as, the nature of the instrument, the size of the forces used in performance, the acoustic, and a number of other factors. A noticeably wrong tempo is, however, detrimental to a performance because it indicates a failure of the performer to understand the character of the piece. 'Every good composition has', according to Türk, 'a certain (predominant) character'.[18] Choosing an appropriate tempo is consequently not merely a matter of observing a set of general performance conventions applicable to movement types (even if these could be established with any certainty, which they cannot), but a question of broader understanding of a composition's style, character, and meaning. A 'correct' tempo does not guarantee that the character of the piece has been understood, but equally, a 'noticeably wrong tempo' implicates other aspects of the

---

[17] *Klavierschule*, trans. Haggh, 109.   [18] Ibid. 111.

performance in a significantly misunderstood reading of that piece's character.

Despite its importance, the methods of notating tempo are among the crudest of performance indications. Efforts to describe tempo by using familiar Italian terms provide the performer with equivocal instructions. The term *allegro*, for instance, is non-specific and clearly does not define a particular quantifiable speed: according to eighteenth-century writers, it has different implications depending on the time signature, the genre of the piece involved, its geographical provenance, and the date of the piece bearing the designation. The meanings of these Italian terms are relative and of value only in so far as they attempt to describe the character of a given movement by comparison with other dissimilar movements. Yet they are, as often as not, the only direct information we have concerning tempo which derives directly from the composer. As such, an initial step is to investigate how a composer understood these terms. This is in itself a complex task. While the relative meaning of most of the common Italian terms is unproblematic (*adagio, moderato, allegro*, for instance) many other terms were the subject of much disagreement among eighteenth-century writers. Table 3.2 is an attempt to list the

TABLE 3.2 *Haydn's tempo categories*

Basic indication	Modifications
Largo	Largo e sostenuto; Largo cantabile
Adagio	Adagio e cantabile; Adagio non tanto; Adagio ma non troppo (cantabile); Adagio pastorale; Poco adagio (cantabile)
Larghetto	—
Andante	Andante con espressione; Andante cantabile; Andante con moto; Molto andante;
Andantino	Andantino più tosto allegretto; Andantino et innocentemente
Moderato	—
Allegretto	Allegretto et innocentemente
Allegro	Allegro moderato; Allegro ma dolce; Poco allegro; Allegro spiritoso; Allegro di molto; Allegro con brio; Allegro assai; Allegro vivace
Vivace	Vivace assai; Vivace molto innocentemente
Presto	Presto ma non troppo innocentemente; Presto assai
Prestissimo	—

tempo indications found in Haydn's keyboard music in a progressive order, from slowest to fastest.

Not least among the difficulties of understanding the meaning of Italian tempo designations is the problem of deciding on the order of slow tempos. The terms *lento, largo, grave, larghetto,* and *adagio* are understood differently by many writers and it is impossible to give an order of increasing tempos for the period as a whole based on contemporary evidence. Some of the many anomalies are suggested by Table 3.3, which lists the various orderings of these terms in ten different treatises.[19]

TABLE 3.3 *The categorization of slow tempos in eighteenth- and early nineteenth-century treatises*

Author of treatise	Ordering of tempos
Hoyle	Adagio Grave Largo Larghetto
Clementi	Adagio Grave Largo Lento Larghetto
Kollmann	Largo Adagio Lento Grave
Cramer	Adagio Largo Larghetto
Broderip	Grave/Adagio Largo/Lento/Larghetto
Hummel	Grave/Largo Larghetto/Lento Adagio
L. Mozart	Grave Largo Adagio pesante Adagio Lente [*sic*]
Ricci–[Bach]	Largo Adagio Lento Larghetto
Koch	Largo Lento/Adagio Larghetto
Türk	Largo Adagio Lento Larghetto

There would appear to be an English tradition which regarded *adagio* as the slowest tempo, but in the Germanic world *largo* seems to be regarded with a considerable degree of unanimity as a slower tempo than *adagio*.[20] *Grave* seems to have been regarded as a more general indication of mood rather than a specific tempo designation; hence,

[19] See J. Hoyle, *A Complete Dictionary of Music* (London, 1791); Clementi, *Introduction*, 13–14; A. F. Kollmann, *An Essay on Musical Harmony* (London, 1796), 71; J. B. Cramer, *Instructions for the Piano Forte* (London [1812]), 44–5; R. Broderip, *Plain and Easy Instructions for Young Performers on the Pianoforte or Harpsichord* (London [1788]), 8; Hummel, *Instructions*, pt. I, pp. 68–9; L. Mozart, *Versuch*, trans. Knocker, 50–2; P. Ricci [and J. C. Bach], *Méthode ou recueil de connoissances* [sic] *élémentaires pour le forte-piano ou clavecin* (Paris, 1786), 3–4; Koch, *Lexikon*; Türk, *Klavierschule*, trans. Haggh, 105–7.

[20] H. C. R. Landon misleadingly asserts that in Haydn's music *adagio* is a slower tempo than *largo*, or even *largo assai* (*The Symphonies of Joseph Haydn* (London: Universal & Rockliff, 1955), 129).

presumably, its variable placement in relation to other terms.[21] The placement of *lento* among the slower tempos is not entirely consistent, but it seems to be agreed, contrary to some modern understandings of the term,[22] that it indicated a faster tempo than *largo*: it is usually described as a tempo similar to *adagio*.[23]

Among Germanic writers Hummel is exceptional in regarding *lento* as slower than *adagio* and since he regarded *lento* and *larghetto* as equivalent, Hummel is at odds with the majority of writers in regarding *larghetto* as slower than *adagio*. For the majority of writers *larghetto* is a faster tempo than *adagio*. Koch writes that the *larghetto* is usually like the *andante*, while the Ricci–[J. C. Bach] treatise regarded *larghetto* as a tempo between *largo* and *andante*, close to *andantino* (which these writers regarded as slightly slower than *andante*).[24] This view is confirmed by Quantz and Marpurg. Both authors group tempos into categories without making the internal ordering entirely clear in each category, but they place *larghetto* in a faster tempo category. Marpurg, for instance, lists *larghetto* along with *andante*, *poco adagio*, *andantino*, *poco largo*, and *poco lento* in the category of moderately slow tempos, while *adagio* is placed in the category of slow tempos with *largo* and *lento*.[25]

It has been suggested that Haydn employed the terms describing slow tempos in the following order (beginning with the slowest): *largo*, *lento*, *grave*, *adagio*.[26] The ordering for slow movements in Haydn's keyboard music is less complicated, since he uses only three

[21] Türk includes *grave* among those terms by which 'careful composers are accustomed to indicate the character of a composition as well as its tempo': it is thus listed along with terms such as *cantabile*, *brillante*, and *espressivo* (rather than with *largo*, *adagio*, and similar terms), and is described as 'serious, grave with dignity' (see Türk, *Klavierschule*, trans. Haggh, 111–12). Similarly, in Koch's *Lexikon* the entry on 'Grave' refers the reader to the article 'Con gravità' and, unlike other terms, *grave* is not here defined as faster or slower in relation to other tempo indications.

[22] e.g. P. and E. Badura-Skoda (*Interpreting Mozart*, 34) imply that *lento* is a slower tempo than *largo*.

[23] Koch's *Lexikon* describes *lento* as 'slowly, often means the same degree of slow movement . . . as the *adagio*' ('gemächlich, bedeutet oft den nemlichen Grad der langsamen Bewegung . . . wie das Adagio'). For Türk (*Klavierschule*, trans. Haggh, 105) *lento* is 'somewhat similar to *adagio*, but not quite as slow', and similarly Kollman describes *lento* as 'slow, rather less than *largo* and *adagio*'. (*Essay on Harmony*, 71).

[24] 'Das Zeitmaaß [Larghetto] ist dabey gewöhnlich dem des Andante gleich' (Koch, *Lexikon*, s.v. 'Larghetto'); 'LARGHETTO, annonce le Mouvement un peu moins lent que *Largo*, & plus que l'*Andante*, & très-approchant de l'*Andantino*.' (P. Ricci–[J. C. Bach], *Méthode*, 4).

[25] Marpurg, *Anleitung*, 16; see also Quantz, *Versuch*, trans. Reilly, 284.

[26] See Rosenblum, *Performance Practices*, 314; I. Saslav, 'Tempos in the String Quartets of Joseph Haydn', D.M. diss., Indiana University, 1969, pp. 36–7, 55–8.

basic terms: *largo, adagio, larghetto*. That we should regard *largo* as the slowest tempo is confirmed by the modification *e sostenuto*, which he avoids in connection with *adagio* movements: characteristically Haydn's modifications of *adagio* are on the fast side, indicated by *non tanto, ma non troppo*, and *poco adagio*.[27] Indeed, an important genre distinction may be identified here. In his keyboard music Haydn's normal slow movement is marked *adagio*, frequently with modifications on the fast side of that tempo category. *Largo* is rarely used in keyboard slow movements, *grave* never occurs, and *adagio* is never modified by terms such as *sostenuto* which might imply that it approaches a *largo* tempo. Haydn thus seems to have avoided the slowest tempos in his keyboard music to a far greater extent than in other genres, perhaps because of the relative lack of sustaining power in the keyboard instruments for which he wrote. The generally florid style of the slow movements in Haydn's keyboard music does not require exaggeratedly slow tempos, and many *adagio*s are closer to the *andantino-andante*, rather than the *largo*, tempo category.

The Meaning of Andantino

The term *andantino* gave rise to greater ambiguity than any other of the common Italian tempo indications used in the eighteenth century. To some writers it indicated a tempo slower than *andante* and to others a tempo somewhat faster than *andante*. Indeed, such was the extent of the ambiguity in the eighteenth century that a number of theorists drew attention to what they considered the commonplace misunderstanding of the term among other writers. Türk explained that *andantino* meant 'somewhat, and therefore not too much, of a walking tempo, that is, somewhat slower than *andante*' and, in a much-quoted footnote, emphasized his view:

In most instruction books, *andantino* is translated as somewhat faster than *andante*. If one considers, however, that for molto andante (a brisk walking tempo), a greater degree of speed is required than for an andante, then it may perhaps be found that my translation of andantino which indicates only a diminutive degree of walking speed—or of the tempo—is suitable in this connection.[28]

---

[27] That *larghetto* is indeed faster than *adagio* is suggested by xviii: 11/ii, which is marked *Un poco adagio*, but in some parts *larghetto* occurs as a variant reading. See *JHW* XV/2 (Munich: Henle, 1983), 'Kritischer Bericht', 192.

[28] Türk, *Klavierschule*, trans. Haggh, 106, 450 n. 125.

Similarly, Hummel commented that 'many authors assign a quicker degree of movement to the *Andantino*, than to the *Andante*; but this is incorrect, for it is evident that *Andantino* is the diminutive of the original word *Andante*, and therefore that it implies a less degree of movement than it'.[29] Such 'corrections' evidently failed to establish a common understanding of the term as Beethoven's much-quoted letter of 19 February 1813 makes clear:

If among the airs that you may send me to be arranged in the future there are Andantinos, please tell me whether Andantino is to be understood as meaning faster or slower than Andante, for this term, like so many in music, is of so indefinite a significance that Andantino sometimes approaches a[n] Allegro and sometimes, on the other hand, is played like Adagio.[30]

Among those authors who agreed with Türk and Hummel that *andantino* indicates a tempo slower than *andante* may be numbered Ricci–Bach, Fétis–Moscheles, Clementi, Cramer, and Adam.[31] On the other hand Koch described *andantino* as 'a tempo which is somewhat faster than *Andante*. One finds it often in compositions which require a markedly faster tempo than the usual *Andante*.'[32] The writers who agree with Koch (Kollmann, Galeazzi, Cartier, Muller, and Czerny) are, perhaps, numerically in the minority, and it has been suggested that they belong to a slightly later tradition,[33] but no simple chronological trend is apparent and the ambiguity in treatises is also witnessed in eighteenth-century usage by composers.

In Mozart's music the modification of the term *andantino* by the qualifier *sostenuto* would seem to suggest that, at least sometimes, he regarded *andantino* as a slower tempo than *andante* and among modern writers Rosenblum and Zaslaw have persuasively argued this

[29] *Instructions*, pt. I, p. 69.

[30] Anderson, ed., *Letters of Beethoven*, i. 406. Trans. in A. Thayer, *Thayer's Life of Beethoven*, ed. E. Forbes (rev. edn., Princeton: Princeton University Press, 1967), 555.

[31] Ricci–[J. C. Bach], *Méthode*, 3; F. J. Fétis and J. Moscheles, *Méthode des méthodes de piano* (Paris, 1840; facsimile repr., Geneva: Minkoff, 1973), p. v; Clementi, *Introduction*, 13; Cramer, *Instructions*, 44–5; L. Adam, *Méthode de piano du conservatoire* (Paris, 1805; facsimile repr., Geneva: Minkoff, 1974), 161.

[32] 'Andantino bezeichnet . . . eine Bewegung, die etwas geschwinder ist, als *Andante*. Man findet es auch sehr oft in Tonstücken gebraucht, die eine merklich geschwindere Bewegung erfordern, als das gewöhnliche *Andante*' (*Lexikon*, s.v. 'Andantino').

[33] Rosenblum suggests that the tradition of regarding *andantino* as faster than *andante* emerges in the 1780s and was 'widely adopted only well into the nineteenth century' (Rosenblum, *Performance Practices*, 316).

view.[34] Haydn used the term *andantino* less frequently than Mozart; in the keyboard music it occurs rarely, and, although it is difficult to draw conclusions from these few occurrences, the designation Andantino più tosto Allegretto in Hob. xv: 16/ii would seem to make little sense if he regarded *andantino* as a tempo significantly slower than *andante*: significantly, Haydn, unlike Mozart, never qualified *andantino* with the term *sostenuto* or other such term which would suggest a slower tempo. It is also of interest that the keyboard movements in 6/8 bearing the designation *andantino, innocentemente, allegretto,* or a combination of these, have much in common,[35] and that the arrangement of the Allegretto first movement of the Sonata, Hob. xvi: 3 in the Baryton Trio, Hob. xi: 37 has the tempo marking *andantino.* Haydn therefore on a number of occasions seems to have associated *andantino* with *allegretto* or a tempo approaching *allegretto.* There are no similar associations of *andantino* with a tempo slower than *andante.* On the other hand, *andantino* and *andante* must have been for Haydn quite similar tempos: *andante,* like *andantino,* is not modified in the keyboard music by a slower qualifying term (such as *sostenuto*) but very frequently by such qualifiers as *con moto,* or *molto.* Indeed *più tosto allegretto* occurs as a modification of both *andante* and *andantino*: Andante più tosto Allegretto occurs, for instance, in Symphony No. 103, but is not used in Haydn's keyboard music. It seems likely that *andantino* in Haydn's usage signified a tempo extending from the faster side of the *andante* category (*andante con moto, molto andante,* and *andante più tosto allegretto*) to *allegretto.*

The terms describing faster tempos given in Table 3.2 are less problematic than those discussed above. *Vivace,* like *grave,* seems to describe a movement of a particular character. Koch's definition, for instance, does not describe *vivace* as a particular speed located in relation to other terms, but emphasizes the character of the performance associated with the term: '*Vivace,* lively [vivacious], as well as a brisk

---

[34] See ibid. 317; N. Zaslaw, 'Mozart's Tempo Conventions', in *Report on the Eleventh Congress of the International Musicological Society, Copenhagen, 1972,* 2 vols. (Copenhagen: Hansen, 1974), ii. 722, 727; id., *Mozart's Symphonies: Context, Performance, Reception* (Oxford: Clarendon Press, 1989), 495. W. S. Newman concludes that Beethoven 'must have arrived at no final answer, but contrary to Mozart's use of "andantino" . . . Beethoven's twenty-three uses of that term seem to interpret it more often as meaning faster instead of slower than "andante"'. (Newman, *Beethoven on Beethoven,* 101).

[35] Cf. Hob. xv: 16/ii (Andantino più tosto Allegretto), xv: 29/ii (Andantino et innocentemente), xvi: 40/i (Allegretto e innocente).

movement, also a lively, and light flowing performance.'[36] Hence *vivace* is frequently used as a qualification of the term *allegro*. When used independently Haydn reserves the term *vivace* mainly for finales. Its placement in Table 3.2 in relation to *allegro* is therefore somewhat arbitrary: *vivace* does not necessarily indicate a faster tempo than *allegro*, but a particularly lively and light type of *allegro* movement. Haydn's description of the finale of Symphony No. 96, a movement marked Vivace assai, is consistent with this view. In a letter of 17 November 1791, he recommended 'the softest *piano* and a very quick *tempo* [*einem sehr geschwinden Tempo*]' for this movement:[37] as regards speed alone *vivace assai* would seem to have the same implication as *allegro assai*. This reference also clarifies an ambiguity in eighteenth-century writings concerning the meaning of the term *assai*. The term was variously understood as meaning both 'very' and 'somewhat': clearly Haydn understood it as meaning the former, that is, in its more conventional meaning (*assai* = *sehr*).[38]

Metre, Metronomes, and Tempo

It should be reiterated here that tempo markings do not define strict categories, quantifiable in absolute measurements of speed, as for instance in metronome markings. Any given metronome marking may be appropriate for movements bearing different tempo markings; equally, movements bearing the same tempo marking may require radically different metronomic speeds, since Haydn wrote an infinite variety of movement types bearing similar or the same tempo marking. In determining the tempo of any movement the particular combination of tempo designation and time signature is of great importance, although this is not to say that any system of proportional relationships or a fixed *tactus* is operable in Haydn's music. Haydn certainly in general associated specific time signatures with particular tempos: for instance, in his fastest movements Haydn avoids 𝄴, preferring 2/4, 3/4, 6/8, and, in early works, 3/8. However, in the body

---

[36] '*Vivace*, lebhaft, bestimmt sowohl eine muntere Bewegung, als auch einen lebhaften, und leicht dahinfließenden Vortrag' (*Lexikon*, s.v. 'Vivace').

[37] *CCLN*, 121; D. Bartha, ed., *Joseph Haydn: Gesammelte Briefe und Aufzeichnungen* (Kassel: Bärenreiter, 1965), 265.

[38] On the meaning of *assai* see Rosenblum, *Performance Practices*, 320–1; Newman, *Beethoven on Beethoven*, 101; and *New Grove*, s.v. 'Tempo'. Presumably the controversy arose at least in part from the confusion of the French *assez* and the Italian *assai*.

of his keyboard music as a whole, Haydn used the time signatures **C**, 2/4, 2/2, 6/8, 3/4 in a range of tempos from *adagio* to *allegro*, which clearly implies that time signatures are not in themselves determinants of tempo. Even the time signature 3/8, which has particular associations with fast movements, and occurs for the most part only in fast finales in the early works of Haydn, cannot be said to have an exclusive association with a particular tempo, since it also appears in the Andante second movement of Hob. XVI: 22 (1773).[39] In the special case of the relationship between *alla breve* and **C**, the former, which according to Türk and others implies a tempo 'once again as fast as usual',[40] does not in practice necessarily define a tempo proportionally twice as fast as a movement in **C**. *Alla breve* movements frequently require, because of their accentuation, prevalent note values, and harmonic rhythm, a tempo somewhat faster than movements in common time bearing the same tempo marking—perhaps even a tempo twice as fast as some Allegro **C** movements.[41] There is, however, no possibility of a proportional relationship between 2/2 and **C** in Haydn's keyboard music: 2/2 might suggest a proportionally faster tempo were the time signature **C** altered to 2/2 in the same movement without a change in tempo indication, but this occurs nowhere in Haydn's keyboard music. Since 2/2 occurs in a range of tempos from *adagio* to *allegro* is cannot be said to have particular associations with any one tempo.

It is true that while the category of, for instance, 'Allegro movements' in Haydn's keyboard music encompasses a heterogenous group of movements, which in terms of absolute tempo would require a very wide range of metronome markings overlapping with numerous other tempo categories, subcategories of tempo associated with various time signatures form more homogenous groups with a narrower range of feasible performance speeds. It is in subcategories of tempo and time signature combinations that the logic of Haydn's

[39] For many 18th-cent. writers different time signatures, while not determining tempos, had implications for the types of execution expected. Thus, Türk explains that a composition in 3/2 is 'played more heavily' than one in 3/4 or 3/8; likewise, in an *adagio* in 3/8 or 2/4 'a good player would not play . . . with as much emphasis as in the alla breve'. See Türk, *Klavierschule*, trans. Haggh, 348–50.

[40] Ibid. 105.

[41] If one compares e.g. the Andante **C** movement, Hob. XVI: 8/iii and the Andante alla breve movement Hob. XVI: 11/ii, workable tempos for each might be considered to be approximately ♪ =108 and ♩ = 108 respectively. The **C** signature which appears in some sources of XVI: 11/ii must be an error.

tempo markings is apparent. Presto 2/4 movements such as the finales of Hob. XVI: 46, 23, 48, and 52 are similar in rhythmic construction and harmonic rhythm, and seem to require tempos which are not hugely different from one another. By comparison, the Allegro 2/4 indication of XVI: 47 and the Allegro moderato 2/4 of XVI: 18 appear as carefully gauged gradations which reflect significantly different rhythmic construction and harmonic rhythm: the latter has a significantly faster harmonic rhythm and an abundance of triplet semiquaver and demisemiquaver figuration which is lacking in Presto 2/4 movements. Similarly, Adagio 3/4 movements and 6/8 movements marked Andante, Andantino, or Allegretto form relatively homogenous subcategories with fairly narrow ranges of feasible performance speeds. Comparisons of this type reveal the logic of Haydn's tempo markings when broader (and vaguer) analogies appear anomalous: for instance, the fastest reasonable tempo for the Presto 2/4 movement Hob. XVI: 48/ii, must quantatively have a radically slower crotchet pulse than the Presto 3/4 movement Hob. XVI: 51/ii.

There are, even within relatively homogenous tempo–time-signature subcategories, movements of subtly different character. The crotchet upbeat (or more specifically two quavers) in Hob. XVI: 48/ii distinguishes this movement from other movements in Presto 2/4 subcategory (e.g. XVI: 46/iii, 23/iii, 52/iii) which are characterized by a single quaver upbeat: in this same group the virtually continuous semiquaver movement and frequent passages of more than two changes of harmony in a bar suggest that the Presto 2/4 of XVI: 46/iii lies on the border of the Presto 2/4 tempo and perhaps closer to many movements in Allegro 2/4. The relationship between tempo, metre, rhythm, and harmonic rhythm is infinitely variable and complex, allowing few precise analogies, and it is for this reason that apart from explaining the meaning of Italian terminology, eighteenth-century theorists for the most part content themselves with the useful rule of thumb that tempo depends on the number and type of the shortest note values in a piece, as in the following passage from Türk:

If one only knows, for example, that an allegro must be played faster than a largo, then one still has a very uncertain concept of tempo. The question is, therefore: how fast is the tempo of an allegro assai and of relative tempos in other compositions? This question cannot be answered with assurance because certain other secondary circumstances make many modifications necessary. For example, an allegro with some thirty-second notes intermingled, should not be played as fast as when its most rapid passages consist of only eighth notes.[42]

Although generalizations can be made about the rhythmic construction characteristic of Allegro 2/4, Vivace 6/8, or other tempo–time-signature subcategories, each movement has its own individual features which set it somewhat apart from like movements. It is perhaps this that L. Mozart had in mind when he said that 'Every melodious piece has at least one phrase from which one can recognize quite surely what sort of speed the piece demands.'[43]

Metronome markings are more precise in describing the speed of a composition and have the merit of suggesting absolute tempos, as opposed to the relative tempos suggested by tempo indications and time signatures. They are, however, no more successful in defining the indefinable, the meaning or character of a piece, the *raison d'être* of all tempo and metronome indications. A metronome marking provided by the composer for a particular movement gives us an absolute speed which is compatible with the composer's understanding of that movement's character: it does not tell us of the character of other movements which bear the same tempo designation. The apparent precision of metronome markings should not therefore be confused with absolute authority, nor can they be applied easily to movements other than those to which they are appended.[44] An additional and even more important reason for caution applies when the metronome markings derive from individuals other than the composer. There are no extant metronome markings for Haydn's works which derive from the composer himself, but sets of metronome markings for Haydn's *Creation* and 'London' Symphonies survive from the 1830s and 1840s, the former prepared by Haydn's pupil Neukomm (and brought to light by Nicholas Temperley) and the latter supplied by Carl Czerny.[45] These obviously create the

[42] *Klavierschule*, trans. Haggh, 107.　　　　[43] *Versuch*, trans. Knocker, 33.

[44] On the general problems of interpreting the evidence of extant metronome markings see J.-P. Marty, 'Mozart's Tempo Indications and the Problems of Interpretation', in *Perspectives on Mozart Performance*, 55–73; Rosenblum, *Performance Practices*, 324–8; Newman, *Beethoven on Beethoven*, 83–9.

[45] See N. Temperley, 'Haydn's Tempos in *The Creation*', *EM* 19/2 (May 1991): 235–45; W. Malloch, 'Carl Czerny's Metronome Marks for Haydn and Mozart Symphonies', *EM* 16/1 (Feb. 1988): 73–82. Other attempts to establish absolute tempos in Haydn's music centre on the music preserved on musical clocks (see E. F. Schmid, 'Joseph Haydn und die Flötenuhr', *ZfMw* 14 (Jan. 1932): 193–221; and Saslav, 'Tempos', 58–62). This evidence is now viewed with scepticism by most scholars because so much relies on the tension of the springs and the instruments were in any case adjustable. See esp. *JHW* XXI.

expectation that we have here some insight into the absolute tempos appropriate for at least some of Haydn's music.

Leaving aside for the moment the major problem of whether the indications reflect Haydn's intentions or the taste of the 1830s and 1840s, there are other dangers in the possible assumption that these metronome markings can inform us about tempo in Haydn's keyboard music. In the first place, the transference of tempo indications between genres is highly problematic. For instance, Czerny gives the tempo ♩ = 69 for the slow introduction to Symphony No. 103, which is marked Adagio 3/4 by Haydn with the indication 'P[iano] e sostenuto' over the bass-line. If this seems unreasonably fast, the reason in this instance may quite possibly be related to the fact that Czerny's indications are appended to a piano arrangement of Haydn's symphonies, and not to an orchestral score (Neukomm gives the marking ♪ =112 for an Adagio 3/4 and a Poco adagio 3/4 movement in the *Creation*). Yet even as a 'keyboard Adagio 3/4 tempo' ♩ =69 is of little use to performers of Haydn's original keyboard music since there is no keyboard Adagio movement in 3/4 which even remotely resembles the distinctive slow introduction to Symphony No. 103. (Movements like the Adagio 3/4 from Haydn's Sonata, Hob. XVI: 49 must, because of the degree of embellishment, surely be closer to ♩ =56 than ♩ = 69). With regard to Neukomm's metronome markings it cannot be assumed that tempos which may be appropriate for a work involving soloists, chorus, and orchestra transfer to keyboard music. Neukomm gives ♪ =120 and ♪ =132 as the tempos for the two Andante 6/8 movements in *Creation*, but in Haydn's keyboard music Andante 6/8 movements characteristically contain far more extensive demisemiquaver figuration (or even faster note-groups) than is present in either of these *Creation* movements. For this reason ♪ =120 seems sometimes to be excessive and sometimes a maximum feasible tempo for keyboard movements marked Andante 6/8 (such as XV: 7/i, XV: 18/ii, XV: 12/ii, and XV: 24/ii): only in 6/8 movements marked Andantino and Andantino più tosto Allegretto (XV: 29/ii, XV: 16/ii) does the rhythmic profile allow one to contemplate the tempo range ♪ =120–32.

Even if the Neukomm–Czerny metronome markings are appropriate for the works to which they are appended, and ignoring the question of genre, these markings would remain of little use to the keyboard-player, for the simple reason that any metronome marking is specific to a particular movement and takes account of the individuality of that movement. Only in instances where very specific analogies between two movements suggest an identical or near-identical tempo (considering tempo indication and time signature, but also such criteria as rhythmic construction, harmonic rhythm, embellishment, etc.) can one contemplate applying the metronome marking of one movement to another.[46] The Neukomm–Czerny metronome markings are insufficient in number and type to provide worthwhile specific analogies with Haydn's keyboard music. In order to pursue this point further, and to consider the problematic question of whether extant metronome markings represent Haydn's intentions or the taste of the 1830s and 1840s, it is useful to consider minuet tempos in some detail. The minuet makes an especially interesting case study because the most controversial aspect of Czerny's metronome markings is undoubtedly the consistently fast speed indicated for the minuets in Haydn's 'London' Symphonies.

Haydn's Minuets and Czerny's Metronome Markings

Mozart remarked in a letter of 24 March 1770 that 'The minuets in Milan, in fact the Italian minuets generally, have plenty of notes, are played slowly and have several bars, e.g., the first part has sixteen, the second twenty or twenty-four.'[47] Minuets in Milan may have been slower than in Vienna, but what is also significant about the comment is that Mozart, like most eighteenth-century writers, relates the tempo of a piece to the content and, in particular, to the fastest note values in the movement. There is clearly no single minuet tempo in the same way that there is no single *allegro* tempo. Viewed from the standpoint of their rhythmic profiles, Haydn's minuets are very diverse, ranging from those which move primarily in crotchets and have a slow harmonic rhythm (mostly one harmony per bar) to those with fairly continuous quaver, or quaver-triplet, movement and

[46] Even in the case of Beethoven's music where there are extant metronome markings which derive from the composer, it is widely agreed that only the most rigorous of analogies between the rhythmic characters of movements allow one to transfer an extant metronome marking to a similar movement for which there is no metronome marking. See R. Kolisch, 'Tempo and Character in Beethoven's Music', *MQ* 29/2 (April 1943): 169–87, 29/3 (July 1943): 291–312; slightly revised version in *MQ* 77/1 (Spring 1993): 90–131, 77/2 (Summer 1993): 268–342, with an introd. by T. Levin, 'Integral Interpretation: Introductory Notes to Beethoven, Kolisch and the Question of the Metronome', *MQ* 77/1 (Spring 1993): 80–9. See also Rosenblum, *Performance Practices*, 348–51; Newman, *Beethoven on Beethoven*, 89–110.

[47] Anderson, ed., *Mozart Letters* (rev. 3rd edn.), 121.

frequent semiquaver passages (and with a faster harmonic rhythm, with one, two, or three changes of harmony in a bar). Minuets with longer note values and slower harmonic rhythm occur frequently in Haydn's late symphonies and string quartets, but even these do not form a homogenous group. The diversity in minuet type is reflected clearly in Haydn's tempo indications. In the 'London' Symphonies the minuet movements are marked variously Menuet, Menuet Moderato, Menuet Allegretto, Menuet Allegro, and Menuet Allegro molto: Haydn's String Quartets, Op. 76 have minuets marked Menuet Allegro ma non troppo, Menuet Allegro, and, Haydn's fastest tempo marking for a minuet, Menuet Presto. The fastest of these indications occur in Haydn's late symphonies and string quartets and accompany movements which are in effect scherzos in everything but name. However, in earlier works Haydn also made some terminological distinctions in his symphonies and string quartets, albeit describing a more restricted tempo range: the String Quartets, Op. 9 have movements marked variously as Menuet, Menuet un poco allegretto, and Menuet allegretto. Even without considering issues such as harmonic rhythm or the character of individual movements, the rhythmic patterns of the incipits alone suggest that there is a relationship between Haydn's tempo markings and the rhythmic profile of a movement. In Op. 9 No. 4, the frequent quavers, semiquavers, and occasional triplet-semiquavers of the Menuet contrast noticeably with the predominant crotchet movement, with only occasional quavers or triplet-quavers, in the Menuet allegretto movements of Op. 9 Nos. 3 and 5: in Op. 9 No. 1 the Menuet un poco allegretto occupies rhythmically the middle ground between Op. 9 No. 4 and Op. 9 No. 3.

We should not assume that Haydn's tempo markings in minuets describe strict categories of minuet or precise descriptions of tempo which operate consistently throughout the composer's career. It is not certain that a Menuet allegretto marking in Op. 9 describes the same type of minuet and/or the same tempo as it does in the late string quartets and the 'London' Symphonies. Nevertheless, a number of important points emerge from a consideration of Haydn's tempo markings in minuets. First, there is no single minuet tempo and, secondly, Haydn maintains a distinction between a movement entitled Menuet, or Tempo di Menuetto, and minuet movements which are qualified by tempo indications such as *allegretto*, *allegro*, and *presto*. By any criteria, such as the fastest note values, the harmonic rhythm, or the amount of embellishment, movements simply entitled Menuet, Menuetto, or Tempo di Menuetto, unqualified by a tempo designation, represent Haydn's slowest minuet tempo, and although faster minuets are more common in the later string quartets and symphonies, this relatively slower minuet type continues to occur throughout Haydn's career. The (unqualified) Menuet indications in Op. 71 No. 3, Op. 74 No. 2, and Symphony No. 103 are justifiable by comparison with the predominantly longer note values and slower harmonic rhythm in the minuets of contemporaneous symphonies and string quartets. Haydn's *Raccolta de Menuetti Ballabili* written for orchestra and published by Artaria in 1784 is also a witness to the continuation of a tradition of slower minuets: none of these minuets have tempo qualifications and their rhythmic profile suggests that the lack of such qualifications was purposeful.

Haydn's terminological distinctions in the string quartets and symphonies are important to the present discussion of his keyboard music because they highlight an important, and hitherto unremarked, genre distinction in Haydn's minuets. Rosenblum makes a distinction between moderate and fast minuets and claims that 'The majority of minuets by Haydn, Mozart, and Beethoven are of the fast type, but those composers wrote some of the slower type as well.'[48] Even if this observation is supportable statistically for these composers in general it is demonstrably untrue of Haydn's keyboard music. In the keyboard music, only the minuet of Hob. XVI: 36/iii is qualified by a tempo designation and significantly this movement is entitled Menuet Moderato. Otherwise all keyboard pieces entitled Menuet, Menuetto, Tempo di Menuet, or equivalent term, lack the faster tempo indications such as *allegretto*, *allegro*, or *presto* which appear in other genres. It is particularly striking that when Haydn began to distinguish between the Menuet, Menuet Allegretto, and Menuet Allegro movements in his symphonies and string quartets, such tempo distinctions were not transferred to his keyboard music, and, furthermore, that the keyboard minuets develop along very different stylistic lines. When minuets with longer note values and slower harmonic rhythm begin to appear in the symphonies and string quartets, keyboard minuets continue to have faster note values and a faster harmonic rhythm. Moreover, many keyboard Menuet or Tempo di Menuetto movements from the mid-1760s contain the elaborately

---

[48] Rosenblum, *Performance Practices*, 338.

notated embellishments, such as those discussed in relation with Hob. XVI: 30 (Ex. 5.5), or the elaborate embellishments in hybrid variation movements such as Hob. XVI: 22/iii. In the latter, even before the written-out embellishments of the reprises, the original statement of the Tempo di Menuet theme is itself replete with semiquavers and numerous embellishments, and has a relatively fast harmonic rhythm (only four bars of the sixteen-bar theme have one harmony per bar; all others have two or three harmonies per bar): the varied reprises have virtually continuous semiquaver or quaver movement. In Haydn's later keyboard trios and sonatas minuet and trio movements occur infrequently, but a tradition of Tempo di Menuet movements with varied reprises or hybrid variations continues: such movements, with their characteristically rich embellishment and variation, are in marked contrast to the faster minuets of the late symphonies and string quartets. Fast movements in 3/4 do, of course, occur in Haydn's keyboard music, particularly as finales (see e.g., Hob. xv: 29/iii, Finale in the German Style Presto assai, and Hob. XVI: 51/ii, Finale Presto): such movements are, however, never entitled Menuet or Tempo di Menuet.

The numerous authors who have advocated faster minuet tempos in the works of Haydn and Mozart almost invariably cite as part of their argument the metronome markings preserved for selected Haydn and Mozart symphonies by Hummel and Czerny.[49] It cannot be assumed that these markings are necessarily appropriate even for the works concerned, but, more important in the present regard, is that they cannot be applied to Haydn's keyboard music because of the evident differences between minuets in keyboard music and in symphonies. In Table 3.4 Czerny's metronome markings for Haydn minuets are grouped according to the tempo markings.

For a number of reasons these metronome markings should be viewed as modification by Czerny of Haydn's intentions. Haydn's distinction between various minuet tempos are treated in a cavalier manner. Movements marked simply Menuet are, according to Czerny, sometimes faster than movements marked Menuet Allegretto; a movement marked Allegro molto has a slower metronomic speed than one marked Allegro. Moreover, these tempo indications as given by Czerny differ in four instances from Haydn's original tempo markings: three movements marked Allegro by

[49] For Hummel's metronome markings see R. Münster, 'Authentische Tempi zu den sechs letzten Sinfonien W. A. Mozarts?', *MJb* (1962–3), 185–99.

TABLE 3.4 *Czerny's metronome markings for Haydn minuets*

Tempo marking	Metronome marking
Menuetto	$\downarrow. = 72\text{--}80$
Menuetto Moderato	$\downarrow. = 66$
Menuetto Allegretto	$\downarrow. = 66\text{--}80$
Menuetto Allegro	$\downarrow. = 84\text{--}96$
Menuetto Allegro molto	$\downarrow. = 92$

Haydn are modified to Allegretto and one movement marked Allegretto is modified to Allegro. All of the movements, even those which Czerny modified to a slower tempo indication, have metronome markings which indicate unusually fast tempos and one pulse in a bar. Interestingly, these markings (which range from $\downarrow. = 66\text{--}96$) and Hummel's markings for minuets in Mozart's last six symphonies ($\downarrow. = 66\text{--}88$) approach the Beethovenian range for one-in-a-bar scherzo tempos, that is $\downarrow. = 69\text{--}132$. While some of the minuets in the 'London' Symphonies arguably move stylistically in the direction of the Beethovenian scherzo, and are in many cases rather different from the three-in-a-bar minuets of Haydn's earlier works and of his keyboard music in general, it is by no means clear that what in effect are Beethovenian scherzo metronome markings are appropriate even for the 'London' Symphonies. Haydn's tempo marking for the minuet of Symphony No. 99 is Menuet Allegretto: Czerny modified this to Menuetto Allegro and added the metronome marking of $\downarrow. = 96$. William Malloch, an advocate of Czerny's tempos in Haydn 'London' Symphonies, writes concerning this metronome marking as follows:

The most surprising Czerny tempo for a minuet is the one for Haydn's 99th Symphony, an unbelievable dotted minim equals 96; unbelievable, that is, until one hears it. Then the impression of such a movement as the Scherzo from Beethoven's 4th Symphony, with its hemiola figures, comes to mind (dotted minim equals 100).[50]

While the Menuet of Symphony No. 99 is undoubtedly of the one-in-a-bar type, with an opening moving exclusively in crotchets and with a slow harmonic rhythm, Haydn's indication Allegretto may be justified by the fairly continuous quaver movement from bar 19

[50] 'Czerny's Metronome Marks', 81.

onwards, by the ornamental formulas of bars 30 ff. and 59, and by the numerous bars with two or even three harmonies per bar, which depart from the admittedly prevailing harmonic rhythm of one harmony per bar. The scherzos of Beethoven's Fifth and Seventh Symphonies are rhythmically very different, with slower harmonic rhythms and movement in crotchets and longer note values for which Beethoven's metronome markings, ♩. =96 for the former and ♩. =132 for the latter, indicate relatively moderate and unsurprising tempos. The tempo ♩. =96 for the Menuet Allegretto of Haydn's Symphony No. 99 is unjustified stylistically by comparison with the Beethoven scherzos and it seems to me more than likely that Czerny's metronome marking is closer to the spirit of Beethoven than Haydn. It is hardly a safe assumption that even the minuets in Haydn's late symphonies and string quartets should be performed at the faster tempos in the Beethovenian range of scherzo tempos, although they undoubtedly require a tempo faster that Haydn's Tempo di Menuetto movements.

In any case, it should be emphasized that these Beethovenian scherzo tempos have no relevance to Haydn's keyboard minuets. The Beethoven metronome markings which are of greater relevance to Haydn's keyboard music are the three extant Beethoven markings which document the continuation of a moderate minuet tempo, with three pulses in a bar. These are as follows:[51]

Beethoven Symphony No. 8/iii, Op. 93, Tempo di Menuetto ♩ = 126
Beethoven Septet, Op. 20/iv, Tempo di Menuetto ♩ = 120
Beethoven String Quartet Op. 59 No. 3/iii, Menuetto grazioso ♩ = 116

These metronome markings are for the reasons outlined above more relevant to Haydn's keyboard music than are Beethoven's scherzo tempos (♩. = 69–132), but they probably represent too narrow a range for Haydn's Tempo di Menuetto movements. Gerstenberg, Rudolf and others have referred to Tomasek's tempo of ♩ = 96 for a Mozart minuet in Act I of Don Giovanni,[52] a tempo which is often appropriate for many of Haydn's Tempo di Menuetto movements,

---

[51] On Beethoven's metronome markings see esp. Rosenblum, *Performance Practices*, 323–51, 355–61; Newman, *Beethoven on Beethoven*, 83–120.

[52] See W. Gerstenberg, 'Authentische Tempi für Mozarts "Don Giovanni"?', *MJb* (1960–1): 58–61; and M. Rudolf, 'Ein Beitrag zur Geschichte der Temponahme bei Mozart', *MJb* (1976–7): 204–24, esp. 222.

given their frequently larger number of short notes and greater amount of embellishment by comparison with the three Beethoven movements listed above. $\bullet$ = 126 should be regarded as a tempo appropriate for Haydn's less embellished Tempo di Menuetto movements, and indeed some keyboard minuets seem to require a somewhat faster tempo, perhaps $\bullet$ = 130–5: the Beethoven range of $\bullet$ = 116–26 should probably be extended to approximately $\bullet$ = 96–135 to allow for the greater number and variety of 'moderate' minuets in the Haydn keyboard repertoire. Zaslaw is undoubtedly correct in stating that we still need to guard against 'the Wagnerian slowing of classical-period tempos, the "powdered-wig" image of the *ancien régime* in general and of the minuet in particular',[53] but equally we need to beware the recent trend in early-music performances towards Beethovenian scherzo tempos in the performance of Haydn's minuets. The trend is particularly injurious to performances of Haydn's keyboard minuets which never moved stylistically in the direction of the minuets in the composer's late string quartets and symphonies, but remained within the tradition of the slower Tempo di Menuetto.

Haydn and Tempo Trends

Since it is impossible to establish reliable absolute tempos for eighteenth-century music, many authors have attempted to establish changing trends in tempo, based on general contemporary observations. Among the most frequent observations is that tempos have been getting faster since the eighteenth century. Although the comments of Quantz and Türk, discussed below, and the often problematically fast metronome markings of Beethoven, Czerny, and others do indeed suggest such a trend, W. S. Newman has recently commented reasonably that 'the evidence is far from conclusive' and that the available information 'leaves the impression of vacillating preferences, depending simply on personal tastes and technical abilities'.[54] Rosenblum's provocative discussion of tempo trends also assumes an increase in tempo from the eighteenth century, but, in the strongest section of this discussion, she argues that Habeneck, and Wagner especially, were responsible for a reversal of this trend and for the popularity of generally slower tempos. 'This tradition of Wagnerian

[53] *Mozart's Symphonies*, 497.   [54] *Beethoven on Beethoven*, 119.

tempos', she continues, 'especially in regard to slow movements and "moderate" minuets is very much alive today.'[55] The relatively recent trend in performances on 'original instruments' and performances influenced by the early-music movement is decidedly towards faster tempos. This is seen by Rosenblum and Zaslaw as a necessary corrective to the lingering influence of Wagnerian tempos, but, to me at least, there seems to have been an overcompensation and the results are erratic.[56] Sometimes there is a clear historical foundation for the faster tempos (as in the case of many of Beethoven's works); often, however, the faster tempos are based on weak evidence (that is, on vague general comment, or on the application of frequently problematic, and obviously very incomplete, information on absolute tempo) and represent the triumph of a new dogma in the name of historicism. Some interesting, experimental performances have resulted, which are a welcome challenge to our preconceptions, but, more frequently, dubious historical information is misapplied, regardless of the evidence of the music (as in the case of Haydn's minuet tempos) giving rise to performances which are undoubtedly striking, but which rely for their impact on an empty surface energy, or, to use C. P. E. Bach's epithet, 'shallow fleetness'.

Tempo trends in eighteenth-century performance are more difficult to establish than those in the latter half of the nineteenth century and the twentieth century. General comments by a variety of commentators give the impression of a general diversity of tastes and some strong regional distinctions. On two occasions in his *Versuch* C. P. E. Bach pointed out that *adagios* were played slower and *allegros* faster in Berlin than elsewhere;[57] other sources would seem to corroborate this view.[58] Yet, the general conclusion that 'tempos were more moderate in Italy, England, and France than they were in

[55] *Performance Practices*, 335. There is some evidence from a late-1790s report that Haydn found some contemporary performances of his minuets too fast. See C.-G. Stellan Mörner, 'Haydniana aus Schweden um 1800', *H–St* 2/1 (Mar. 1969), 5–6, trans. in H. C. R. Landon, *Haydn: Chronicle and Works*, iv (London: Thames & Hudson, 1977), 455–6.

[56] I concur with Temperley's observation in connection with his study of tempos for Haydn 'The Creation' that recent recordings 'influenced by "early music" ideas, have over-corrected' in a reaction to Wagnerian tempos. See Temperley, 'Haydn's Tempos in *The Creation*', 244.

[57] 'In certain other countries there is a marked tendency to play adagios too fast and allegros too slow' (*Versuch*, trans. Mitchell, 148): 'These remarks [on accompaniment] will be based on tempos as they are performed here [i.e. in Berlin], where adagio is far slower and allegro far faster than is customary elsewhere'. (Ibid. 414)

[58] Cf. Sulzer, *Allgemeine Theorie*, s.v. 'Vortrag'.

Germany',[59] would form a dangerous basis for the selection of tempos in eighteenth-century music: remarks such as those of C. P. E. Bach should very probably be taken in conjunction with the stylistic characteristics of local repertoires rather than as a general advocacy of generally slow *adagios* and generally fast *allegros*. Certainly, generalizations about German tempos in the eighteenth century lack compelling evidence.

The two most famous and seemingly dramatic remarks about eighteenth-century tempo derive from Quantz and Türk. Quantz commented as follows on changing tempos in the eighteenth century:

What in former times was considered to be quite fast would have been played almost twice as slow as in the present day. An Allegro assai, Presto, Furioso, &c., was then written, and would have been played, only a little faster than an Allegretto is written and performed today. The large number of quick notes in the instrumental pieces of the earlier German composers thus looked much more difficult and hazardous than they sounded. Contemporary French musicians have retained this style of moderate speed in lively pieces to a large extent.[60]

If this passage, and a similar comment in the second edition of Türk's *Klavierschule*,[61] are taken as an indication of a teleological progression, such that by the late eighteenth century tempos similar to the most problematically fast Beethoven metronome markings had become the norm, then there would indeed be grounds to claim, as many authors have done, that there is a radical difference between today's norms in performance and those of the eighteenth century. This would be a gross overinterpretation of Quantz's evidence and ignores, crucially, the clear relationship which he makes between tempo and the 'number of quick notes'. If, however, one takes account of the major style change in the eighteenth century, that is the radical slowing of harmonic rhythm, then Quantz's comments are understandable and do not imply near-Beethovenian tempos in the second half of the eighteenth century. In a Baroque trio-sonata Allegro C movement with a typical 'walking bass' in quavers and fast rate of harmonic change, the crotchet pulse will naturally be much slower than in a later Allegro C movement where crotchet movement articulates a slower harmonic rhythm with typically one or two

[59] Rosenblum, *Performance Practices*, 333, after C. Sachs, *Rhythm and Tempo* (New York: Norton, 1953), 314, 317, 320–4.
[60] *Versuch*, trans. Mitchell, 285.
[61] (2nd. edn., Leipzig and Halle, 1802), 106.

changes of harmony in a bar. Even within Haydn's lifetime the slow-ing down of harmonic rhythm produced a faster crotchet pulse in later Allegro 𝄵 movements, but this does not imply an unusually fast tempo for the later movements. If one compares the Allegro 𝄵 move-ment of Hob. XVI: 6/i and XVI: 50/i, relatively safe conventional tempos for each (say ♩ = 65 and ♩ = 100) would broadly speaking support Quantz's observation without recourse to the much faster metronome markings (ranging from ♩ = 152 to ♩ = 160) which Haslinger, Czerny, and Moscheles suggest for the Allegro 𝄵 finale of Beethoven's Sonata, Op. 10 No. 3.[62] In short, changes in composi-tional style account for the seemingly radical comments of Quantz and Türk about the increase in tempo in the eighteenth century, which lends no support to the view that Haydn's tempos approached those apparently prevalent in the first few decades of the nineteenth century.

Quantz is careful to associate tempo with the content of a piece, especially with the character of the work and the number of fast notes. Haydn's few extant comments on tempo do likewise, although they are generally taken out of context to support the notion that Haydn was an important figure in the supposed general increase in tempo throughout the eighteenth century and through to Beethoven. At face value Haydn's much-quoted 'Applausus' letter of 1768 is unambiguous: here the composer supplies quite spe-cific instructions for a forthcoming performance of his cantata, including, in the second paragraph, direct instructions on appropri-ate tempos:

First, I would ask you to observe strictly the tempi of all the arias and recita-tives, and since the whole text applauds, I would rather have the allegros taken a bit more quickly than usual, especially in the very first ritornello and in one or two of the recitatives; but no less in the two bass arias.[63]

Although this letter clearly is of great value in relation to the 'Applausus' Cantata, general inferences from it regarding Haydn's supposed preference for fast *allegro* tempos are misleading. Haydn is not here in effect saying anything that eighteenth-century writers in general do not make abundantly clear, namely, that tempo is related to the character of the music. Haydn relates the request for a quicker

---

[62] For a summary of metronome markings in early editions of Beethoven's sonatas see Rosenblum, *Performance Practices*, 355–61.

[63] *CCLN*, 9.

'than usual' tempo to the nature of the text and, moreover, it becomes clear when one looks at the music that when Haydn refers to 'allegros' he is referring not to a specific *allegro* tempo but to the category of fast movement. Haydn marks the opening ritornello Allegro di molto in the score and the two bass arias are marked Allegro e con spirito and Presto respectively. Haydn's preference for Allegros that are 'taken a bit more quickly than usual' applies to movements with a particular affect and which are marked with tempo designations on the faster side of the *allegro* category of movement. The statement cannot be taken as an indication of a preference for unusually fast tempos in all movement marked Allegro, without the appropriate qualification and irrespective of affect.[64] Similarly, when Haydn recommends, as mentioned above, in his letter of 17 November 1791 the 'softest *piano* and a very quick tempo' for the last movement of Symphony No. 96 he tells us no more than that movements marked Piano and Vivace assai should be played as marked and suggests at most that Haydn generally preferred finales in his symphonies which are faster than Allegro: again there is no support here for the view that Haydn generally preferred faster tempos or that movements marked Allegro should be played faster than usual.

In reaching decisions on appropriate tempos for Haydn's keyboard music the composer's tempo markings and the music itself are the only sure guides. Table 3.2 is an attempt to establish Haydn's particular usage with regard to the common Italian terminology. A useful process in determining the 'natural speed' (L. Mozart's phrase) of a particular movement is to compare it with other movements in the same time-signature–tempo-designation category. Thus, in determining the tempo of the Adagio 3/4 movement of Hob. xvi: 52, it helps to decide how the rhythmic profile of this movement

---

[64] Apart from references to the 'Applausus' letter, Saslav and Rosenblum also use the fact that Haydn wrote faster minuets as an argument for his role in the increase in tempo in the 18th cent. (see Saslav, 'Tempos', 97–101, 160; Rosenblum, *Performance Practices*, 319, 338). Although it is undoubtedly true that some of Haydn's later minuets move stylistically in the direction of the Beethovenian scherzo, it does not follow, as discussed above, that Beethoven's scherzo tempos are applicable to Haydn's music. On Haydn's use of the term scherzo in the String Quartets, Op. 33 David Wyn Jones comments that these scherzos 'are minimally faster than the average minuet' but 'are certainly not early examples of the one-in-a-bar movements associated with Beethoven, Schumann, Bruckner etc.' (H. C. R. Landon and D. W. Jones, *Haydn: His Life and Music* (London: Thames & Hudson, 1988), 193).

compares with, for instance, the Adagio 3/4 movements of Hob. XVI: 49 and XVI: 50.[65] To base decisions regarding tempo on the content of the music in this manner, as all eighteenth-century writers say we must, is, of course, subjective, but this seems to me to be ultimately far preferable in the case of Haydn's keyboard music than trusting the metronome markings of later generations of musicians or relying on the sparse gleanings of scholars regarding general tempo trends. Tempo remains one of the most problematic issues in the performance of Haydn's music. It was ever thus: L. Mozart counted decisions concerning the tempo of a piece as 'among the chiefest perfections in the art of music' which require 'long experience and good judgement'.[66]

---

[65] Hob. XVI: 50/ii and XVI: 52/ii work reasonably well at similar tempos (perhaps ♪ = 90) while XVI: 49 seems to require a somewhat faster tempo (*c.* ♪ = 100+). Of these movements it is perhaps XVI: 52/ii which has suffered most from 'Wagnernian' slow *adagio* tempos, yet in rhythmic profile it is quite close to XVI: 50/ii and should not be radically slower than XVI: 49/ii.

[66] *Versuch*, trans. Knocker, 33.

4

Repeat Conventions and Embellishment

◊

The practice of omitting certain formal repeats in eighteenth-century music (in particular, the omission of the second repeat in a binary movement and the omission of both repeats in the da capo of minuets) has become so commonplace that it may be regarded as a modern convention. The reasons for the adoption of this practice are complex and to some extent actually have their origins in some late eighteenth-century music; extra-musical factors associated with modern performance are, however, probably equally responsible for the widespread present-day practice. Whatever the reasons, and the justifications, for the omission of certain repeats in modern performance may be, it seems to be clear that there is little eighteenth-century evidence to support modern convention.[1] Studies by Macdonald, Broyles, and others have described repeat conventions in a large amount of eighteenth-century music in various genres. My purpose here is to study the repeat conventions operable in Haydn's keyboard music and to compare these with trends observable in the eighteenth century as a whole.

The notation in the sources must be the starting-point for any such study. The general trend in the notation of repeats is, as Broyles demonstrates, clear in the eighteenth century as a whole:

Before 1780, both halves of a binary structure were almost always repeated. It was possible to repeat only the first, but this was done so seldom as to be insignificant in determining stylistic norms. In the 1780s, the pattern began to change, and there was a steady trend towards eliminating the repeat of the development and recapitulation throughout the latter two decades of

---

[1] See H. Macdonald, 'To Repeat or Not to Repeat?', *PRMA* 111 (1984–5): 121–38; M. Broyles, 'Organic Form and the Binary Repeat', *MQ* 66/3 (July 1980): 339–60.

the eighteenth century until by 1800 the use of the second-half repeat sign appeared archaic. It might still be found, but as the exception rather than the rule.[2]

This general trend is apparent in Haydn's music taken as a whole, but not on the time-scale indicated by Broyles as being typical for the century, and is more prevalent in Haydn's symphonies than in his keyboard music. In Haydn's keyboard music before *c.*1780 the indication of two repeats in binary and two repeats each in minuet and trio movements is clearly the norm: there is not a single exception to this practice in the *Werkgruppe* XIV, or in the trios of *Werkgruppe* XV written before 1785. The exceptions to this norm, which Broyles regards as 'insignificant in determining stylistic norms', are, however, worth noting since they provide evidence of a practice independent of the general trend in the late eighteenth century; the early exceptions to the standard formal repeat occur in the slow movements of a number of solo sonatas (see Table 4.1).

Clearly, in a significant number of slow movements Haydn did not require the second or in some instances either repeat. Those move-

TABLE 4.1 *Haydn's repeat conventions: patterns of omission in slow movements before 1780*

Hob. no.	Tempo	1st repeat only	No repeat	Ending
XVI: 2/ii	Largo		x	tonic
XVI: 6/iii	Adagio		x	tonic
XVI: 47/i	Adagio	x		dominant
XVI: 33/ii	Adagio	x		dominant
XVI: 24/ii	Adagio		x	dominant
XVI: 29/ii	Adagio		x	tonic
XVI: 37/ii	Largo e sostenuto	x		dominant
XVI: 38/ii★	Adagio	x		dominant
XVI: 39/ii	Adagio	x		tonic
XVI: 34/ii	Adagio	x		dominant of relative minor

★ Although there are no formal repeats in this movement, there is a written-out varied reprise of the first part.

---

[2] 'Organic Form and the Binary Repeat', 340–1.

ments which end on the dominant are usually marked *attacca* or an
equivalent and this may be advanced as a reason for the 'missing'
repeat of the second half. Equally it may be said that this is not the
sole determining factor, since a tonic ending may lack the second or
both repeats; nor apparently does the dominant ending of some of the
movements determine whether the first half of the movement is
repeated. The omission of one or both repeats in some slow movements is independent of the general trend in the late eighteenth
century which Broyles attributes to changing aesthetics; slow movements in various galant styles dating from early in Haydn's career,
which cannot be associated with the tendency towards 'organic'
compositional procedures in the later part of the eighteenth century,
may lack repeats, although statistically the slow movements in later
works may be more likely to do so.[3] Until Haydn's late keyboard
music, however, binary first movements almost invariably contain
two formal repeats, a rare and interesting early exception being Hob.
XVI: 30/i. Although in binary ('sonata') form, this movement lacks a
second repeat, presumably because after the 'recapitulation' an *adagio*
coda leads the movement to a close on the dominant; it is therefore exceptional in more than one respect[4] and can be associated
with the 'missing' repeats in the category of movements listed in
Table 4.1.

It is also worth noting, as other authors have done, that certain
genres, notably the concerto and the overture, remain outside the
normal repeat conventions associated with binary movements. Hugh
Macdonald summarizes the general practice as follows: 'Concertos
never repeat . . . except in minuet movements, nor do overtures,
nor do fugues; nor do rondos, for obvious reasons, except when
sections within the movement contain internal repeats.'[5] There are,
of course, exceptions: the Largo cantabile second movement from
Haydn's keyboard concerto Hob. XVIII: 3 (*c.*1762–6) contains a formal repeat of the first part, excluding the introductory ritornello, but
the second part is not repeated.[6] However, rather than refuting the
link between genre and repeat conventions this movement highlights

---

[3] In the solo sonatas two formal repeats in slow movements appear for the last time in
Hob. XVI: 35; all the slow movements of *Werkgruppe* XIV (all early works) have two formal
repeats; after 1785 slow movements in the piano trios generally lack one or both repeat.

[4] See Ch. 5 n. 51. [5] 'Repeat', 124.

[6] In the 1780s exceptions to Macdonald's statement may also be found: there are e.g.
internal repeats in the *minore* episode of the second movement from Mozart's Concerto in
D minor, K.466.

the more complex nature of genre (and subgenre) definition pertaining in the third quarter of the eighteenth century compared to the more clearly defined categories of the 1780s.[7] In this regard it is striking that movements in Haydn's early sonatas which lack one or both formal repeat (i.e. many of the slow movements listed in Table 4.1) often display generic traits of concerto slow movements, containing in some instances cadenzas, an obvious hallmark of such movements. Such early departures from the normal repeat conventions of sonatas may be in part due to the interaction of generic conventions.

The examples listed above of movements lacking one or both repeats may be statistically insignificant in relation to common practice but they illustrate a fundamental point concerning repeats, in effect being the exceptions which demonstrate (if not exactly proving) the rule. It must be assumed since Haydn omitted repeat indications on occasion even in his earliest works that the normal presence of two repeat marks in a binary movement should be taken quite literally by performers as an indication of the composer's intention.[8] There is no reason to believe that repeat indications are merely a calligraphic convention which may be observed or ignored at the performer's discretion; the frequency of *prima* and *seconda volta* bars contradicts this point of view, although there is no reason to regard these repeats as in any way more essential than formal repeats without *prima* and *seconda volta* bars. Eighteenth-century theorists offer no suggestion that repeats may be treated liberally by the performer, and for the most part their comments simply explain what the various repeat signs mean. In the famous preface to his *Sonaten mit veränderten Reprisen* C. P. E. Bach comments that 'today [1760] varied reprises are indispensable, being expected of every performer'.[9] The nature of

---

[7] Michelle Fillion has pointed out that the Concertini and Divertimenti of *Werkgruppe* XIV share characteristics with the concerto, despite the fact that the former as a rule contain indications of two formal repeats in each movement: see Fillion, 'Scoring and Genre in Haydn's Divertimenti Hob. XIV', in E. Badura-Skoda (ed.), *Haydn Kongress, Wien, 1982*, 435–44.

[8] The functional nature of repeat indications is even more obvious in non-Viennese music. From an early date C. P. E. Bach omits both repeats as a rule in the slow movements of his keyboard sonatas; MacDonald points out that in Bach's symphonies repeats are the norm only in finales (Macdonald, 'Repeat', 124), again, perhaps, reflecting generic traits of the concerto; in the works of Bach, a composer who devoted considerable attention to details of notation, it is a particularly dubious practice to omit repeats when they are indicated by the composer (on this point, see esp. S. Wollenberg, 'A New Look at C. P. E. Bach's Musical Jokes', in Clark (ed.), *C. P. E. Bach Studies*, 298–9).

[9] *Sechs Sonaten mit veränderten Reprisen*, H.126, 136–40 (Berlin: Georg Winter, 1760), in C. P. E. Bach, *Versuch*, trans. Mitchell, 166.

the varied reprises in these works and their relationship to Haydn's music is discussed below, but Bach's statement is, on another level, an indication that repeats were observed. Türk in his *Klavierschule* explains the various signs used to indicate repeats (whether of one or both halves of a binary movement) and advocates that 'The teacher should insist that his students accustom themselves to playing every repeated section immediately for the second time without interruption'.[10] Various comments from the late eighteenth century objecting to the formal repeat are quoted below, but it is of interest that the authors were apparently questioning prevalent compositional norms and not the performance practice of observing repeats when indicated by the composer.

Broyles points out that in eighteenth-century sources the notation of formal repeats is 'remarkably consistent': 'To deny these indications and this consistency would require an extremely compelling argument, with solid evidence; until such an argument is advanced, the markings themselves must be taken at face value'.[11] In Haydn's keyboard music, there are individual movements in which the notation of the sources is ambiguous, but text-critically most of the contradictions can be shown to be irrelevant and they do not alter the overall appearance of consistency referred to by Broyles.[12] Moreover there are instances in which the notation of the sources provides positive evidence that formal repeats were observed in practice. In the Largo cantabile from the Concerto, Hob. xviii: 3 referred to above, the repeat in the first part is indicated in the normal way by a sign, but in a contemporary manuscript copy of the viola and basso parts the repeat is written out in full.[13] Haydn frequently wrote out

---

[10] Trans. Haggh, 116.   [11] 'Organic Form and the Binary Repeat', 342.

[12] In the 1st movement of Hob. xv: 24 (Artaria edn., op. 75, plate no. 624) bar 70/71 has the indication ‖ in the violin and cello parts but ‖ in the keyboard part. Since there is no corresponding mark ‖ at the end of the movement and since a different (and generally less accurate) engraver prepared the string parts than the keyboard part, the reading of the keyboard part should be preferred. On other occasions errors in the notation of repeats may be suspected although they cannot be proven: in Hob. xvi: 39/iii and 41/i the notation at the end of the first part (‖) is not matched by a corresponding indication ‖ at the end of these movements in the primary sources, the first edns. of Artaria (op. 30, plate no. 7) and Bossler (œuvre 37, plate no. 33). The second repeat indication is added editorially in the modern editions of C. Landon and Feder, presumably on the basis of common practice. The finale of Hob. xvi: 19 is a set of variations in which each variation contains two repeat indications. In the last variation, however, the repeat of the second half is written out in full but is nevertheless followed by a 'dotted double bar'. Although the source is Haydn's autograph manuscript, it is reasonable in this instance to regard the final repeat indication as an error.

repeats with embellishments in his 'hybrid' variation movements; this point may also be considered as evidence for the observation of repeats and will be examined in more detail in connection with da capo repeats. In binary movements an interesting and very late exception to Haydn's normal manner of indicating repeats occurs in the Sonata, Hob. XVI: 51/ii; in this movement the repeat of the first part is indicated in the usual manner but the repeat of the second part is written out in full, without alterations, in the first edition of Breitkopf & Härtel.

In the late 1760s and the 1770s formal binary repeats begin to disappear from the finales in Haydn's instrumental music, not, it must be assumed, because of any disaffection with formal repeats (they, of course, continue to be the norm in binary first movements and also occur, though not consistently, in slow movements and binary finales) but because Haydn increasingly preferred new formal types, in particular rondos, variations, and 'hybrid' variations. These latter forms often contain internal repetitions, sometimes indicated by the 'dotted double bar', sometimes written out in full, with or without embellishment or variation, but the formal repeat of each half in the manner of binary first movements and binary finales is not in general a feature.

The trend in the 1780s, observed by Broyles, towards the omission of repeats in binary movements is not immediately apparent in Haydn's keyboard music. It is true that, in general, more and more movements without two formal repeats appear but this is due, on the one hand, to the increasing variety of formal types in the music and, on the other hand, to the continuing practice of omitting formal repeats in slow movements, which, as demonstrated in Table 4.1, is not a reflection of a new aesthetic but a continuation of an earlier practice. The percentage of slow movements lacking one or both repeats does, however, increase in the 1780s and 1790s and it is also noticeable that this practice is not confined to the slowest movements but increasingly applies to moderate tempos (see Table 4.2).

The examples listed in Table 4.2 could be multiplied, and it is especially noticeable in the late piano trios that binary movements in slow and moderate tempos as a rule lack one or both repeats. This tendency is not, however, apparent in binary movements with fast tempos until Haydn's very last keyboard compositions. Keyboard music

---

[13] See *JHW* XV/2, 'Kritischer Bericht', 173.

TABLE 4.2 *Haydn's repeat conventions: patterns of omission in slow and moderate movements in trios from the mid-1780s*

Hob. no.	Tempo	1st repeat only	No repeat	Ending
XV: 5/i	Adagio non tanto		x	tonic
XV: 7/ii	Andante	x		dominant
XV: 9/i	Adagio	x		tonic
XV: 12/ii	Andante		x	tonic
XV: 16/ii	Andantino più tosto Allegretto	x		dominant
XV: 18/ii	Andante	x		dominant
XV: 19/iii	Adagio ma non troppo		x	tonic

would therefore seem to be outside the trend towards the elimination of the second repeat in fast binary movements which is clearly established in Haydn's 'London' Symphonies. Of the twelve 'London' Symphonies all except No. 96 ('The Miracle') omit the second repeat, a practice which is established much earlier in Mozart's symphonies.[14] The question of genre is of paramount importance here, since the string quartets of Haydn, like his keyboard music, retain both formal binary repeats.

The practice of the 'London' Symphonies can, however, be seen in a small number of fast binary movements in Haydn's late keyboard works. An isolated example from 1789 occurs in the finale of the Trio, Hob. XV: 13, in which the second repeat is lacking: although this movement may be described as a binary form, it displays characteristics of Haydn's hybrid variations and minuet-cum-rondo form which may account for the exceptional (for Haydn, in this genre and at this date) elimination of the second binary repeat. Only in the years 1794–5 can one identify a trend of omission in any way comparable to that in the symphonies (see Table 4.3). Nevertheless, a comparison with other fast binary movements contemporary with those listed in Table 4.3 (the last solo sonatas, the trio sets XV: 21–3, 24–6, 27–9) reveals that Haydn did not abandon the formal binary repeats in keyboard music to the extent that he did in the symphony: Haydn

---

[14] Macdonald, 'Repeat', 125 and *passim*; see also Zaslaw, *Mozart's Symphonies*, 501–4.

TABLE 4.3 *Haydn's repeat conventions: patterns of omission in fast movements from the 1790s*

Hob. no.	Tempo	1st repeat only	No repeat
xv: 23/iii	Finale Vivace	x	
xv: 24/i	Allegro	x	
xv: 27/i	Allegro	x	
xv: 28/i	Allegro moderato	x	
[xvi: 51/i	Andante		x]
xvi: 52/i	Allegro	x	
xvi: 52/iii	Finale Presto	x	

retained both repeats in, for instance, Hob. xv: 21/i, 22/i, 22/iii, 26/i, 27/iii, 30/i, 32/ii, xvi: 49/i, 50/i, and 51/ii.

Repeats in Da Capo Forms

It is also a modern convention to omit the internal formal repeats in the da capo of minuet and trio, and minuet and trio-type movements. It must be stated that there is no theoretical evidence to support this practice, but an examination of Haydn's written-out varied reprises in ternary and various hybrid variation forms involving a da capo-like repeat suggests that, while internal formal repeats should be observed in the greater part of Haydn's keyboard music, there is some evidence of a trend of omission in the composer's last keyboard compositions.

Haydn's general practice in minuet and expanded da capo movements, which contain, in place of a literal da capo repeat, a written-out variation of material presented initially, is to repeat both halves. Some basic schematic representations may be used to demonstrate, in outline, characteristic practices:

Hob. xvi: 22/iii

```
    A      B              A           B            A
  a ‖ b ‖  c ‖ d(=link)  a, var. 1 of a;  c' ‖ d(=link)  a, var. 2 of a;
                          b, var. 1 of b;               b, var. 2 of b
```

Hob. xv: 6/ii

```
    A          B         A
  a ‖ b a ‖  c ‖ d c ‖   a, var. 1 of a; b a, var. 1 of b a codetta
```

Hob. xv: 11/ii

A   B   A

a ‖ b a‖   c ‖ d c‖ (link) a, var. 1 of a; var. 1 of b a, b a coda

In one particular movement the A material reappears twice in succession in varied forms, on both occasions with its internal repeats:

Hob. XVI: 29/iii

A   B   A

a‖ b‖ c ‖ d c ‖ a(var. 1) ‖ b (var. 1) ‖ a, var. 2 of a; b, var. 2 of b

In the absence of evidence to the contrary, it is probable that in those movements where the return of the A section is simply indicated by 'da capo' or 'menuet da capo' the internal formal repeats should be observed. However, in some piano trios from the years 1794–5 a change in practice is evident. Again, the point may be illustrated schematically:

Hob. XV: 25/ii

A   B   A

a‖ b‖   c‖ d c link   a b

Hob. XV: 28/iii

A   B   A

a‖ b a‖   c‖ d c   a b a coda

Hob. XV: 30/iii

A   B   A

a‖ b   Minore   a b coda

The change in practice evidenced in these works is confirmed by the composer's written instructions in the autograph manuscript of the Trio, Hob. XV: 31, first movement. After the A (a ‖ b a:‖) and B (c ‖ d c ‖) sections the composer writes 'Da Capo il minore [i.e. A] senza repetizione'; after another episode (C: e ‖ f:‖ g) a variation of the A section returns, this time with the first part repeated but with no repetition of the second part (A: var. 1 of a ‖ var. 1 of b a). This appears to be the only instance of the instruction 'Da Capo . . . senza repetitione' occurring in Haydn's music but its presence here suggests that its absence elsewhere is intentional, and that in works other than Haydn's late piano trios formal repeats should be observed in the da capo reprise.[15] Two movements in the late trios (XV: 24/iii and 26/iii) occupy an ambiguous position in relation to Haydn's apparent

[15] Macdonald is incorrect in his statement that 'Haydn himself never wrote "senza replica"'. See Macdonald, 'Repeat', 134.

changing practice. In these two movements the end of the middle section is simply followed by the written instruction 'Da Capo'; the editors of *JHW* XVII/3 reproduce the initial section but without its internal repeats. This decision, which would be unjustifiable in earlier works, is here at least a valid interpretation given the practices in the contemporaneous works mentioned above.

The whole question of the formal repeat is surrounded by ambiguities. It is not immediately apparent why, in the early works, some slow movements have no repeats, some one repeat, while others retain both repeats. A general change in practice is apparent in the late eighteenth century, but many ambiguities within the new practice remain unexplained. It is not clear why one movement has only one repeat indication while a movement in many ways quite similar retains both repeats. It would seem to be the case that the impetus for change in the late eighteenth century gradually brought about a different attitude to the formal repeat, but that the new attitude did not affect every composer or every genre equally and that even within a single genre, a great degree of flexibility was practised by composers with regard to repeat conventions.

Towards a Modern Convention

Broyles argues with some validity that the omission of repeats in the late eighteenth century was the result of the emergence after 1780 of a new aesthetic, and that there was a fundamental change in musical style in which 'Drive and intensity replace symmetry and balance; the Classical ideal becomes the dramatic ideal.' He continues:

Within a form governed by symmetry, balance, and elaboration, the repetition of both halves is logical and consistent. As part of a tonal drama, the repetition of the second half results in a severe dilution of the dramatic effect. That composers almost always repeated the second half before 1780, began dropping the second-half repeat marks in the 1780s, and by the late 1790s normally omitted them is in precise correspondence with the nature of the stylistic change as described by modern writers and suggests that it was of some importance.[16]

That a change in aesthetics did occur is undeniable. That strong objections to the formal repeat began to be made in the 1790s is also

---

[16] 'Organic Form and the Binary Repeat', 352.

clearly established by Broyles. He quotes Reichardt's comment that 'above all unnatural and senseless is the continuous repetition at the end back the same way' and Grétry's much-quoted denunciation of the formal repeat.[17] Most commentators would also agree that a degree of stylistic change occurred in the music of, in particular, Haydn and Mozart in the 1780s and it is reasonable to propose that there is a connection between changes in aesthetics, style, and repeat conventions. It is, however, problematic to accept, as Broyles does, 'repeat signs as benchmarks of a composer's orientation'.[18] Inherent in Broyles's argument is the assumption that the 'new' repeat conventions are progressive and associated with mature Classical sonata form. He characterizes the string quartet as 'conservative', and keyboard music as scarcely less so,[19] a point of view which is at variance with stylistic developments in the second half of the eighteenth century. Haydn's string quartets retained both formal repeats after the composer had abandoned the second repeat in the symphony, but stylistically the former are in no way more conservative than the latter. Haydn's Sonata in E flat, Hob. XVI: 52 may be regarded as a progressive work both in respect of style and in the omission of repeats; the Sonata in C, Hob. XVI: 50, written around the same time, retains both formal repeats in the sonata form first movement but is none the less as intense, organic, and Classical (in Broyles's understanding of the term) as Hob. XVI: 52.[20]

Undoubtedly there is a connection between the musical style of the 1780s and the tendency to omit repeats. It is also certain that some repeats may be justified and explained analytically more readily than

---

[17] Ibid. 343. That this attitude persisted and indeed intensified throughout the nineteenth-century is clear from Ferdinand Praeger's article 'On the Fallacy of the Repetition of Parts in the Classical Form', *Papers of the Musical Association*, 9 (1882–3): 1–16. In the discussion following this paper a Mr Banister refers to a conversation in which Sterndale Bennett stated that he 'should like to abolish all repetitions in music' (p. 8). Obviously repeats were not 'abolished' in the 19th cent., but it is significant that such an opinion should have been expressed.

[18] 'Organic Form and the Binary Repeat', 357.   [19] Ibid. 359.

[20] Jonathan Dunsby has convincingly argued the continuing importance of the formal repeat and is of the opinion that 'Historically, the non-observance of Classical repeats is indefensible' (J. Dunsby, 'The Formal Repeat', *JRMA* 112/2 (1987): 206), but his proposition that formal repeats can be 'more and less structurally effective' (ibid. 203) is similar in spirit to Rosen's view: 'some repeats are dispensable, others absolutely necessary' (Rosen, *The Classical Style: Haydn, Mozart, Beethoven* (London: Faber & Faber, 1971), 395). Both opinions imply an ultimately insupportable hierarchy and by emphasizing structuralist criteria alone seem to encourage an attitude whereby 'effective', 'necessary' (observed?) repeats are only those which an analyst can explain satisfactorily.

others. None of these explanations can alone possibly hope to account for the ambiguities of eighteenth-century practice. Seemingly superficial criteria, such as size, play a role in determining the presence or absence of repeats,[21] but clearly this is not always a factor, as a comparison between Hob. XVI: 50/i and XVI: 52/i will demonstrate. Tempo, the placement of a movement within a sonata cycle, the presence or absence of through-compositional procedures, and, perhaps most importantly, generic cross-references may also be advanced as reasons for the presence or omission of repeats.[22] The reasons for a composer's notation of repeats may sometimes be apparent; often they are not. Ultimately the repeat markings in Haydn's music must be regarded in the same way as any other performance instruction, whether they can be justified by the analyst or not, if, as we must assume it to be, the notation is a reflection of the composer's intention.

In his *Introduction to the Art of Playing on the Pianoforte* (1801) Clementi makes a brief but significant reference to the notation of repeats:

The DOTTED bars 𝄇 or 𝄆 denote the repeat of the foregoing, and following strain. N.B. The second part of a piece, if VERY LONG, is seldom repeated; notwithstanding the DOTS. When the bars are marked thus 𝄇 or 𝄆 then the strain, only on the side of the DOTS is to be repeated.[23]

---

[21] Kollmann e.g. makes a connection between the omission of repeats and large compositions: 'In its *outlines*, a long movement is generally divided into *two sections*. . . . These two sections are either separated by a *double bar* or *repeat*, or not distinguished by any particular mark; which latter commonly is the case in concertos or those pieces which would become too long by a repetition.' (Kollmann, *An Essay on Practical Musical Composition* (London, 1799), 5).

[22] Just as there is a difference between the repeat conventions of sonatas and concertos, so too theorists comment on the differences between repeat conventions in sonatas and symphonies. 'The first allegro of a symphony . . . has two parts, which the composer often plays with, but also often without, a repetition. . . . For the sonata employs all the forms that we have already described for the symphony. For example, the first allegro has the same two parts which are usually repeated.' (Koch, *Versuch einer Anleitung zur Composition* (1793), quoted in Broyles, 'Organic Form and the Binary Repeat', 343–4.) Koch here describes the flexible practice with regard to repeats in compositions of the 1780s and 1790s. His distinction between sonata and symphony is exemplified by the contrast in general practice between the repeat conventions of Haydn's sonatas and his 'London' Symphonies. The tendency, identified above, in a small number of Haydn's late sonatas and trios to omit the second repeat in sonata-form movements may be connected with the influence of the symphony on some of Haydn's late keyboard works, just as in earlier Haydn sonatas the omission of repeats in some slow movements may be attributed to the concerto-like character of these movements.   [23] p. 8.

It is of interest that Clementi, like Kollmann and others, associated the omission of the second repeat with larger works.[24] Of greater significance, perhaps, is that Clementi advocated in such works the omission of the second repeat 'notwithstanding the dots', implying that the decision to omit or include the repeat was the prerogative of the performer and not the composer. As far as can be ascertained, Clementi is the first writer to make such a claim. Other theorists, whether advocating the omission or inclusion of repeats, are concerned with the notation by which the composer makes his intentions known: those writers to whom the repeat is abhorrent address their comments to the composer, not the performer. Clementi's comment is thus important since it represents a change in attitude to performance which affects the repeat as fundamentally as the change in aesthetics and style affected the composer's notation of repeats. It is in effect as concise a statement of our 'modern' convention concerning repeats in Classical music as could be wished for. The convention therefore has a certain historical validity, but it represents an attitude which post-dates the works of Haydn which are the present concern. It has been pointed out that modern practices concerning the repeat are unlikely to alter fundamentally,[25] and there are many reasons why modern performers might not wish to observe every repeat indicated by the composer. It should, however, be accepted that a performance which ignores Haydn's notation of repeats is not, in this respect, in the manner of Haydn, but in the manner of Clementi.

EMBELLISHMENT

The Theoretical Evidence

The role of improvised embellishment is one of the most problematic issues in the performance practice of music from the second half of the eighteenth century. The issue is replete with dichotomies, within the corpus of eighteenth-century theory and between eighteenth-century theory and modern understanding of eighteenth-century style. Moreover, the best evidence available, both for and against a practice of improvised embellishment, is, in one respect,

---

[24] Cf. n. 21, above.
[25] See Macdonald, 'Repeat', 137 and Dunsby, 'Formal Repeat', 206–7.

suspect since it relates to written traditions and not to a live tradition of improvisation. Descriptions of improvised embellishment in eighteenth-century theory are frequently devoid of a specific stylistic context, or refer to a style which cannot be taken as a model for Haydn's music; it can be argued that written-out embellishments in actual compositions (e.g. C. P. E. Bach's *Sonaten mit veränderten Reprisen*) tell us more about that composer's compositional style than about a practice of improvisation, since the process of writing involves the composer in compositional decisions which frequently take account of questions of large-scale structure. Contemporary theory clearly establishes that a strong tradition of improvised embellishment existed throughout the eighteenth century and even into the nineteenth century,[26] yet, as is the case in relation to other questions of performance practice, the composite view of eighteenth-century theory is not necessarily applicable equally to each genre or to each composer irrespective of questions of style and chronology.

Theoretical writings are consistent on two points in relation to improvised embellishment and to ornamentation in general, namely advocacy and admonition. Just as writers throughout the seventeenth and eighteenth centuries supply examples of how a performer might embellish music, their illustrations and prescriptions are accompanied by the ubiquitous rejoinder on the abuse of the practices they advocate. Although far removed in stylistic orientation, the advice of Caccini in *Le nuove musiche* (1602) and of Türk in his *Klavierschule* (1789) is fundamentally in agreement on these points. Metaphors comparing embellishment to the careful use of spices in cuisine are employed by Printz (1696), Quantz (1752), and Hiller (1780). The eighteenth-century sources which contain the strongest, most extensive, or most influential advocacies of embellishment are also those which contain the strongest obloquy. The importance of improvised embellishment in the performance practices advocated by Quantz is clear, since he devotes three whole chapters of his *Versuch* to the subject.[27] Quantz's purpose is clearly not to initiate a new practice but to improve the standard of the general practice and, notwithstanding the extent of the embellishment in many of his examples, he comments that 'so many incorrect and awkward ideas appear that it

[26] For summaries of 18th-cent. writings on embellishment see R. Stowell, *Violin*, 337–67; *New Grove*, s.v. 'Improvisation'; Rosenblum, *Performance Practices*, 287–92.

[27] Trans. Reilly: chs. 13 'Of Extempore Variations on Simple Intervals', 14 'Of the Manner of Playing an Adagio', 15 'Of Cadenzas'.

would be better in many cases to play the melody as the composer has set it rather than to spoil it repeatedly with such wretched variations'.[28] Even with regard to the *locus classicus* of improvised embellishment, the Adagio in the Italian style, Quantz's lengthy excursus contains a severe restriction on the use of the procedures which he describes:

Neither do I demand that all Adagios be ordered like this one, and thus overloaded with graces; the graces should be introduced only where the simple air renders them necessary, as is the case here. In other respects I remain of the opinion previously mentioned: the more simply and correctly an Adagio is played with feeling, the more it charms the listeners, and the less it obscures or destroys the good ideas that the composer has created with care and reflection. For when you are playing it is unlikely that you will, on the spur of the moment, improve upon the inventions of a composer who may have considered his work at length.[29]

Similar attitudes are also found in those other sources notable for their detailed descriptions of improvised embellishment, namely the treatises of Tosi, Tartini, L. Mozart, C. P. E. Bach and the latter's preface to his *Reprisen Sonaten*.

In German theory there is a standard division of ornamentation into two categories, the *wesentlichen Manieren* or *Spielmanieren*, that is standard, essential ornaments indicated by symbols, and the *willkürlichen Manieren* or *Setzmanieren*, that is the arbitrary ornaments which are not indicated by the composer, but which are improvised in performance.[30] The distinction has its origins in the characteristically French and Italian attitudes to ornamentation prevalent from the end of the seventeenth century and became codified in mid-eighteenth-century German theory.[31] In theory at least the *wesentlichen Manieren* should be set by the composer, while the *willkürlichen Manieren* derive from the practice of the performer. Such a clear categorization is not, however, without contradictions, particularly in relation to music dating from the second half of the eighteenth century. First, the *wesentlichen Manieren* were not necessarily indicated with the precision or consistency advocated by German theorists: Italian keyboard music from this period contains few ornament symbols and with regard to Haydn's keyboard music a number of different practices can

---

[28] Ibid., p. 136.   [29] Ibid. 169.

[30] See e.g. Marpurg, *Anleitung*, 36–7, 43; Quantz, *Versuch*, trans. Reilly, 91 ff., 136 ff.

[31] The derivation of this categorization is made clear in Quantz, *Versuch*, trans. Reilly, 113, 136, 162–3.

be associated with specific periods in his career. The *wesentlichen Manieren* might therefore, depending on the composer, style, or date of a particular composition, derive from the improvisation of the performer rather than from the notation of the composer. Secondly, although the addition in performance of *willkürlichen Manieren* was undoubtedly widely practised, these ornaments were increasingly specified by the composer: the highly embellished alternative versions of the Courante, Sarabande, Gavotte, and Menuet in F. Couperin's *Premier Ordre*, and the slow movement of J. S. Bach's 'Italian' Concerto are early and notable examples of this tendency, and, as will be argued below, Haydn began to specify the *willkürlichen Manieren* in his keyboard music at approximately the same time that he adopted a more precise notation for the *wesentlichen Manieren*.

In instrumental music[32] improvised embellishment is associated with the following contexts: fermatas, slow movements in general, and repeats in all forms. The embellishment of repeats is, according to some theorists, *de rigueur*, but there is reason to believe that in music dating from the second half of the eighteenth century not all repeats were embellished. On the other hand areas of thematic recurrence (as distinct from formal repeats) such as the 'recapitulation' in 'sonata form' and the refrains in rondos may have been embellished, and immediate phrase repetition written out within a composition should also be considered as a possible context in which improvised embellishments were introduced by the performer.

As regards Haydn's keyboard music, it may be assumed that improvised embellishment is requisite at least in some of the contexts mentioned above, if not in every chronological stage of the output then at least in certain periods. The questions which must be addressed in this light are: what models should be used in reconstructing the improvisatory practices and in which periods and in which specific contexts is improvised embellishment necessary?

---

[32] The question of embellishment in Haydn's vocal music is not considered here. Concerning embellishment specifically in Haydn's vocal music see E. F. Schmid, 'Joseph Haydn und die vokale Zierpraxis seiner Zeit, dargestellt an einer Arie seines Tobias-Oratoriums' in B. Szabolcsi and D. Bartha (eds.), *Bericht über die Internationale Konferenz zum Andenken Joseph Haydns, Budapest, September 1959* (Budapest: Akadémiai Kiadó, 1961), 117–30; E. Melkus, 'Zur Auszierung der Da-Capo-Arien in Mozarts Werken', *MJb* (1968–70): 159–85 (specifically on Haydn see pp. 174–8); Brown, *The Creation*, 44–61. See also F. Neumann, *Ornamentation and Improvisation in Mozart* (Princeton: Princeton University Press, 1986), 179–239; W. Crutchfield, 'Voices', in Brown and Sadie (eds.), *Performance Practice: Music after 1600*, 292–319.

Many theoretical descriptions of improvised embellishment illustrate in an abstract manner standard compositional figures which may be employed as subdivisions of a beat in ornamenting specific intervals. Descriptions of passing-notes, various types of arpeggio figuration, and so on, often have much in common with elementary harmony and composition textbooks in distinguishing between 'harmonic' and 'non-harmonic', i.e. ornamental, notes. Marpurg's discussion of *Setzmanieren* and Quantz's description 'Of the extempore variations of simple intervals' are intended to provide basic instructions for the beginner and to prevent infractions of standard harmonic practice.[33] Although providing illustrations of the basic procedures of variation and improvisation, such didactic texts are not intended as models *per se* of variation and improvisation. There are, however, in Quantz and in other eighteenth-century textbooks more sophisticated examples of embellishment which can be associated with specific stylistic contexts, but it is doubtful if these can be advanced as models for embellishment in the context of Haydn's keyboard music. The most frequent and elaborate examples of instrumental embellishment are associated with Adagios in the Italian violin tradition. The practices of Corelli provided models for elaborate embellishment which continue to be part of the violinistic tradition at least until the end of the eighteenth century.[34] In German theory the improvised embellishment associated with the Italian violin tradition was described in L. Mozart's treatise,[35] which relies heavily on Tartini, and although quintessentially violinistic, this Italian tradition influenced the performance practices associated with other instruments; it is for instance the basis for Quantz's most extensive illustrations of embellishment, found in chapter 14 of his *Versuch*, 'Of the Manner of Playing the Adagio'. Despite the undoubted relevance of the Italian manner of performing an Adagio to string and wind music written over the period of perhaps a century, embellished Adagios in keyboard music would seem to have little in common with the elaborate divisions of Corelli, Geminiani, or Franz Benda.

The most frequently cited examples of embellishment in keyboard music are the various works of C. P. E. Bach which contain varied

---

[33] Marpurg, *Anleitung*, 37–43; Quantz, *Versuch*, trans. Reilly, 136–61.

[34] See H. J. Marx, 'Some Unknown Embellishments of Corelli's Violin Sonatas', *MQ* 61/1 (Jan. 1975): 65–76; D. A. Lee, 'Some Embellished Versions of Sonatas by Franz Benda', *MQ* 62/1 (Jan. 1976): 58–71; Stowell, *Violin*, 337–67.

[35] *Versuch*, trans. Knocker, 203–14.

reprises (*veränderte Reprisen*), and yet, despite the undoubtedly idiomatic nature of the embellishment as keyboard music, it is again problematic to regard these works as models for improvised embellishment in Viennese keyboard music, even in the music of Haydn, who was clearly influenced by the keyboard style of C. P. E. Bach (see Ch. 5). In his preface to the *Sonaten mit veränderten Reprisen* Bach states that 'Today varied reprises are indispensable, being expected of every performer' and in the *Versuch* Bach refers to the F major 'Probestück' as 'an illustration of the present practice of varying extemporaneously the two reprises of an allegro'.[36] Yet Bach's use of varied reprises can hardly be considered as an illustration of a general practice of extempore embellishment. First, these varied reprises are stylistically very typical of Bach's unique keyboard style and are not easily compatible with other keyboard styles; secondly, the *Reprisen Sonaten* are the product of a carefully crafted process of variation which was subject to revision over a period of more than twenty years.[37] Bach's process of variation has formal implications and is quite distinct from a practice of improvised embellishment. Characteristically Bach employs the varied reprise to create formal ambiguity and obscure the 'structural downbeat' in a way which may well have influenced Haydn but which remains none the less uniquely Bachian.

Each of the above-mentioned sources may be seen to have certain disadvantages as models for improvised embellishment in Haydn's keyboard music. The one remaining source, which is the most obvious and perhaps the best model, is Haydn's own music, and particularly the style of writing in passages which may be identified as highly embellished by comparison with simpler statements of the same basic material. Such passages provide the most specific models to which extempore embellishment should aspire and, considering the evidence that eighteenth-century embellishment was often prepared (as it almost invariably is today),[38] 'improvisation' may usefully be 'prepared' as pastiche of Haydn's written-out embellishments. Studying these passages in Haydn's keyboard music also informs the performer concerning the specific contexts in which Haydn embellished thematic material and raises interesting questions concerning

---

[36] *Versuch*, trans. Mitchell, 166, 165.

[37] See H. Serwer, 'C. P. E. Bach, J. C. F. Rellstab, and the Sonatas with Varied Reprises', in Clark (ed.), *C. P. E. Bach Studies*, 233–43.

[38] See *New Grove*, s.v. 'Improvisation', 43.

the place of embellishment in the various styles encountered in Haydn's keyboard music.

Willkürliche Manieren *in Haydn's Keyboard Music from c.1766*

The practice of writing out the *willkürlichen Manieren* is noticeable in Haydn's keyboard music from *c.*1766 at the same time that Haydn began to specify the *wesentlichen Manieren* with an increasing variety of ornament symbols. This new practice is a significant factor in the compositional style which emerged in Haydn's keyboard music at this time. Initially Haydn's embellishments take the form of, at times, almost obsessive experimentation with stereotyped ornaments indicated by symbols; but increasingly *willkürliche Manieren* as well as *wesentliche Manieren* become part of the variation process. Examples abound in almost every sonata written in the second half of the 1760s and the early 1770s, and certain generalizations may be made concerning the contexts in which Haydn employed ornamentation as variation.

The most common use of variation is in the embellishment of immediate phrase or subphrase repetition, a practice which is found equally in slow and fast movements. Characteristically the statement and counterstatement opening to movements takes the form of a simple and embellished version of what is basically the same thematic material. The extent of the embellishment in this context is quite variable. In the second movement of Hob. XVI: 19 (see Ex. 4.1) the upper auxiliary note and passing-note which ornament the third beat of bar 1 become in bar 5 a decorated returning-note figure with a more complex rhythm, but the melodic shape is otherwise retained. More remarkable in this example is the alteration of the left-hand part, which moves in thirds on the second and third beats of bars 5–7, and the extra quaver on the first beats of the right-hand part, which alters the characteristic part-writing of the initial statement. The opening of the second movement of Hob. XVI: 45 is structurally similar (see Ex. 4.2), but the embellishment of the counterstatement is somewhat more melismatic. The second beat of bar 1 is ornamented with an appoggiatura, while in bar 5 this is changed to an inverted *Doppelschlag*, but bars 2–3 are subjected, in bars 6–7, to more extensive changes involving an alteration to the actual shape of the melody. In bars 6–7 the structurally important notes are retained, but the descent of a third to *c″* in bar 2 is inverted to an ascending sixth,

Ex. 4.1. Hob. XVI: 19/ii

filled in with sextuplet passing-notes. The third beat of bar 6 prepares
a descending suspension *d″* and not the ascending suspension of bar
3, while the ascent to *e♭″* on the fourth quaver beat of bar 7 involves
an actual change to the harmony (a 6–3 on the mediant by comparison with the 5–3 on the submediant in bar 3).[39]

Comparable changes can be seen in the embellishment of internal,
immediate phrase repetition. In Hob. XVI: 47/i the quaver movement of bar 13 is expanded to demisemiquaver movement (bar 16)
using auxiliary and arpeggio notes as decoration (see Ex. 7.21), while
in Ex. 4.3 semiquavers are expanded to sextuplet figures using only
passing-notes as decoration: in the latter example, however, the
cadence figure is altered more extensively, the expanded tessitura in
bars 47–8 giving rise to a different cadential trill (see Ch. 6) and
necessitating a slight change in the bass (*g♯′* in bar 48 by comparison
with *e′* in bar 43) to avoid consecutive fifths.

The second movement of Hob. XVI: 18 (see Ex. 4.4) is particularly
rich in embellishment, containing embellishment in the counterstatement of the first theme (cf. bar 1 and bar 9), an embellishment of
bar 3 in the transposition of the first phrase beginning at bar 46, and
the most elaborate embellishment of the whole first phrase beginning
at bar 67. The latter is perhaps of greatest interest in that the embellishment is particularly elaborate, occurs in a context which is charac-

---

[39] Although embellishment in Haydn's keyboard music is mainly confined to the right-
hand part, changes to the left-hand part do occur; in general the harmony is not altered, but
there are exceptions. On this matter Türk comments that 'In pieces for the keyboard it is
also permissible to vary the bass, but the basic harmony must be retained thereby' (Türk,
Klavierschule, trans. Haggh, 314).

Ex. 4.2. Hob. XVI: 45/ii

teristic of Haydn's music dating from the second half of the 1760s, and raises an interesting question concerning editorial policy. The embellishment of bars 67 ff. is mostly the result of the extensive addition of *wesentliche Manieren* (trills, *Doppelschlag*, *Vorschlag*, and *Praller*) by comparison with the autograph version of bars 1–8. In the edition of Georg Feder (*JHW* XVIII/1) the ornaments in square brackets in bars 1–8 (as in Ex. 4.4) are added apparently on the basis of the parallel reading of bars 67 ff., which, given Haydn's characteristic practices at this time (*c.*1766), can be seen as a rare instance of misguided

Ex. 4.3. Hob. XVI: 47/ii

editorial intervention in *JHW*.[40] The embellishment of counterstatements and recapitulations in sonata-form movements became a
prominent stylistic feature of Haydn's keyboard music from the mid-
1760s: the practice is particularly noteworthy since counterstatements
and recapitulations are not mentioned specifically in contemporary
theory as a context suitable for improvised embellishment. In Hob.
XVI: 18/ii it is therefore unwise to look to the recapitulation to supply parallel readings, since the practice weakens the impact of the
embellishment in the recapitulation. In the present example *willkürliche Manieren* are also used in the recapitulation (cf. bars 3–4 and
69–70) so that, even in the text of *JHW*, the intention to embellish is

[40] On the editorial policy of *JHW* see G. Feder and J. P. Larsen, 'Haydn-Ausgabe', in G.
von Dadelsen (ed.), *Editionsrichtlinien musikalischer Denkmäler und Gesamtausgaben*, (Kassel:
Bärenreiter, 1967), 81–98.

clear, but the extensive use of *wesentliche Manieren* (and also perhaps the additional indications regarding articulation) should be reserved for the recapitulation (as they are in C. Landon's edition). In later embellished recapitulations Haydn relies less on *wesentliche Manieren*, and the extent of the embellishment ranges from minor changes (as in XVI: 24/i; cf. bars 5–7 and 103–5) to the more extensive alterations of Hob. XVI: 19/i (see Ex. 4.5). This movement is particularly interesting in that the recapitulation exploits the embellished versions of the first two subphrases (bars 1–3, 4–8) which occur in the counterstatement (cf. bars 9–11, 12–16 and 69–71, 72–6), the initial unornamented version being omitted in the recapitulation. The embellishment in this example is also notable for its sophistication, since the embellished version of bar 2 (the transformation of the dotted rhythms to semiquaver triplets) derives from the dotted-rhythm–triplet-semiquaver contrast in the immediate half-bar repetition and embellishment of bar 3; it is also noteworthy that the rhythmic contrast of bars 1–3 and 4–8 is retained in the embellished versions of these subphrases (in the latter the contrast is between triplet semiquavers and demisemiquavers).

Another potentially rich source of models for improvised embellishment in Haydn's keyboard music is to be found in movements where Haydn writes out varied reprises in place of formal repeats and in those movements which Sisman labels generically as 'hybrid' variations.[41] In this latter category may be counted Haydn's characteristic double variation movements and movements akin to a minuet and trio or a rondo which are combined with variation procedures (Sisman's 'alternating variations' and 'rondo variations'). Of particular relevance here are those passages where areas of thematic recurrence are replaced by variations and where formal repeats are replaced by written-out varied reprises. For instance, Hob. XVI: 38 and XVI: 49 provide striking models for the embellishment of formal repeats and passages of thematic recurrence in slow movements. In Hob. XVI: 38, bars 1–13 are followed by a written-out varied reprise which is characteristic of Haydn's manner of embellishment in the 1770s. In bars 20–1 there are subtle changes to the *Spielmanieren* employed by comparison with bars 7–8 and the more florid embellishment is, typically, concentrated in the middle of the varied reprise

---

[41] See 'Haydn's Hybrid Variations', in Larsen *et al.* (eds.), *Haydn Studies*, 509–15; and ead., *Haydn and the Classical Variation* (Studies in Music History, 5; Cambridge, Mass.: Harvard University Press, 1993), 150–63.

(bars 18–22), leaving the first phrase virtually unaltered. Particularly elaborate examples of embellishment in a later style may be observed in the slow movement of Hob. XVI: 49. The first phrase, bars 1–8, is followed by a particularly subtle varied reprise of this phrase and throughout the movement virtually all instances of thematic recurrence are embellished profusely (cf. in particular bars 1–8, 9–16, and 81–8; 27–36, 47–56, and 99–108). These and many other passages may be advanced as illustrations 'of the . . . practice of varying extemporaneously' in formal repeats in the same way that C. P. E. Bach offered his *Reprisen Sonaten* as such an illustration. Yet not all of Haydn's hybrid variation movements and varied reprises are equally suitable as models for improvisation. In the third movement of Hob.

Ex. 4.4. Hob. XVI: 18/ii

XVI: 22 written–out variations replace formal repeats on each occasion the E major theme recurs:

A (maggiore) B (minore) A (maggiore) B (minore) A (maggiore)
a:‖ b ‖   c ‖ d   a a′bb′   c′ ‖ d′   a a² b b²
8 ‖ 8 ‖   8 ‖ 6   8 8 8 8   8 ‖ 6   8 8 8 8

The variation in bars 39–46 of Hob. XVI: 22/iii is, however, rather similar to the obligatory 'semiquaver variation' of independent strophic variation sets, and although it is not possible to draw a clear distinction between the types of figuration characteristic of strophic variations and embellishment of the type illustrated in Exx. 4.1–5, the former does not transfer well to, for instance, the contexts in sonata-form movements in which Haydn chose to introduce embellished versions of themes or to slow movements. The double-variation

Ex. 4.5. Hob. XVI: 19/i

second movement of Hob. XVI: 44 has a less regular structure, but again contains written-out reprises:

A (minore)	B (maggiore)	A (minore)	B (maggiore)
a ‖ b a ‖	c d link	a x b′ a a′	c Codetta
6 ‖ 12 6 ‖	10 18 4	6 6 12 6 6	10 7

In this movement the six-bar phrase labelled x above (bars 63–8) begins as an embellishment of first phrase, but the continuation is totally new, harmonically and melodically, and the cadential figure is borrowed from the ending of the b phrase (bars 23–4), cadencing on the tonic, rather than corresponding to the cadence on the dominant at bars 5–6. Clearly the compositional decisions made by Haydn here are beyond the scope of what the performer should legitimately attempt. On the other hand Haydn's variation of phrase b of this movement at bars 69–80 and of phrase a at bars 87–92 might more realistically be advanced as illustrations of embellishment, since they decorate pre-existing phrases without departing from their established structures and without creating a totally new thematic character (see Ex. 4.6).

Applicatio

If the examples quoted above can be taken as putative models for embellishment, questions remain concerning the extent to which improvised embellishment is requisite in Haydn's music. Charles Rosen is of the opinion that 'The music of Haydn after 1775 cannot be ornamented'[42] and it is a common assumption that in the 'classical' style of the late eighteenth century, composers 'notated nearly everything with unusual care and finality'.[43] However, in view of what has been said in the present chapter and the detailed discussion in Chapters 6–9 of Haydn's notational practices from the mid-1760s, the association of Haydn's later compositions with notational precision is in need of revision. In most of the keyboard compositions written in perhaps a decade from 1766 Haydn adopted a more ornamental style of writing. It is in these works that he developed

---

[42] *The Classical Style*, 101.

[43] *New Grove*, s.v. 'Improvisation', 46. Similar statements are to be found in Rosenblum, *Performance Practices*, 289; L. Ratner, *Classic Music: Expression, Form, and Style* (New York: Schirmer, 1980), 197. This attitude to embellishment in classical music is to some extent based on late 18th- and early 19th-cent. writings; see e.g. the references to Milchmeyer and Baillot in Stowell, *Violin*, 346–8.

Ex. 4.6. Hob. XVI: 44/ii

practices of notation which were more explicit, with regard both to *wesentliche* and *willkürliche Manieren*, than in previous works. It would be an overstatement to say of this music, as Rosen does for the post-1775 music, that 'it cannot be ornamented [by the performer]': for instance, the internal phrase repetition in Hob. XVI: 47/ii and the recapitulations in Hob. XVI: 25/i and 26/i, might be embellished as suggested in Ex. 4.7*a*, *b*, and *c*. The scope for such embellishment is

Ex. 4.7(*a*) Hob. XVI: 47/ii, (*b*)Hob. XVI: 25/i, (*c*) Hob. XVI: 26/i

(*a*)

(b)

(c)

not as wide as might appear; from the mid-1760s virtually all counter-statements in expositions are embellished by Haydn and the performer should not, by improvising additional embellishment, attempt to 'gild the lily', thereby embellishing an embellishment. Even when an opportunity for embellishment does arise it may be advisable to forgo the opportunity in order to preserve Haydn's careful balance between unembellished and embellished versions of thematic material.

The application of the type of embellishment discussed in connection with the sonatas of *c.*1766 to *c.*1776 to Haydn's later keyboard music is also relatively limited. Haydn's notational practices changed considerably in the 1780s: his notation of *wesentliche Manieren* is simplified by comparison with the preceding works, very probably as a consequence of Haydn's writing increasingly for publication. Stylistically it is noticeable that *wesentliche Manieren* are far less prominent than in the works of the late 1760s and 1770s. *Willkürliche Manieren* on the other hand are as prominent, or perhaps more prominent, than before; the tendency already noticeable in the 1760s to write out the *willkürlichen Manieren*, rather than leaving them to the discretion of the performer, is intensified. Certainly, in the last seven sonatas and the late trios literal phrase repetition is rare, the recurrence of themes is often varied, and, as Rosen has pointed out, Haydn's conception of the recapitulation as 'a dramatic reinterpretation' of the exposition rather than as a restatement with the necessary tonal adjustments, is a strong argument against adding embellishments in this context.[44]

Improvised embellishment in the usual two reprises of sonata-form movements, the six reprises in minuet and trio movements, and in the refrain and transition sections of rondos is also increasingly less necessary from the 1770s. Unembellished minuet and trio movements become increasingly less common in Haydn's music from the 1770s and are replaced by movements in 3/4 time, in a moderato tempo, or Tempo di Menuetto, which contain written-out variations in place of a da capo repetition, and/or varied reprises in place of a formal repeat within the larger sectional recurrence or variation. These new forms require little added embellishment by comparison with the earlier minuet and trio movements. Rondos are often mentioned in connection with improvised embellishment, but from the

---

[44] See *Classical Style*, 100–1.

second half of the 1760s rondo refrains are characteristically subjected to variation by Haydn in the new hybrid forms. Another aspect of rondos associated with improvised embellishment is described by Türk:

Other than fermatas, rondos and similar pieces which are so much in favor now, also give opportunities for extempore embellishments; therefore, I will say a few words concerning them. Since these fermatas—if they may be so named—generally bring an important musical idea to a close in some neighboring key, after which the theme (principal subject) usually appears again in the main key, it is chiefly a question here of a skillful transition. Many composers prescribe these transitions; however, if this is not the case, then the following rules should be especially observed.[45]

Türk here seems to comment on the transition between the end of a rondo episode and the recurrence of the rondo refrain and goes on to give instructions for appropriate improvised links. Yet, here again the opportunity for improvisation does not arise in Haydn's rondos, since Haydn must certainly be regarded as one of those composers who 'prescribe the transitions [to the reprise of the rondo refrain]'.

As regards the usual two formal repeats in a sonata-form movement, the tendency among theorists to exclude elaborate embellishment from the reprises in Allegro movements, which is already apparent in the 1750s, increases towards the end of the eighteenth century. Türk comments that 'in general it is customary now and then to vary a passage at the repetition of an Allegro, and the like. However, longer elaborations are most frequently used in compositions of a gentle, pleasing character in slow tempo, and particularly in an Adagio.'[46] In this regard it is at least highly suggestive that, unlike C. P. E. Bach, Haydn never wrote varied reprises in sonata form movements, whereas he did in hybrid movements related to minuet and trio and rondo forms.

It is increasingly apparent in Haydn's keyboard music from the mid-1760s that the practice of embellishment is subsumed into Haydn's compositional style. Rosen has observed that 'The decoration of the classical style . . . articulates structure. The chief ornament retained from the Baroque is, significantly, the final cadential trill.'[47] However, the cadential trill is but one of the conventional elements of decoration which Haydn uses to slow harmonic rhythm

---

[45] *Klavierschule*, trans. Haggh, 293–4.   [46] Ibid. 311.
[47] *Classical Style*, 108.

and emphasize structurally important cadences. While in some early works fermatas obviously require an improvised cadenza or *Eingang*, it is characteristic of Haydn's later keyboard music, particularly the late piano trios, that structurally important cadences are decorated by the composer, using the conventional cadential figures characteristic of cadenzas, but written out in the metre of the movement,[48] or using a combination of large and small notes.[49] Undecorated *fermatas* which occur frequently in Haydn's keyboard music from the mid-1760s are contextually very different from those occurring in earlier works. Some of these *fermatas* may be decorated slightly, and some interesting contextual analogies may be found in the late works between decorated and undecorated fermatas (see e.g. Ex. 4.8). The majority of *fermatas* would appear however to have a rhetorical function in emphasizing chromaticism, unusual harmonic juxtapositions (in the late works frequently a tertiary key relationship), or simply indicating a dramatic pause, the effect of which would be vitiated by embellishment.[50]

Ex. 4.8(*a*) Hob. XVI: 52/iii, (*b*) Hob. XVI: 42/ii

---

[48] See Ch. 6 and Ex. 6.27.

[49] See e.g. Hob. XVI: 24/ii, bar 21; XVI: 49/i, bar 131; and XVI: 52/iii, bars 200–3.

[50] It is not obligatory to embellish every *fermata*. C. P. E. Bach states that *fermatas* 'over rests . . . are not embellished' (*Versuch*, trans. Mitchell, 143); Türk commented that *fermatas* could either be 'played without extempore elaborations (simple fermatas) or they are embellished' and that 'fermatas occur now and then for which an appropriate embellishment would

The widest scope for embellishment is to be found in the pre-1766 compositions. In these works Haydn's notation is in the Italian tradition, in that few symbols are used to indicate the *wesentlichen Manieren* and their occurrence is infrequent. The addition of suitable *wesentliche Manieren* is therefore largely the task of the performer, for which the extensive eighteenth-century literature provides plentiful information on the appropriate contexts; Haydn's later, specific notation of *wesentliche Manieren* also provides useful instruction. The *willkürlichen Manieren* are not written out by Haydn in the pre-1766 keyboard music and these also may, with less restraint than in later works, be added by the performer. Minuet and trio movements are written with six formal repeats rather than with written-out variations or varied reprises; because of the amount of repetition stipulated by repeat signs it would appear that embellishment is essential in these early minuet and trio movements. On the other hand, rondos, which are often associated with improvised embellishment, do not occur in Haydn's keyboard music until after the mid-1760s, when he began the practice of writing out the *willkürlichen Manieren*. Formal repeats in other movements might well be embellished also, but even in the 1750s theorists qualify the general instruction to embellish repeats. C. P. E. Bach's advocacy of the practice of 'varying extemporaneously the two reprises of an Allegro' is much quoted, but it should be taken in the proper context. Bach qualified this statement as follows:

Not everything should be varied, for if it is the reprise will become a new piece. Many things, particularly affettuoso or declamatory passages, cannot be readily varied. Also, galant notation is so replete with new expressions and twists that it is seldom possible even to comprehend it immediately. All variations must relate to the piece's affect, and they must always be at least as good as, if not better than, the original.[51]

Quantz also comments that certain affects are less suited to embellishment and remarks that in general 'Few extempore variations are allowed in the Allegro, since it is usually composed with melodies and passages of a kind that leave little room for improvement.'[52] The performer is required to supply cadenzas for a number of Haydn's early works,[53] and phrase repetition, which in the early works is

be of good effect' (*Klavierschule*, trans. Haggh, 290); see also Stowell, *Violin*, 358–67 and the discussion of *fermatas* in Ch. 10.

[51] *Versuch*, trans. Mitchell, 165.   [52] *Versuch*, trans. Reilly, 134.

[53] In Haydn's early keyboard sonatas cadenzas are required in Hob. XVI: 6/iii, 19/ii, and 46/ii; see R. Steglich, 'Kadenzen in Haydns Klaviersonaten', *ZfM* 99 (Apr. 1932): 295–7; and

frequent and usually literal, also invites embellishment. The embellishment of counterstatements and recapitulations mentioned above
may, however, be a particular characteristic of later works and therefore inappropriate in the pre-1766 compositions. There are no precise models for the embellishment of this early repertoire, but the
written-out embellishments in Haydn's later works, some of which
are illustrated in Exx. 4.1–6, provide general illustrations of the
possibilities.

There is clearly a relationship between the notational precision of
any work and the extent of the embellishment that is requisite in that
work. In Haydn's keyboard music three chronological stages of notation may be identified: first, in the pre-1766 music where neither
wesentliche nor *willkürliche Manieren* are specified precisely and must be
supplied by the performer; secondly, in the late 1760s and for most of
the 1770s, where both *wesentliche* and *willkürliche Manieren* are a
prominent feature of Haydn's style and are generally notated in great
detail; thirdly, in the late keyboard music, where *wesentliche Manieren*
are less frequent but *willkürliche Manieren* continue to be written out
by the composer. While the general trend towards notational precision and the consequent restriction in the scope for embellishment is
apparent, dogmatic strictures on embellishment after 1775, or indeed
any other date, are inadvisable.[54] It should also be allowed that
Haydn's notation in post-1766 works is not always as detailed and
precise as, for instance, in Hob. XVI: 20 or 49; embellishment of the
type illustrated in the above examples may be appropriate, regardless
of chronology, in works where Haydn has not prescribed embellishment in contexts which lend themselves to embellishment.

C. Landon, preface to *Haydn: Samtliche Klaviersonaten*, i. 163, 176. It could also be argued
that cadenzas are required in Hob. XVI: 2/ii (at bars 21, 49, and possibly 52 (third beat))
although *fermatas* are not indicated in the sources. For the extant inauthentic cadenzas for
Haydn's concertos see *JHW* XV/2; see also Haydn's own cadenza in the Sonata, Hob. XVI:
39/ii, bars 47–59. On the subject of cadenzas in Mozart's music see P. and E. Badura-Skoda,
Interpreting Mozart, 214–41; R. Levin, 'Instrumental Ornamentation, Improvisation, and
Cadenzas', in Brown and Sadie (eds.), *Performance Practice: Music after 1600*, 267–91;
Neumann, *Mozart*, 257–74. On the history of the cadenza see P. Whitmore, *Unpremeditated
Art: The Cadenza in the Classical Keyboard Concerto* (Oxford Monographs on Music; Oxford:
Clarendon Press, 1991).

[54] The six sonatas of Artaria's op. 30 (published in 1780) and the three sonatas Hob. XVI:
33, 34, and 43 are, as mentioned in Ch. 1, diverse stylistically; some of them belong to the
tradition of the sonatas dating from the earlier 1770s and the comments made above on the
embellishment of the sonatas from *c.*1766 to *c.*1776 are perhaps more appropriate for these
works than is Rosen's rejoinder regarding embellishment in post-1775 works.

Robert Levin has argued that modern performances of Classical music are the products of performance traditions which stress 'technical security over imagination, and absolute respect for the sanctity of the printed text over creativity'.[55] Levin's discussion centres, appropriately enough, on slow movements in Mozart's keyboard music and on his concertos in general, but Haydn's slow movements are very different to Mozart's, and the very special case of incomplete notation in Mozart's concertos (arising from Mozart's role as a composer-performer) has little relevance to Haydn's late keyboard music. Improvised embellishment clearly played a greater role in eighteenth-century performance than it does in twentieth-century performance, but the recovery of eighteenth-century practices of improvisation ought not be promoted uncritically as a general practice equally appropriate to every composer, every genre, and every work. Depending on the notational precision of the work, respect for the 'sanctity of the printed text' may be needed more than 'risk-laden' improvisation, and, of course, respect for the text need not exclude creativity. With regard to Haydn's late keyboard music there is reason to believe that a cautious attitude to embellishment is appropriate. A. P. Brown has suggested with regard to the *Creation* that 'Haydn wished for few added embellishments':[56] that the trend away from improvised embellishment apparently extended to vocal music, the traditional home of exuberant embellishment, and is supported for Haydn's late vocal music by the testimony of Dies,[57] suggests that Haydn's late keyboard music should also be performed without elaborate embellishment (notational precision is generally associated with keyboard music rather than with vocal music). Yet the strongest reason for discernment in embellishment is perhaps provided by the common statement of eighteenth-century theorists regarding the exacting standard expected of improvised embellishment, which must equal or improve on the quality of the original, unembellished melody. In his preface to the *Reprisen Sonaten* C. P. E. Bach qualified his general advocacy of varied reprises with two challenging, rhetorical questions, which imply a stringent standard of self-criticism:

---

[55] 'Improvised Embellishment in Mozart's Keyboard Music', *EM* 20/2 (May 1992): 221.
[56] *The Creation*, 46.   [57] Ibid. 44–6.

Is not the most important consideration in varying, that the performer do honor to the piece? Must not the ideas that he introduces into the repetition be as good as the original ones?[58]

[58] In C. P. E. Bach, *Versuch*, trans. Mitchell, 166. The quality of improvised embellishment is also a constant concern of other 18th-cent. writers. Quantz comments that 'If, however, through the oversight of the composer, too-frequent repetitions do occur, which could easily arouse displeasure, the performer is in this case justified in improving them through his skill. I say improve, not disfigure. Many believe that to remedy something they need do no more than vary it, although by doing this they often spoil more than they improve', and again that 'A well-written melody, which is already sufficiently pleasing in itself, must never be varied, unless you believe it can be improved' (Quantz, *Versuch*, trans. Reilly, 135, 139). Similarly, Türk states that 'The variation must be of significance and at least as good as the given melody. If the opposite is true then it would be better to leave the composition unvaried'. (Türk, *Klavierschule*, trans. Haggh, 312.)

5

C. P. E. Bach and Haydn:
The Question of Influence Revisited

◊

The question of C. P. E. Bach's influence on Haydn is a perennial subject in the literature on Haydn and is addressed in some detail here because of, as I see it, its direct relationship to problems of performance practice discussed in Chapters 6–9. Musicologists have generally accepted that Haydn was influenced by C. P. E. Bach and there is what appears to be a very solid documentary basis for this assumption. The legend of this influence dates from the eighteenth century and appeared first in a review of Haydn's Sonatas, Hob. XVI: 21–32 in the *European Magazine and London Review* in October 1784. Various other, mostly obscure, references date from the 1780s and 1790s but more precise information is found in two contemporary biographical sketches of Haydn, the *Biographische Notizen* of Georg August Griesinger and the *Biographische Nachrichten* of Albert Christoph Dies.[1] Following a description of Haydn's dismissal from St Stephen's and his early life in Vienna, Griesinger's account has the following passage:

About this time Haydn came upon the first six sonatas of Emanuel Bach. 'I did not come away from my clavier till I had played through them, and whoever knows me thoroughly must discover that I owe a great deal to Emanuel Bach, that I understood him and have studied him diligently'.[2]

Dies also places the influence of Bach early in Haydn's career:

That Haydn sought to make Bach's principles his own, that he studied them untiringly, can already be noted in his youthful works of that period. Haydn

---

[1] For a summary of the relevant documentation see Brown, *Keyboard Music*, 203–29, esp. 203–13.

[2] Griesinger, *Notizen*, trans. in Gotwals, *Haydn*, 12.

wrote in his nineteenth year quartets that made him known to lovers of music as a profound genius, so quickly had he understood.[3]

The specific source of the influence mentioned in Dies's account is Bach's treatise *Versuch über die wahre Art das Clavier zu spielen*; Dies comments that 'In his [Haydn's] opinion Bach's writings form the best, most basic and useful textbook ever published.'[4]

While references in the two authentic Haydn biographies testify to the influence of C. P. E. Bach on Haydn, there are considerable problems in stipulating how and when this influence is manifest in Haydn's music. Among modern Haydn scholars E. F. Schmid, Geiringer, Landon, and others have all accepted the influence of Bach on Haydn, but it must be said that the thematic and stylistic analogies which they cite as evidence of this influence are, at best, unconvincing.[5] The unproductive search for Bach's influence on Haydn's early works, those works mentioned by Griesinger and Dies, prompts questions regarding the date of the supposed influence and the chronological accuracy of the contemporary biographies. As increasing bibliographic control is established over eighteenth-century music in general and over the distribution of Bach's works in the eighteenth century in particular, it has emerged that supposed instances of Bach's influence on Haydn are unlikely or impossible in respect of chronology:[6] it is necessary that discussions of the subject be credible with regard to the chronology of the works of Bach and Haydn, and the availability of Bach's works in Vienna.

The first important steps in reassessing the question of Bach's influence on Haydn were taken by A. Peter Brown in two important papers which make a major contribution to the clarification of some of the documentary issues involved in this subject.[7] Brown convinc-

---

[3] *Nachrichten*, trans. ibid. 95.   [4] Ibid.

[5] See E. F. Schmid, 'Joseph Haydn und Carl Philipp Emanuel Bach', *ZfMw* 14 (Mar. 1932): 299–312; K. Geiringer, *Haydn: A Creative Life in Music* (2nd edn., London: Allen & Unwin, 1964), 244–5, 251, 274–8, and *passim*; H. C. R. Landon, *Haydn: Chronicle and Works*, ii. 337–40. For a brief, important, critical review of the modern literature on the subject see Brown, *Keyboard Music*, 213–15.

[6] Brown (*Keyboard Music*, 213–15) cites a number of such instances, which could easily be multiplied. Tovey's assertion that Haydn's Fantasia in C major, Hob. xvii: 3 and Capriccio in G major, Hob. xvii: 1 are 'obviously late piano pieces' and influenced by C. P. E. Bach's Rondos similarly cannot withstand scrutiny (Tovey, 'Haydn's Chamber Music', in *Essays and Lectures on Music*, ed. H. Foss (London: OUP, 1949), 28): we now know that the Capriccio dates from 1766 while the Bach Rondos are late works which could not have been available to Haydn until the 1780s.

[7] 'Joseph Haydn and C. P. E. Bach: The Question of Influence', in Larsen *et al.* (ed.), *Haydn Studies*, 158–64; and *Keyboard Music*, ch. 7, pp. 203–29.

ingly contests the chronology of the Griesinger and Dies accounts, which place Haydn's encounter with Bach's music and/or his *Versuch* in the 1750s. He cites a little-known account by Maximilian Stadler who wrote that in his early works Haydn 'had modeled himself after Wagenseil and his kind. Later he took in hand the foreign "products" such as those of C. P. E. Bach, etc., studied them, and while remaining faithful to his own special tastes, through this study he still molded more and more the realization of his own ideas'.[8] The chronology of this account is attractive since it is compatible with our modern understanding of Haydn's stylistic development,[9] and it is in accordance with the extant information of the availability of Bach's music and of his *Versuch* in Vienna. Recent research by Brown and others suggests that little of Bach's music was available in Vienna in the 1750s, that there is an increasing possibility of Haydn's access to Bach's music in the 1760s and 1770s but that irrefutable proof of Haydn's acquisition of Bach's music exists only for the 1780s.[10] With regard to Bach's *Versuch*, clearly there are problems with the implication in Dies's account that Haydn studied this treatise in the early 1750s.[11] It seems likely that the *Versuch* was not available in Vienna in the 1750s; part I was published in 1753 and part II in 1762, but the first known advertisement for the *Versuch* in Vienna appeared only in 1763.[12] The point should be made that if Haydn studied the *Versuch* in the 1750s, then it left no discernible trace on his early keyboard music, which is very much in the contemporary Viennese tradition. It might be argued that one should not necessarily expect to find

---

[8] Quoted in *Keyboard Music*, 209.

[9] In her study of Haydn's early keyboard music, B. Wackernagel (*Joseph Haydns frühe Klaviersonaten: Ihre Beziehungen zur Klaviermusik um die Mitte des 18. Jahrhunderts* (Tutzing: Schneider, 1975)) emphasizes the influence of the Viennese and Italian repertoires on Haydn's early sonatas and casts doubt on customary assertions regarding the influence of C. P. E. Bach.

[10] See H. Gericke, *Der Wiener Musikalienhandel 1700–1778* (Wiener Musikwissenschaftliche Beiträge, 5; Graz, Hermann Böhlaus, 1960); Brown, *Keyboard Music*, 210–11, 215–19; H. Krones, 'Carl Philipp Emanuel Bachs Präsenz im Wien des 18. Jahrhunderts', in *Konferenzbericht der XVI. Wissenschaftlichen Arbeitstagung, Michaelstein, 9. bis 12. Juni 1988: Studien zur Aufführungspraxis und Interpretation der Musik des 18. Jahrhunderts*, 39: 39–51.

[11] Regarding the problematic chronology of the Dies and Griesinger accounts with regard to the early Haydn string quartets see J. Webster, 'The Chronology of Haydn's String Quartets', *MQ* 61/1 (Jan. 1975): 17–46, esp. 35–44 and L. Finscher, *Studien zur Geschichte des Streichquartetts*, i *Die Entstehung des klassischen Streichquartetts: Von den Vorformen zur Grundlegung durch Joseph Haydn* (Saarbrucher Studien zur Musikwissenschaft, 3; Kassel: Bärenreiter, 1974), 137–67, esp. 137–44.

[12] In the *Wiener Diarium*. See Gericke, *Wiener Musikalienhandel*, 83.

an overt stylistic influence, if Haydn merely studied the *Versuch* as an elementary textbook on composition. Yet even this quite general notion appears unlikely. Part I of the *Versuch*, the only part even hypothetically available to Haydn in the 1750s, deals exclusively with matters of performance, while part II, which would undoubtedly be of interest to a composer learning his craft, was not available until 1762 at the earliest. Part II of the *Versuch* cannot therefore have been Haydn's basic textbook in composition. Yet it is the *Versuch* which provides the strongest link between C. P. E. Bach and Haydn. Brown considers the *Versuch* 'in many respects the strongest candidate for a Haydn connection' and in this regard has suggested a link between certain of Haydn's compositions and Bach's essay on the free fantasia which concludes part II of the *Versuch*.[13] However, there is a more specific link than that posited by Brown, namely the clear correlation between Bach's discussion of the two main topics in the *Versuch*, performance and figured bass (the subjects of part I and part II of the *Versuch* respectively), and changes in the orthography of Haydn's music which date from 1765/66. This correlation establishes more clearly that Haydn did study the *Versuch* and that he did so *c*.1765/6 and not in the 1750s; it raises interesting broader questions regarding Haydn's style in the mid-1760s and provides important information regarding the relevance of the *Versuch* to the discussion of ornamentation in Haydn's music in Chapters 6–9.

C. P. E. BACH'S *VERSUCH* AND HAYDN'S ORTHOGRAPHY

For present purposes I am not concerned with the interpretation of ornaments in the music of C. P. E. Bach or Haydn but simply with the manner in which ornaments are notated. In this regard Bach's *Versuch* represents a very distinctive tradition which in the second half of the eighteenth century was decidedly not the norm, but it is precisely Bach's characteristic notation which can establish a firm connection between the *Versuch* and Haydn's keyboard music from the latter half of the 1760s and first half of the 1770s. Bach's notation of ornaments is strongly influenced by the earlier French *clavecin* tradition, both directly through his own study of French music and indirectly through his knowledge of J. S. Bach's keyboard music. The

---

[13] *Keyboard Music*, 219–29.

precision and notational complexity of French ornament tables are a direct influence on the *Versuch*, although the notation and contextual setting of individual ornaments is different in each tradition. In the second half of the eighteenth century the elaborate ornament tables of the French keyboard tradition were positively *démodé* and generally only in North Germany did an attitude which required precision in notation survive. Bach specifically remarks on this in the *Versuch*:

The French are especially careful in setting the signs of their embellishments. But unfortunately we have so far removed ourselves from their music and their fine style of playing that the exact meaning of their embellishments is vanishing to the point where signs once well known are becoming unrecognizable even to keyboardists.[14]

Over thirty years later E. W. Wolf published an ornament table clearly derived from C. P. E. Bach's *Versuch* concerning which he commented as follows:

A further elaboration of these signs would be useful to young clavichord players. Even though Bach and Marpurg have already explained them, I see that in most pieces, with the exception of occasional grace-notes [*Vorschlägen*], *the only ornaments indicated by most composers are turns and trills* [italics added]. I have recorded all these ornaments because I consider them to be the most natural and the best and am therefore passing them on for the benefit of young clavichord players who do not know them. Also, since the use of ornaments in performance is a constituent of good taste, *I feel justified in publishing them in order to prevent their being completely forgotten* [emphasis added][15]

Even in France the complicated system of diacritic symbols formerly used to indicate ornaments was dispensed with increasingly from the mid-eighteenth century as Italianate, galant keyboard music gained the ascendancy over the native keyboard tradition. Popular keyboard composers and players in France in the generations after François Couperin, such as Schobert, did not indicate ornaments with the precision found in earlier French keyboard music, and the ornament tables, obligatory in earlier publications of keyboard music, disappear in the mid-eighteenth century.[16] In Viennese and Italian keyboard

[14] Trans. Mitchell, 83.

[15] Quoted in C. Hogwood, 'A Supplement to C. P. E. Bach's *Versuch*', 143.

[16] The keyboard works of Armand-Louis Couperin provide a particularly interesting case in point. Regarded by his contemporaries as one of the last proponents of the French *clavecin* tradition, he none the less published accompanied keyboard sonatas in a decidedly more galant style than his *Pièces de clavecin*. Interestingly, the stylistic differences between the two

music of the 1750s and 1760s, whatever ornamentation may have been added in performance, few ornament signs are actually notated in the written sources and those symbols that are used are usually generic indications. Clearly the reliance on improvised embellishment and non-specific notation of occasional ornaments belongs to the Italian tradition rather than to the French–North German tradition. For instance, the *tr* symbol, which is the most common symbol in Viennese music at this time, does not distinguish between various types of trill, as does French–North German notation, and indeed it is arguable that the *tr* symbol is here sometimes employed in an even looser sense, merely indicating that 'an appropriate ornament' should be played.[17] Haydn's early keyboard music is manifestly in this tradition; few ornament signs are employed, those used are often employed generically and the notation of appoggiaturas is conventional, in the sense that the performer must decide on the duration of appoggiaturas based on convention and context rather than on the basis of the literal meaning of the notation. Against this background of the trend away from the precise notation of ornaments the very sudden change in Haydn's attitude to the notation of ornaments, which is apparent in the autograph manuscripts beginning in 1765–6, is particularly striking and there is a close correlation between Haydn's new orthography and the advice on notation found in Bach's *Versuch*.

The first clear indicator of notational change in Haydn's keyboard music concerns the way in which appoggiaturas are written. In his music before 1762 when small notes are used to notate appoggiaturas the written value of the small notes is invariably a quaver. Obviously the duration of appoggiaturas in performance must be decided by the performer, rather than being explicit in the notation. Although the rules for the durations of appoggiaturas advocated by Quantz and others cannot be applied literally to Haydn's early music, Haydn's notation is, like Quantz's, conventional. In Haydn's dated autographs from 1766 (and possibly from 1765) a significant change in the notation of appoggiaturas is apparent. Small notes of various values, from

---

traditions in Armand-Louis Couperin's output are emphasized by differences in ornamentation, e.g. cf. 'Les tendres sentimens' and the accompanied Sonata, Op. 2 No. 5 in D. Fuller, ed., *Armand-Louis Couperin: Selected Works for Keyboard*, pt. ii (Recent Researches in the Music of the Pre-Classical, Classical, and Early Romantic Eras; Madison: A-R Editions, 1975).

[17] See Ch 6.

demisemiquaver to minim, are used to indicate appoggiaturas, and the contexts in which the different values occur strongly suggest that the values of the small notes indicate the 'real' value of the appoggiaturas in performance. Such precision in the indication of a great variety of durations for these small notes is not at all common in keyboard music of the 1760s and 1770s, but it is characteristic of North German keyboard music, and is advocated as the best means of notating appoggiaturas in Bach's *Versuch*. Bach comments on the notation of appoggiaturas as follows:

Because of their variability, . . . appoggiaturas have been notated of late in their real length. . . . Prior to this all were written as eighths. At that time, appoggiaturas as diverse as ours were not yet in use. Today, we could not do without the notation of their real values, for the rules covering their length in performance are insufficient to cover all cases, since all types appear before every kind of note.[18]

In his 'real' notation Haydn prescribed a wide range of values, and not simply half that of the main note, for appoggiaturas written as small notes (for instance, the quaver small note may occur before dotted crotchets and minims as well as before crotchet main notes: a minim main note may be preceded by semiquaver, quaver, or crotchet small note; see Table 7.1).[19] The earliest autograph in which real notation is used consistently is that of the Sonata, Hob. XVI: 45, dated 1766: it is possible that the notation of appoggiaturas in the Capriccio in G (dated 1765) and the Sonata, Hob. XVI: 47 in the E minor version (which can tentatively be dated to 1765 although no autograph is extant) may indicate real values, although there are some problems concerning these works.[20] In Haydn's keyboard works from 1766 the situation is clear: Haydn consistently notates appoggiaturas with the same precision which characterizes Bach's real notation.

Haydn's notation of other ornaments supports the thesis that he

---

[18] Trans. Mitchell, 87.

[19] From 1762 until 1765 Haydn notated appoggiaturas in what Feder has referred to as *Halbwertnotierung*, that is he uses a few different values of small note, half the value of the main notes they precede. It should be pointed out that *Halbwertnotierung* is quite commonplace in mid-18th-cent. keyboard music. Such notation remains conventional: the duration of the small note does not necessarily indicate the duration in performance. It is therefore not synonymous with 'real notation' as described by Bach, as has erroneously been assumed by Brown, Somfai, and Rosenblum. See Ch. 7.

[20] See Ch. 7.

read the *Versuch c.*1765/6. In early autographs the *tr* symbol either on its own or preceded by a lower appoggiatura (♪ , indicating a *Triller von unten*) is the only indication for the various types of trill. From 1765, however, Haydn begins to distinguish the *Triller* (indicated by the *tr* symbol) from the short- or half-trill (*Praller*) which is now indicated by the short chevron symbol. Trills ornamenting long notes or tied notes have distinctive symbols and Haydn experimented with various ways of indicating the *Triller von unten*, including the typically French-North German symbol for the *Triller von unten*, i.e. a hook before a chevron (ᴄᴡ). In a number of autographs Haydn also adopts the characteristic typically French-North German manner of indicating a *Nachschlag* to a trill by a hook following a chevron (ᴡᴜ). These changes in notation are discussed in more detail in Chapter 6. It would appear from Table 6.1 that in the decade from roughly 1765 to 1775 Haydn experimented extensively with various means of indicating trill types more accurately, and while some of the symbols he employs are hybrid, many are derived from the French-North German tradition. The period of Haydn's experimentation with North German manners of notating trills coincides exactly with his adoption of real notation of appoggiaturas.

It is perhaps the notation of the *Doppelschlag* which most convincingly establishes the connection between Haydn and C. P. E. Bach's *Versuch*. The typically Haydnesque symbol (∾) is the only indication of the *Doppelschlag* in the early autographs. The more conventional *Doppelschlag* symbol (∿) occurs in a dated autograph for the first time in the C minor Sonata of 1771, but is found earlier in the fragmentary undated autograph of the Sonata in B flat, which may be dated to *c.*1766. Most suggestive, however, is the occurrence in the C minor Sonata (dated autograph 1771) of the symbol for the *prallende Doppelschlag* (⁑), and, in the D major Sonata, Hob. XVI: 24, dating from 1773, of the symbol for the *geschnellte Doppelschlag* (♪). These symbols, like the real notation of appoggiaturas, have paticularly strong associations with North Germany and their occurrence in Haydn's music at this time is especially revealing. The symbol for the *prallende Doppelschlag* may derive from the French tradition,[21] but in the second half of the eighteenth century is found only in North German music and in music influenced by the North Germans.[22]

---

[21] The symbol ᴡ is used by François Couperin (e.g. in 'Les Moissonneurs' from his *Sixième Ordre*) but is not listed in his ornament table.

The symbol for the *geschnellte Doppelschlag* is even more useful in establishing a direct link to C. P. E. Bach's *Versuch*, since the notation was actually invented by C. P. E. Bach, who says in the *Versuch* that this ornament is 'discussed in no other writings'.[23] While historically the ornament itself does not originate with Bach, its manner of notation in the *Versuch* was Bach's invention and the appearance of this notation in a Haydn sonata in 1773, albeit in a non-autograph source, establishes a direct connection with C. P. E. Bach's notational practices. Haydn used Bach's symbol for the *geschnellte Doppelschlag* only once and in later works he preferred to use four small notes to indicate this ornament: this latter manner of notation also has North German associations since it is derived from Marpurg's *Anleitung zum Clavierspielen*, a treatise which is very much in the tradition of Bach's *Versuch* and which we know Haydn owned.

Haydn is also more precise in his notation of other ornaments at this time although theoretically the notation may derive from a number of sources and cannot for the most part be directly connected with North German influences.[24] Overall the sonatas of the period 1765 to 1775 give the impression of almost obsessive experimentation with the notation of a range of ornaments which is uncharacteristic of Haydn's earlier music and of contemporary Viennese keyboard music. Haydn's 'new' concern for precision in the notation of ornaments is redolent of Bach's careful explanations throughout the *Versuch* of the importance of the precise notation of ornaments. Given the occurrence in Haydn's music from 1765/6 of characteristically French-North German symbols, specifically North German notation, and notation which actually originated with Bach, 1765 or 1766 may be proposed with some confidence as the date of Haydn's reading of the *Versuch*. The likelihood of this rather than an earlier date for Haydn's reading of the *Versuch*, and the further suggestion that Haydn read both part I and part II of the *Versuch* at this time, find further support in, hitherto unremarked, changes in Haydn's manner

---

[22] See e.g. the sonatas of W. F. Bach and Müthel. Its occurrence may also be associated with certain North German publishers and engravers who were obviously familiar with North German notation of ornaments and used the symbols sometimes irrespective of the composer's notation. See e.g. the 'Zweystimmige Fuge von Herrn Handel', the fourth piece in 'Tonstücke für das Klavier, | vom | Herrn C. P. E. Bach, | und | einigen andern classischen Musikern', published by Breitkopf in 1762.

[23] Trans. Mitchell, 125.

[24] See e.g. the discussion of Haydn's notation of arpeggios in Ch. 9. Haydn's notation of the *Schneller* in Hob. XVI: 39/i may derive from C. P. E. Bach: see Ch. 6.

of notating figured bass parts which, chronologically, closely parallel the changes in his notation of ornaments.

When Haydn writes figured bass parts in his early works the notation is fairly routine, involving the common figures 7, 6, 5–3, 6–4, and occasional suspensions:[25] the notation is not especially detailed nor is it complete. In general his notation of figured bass from the mid-1760s, certainly from the Missa Cellensis of 1766 onwards, is noticeably more elaborate and punctilious. Apart from the general precision from this date there are a number of features which become established in Haydn's notational practice and which correspond to passages of detailed discussion in Bach's *Versuch*. The most distinctive feature of Haydn's new notation is seen in his concern to indicate specifically passages which are not intended to be realized in four parts. This also is a constant concern throughout the *Versuch*. In one instance, Bach follows a description of 'cases [where] the entire chord is played' with the following comment:

But there are times when a series of threes is written over a rapid passing bass as a means of informing the accompanist that the right hand is to play only parallel thirds with the bass.[26]

From the mid-1760s Haydn consistently indicates such passages with consecutive threes or tens.[27] Similarly in the figured bass parts of Haydn's church music from the mid-1760s the composer takes great care to distinguish passages which require chordal harmonizations from those which should be in unison or simply doubled at the octave. C. P. E. Bach deals with *all'unisono* and *tasto solo* passages in greater detail than any other treatise.[28] Concerning the former he comments as follows:

The octave is included in the meaning of the term *unison*. Thus when parts progress either in real unisons or in octaves, they are said to move in unison (*all'unisono*) . . .

---

[25] See e.g. the Organ Concerto, Hob. XVIII: 8 (1755–60) which is typical of Haydn's earlier manner of notation in figured bass parts.

[26] Trans. Mitchell, 207, see also 388 ff.

[27] Although this is found occasionally in some early works, it is particularly evident in compositions from the mid-1760s. See e.g. the Gloria from the *Grosse Orgelmesse*, Hob. XXII: 4, (c.1768–9); the first number in the 'Applausus' Cantata, Hob. XXIVa: 6 (1768). See also Ex. 5.1. In indicating a bass realization with the right hand playing in parallel thirds with the left hand Haydn used the figures 3 and 10 interchangeably (as e.g. in the Gloria from the *Grosse Orgelmesse*).

[28] *Versuch*, trans. Mitchell, 313–19.

There is no need to commend this technique, which attains its beauty through the omission of harmony, for the many examples of it to be found in the works of good composers provide a dependable testimony.

Yet it is surprising that some composers do not always specify a unison accompaniment in scoring the bass.[29]

On the other hand Bach specifies that in *tasto solo* passages 'the left hand alone plays the bass without octave duplication'.[30] Dramatic unison passages became a striking new feature of Haydn's compositional style in the church music from the mid-1760s and the importance of such passages requires clear notation. Haydn employs two manners of notation, a series of ones above the bass and the words *tasto* or *tasto solo*.[31] It seems likely that in this distinction Haydn intended a similar differentiation between bass parts which may be doubled at the octave (Bach's *all'unisono* and Haydn's series of ones) and parts where the left hand of the keyboard bass plays alone without octave duplication.

The successive use of the figures 3, 10, and 1, and the occurrence of *tasto solo* indications are a witness to Haydn's new precision in his figured bass parts and to his concern to identify those passages which do not require conventionally full harmonizations. These features are commented on in Bach's *Versuch*, although this source is by no means unique in so doing. A more special feature of Haydn's music from this period is the composer's practice of using rather unusual figuring of the bass part to indicate thin textures in his accompaniments in which the part-writing is specified in such a way that the figured bass doubles the part-writing in orchestral or, more frequently, vocal parts in the chorus. Such figuring becomes a striking characteristic of Haydn's bass parts from the mid-1760s through to his late vocal works. Bars 61 to 97 of Haydn's Salve Regina, Hob. xxiiib: 2 (1771) exemplify many of the new features of Haydn's figured bass parts from this period (see Ex. 5.1): on the upbeat to bar 61 a unison passage is indicated by a series of ones (indicating octave doubling of the bass); this is succeeded in bars 63–8 by the resumption of conventional figuring (Bach explains that the 'Termination of a unison

[29] Ibid. 313.　　　　　　　　　　　　　　　　　　　　[30] Ibid. 316.

[31] Examples of unison and *tasto solo* indications are widespread in Haydn's music from this time. See e.g. *Missa Cellensis* (1766)—Kyrie II, Gloria, etc.; Salve Regina, Hob. xxiiib: 2; *Kleine Orgelmesse*—Credo, Sanctus, Benedictus, etc. Haydn occasionally uses the term 'unisono' in place of a series of ones, as in bar 13 of the Gloria and bar 73 of the Agnus Dei from the *Mariazellermesse* (1782). In modern eds. the numeral 1 is frequently transcribed as a staccato *Strich*: on this point see *JHW* XXIII/1a, 'Vorwort'.

Ex. 5.1. Salve Regina, Hob. XXIIIb: 2, vocal parts and continuo

Ex. 5.1. *cont.*

accompaniment is indicated by figures placed over the bass at the
point where a chordal setting is resumed'[32]); the *tasto solo* indication
at bar 69 holds force until bar 91 and from 92 to 97 the unusual figuring of the bass part yields a two- or three-part realization which
doubles the vocal parts. Characteristically Haydn is considerate in
doubling vocal entries: for instance, the figures 1 and 10 in bar 92 give
part-writing which doubles initially the Bass, then the Alto entry, and
when the sequence of tens is broken in bar 93 by the figure 6, it is to
cue the Tenor entry. Haydn is careful to indicate by successive ones
that the bass entry is not accompanied by chords and the use of 8–3,
instead of 5–3, and 9–7♭, instead of 7♭–4–2, specifies precisely the
voice-leading in a two- or three-part realization as opposed to a four-
part chordal realization. The use of rather unusual figuring to specify
voice-leading, which is wholly characteristic of Haydn's figured bass
parts from *c.*1765, may well derive from Bach's *Versuch*. In some pre-
liminary exercises Bach, unusually, figures the bass part in such a way
that 'The numerals denote the best intervals for the upper voice' (see
Ex. 5.2).[33] Perhaps more suggestive is the occurrence in both the

[32] *Versuch*, trans. Mitchell, 315. Although clearly not uniquely associated with C. P. E.
Bach and Haydn, the careful notation of unison and *tasto solo* passages is by no means commonplace. On problems of interpreting Handel's less than precise notation see P. J. Rogers,
Continuo Realization in Handel's Vocal Music (Studies in Music, 104; Ann Arbor: UMI, 1989),
ch. 6, pp. 95–108.
[33] *Versuch*, trans. Mitchell, 208.

Ex. 5.2. C. P. E. Bach, *Versuch*, trans. Mitchell, p. 208, fig. 243 (extract)

Versuch and in Haydn's figured bass parts of compound figures, a feature which was common in the figured bass parts of Caccini and others in the early history of figured-bass, but which generally is not found in later figured bass writing.[34] Bach describes the use of such figures in the first chapter of part II of this *Versuch*:

Primes, tenths, elevenths, and twelfths are nothing more that octaves, thirds, fourths, and fifths. They are denoted by the numerals, 1, 10, 11, and 12, and appear often in galant notation and three-part accompaniment. Such figures are used to specify the exact progression of the voices . . .[35]

Haydn's use of unusual figures such as 10, 10–5, 8–6, and 8–3 instead of 5–3 or 6–3 clearly derives from his desire to 'specify the exact progression of the voices' in two- or three-part realizations.[36]

One further detail of Haydn figured bass parts concerning the notation of appoggiaturas in the bass is worthy of note. Bach comments on the notation of such appoggiaturas as follows:

When one prefers not to figure the accented note [*anschlagende note*, i.e. the appoggiatura or *transitus irregularis*] one may set figures over the succeeding notes, or place over the accented notes either an oblique stroke, a circle, a semicircle, or an m, which, on occasion, may be lengthened [see Ex. 5.3]. The sign of the oblique stroke in number (2) is the best.[37]

---

[34] See F. T. Arnold, *The Art of Accompaniment from a Thorough-Bass as Practised in the XVIIth and XVIIIth Centuries* (1931; repr. New York: Dover, 1965), vol. i, ch. 1, esp. pp. 33–67, ii. 878–9; and P. Williams, *Figured Bass Accompaniment* (Edinburgh: Edinburgh University Press, 1970), ii. 83–7.

[35] Trans. Mitchell, 183; see also 184, 309.

[36] Such figuring is not unusual in Haydn's music from the mid 1760s: see e.g. 'Applausus' Cantata, Nos. 1 and 8.b; *Grosse Orgelmesse*—Gloria; Salve Regina; *Kleine Orgelmesse*—Sanctus; Non nobis Domine (Hob. xxiiia: 1). Indeed, it is not unusual for Haydn to abandon figured bass notation for a few beats or bars at a time and write a two-part realization in the continuo part (as e.g. in the *Missa Cellensis* (1766) and the 'Applausus' Cantata).

[37] 'Wenn man die anschlagende Note nicht beziffern will, so setzt man entweder die Ziffern über die nachschlagende Noten allein, oder bezeichnet die anschlagenden Noten noch oben ein entweder mit einem Seitenstrich, einer Null, einer halben Null, oder einem m, welches, wenn es nöthig ist, verlängert wird: . . . Das Zeichen mit dem schrägen Strich bey Numer (2) ist das beste.' *Versuch*, pt. II, p. 31 (trans. Mitchell, 196).

Ex. 5.3. C. P. E. Bach, *Versuch*, part II, p. 31

Bach's favoured manner of indicating appoggiaturas in the bass by an
oblique stroke, apparently Bach's invention, has become standard in
modern figured bass notation, but had little currency in the eighteenth century.[38] The occasional occurrence of Bach's innovatory
method of notating appoggiaturas in the bass in Haydn's music is
therefore significant (see Ex. 5.4).[39] Separately the occurrence of any
of these features in Haydn's figured bass parts might be coincidental.
Taken together they point to a significant revision in Haydn's notation of figured bass parts. Haydn's 'new' notation in figured bass parts
may be associated with specific passages in Bach's *Versuch*, some of
which represent common practice, particularly in church music, but
some of which represent relatively unusual or unique practices by
comparison with common practice. It can be no mere coincidence
that the changes in Haydn's figured bass parts occur in the body of
church music which Haydn composed from *c.*1765. Given the docu-

Ex. 5.4(*a*) Salve Regina, Hob. xxiiib: 2, continuo; (*b*) Missa Cellensis
(Mariazellermesse), Hob. xxii: 8, continuo Kyrie; (*c*) Missa Cellensis
(Mariazellermesse), Hob. xxii: 8, continuo Sanctus

(*a*)

(*b*)

(*c*)

---

[38] See Arnold, *Accompaniment*, ii. 717 n. 2, and 880–2.

[39] Prior to Haydn's use of the oblique stroke to indicate appoggiaturas in the bass, he had
in the *Missa Cellensis* of 1766 employed Bach alternative practice of setting 'figures over the
succeeding notes'. See *JHW* XXIII/1a, p. xii.

mentary information on the availability of Bach's *Versuch* in Vienna, Haydn's new orthography with regard to ornaments and the 'new' manner in which he notates figured bass parts support the thesis that Haydn studied Bach's *Versuch* in 1765 or 1766 and not the 1750s. The notational evidence would also seem to imply that Haydn continued his study of Bach's *Versuch*, or returned periodically to the *Versuch*, for some time, perhaps for the greater part of a decade, after this date. Most of the notational features described above appear in Haydn's music in 1765 or 1766, but some apparently appear for the first time in Haydn's music in the early 1770s (the use of the *prallende Doppelschlag* and the oblique stroke in figured bass parts seem to appear for the first time in 1771; the symbol for the *geschnellte Doppelschlag* appears in 1773).

EXTENT AND NATURE OF INFLUENCE

If we can date the influence of Bach on Haydn to a period beginning in 1765 or 1766, the obvious question still remains. What is this influence? Is it simply the case that Haydn adopted a few of Bach's notational conventions? This seems unlikely since it is in general true that notation is rarely an end in itself. Arguably, however, the new notational features in Haydn's music from 1765 are an indicator of what Haydn absorbed from Bach's *Versuch* into his own compositional style. In this regard it is of interest that the notational features which Haydn absorbed from the *Versuch* are all performance related and that many of the most striking new stylistic features in Haydn's keyboard music from 1765 are also performance-related. It may be observed that a principal difference between Haydn's earlier sonatas and the sonatas from 1765 is that details of performance practice, including, but not exclusively, matters of ornamentation, are no longer an appendage to Haydn's style, left in the domain of the performer, but rather, become an essential part of the compositional process, and consequently, as in Bach's music, require precise notation. The exploitation of details of performance practice as a facet of compositional style is therefore, I would suggest, the first lesson that Haydn learnt from C. P. E. Bach.

Haydn's extensive experimentation with the notation of stereotyped ornaments indicated by symbols (*Spielmanieren*) is indicative of the composer's new concern with the potential of ornamentation as part of his keyboard style, of a move away from a rather simple keyboard style to a more complex and expressive ornamental style.[40] The profusion, in number and type, of *Spielmanieren* does not merely render Haydn's music more decorative, but exploits the virtuosic and expressive potential of ornamentation. Throughout the *Versuch* Bach describes ornaments in terms of their expressive character and Haydn's concern to distinguish one ornament type from another by increasingly complex notation would undoubtedly have had more to do with prescribing the expressive affect of a particular passage than with merely imitating notational conventions.

Haydn's most characteristic exploitation of ornamentation is as a means of variation. The second movement of Haydn's Sonata, Hob. XVI: 30 (*c*.1776), a set of variations, is unusual in that, while variations 1 to 5 are customary figurative variations, variation 6 utilizes *Spielmanieren* in a way which is uncharacteristic of strophic variations (see Ex. 5.5). The variety of *Spielmanieren* employed here, the knowledge of the contexts associated with each type and the degree to which they are interchangeable in certain contexts, are not found in Haydn's keyboard music before *c*.1765 and are redolent of the many passages in Bach's *Versuch* which discuss such matters.[41] The use of a wider range of *Spielmanieren* witnessed here and the manner of their exploitation as a means of variation first appear in Haydn's Sonata, Hob. XVI: 18 (*c*.1766), especially in the second movement (see Ch. 4). In this movement, as in Hob. XVI: 30/ii, the extensive use of *Spielmanieren* is accompanied by the exploitation of written-out embellishments (*Setzmanieren*), which as pointed out in Chapter 4, is a new feature of Haydn's music which emerges at the same time. From this time Haydn uses *Setzmanieren* or *Spielmanieren*, or more often a combination of the two, to vary phrase repetition and to embellish counterstatements and recapitulations in sonata form movements. Therefore, while only individual features of Haydn's notation of *Spielmanieren* may be directly linked with Bach's *Versuch*, the notation is an indicator of a more fundamental change in Haydn's music, whereby ornamentation, whether or not indicated by symbols, became an essential part of his compositional style. It is also

[40] This is undoubtedly part of a wider style change in Haydn's keyboard music in the mid-1760s. See Brown's discussion of what he terms 'Six Progressive Solo Sonatas' in *Keyboard Music*, 293–300.

[41] Compare e.g. Haydn's use of both *Anschlag* and inverted *Doppelschlag* (Bach's slide) in parallel passages to ornament an appoggiatura and Bach's discussion of these ornaments (*Versuch*, trans. Mitchell, p. 134 and fig. 152.b and f, pp. 137–8).

Ex. 5.5. Hob. XVI: 30/ii

Ex. 5.5. cont.

notable that Haydn's exploitation of articulation as a means of variation dates from this period (see Ch. 2); and, as argued in Chapter 1,
the dynamic markings in the Sonata in C minor, Hob. XVI: 20 (1771)
are an experiment, unprecedented in extent (for Haydn at this time)
which may be related to the North German clavichord tradition, but
which in any case represents another feature of performance practice
emerging with precise notation in Haydn's music at this time, when
it was absent in earlier works.

The sixth variation in the second movement of Haydn's Sonata,
Hob. XVI: 30 also raises the question of the occurrence in Haydn's
music from the mid-1760s of 'varied reprises' (that is, written-out
embellishments of a passage in place of a formal repeat indicated by a
repeat sign) which has been widely regarded by Haydn scholars as the
most tangible evidence of Bach's influence on Haydn. Tovey saw in
the varied reprises of the slow movements from Haydn's String
Quartets, Op. 9 Nos. 2 and 4, Op. 20 No. 6, and Op. 33 No. 3 'the
only art-form [which] Haydn owes to Bach (C. P. E.)'[42] and Elaine
Sisman sees the sixth of Bach's *Reprisen Sonaten* as a specific model for
Haydn's hybrid variation movements.[43] That Haydn derived the idea
of employing varied reprises in place of formal repeats from Bach is
wholly credible as regards chronology. The early occurrences of
varied reprises in the slow movements of Haydn's string quartets date
from *c.*1769–70, certainly before 1771, and in the hybrid variation
movements varied reprises instead of formal repeats are commonplace in Haydn's sonatas of the 1770s.[44] Haydn would have encountered Bach's varied reprises in studying the *Versuch* and the
accompanying *Probestücke* which exemplify the practice, and he could

[42] 'Haydn's Chamber Music', 27, see also 28–9.
[43] 'Hybrid Variations', 509–15; ead., *Haydn and the Classical Variation*, 153–4.
[44] If indeed Hob. XVI: 44 dates from *c.*1766, this sonata may represent Haydn's first experiments with varied reprises, although in a less regular structure than customary in later works.
On the chronology of Haydn's use of varied reprises and of his hybrid variation movements
see Brown, *Keyboard Music*, 220; and Sisman, 'Hybrid Variations', 512–13.

possibly also have known Bach's *Sechs Sonaten mit veränderten Reprisen*, published in 1760 and available in Vienna in 1767.[45] It has been pointed out that the manner in which Haydn employed varied reprises is very different from that of Bach.[46] Tovey, writing about Op. 9 No. 2, second movement, noted that Haydn wrote a varied reprise only for the first part, while it was Bach's practice when writing varied reprises to do so for both parts of a movement.[47] It is also true that varied reprises are not characteristic of Bach's slow movements, while slow movements are Haydn's favoured vehicle for varied reprises, and that while Bach wrote varied reprises for sonata-form movements Haydn never did so. Varied reprises in minuet-like hybrid variations are common in Haydn's sonatas, but minuets, with or without varied reprises, are (with a few notable exceptions) not an important feature of Bach's sonatas, although he did compose minuets as autonomous movements. Yet it is entirely consistent with the notion of one first-rate composer influencing another that a borrowed idea, in this case replacing formal repeats with varied reprises, produces quite different results.[48] Moreover, it is arguable that Haydn's exploitation of varied reprises is but another facet of what I have suggested is Bach's primary influence on Haydn; namely, the exploitation of details of performance practice as a facet of compositional style. Rather than leaving the improvisation of embellishments in formal repeats to the discretion of the performer, Haydn 'controlled' the embellishment in specific contexts and in so doing produced, as Bach had done, new formal procedures, the most innovative of which are, perhaps, Haydn's hybrid variation movements.

If Haydn learnt from Bach how to exploit details of performance practice as a facet of compositional style, then Haydn's most striking exploitation of this practice is wholly original. As mentioned above, while Bach wrote varied reprises in sonata-form movements, Haydn chose not to do so. Instead, he characteristically varied details in phrase repetitions, counterstatements of first themes, and recapitulations. The most original and characteristic of Haydn's sonata-form procedures, usually referred to, somewhat misleadingly, but conve-

[45] See Gericke, *Musikalienhandel*, 71 ff. See also Brown, *Keyboard Music*, 215–20; and Krones, 'Carl Philipp Emanuel Bachs Präsenz in Wien', 40.

[46] See esp. Brown, *Keyboard Music*, 220.   [47] 'Haydn's Chamber Music', 29.

[48] On general problems in discussing the influence of one composer on another see Rosen, 'Influence: Plagiarism and Inspiration', *19th Century Music*, 4/2 (Fall 1980): 87–100.

niently, as monothematicism, is also closely associated with variation in details of performance, whether by changing details of ornamentation, articulation, or dynamics. When Haydn utilizes a theme first heard in the tonic in the dominant or relative major key, the procedure is often described as a unifying feature of the movement, which of course it is, but it is equally clear that there are nearly always significant differences between the two versions of the theme: often the differences are more important that the similarities between the two statements. In the style of the late symphonies and string quartets the statement of the 'first theme' in the dominant often contains a new countermelody, frequently in invertible counterpoint, and a new orchestration; the differences between the tonic and dominant statements generate much of what happens subsequently in the movement.[49] It is equally characteristic, especially in his keyboard music, for Haydn to characterize the dominant statement of the theme by altering details of performance practice. In the C sharp minor Sonata, Hob. XVI: 36 the version of the first theme which appears in E major at bar 12, is ornamented differently, is characterized by more legato articulation as opposed to the staccato of bar 1, and the dynamics are implicitly altered from f to p; such changes in performance reinforce the major compositional decision to alter the texture from the strong octave statement in bar 1 to a quasi-contrapuntal texture. Some of Haydn's most ingenious feats concern variation in the articulation of a theme when it occurs in the dominant or relative major, several of which are discussed in Chapter 2. It is not suggested here that Haydn's characteristic 'monothematic' sonata-form movements are necessarily derived from C. P. E. Bach, but simply that Haydn's exploitation of ornamentation, articulation, and other aspects of performance practice, which I believe owes much to Bach, is in no sense superficial, but became an integral part of Haydn's compositional style and has a structural and not merely decorative function. It is significant that the compositional control which Haydn exercised over details of performance arises in those sonatas which can be associated orthographically with C. P. E. Bach's *Versuch*. It is, however, entirely characteristic that Haydn exploits details of performance structurally, while C. P. E. Bach's most striking exploitations of the same features are concerned with the individual expressive moment, with underlining an expressive detail

---

[49] Classic examples are to be found in the 1st and 4th movements of Haydn's Symphony No. 104.

rather than necessarily signifying any large-scale structural significance.[50]

Having identified the period from *c.*1765 to 1775 as the period of
Haydn's greatest interest in Bach it is tempting, and not at all difficult, to suggest stylistic analogies between the composers, beyond the
primary performance-related influence mentioned above. For
instance, the four-bar phrase which ends each half of the binary
movement Hob. XVI: 18/ii and which I have referred to in Chapter
1 as a 'fade-out' technique (see Ex. 5.6*a*) is almost interchangeable
with similar phrases in C. P. E. Bach's second 'Prussian' sonata (H.
25, Wq. 48/2), third movement, bars 34–7 and 92–5 (cf. Ex. 5.6*b*):
the compositional effect, the part-writing, key, and shift in register
are identical in both works and it is possible that Haydn may have
known the 'Prussian' Sonatas since they were available in Vienna
from 1756 and possibly as early as 1746. It is also interesting that in
the first movement of this 'Prussian' sonata the recapitulation is
embellished: Hob. XVI: 18/ii is one of the earliest instances of an
embellished recapitulation in Haydn's works. Similarly, regarding
Hob. XVI: 30 where the ornamental writing and varied reprises discussed above in connection with Ex. 5.5 place the work within the
sphere of influence of C. P. E. Bach's *Versuch*, one might also suggest
a relationship between the through-composition of this work, which
is unusual in Haydn's sonatas, and the commonplace practice of
through-composition in the works of C. P. E. Bach.[51] Tempting
though such analogies are, they are also dangerous: the impression
might be given that our perception of Haydn's originality is reduced
by comparison with C. P. E. Bach, or that the influence of C. P. E.
Bach is the only impetus contributing to Haydn's exciting composi-

[50] See S. Wollenberg, 'A New Look at C. P. E. Bach's Musical Jokes', in Clark (ed.),
C. P. E. Bach Studies, 295–314; P. Fox, 'The Stylistic Anomalies of C. P. E. Bach's
Nonconstancy', in ibid. 105–31.

[51] Both Brown and Webster have written about the unusual nature of this sonata.
Webster notes that 'If Sonata No. 30 is Haydn's most thoroughly through-composed work,
it also remains something of an enigma' (Webster, *Haydn's 'Farewell' Symphony and the Idea
of Classical Style: Through-Composition and Cyclic Integration in his Instrumental Music*
(Cambridge Studies in Music Theory and Analysis; Cambridge: CUP, 1991), 294). Brown
suggests that the 'dramatic intrusion' in this work is similar to C. P. E. Bach's Sonata in A
major, H. 186, Wq. 55/4, but notes that the latter was not available in Vienna until 1779
(Brown, *Keyboard Music*, 308). Neither author associates the unusual through-composition
of Hob. XVI: 30 with what is a common practice in C. P. E. Bach's music. Precedents in
Bach's keyboard music can be found in the *Sonaten mit veränderten Reprisen*, which were
available in Vienna in the late 1760s.

Ex. 5.6(*a*) Hob. XVI: 18/ii, (*b*) C. P. E. Bach, H.25 (Wq.48/2)/iii

tional experiments from the mid 1760s. No doubt further research will reveal more potential analogies between Bach and Haydn, but it seems more urgent to address the rather more basic question: why did Haydn study C. P. E. Bach's *Versuch c.*1766?

The year 1766 is in many regards an *annus mirabilis* in Haydn's career. Gregor Werner died on 3 March 1766 and Haydn added to his other activities the regular composition of church music. David Wyn Jones has summarized Haydn's position in 1765 as follows:

By the end of 1765 the Esterházy *Kapellmeister* Gregor Werner was seriously ill and the promise that Haydn would assume the duties of full *Kapellmeister* would shortly be fulfilled. His master, Prince Nicolaus, had provided him with the responsibilities and the facilities that allowed his music to gain in assurance, craft and flair; the building of the summer palace at Eszterháza with its two opera houses (one for marionette operas) was well under way and doubtless Haydn was eagerly anticipating the challenges that the new facilities would provide.[52]

Haydn may not have viewed these forthcoming challenges without some apprehension and already in 1765 he may have been preparing himself. His study of C. P. E. Bach's *Versuch* at this time influenced both his keyboard music and his church music (as witnessed by the notational features discussed above). The challenge of writing church music also led Haydn to other studies as has been demonstrated by the discovery of the autograph manuscript of the *stile antico* 'Missa sunt bona mixta malis' (dated autograph 1768) and by David Wyn Jones's commentary on this unusual work.[53] The compositional discipline which Haydn imposed on himself in this work is unprecedented in the earlier Haydn canon, but it is wholly understandable at this time. Recent research by Elaine Sisman has suggested that Haydn's activities as a composer for the theatre may be related to his symphonic music. She suggests that 'one of the principal forces for change in Haydn's style of the later 1760s and 1770s was his involvement with theater music of all kinds, an involvement that had begun in the 1750s with his association with Kurz-Bernadon in Vienna, grew steadily during the 1760s, became even more significant with the construction of Eszterháza, and finally came to fruition with Haydn's new position as music director of various theatrical companies from 1769'.[54] As the old orthodoxies about Sturm und Drang lose their former attraction, what seems to be emerging is a picture of the extensive stylistic revision which Haydn undertook beginning *c.*1766. This stylistic revision, which was the most wide-ranging and perhaps the only fundamental revision in Haydn's career,[55] was not

[52] H. C. R. Landon and D. W. Jones, *Haydn: His Life and Music*, 93.

[53] Ibid. 140–4 and D. W. Jones, 'Haydn's Missa "Sunt bona mixta malis" and the Austrian *a cappella* Tradition', paper read at the International Conference on Music in Austria, 1750–1800, Cardiff, July 1991.

[54] 'Haydn's Theater Symphonies', *JAMS* 43/2 (Summer 1990): 340.

[55] I agree wholeheartedly with Webster that the style change of 1765–6 is the only one 'marked by fundamental changes both externally and internally' (Webster, *Farewell*, 360). By comparison with the style change at this time the widely accepted view of the emergence of a Classical style in Haydn's music in 1780 seems poorly defined.

the product of a European *Zeitgeist*, but a response to the new challenges of his employment. The many remarkable works which
Haydn produced in roughly a decade from 1766 are a product of the
cross-fertilization of stylistic *données* in various genres. While Haydn's
study of C. P. E. Bach impinged on his church music as well as on
his instrumental music, equally his compositions for church and
theatre influenced his instrumental music in ways which Haydn
scholars have only begun to investigate in detail. It is because of this
cross-fertilization of genres that it is unwise to attribute too much to
the influence of C. P. E. Bach. This point may be illustrated with
reference to Haydn's dramatic use of unison themes which is such a
striking feature of his music from the 1760s and 1770s, frequently
observed in Haydn's symphonies and regarded by Landon and others
as a characteristic of Haydn's Sturm und Drang works.[56] Sisman frequently refers to such themes in her discussion of the 'reciprocal relationship' between Haydn's symphonic music and music for the
theatre,[57] but similar textures are prominent in Haydn's church music
and non-symphonic instrumental music. As mentioned above, C. P.
E. Bach's discussion of *unisono* textures is the most detailed eighteenth-century account, so that this feature may arise in Haydn's
instrumental music from a number of sources; from the theatre, the
church, Haydn's study of Bach, or more likely a combination of
these. What seems clear is that Larsen's claim that Sturm und Drang
characteristics should be understood in a purely musical framework is
correct,[58] even if it is difficult to untangle the contributions of each
of the three main impetuses for stylistic change (the Church,
C. P. E. Bach, and, somewhat later, the theatre).

If C. P. E. Bach's *Versuch* is but one of a number of influences
which contributed to Haydn's stylistic revision of the mid-1760s, its
position in relation to questions of performance practice is more central. Kirkpatrick described the *Versuch* as follows: 'Its codification and
nomenclature of ornaments is the clearest of any 18th-century
treatise, and . . . its codification and exposition of the elements of

---

[56] Landon, *Haydn: Chronicle and Works*, ii. 266–84, esp. 273.

[57] 'Haydn's Theater Symphonies', 315 ff.

[58] See 'Der Stilwandel in der österreichischen Musik zwischen Barock und Wiener
Klassik', in *Der junge Haydn*, 18–29, trans. U. Kramer as 'The Style Change in Austrian
Music between the Baroque and Viennese Classicism' in J. P. Larsen, *Handel, Haydn & the
Viennese Classical Style* (Ann Arbor: UMI, 1988), 301–13, esp. 311–12. See also J. P. Larsen
and G. Feder, *The New Grove Haydn* (London: Macmillan, 1982), 28–31.

thoroughbass is unsurpassed.'[59] From its publication the *Versuch* had, for the reasons stated by Kirkpatrick, exerted an enormous influence on performance practice. It was reprinted a number of times in the eighteenth century and it influenced Marpurg's *Anleitung*, Agricola's German translation of Tosi, Türk's *Klavierschule*, and is cited in Koch's *Lexicon* and by numerous other German authors in the eighteenth century. The reference from E. W. Wolf, cited above, testifies to the continuing importance of Bach's *magnum opus* in 1785, and if it also marked the incipient decline of the *Versuch*'s influence, even in the nineteenth century its influence did not wane completely: Czerny studied the *Versuch* in his lessons with Beethoven[60] and a new, albeit corrupt, edition of the *Versuch* appeared in the nineteenth century. It is not surprising then that the early modern researchers on perfor-mance drew heavily on Bach's teachings, particularly Dolmetsch on ornamentation and Arnold on figured bass. In retrospect early twen-tieth-century writers can be seen to have been overreliant on Bach's teachings, and the impression was sometimes given of a common practice in performance in the seventeenth and eighteenth centuries, largely identical with Bach's teachings, which cannot now be sus-tained. In the past twenty-five years a rather more diversified view of performance practice has emerged. Kirkpatrick can now be seen to have relied too heavily on Bach's teachings (as filtered through Agricola) in his study of Scarlatti, and in an interesting reappraisal of Bach's *Versuch* in 1976 Kirkpatrick commented that 'it has been more convenient than accurate to use Philipp Emanuel Bach as a source book for J. S. Bach' and that 'the distance of Philipp Emanuel Bach from the French style is much greater than I had recalled'.[61] The strongest reaction to the undoubted overuse of Bach and his follow-ers as a source of information on performance practice is found in the writings of Frederick Neumann:

The German synthesis of the 'essential' ornaments produced what could be called the first distinctly German school of ornamentation. Its headquarters was the Berlin of C. P. E. Bach, Marpurg, and Agricola, and—to a much lesser degree—of Quantz. Possibly influenced by the *genius loci* of Prussian militarism, these authors tried to regiment ornamentation into far more definite patterns than had ever before been envisioned . . .

[59] 'C. P. E. Bach's *Versuch* Reconsidered', *EM* 4/4 (Oct. 1976): 387.
[60] Czerny, *On the Proper Performance of all Beethoven's Works for the Piano*, ed. P. Badura-Skoda, 5.
[61] 'C. P. E. Bach's *Versuch* Reconsidered', 389.

these principles enjoyed their greatest triumph two hundred years later when modern researchers elevated them to a basic law for the whole 18th century, subjecting to their jurisdiction the masters of the late baroque along with those of the classical era for all the countries of Europe.[62]

Neumann has, of course, been the central figure in establishing a truer picture of the diversity of seventeenth- and eighteenth-century performance practices and his reaction to the influence of Bach's *Versuch*, in particular, on modern writers has been a necessary corrective. Yet, in view of the seminal importance of the *Versuch* in the theoretical writings of the second half of the eighteenth century and taking into account the strong connection between Haydn and C. P. E. Bach some degree of rehabilitation seems appropriate for the *Versuch*. Its teachings cannot be projected into the past as a canonical authority on Baroque performance practices, and its relevance to problems of interpretation in the music of J. S. Bach should not be assumed uncritically, but its sphere of influence in the second half of the eighteenth century cannot be denied. In the second half of the eighteenth century writers on performance practice disagree on many central questions, and the clarity and authority with which Bach presents his viewpoint should not blind us to the alternatives. The teachings of the *Versuch* are not, however, an isolated, 'militaristic' phenomenon which can be confined geographically to Berlin, nor temporally to the 1750s. The *Versuch* informs us in the first instance about C. P. E. Bach's own performance practice. It also has a special relevance to matters of performance practice pertaining to those composers known to have been influenced by C. P. E. Bach's music and/or his *Versuch*, chief among whom we must count, for the reasons outlined above, Joseph Haydn.

---

[62] *Ornamentation in Baroque and Post-Baroque Music: With Special Emphasis on J. S. Bach* (Princeton: Princeton University Press, 1978), 39–40.

6

Trill Types

◊

INTRODUCTION

As is the case with regard to many other aspects of performance practice, the most comprehensive commentaries on the notation and
interpretation of the trill are to be found in C. P. E. Bach's *Versuch*
and subsequently in treatises which were strongly influenced by
Bach's *magnum opus*, chief among which we must count the treatises
of Marpurg, Agricola, and Türk. Although it cannot be claimed that
Haydn's attitude to performance practice agreed with Bach's in every
detail, nevertheless a documentary link between Haydn and two
North German treatises, Bach's *Versuch* and Marpurg's *Anleitung zum
Clavierspielen*,[1] is established. For this reason the treatises of Bach and
his followers constitute a central source of information for the
present discussion, and Neumann's view of these sources as a local,
'militaristic' phenomenon in performance practice must be rejected
for the reasons stated in Chapter 5.

The ubiquitous question concerning the trill in modern writings
on performance practice is, of course, whether an upper-auxiliary or
main-note trill is appropriate. North German treatises present a uniform attitude to the question, consistently advocating an upper-
auxiliary start. Concerning ornaments in general Bach states that 'the
other voices including the bass [i.e. those voices not containing the
ornament] must be struck with the initial tone of an embellishment'
and specifically in connection with the trill he states that 'Since it
always begins on the tone above the principal note, it is superfluous
to add a small note . . . unless this note stands for an appoggiatura.'[2]

---

[1] Regarding Marpurg's *Anleitung*, which was listed in the catalogue of books in Haydn's
library, see H. C. R. Landon, *Haydn: Chronicle and Works*, v. 314–16.

[2] *Versuch*, trans. Mitchell, 85, 100.

Marpurg also states categorically that the trill begins with the upper auxiliary (*note accidentelle*),[3] while Türk comments that 'Every common trill is usually begun with the auxiliary note . . ., and consequently the execution in b [i.e. a main-note trill] is incorrect.'[4] Some qualifications of this general rule within the corpus of North German theory will be discussed below, but in general the concept of an upper-auxiliary trill, commencing on the beat, may be viewed as central to the North German tradition. This is also the basic description of the trill found in many other eighteenth-century treatises which are not discussed here, since they add nothing to the more thorough expositions found in North German treatises and cannot be linked specifically with Haydn's music. The treatises, a small number dating from the mid-eighteenth century and a more unified group dating from the early nineteenth century, which advocate or appear to advocate the main-note trill, are discussed in the concluding section of this chapter, but since the overwhelming majority of eighteenth-century sources favour an upper-auxiliary trill and since the North German treatises can be linked by documentation to Haydn, the upper-auxiliary trill is taken as a putative theoretical norm, however frequently it may need to be qualified in practice.

NORTH GERMAN THEORY

The interpretation of the various trill types illustrated in the ornament tables which accompanied publications of French keyboard music in the eighteenth century has, in relatively recent writings, become a matter of some dispute.[5] While this is not of direct relevance to the present discussion, it is noteworthy that the notation and classification of trills found in North German theory derives from a fairly literal interpretation of these ornament tables. Some species of trill take on new characteristics and their contextual associations are significantly different, at least in the case of some authors, from those in the earlier French style. Nevertheless, the descriptions of the trill in the writings of C. P. E. Bach and his followers can clearly be seen

---

[3] 'Le battement commence par la *note accidentelle* [emphasis original]' (*Principes*, 66).

[4] *Klavierschule*, trans. Haggh, 249.

[5] Cf. F. Neumann, 'Misconceptions about the French Trill in the 17th and 18th Centuries', *MQ* 50/2 (Apr. 1964): 188–206; and M. Collins, 'In Defense of the French Trill', *JAMS* 26/3 (Fall 1973): 405–39.

to derive from the typically French penchant for precision in distinguishing the various trill types by specific ornament symbols (a tendency which is perhaps seen in its most extreme form in the complex ornament table of D'Anglebert[6] and the notation of Bach's *Versuch*). In this regard the French-North German notation is strikingly different from the common notation of the second half of the eighteenth century where few symbols are used and ornamentation is to a large extent dependent on the judgement of the performer, a characteristic which derives from an earlier Italian tradition of ornamentation. The French influence on C. P. E. Bach undoubtedly derives from his own familiarity with French keyboard music as well as through his studies with J. S. Bach, whose ornament table, or *Explicatio*, derives directly from the ornament table of D'Anglebert. In the *Versuch* C. P. E. Bach comments on the 'painstaking accuracy' with which the French notate their music and bemoans the current neglect of precise notation (quoted in Chapter 5). Marpurg also had direct experience of the French *clavecin* tradition, since he spent some years in Paris and one of his treatises, *Principes du clavecin*, is particularly French in orientation. Other authors probably owed more to the treatise of C. P. E. Bach than to a personal acquaintance with French keyboard music.

North German treatises commonly distinguish four trill types: the common trill (with and without *Nachschlag* or suffix), the trill from below (the *Triller von unten*), the trill from above (the *Triller von oben*) and the short- or half-trill (the *halbe* or *Prall-Triller*, or simply *Praller*).

The Common Trill

Exx. 6.1–6.3, illustrate standard realizations of the 'common trill' as found in the North German tradition (Ex. 6.1 shows the common trill without *Nachschlag*, Ex. 6.2 the common trill with *Nachschlag* (both as realized by Bach), and Ex. 6.3 the 'adjoining trill' (*Angeschlossene Triller*) as illustrated by Türk, which in Marpurg's terminology is equivalent to the *tremblement appuyé* and *tremblement lié*).[7] Bach and Marpurg use the chevron symbol as their basic indication of this trill, while listing the following alternative symbols also in

---

[6] J. H. D'Anglebert, *Pièces de clavecin* (Paris, 1689; facsimile repr., New York: Broude Brothers, 1965).

[7] The common trill is discussed in Bach, *Versuch*, trans. Mitchell, 100–7; Marpurg, *Principes*, 66–9; Türk, *Klavierschule*, trans. Haggh, 245–58.

current use: $\boldsymbol{tr}$ (preferred by Türk and in keyboard music generally from the second half of the eighteenth century) and + (which Marpurg regards as more typical of music for flute or violin and which, for keyboard music of the second half of the eighteenth century, may be regarded as decidedly old-fashioned). *Nachschläge* are indicated by Bach as semiquavers or demisemiquavers in large notes, while the symbol ∿ is advised against (by Marpurg and Türk as well as Bach) because of the possibility of confusion with the mordent sign. However, Marpurg and Türk also give two other methods of indicating the *Nachschlag*, namely by appending two small notes to the trill and by the symbol ∿, both of which will be seen to be of relevance to Haydn's music. Also of relevance to Haydn's music is Bach's statement, echoed by Türk, that 'Since it [the trill] always begins on the tone above the principal note, it is superfluous to add a small note (*d*) [i.e. Ex. 6.1*d*] unless this note stands for an appoggiatura'.[8] A number of composers, including J. C. Bach, Müthel, and occasionally W. F. Bach, prefix trills by seemingly redundant small notes, in the manner illustrated but cautioned against by Türk. It will be seen that when an appoggiatura, a tone or semitone above the principal note, appears before a trill in Haydn's music, it is almost invariably intended as a long appoggiatura.

Within the category of common trills a basic distinction must be made between those trills which commence *ex abrupto* with the repercussions of the trill *per se*, beginning with the upper auxiliary,

Ex. 6.1. C. P. E. Bach, *Versuch*, table IV, fig. xxiii

Ex. 6.2. C. P. E. Bach, *Versuch*, trans. Mitchell, p.101, fig. 92

Ex. 6.3. Türk, *Klavierschule*, trans. Haggh, p. 250

---

[8] Bach, *Versuch*, trans. Mitchell, 100; Türk, *Klavierschule*, trans. Haggh, 249–50.

and the *Angeschlossene Triller* or adjoining trill, which proceeds legato from a prolonged upper auxiliary to the repercussions of the trill. Türk's illustration of the *Angeschlossene Triller* (Ex. 6.3) is accompanied by the following comment: 'These are the adjoining trills . . . where after an appoggiatura (*a*) or after a slurred note (*c*) the first note of a trill is tied.'[9] North German theorists, apart from Marpurg,[10] viewed the *Ansgeschlossene Triller* as a single type, whether the tied note is a consequence of a prolonged appoggiatura or a legato connection to a preceding note a step higher which is not necessarily an appoggiatura; and, indeed, the performance of the trill is the same in each case, regardless of the nature of the prolonged note. A tied upper-auxiliary note is commonly advocated for the start of the trill *per se* (rather than a main-note start), but, as will be seen with regard to the interpretation of the *Praller*, where the same question arises, this should not be seen as an immutable rule. In practice a tied upper-auxiliary start to the trill will be more or less effective depending on context, and the main-note trill is a valid alternative in contexts associated with the *Angeschlossene Triller*.[11] The choice between the tied upper-auxiliary trill and the main-note trill is a matter of taste in such circumstances and, rather than being regarded as subject to dogmatic prescription, is more realistically viewed as a matter of articulation.

When legato is either notated specifically or is implicit in such a context, the presence or absence of the tied note should be decided in much the same way as one selects a legato or over-legato touch, since the tied note is in reality a manifestation of over-legato in the realization of the trill. The tied note, the means of achieving an over-legato in this context, is perhaps of greatest relevance to the interpretation of the *Praller*, but with regard to both the *Praller* and the

---

[9] Türk, *Klavierschule*, trans. Haggh, 250.

[10] Marpurg's *Principes du clavecin* (p. 68; cf. id., *Anleitung*, 56–7) follows French ornament tables closely in maintaining a distinction, not found in Bach or Türk, between a *tremblement lié* and a *tremblement appuyé*. Bach and Türk group them both together as *Angeschlossene Triller*. Marpurg is also alone in giving the specifically French symbol for the *tremblement appuyé* (⌇⌇): Bach and Türk notate the same ornament by placing an appoggiatura, written as a small note, before the trilled main note. On the relationship between the *tremblement lié* and the *tremblement appuyé* in the French *clavecin* tradition see Collins, 'Defense', 409–10.

[11] Neumann correctly points out that the tied note will be inaudible 'in the absence of a rhythmical support in another voice', but he overstates this point by arguing that the tied note of the *tremblement lié* is merely part of a conventional representation of this ornament which will theoretically 'satisfy the eye on paper as to the dutiful conformance with the "rule" [i.e. the rule that trills begin with the upper auxiliary], but it will disorient the ear by rendering the rhythm unintelligible' (Neumann, 'Misconceptions', 200).

Angeschlossene Triller the tied note should be viewed as a distinct and very often a particularly expressive possibility which may, however, for various reasons and in certain contexts become redundant and therefore be omitted. On the other hand, Marpurg places alongside his illustration of the *tremblement lié* an illustration of the *tremblement detaché* (see Ex. 6.4), an important cautionary reminder that legato is not necessarily implied in connection with every trill preceded by a note a second higher.

Ex. 6.4. Marpurg, *Principes du clavecin*, table IV, figs. 30 and 31

In the sections of their treatises devoted to the common trill North German theorists also consider the problem of when it is appropriate to end a trill with a *Nachschlag*, a problem which is also relevant to the *Triller von unten* and the *Triller von oben*. The contexts listed in which the *Nachschlag* is appropriate are so varied and numerous that it is reasonable to conclude that the inclusion of a *Nachschlag* is the norm.[12] For this reason it is perhaps of greater importance to note the contexts in which the *Nachschlag* is deemed to be inappropriate. C. P. E. Bach lists these as follows:

The unsuffixed trill is best used in descending succession (Figure 96, Example *a*) [see Ex. 6.5] and principally over short notes (*b*). The suffix is omitted from successive trills (*c*) and from trills followed by one or more short notes which are capable of replacing it (*d*). If this substitution is made, the asterisked example must not be played in the slowest tempo. Further, the suffix is not employed over triplets (*e*). It is always omitted from the last of those in Example *e*, although it may be introduced into the first three, but only in very slow tempos.[13]

It is, however, generally recognized by theorists that it is largely a matter of taste whether or not to include a *Nachschlag* and that rules cannot adequately prescribe solutions for every context. Bach in fact

---

[12] Bach, *Versuch*, trans. Mitchell, 103–5; Türk, *Klavierschule*, trans. Haggh, 251–8.
[13] *Versuch*, trans. Mitchell, 104–5.

Ex. 6.5. C. P. E. Bach, *Versuch*, trans. Mitchell, p. 104, fig. 96

comments that his discussion of the subject is for 'the benefit of beginners' and concludes that 'The average ear can always tell whether the suffix should be used.'[14]

The Triller von unten

This trill is notated by C. P. E. Bach, Marpurg, and Türk with a similar symbol to that used by D'Anglebert, J. S. Bach, and many other French or French-influenced composers. In his *Versuch* C. P. E. Bach gives the standard realization and appends two other methods of notating the same ornament, commenting that 'Because, aside from the keyboard, this symbol is not widely known, it is often notated in the manner of the asterisked examples; or the general abbreviation *tr.* is written, the choice of trill being left to the discretion of the performer'[15] (see Ex. 6.6). Türk gives these and other methods of notating the *Triller von unten* (see Ex. 6.7) and while he regards (*a*) and (*b*) as acceptable, the notation of (*c*), (*d*), and (*e*) are considered misleading.[16] It should, however, be noted that the representations of the *Triller von unten* illustrated in particular in (*b*) and (*d*) were widely used in contemporary keyboard music, and that these are synonymous with the symbol ᴄᴍ. In addition, in much music dating from the second half of the eighteenth century no specific symbol for the *Triller von unten* is employed, but, in the appropriate context, this trill type should be understood where the generic symbol *tr* occurs. It is generally acknowledged that the *Triller von unten* should be

---

[14] *Versuch*, 105.   [15] Ibid. 107.   [16] *Klavierschule*, trans. Haggh, 258–60.

Ex. 6.6. C. P. E. Bach, *Versuch*, trans. Mitchell, p. 107, fig. 102

Ex. 6.7. Türk, *Klavierschule*, trans. Haggh, p. 259

concluded with a *Nachschlag*, and for this reason Türk regards the notation of the *Nachschlag*, whether as in (*f*) or (*g*), as virtually superfluous.[17]

The contexts in which a *Triller von unten* may be used are relatively restricted, since the ornament 'can generally take place only on long notes',[18] the reason being simply the large number of notes, including a prefix and suffix, of which the trill is composed by comparison with most other ornaments. This type of trill is, however, characteristically used after cadenzas and embellished *fermatas*, and at prominent cadences which require a trill on a relatively long note.[19] These usages are discussed further specifically in connection with Haydn's keyboard music, together with a variant of the *Triller von unten* not codified in treatises and which Haydn employs in these same contexts.

The Triller von oben

Like the *Triller von unten* this trill is indicated in North German treatises by a symbol derived from French ornament tables. In his *Versuch* (see Ex. 6.8) Bach illustrates this symbol, the realization of the ornament, and the alternative notation by which 'Apart from the keyboard it is occasionally notated.'[20] Because of the large number of notes in this type of trill it is, like the *Triller von unten*, restricted in use to long notes and it too is 'ended even without indication by a termination [*Nachschlag*]'.[21] According to Türk the *Triller von oben* is reserved for long notes, in particular 'the penultimate note of a cadence after the skip of a third (*a*); it may also be utilized for a

---

[17] Ibid. 258.
[19] Ibid. 259–60; Bach, *Versuch*, trans. Mitchell, 107–9.
[21] Türk, *Klavierschule*, trans. Haggh, 260.

[18] Ibid. 259.
[20] Trans. Mitchell, 109.

Ex. 6.8. C. P. E. Bach, *Versuch*, trans. Mitchell, p. 109, fig. 109

descending second (*d*) or above a repeated note (*e*)' (see Ex. 6.9).[22] Noteworthy, however, is Bach's comment that while 'In earlier times it was used widely,'[23] in contemporary music its occurrence is much more restricted. This comment can in fact be seen to be true of much keyboard music from the second half of the eighteenth century: the symbol ᴄᴡ is rarely found and the alternative notation in Ex. 6.8 is also a rare occurrence. If the *Triller von oben* was used it was largely an improvised embellishment (probably on long notes at cadenzas, embellished *fermatas*, and other prominent cadences) deriving from the performer, rather than expressed by any specific notation deriving from the composer. However, a relatively common variant of the *Triller von oben*, in which the prefix anticipates the beat, is of interest. It is illustrated by Türk (see Ex. 6.9) and described as follows:

Ex. 6.9. Türk, *Klavierschule*, trans. Haggh, p. 261

The not unusual arrangement of note values in *c*, in place of the more correct realization in *b*, appears to have originated from the so-called Lombardic style, in which the appoggiaturas are usually changed to terminations.[24]

A variant of the *Triller von oben* which involves anticipation of this kind will be discussed further below.

---

[22] *Klavierschule*, 260.   [23] *Versuch*, trans. Mitchell, 109.
[24] *Klavierschule*, trans. Haggh, 261.

The Praller

The ornament known variously as the *Praller*, the *Prall-Triller*, or the *halbe Triller* has a complicated history with attendant confusion over notation and terminology. In North German treatises it is notated by the chevron symbol (distinctively shorter than the chevron symbol used in notating the common trill) and is realized in illustrations as a four-note trill, usually, because of the contexts associated with it, with the first upper auxiliary tied to the preceding note (see Ex. 6.10). To C. P. E. Bach it is one of the most important ornaments:

Ex. 6.10. C. P. E. Bach, *Versuch*, trans. Mitchell, p. 111, fig. 115

The short trill adds life and brilliance to a performance. It is possible, when necessary, to omit any other ornament, even the other trills, and arrange matters so that easier ornaments may be substituted for them. But without the short trill no one can play successfully. Even if all other ornaments were correctly performed, no one could be happy in the absence of this one.[25]

Bach states that the *Praller* occurs 'only in a descending second regardless of whether the interval is formed by an appoggiatura or by large notes'.[26] The ornament is particularly associated with the resolution of appoggiaturas at cadences, especially if the cadence is prolonged by a *fermata* (see Ex. 6.10c) and, again according to Bach, 'In addition to its employment at cadences and *fermate* it is found in descending passages of three or more tones' (see Ex. 6.11).[27] Although these illustrations represent perhaps the most characteristic usages of the *Praller* (the first and third illustrations in Ex. 6.11 are in fact *loci classici* which will be discussed further below), Bach's statement that this four-note trill is 'only' used to ornament the second note of a descending second interval is disputed by some theorists and manifestly contradicted in practice. Türk, for instance, qualifies Bach's precept in the following way:

Although the short trill (as Agricola and Bach teach) should never occur unless it is preceded by a note a second higher, it [the preceding note] may

[25] *Versuch*, trans. Mitchell, 111.   [26] Ibid. 111.   [27] Ibid. 112.

Ex. 6.11. C. P. E. Bach, *Versuch*, table IV, fig. xlviii

be written as a note of usual size (*a*) or as a small note (*b*); nevertheless, even the best composers at times allow themselves one exception or another in this regard, as in the examples *c*, *d*, and *e*.[28] [see Ex. 6.12]

Ex. 6.12. Türk, *Klavierschule*, trans. Haggh, p. 263

Many composers use the *Praller* in these and other contexts where it is not preceded by a note a second higher. Although Haydn's most frequent use of the *Praller* is in the contexts preferred by Bach, he does, however, use the *Praller* in contexts where a tied upper auxiliary is impossible.

   It should be noted that many composers do not use the chevron symbol to indicate either the common trill or the *Praller* and in these cases the latter ornament must be recognized as appropriate from the context alone. P. and E. Badura-Skoda have pointed out, for instance, that in the sources for Mozart's works the chevron symbol rarely occurs and 'Thus one has to tell, from the particular trill concerned, whether it is an ordinary trill or a half-shake [*Praller*].'[29] The more complicated situation with regard to Haydn's works is discussed below.

   There is a large amount of evidence, both documentary and internal, which suggests that in certain contexts the four-note *Praller* was transmuted into a three-note ornament in a process analogous to the

[28] *Klavierschule*, trans. Haggh, 263.   [29] *Interpreting Mozart*, 123.

elision of vowels in language. Marpurg, in *Principes du clavecin*, illus-trated the *loci classici* referred to above in connection with Ex. 6.11, but the realizations he gives are unambiguous in their omission of a tied upper auxiliary in favour of a three-note form of *Praller*. He explains the reasons for these realizations in some detail:

When in the *tremblement lié* one passes the tied note and immediately begins the beating [of the trill] with the main note, contrary to the rule for the trill, and one then cuts short the beating [*battement*] reducing it to three notes, it is thus that one in truth is making an imperfect trill [*tremblement imparfait*], but which nevertheless in certain cases is a better usage than the normal and perfect trill. Such is the case (a) in a conjunct progression of notes, when the tempo is a little fast, Table V, figure 1 and (b) when a short note [*petite note*] is preceded by a long appoggiatura, figures 2 & 3. When one employs this imperfect trill at a *fermata*, after a long appoggiatura, one should not play the last note except to release it immediately, detaching it. See figure 4. Table V.[30] [Marpurg's table V, figures 1–4 is reproduced as Ex. 6.13].

Bach seems in fact to be somewhat exceptional in his insistence that the *Praller* always retains a four-note format with a tied first note.[31] It is also interesting that in J. C. F. Bach's ornament table, which accompanied his first book of *Musikalische Nebenstunden* in 1787 and which agrees in almost all respects with C. P. E. Bach's *Versuch*, the illustrations of *Praller* contain both four- and three-note forms (see Ex. 6.14). Türk, who rarely departs from the teachings of Bach, also introduces a qualification of Bach's practice with regard to the pas-sages quoted in Ex. 6.12, concerning which he comments that

---

[30] 'Quand dans le tremblement lié on passe la note liée & que l'on commence tout de suite le battement avec la note essentielle, contre la règle du tremblement, qu'on abrége ensuite le battement & qu'on le *reduit à trois notes*, c'est alors que l'on fait à la vérité un trem-blement imparfait, mais qui néanmoins dans de certains cas est d'un meilleur usage que le tremblement régulier & parfait. Ces cas existent (a) dans une progression de notes par dégrés conjoints, quand le mouvement en est un peu vif, Tab.V. fig.1. & (b) quand une petite note est précedée d'un port de voix long, fig.2. & 3. Quand on emploie ce tremblement impar-fait dans une *Fermate*, après un port de voix long, il ne faut toucher la dernière note que pour la lâcher aussitôt en la détachant. Voyez la fig. 4. Tab.V.' (*Principes*, 68.)

[31] The English ornament tables of Hook and Miller distinguish, for example, between the normal trill or shake and a three-note ornament, equivalent to the three-note form of the *Praller* as described by Marpurg, which is termed a 'transient shake': it is interesting that in the case of Miller's ornament table a four-note ornament is preferred in connection with movement in quavers but the three-note transient shake is advocated where the movement is in semiquavers—analogous to Marpurg's realization 'quand le mouvement en est un peu vif'. See E. Miller, *Institutes of Music* and J. Hook, *Guida di Musica: Being a Complete Book of Instructions for Beginners on the Harpsichord or Pianoforte, Op. 37.* (London, [*c*.1785]).

Ex. 6.13. Marpurg, *Principes du clavecin*, table V, figs. 1–4

Effectus

Effectus   Pro

Effectus

Ex. 6.14. J. C. F. Bach, *Musikalische Nebenstunden*

One can see that in examples *c*, *d*, and *e*, which I have borrowed from the works of Bach, C. W. Wolf, and others, the *Pralltriller* has been interchanged with the . . . *Schneller*. How great a crime this may be I will leave to the critics to decide.[32]

Türk is therefore advocating for these passages the three-note form of the *Praller* as used by Marpurg (Marpurg's *tremblement imparfait*) and others, but his comments give rise to problems of terminology, since he identified this usage with the ornament which Bach called a

---

[32] *Klavierschule* (facsimile edn.), 274.

Schneller, but for which Bach had a different notation, namely three small notes rather than the chevron symbol.[33] Bach sometimes uses the three-note *Schneller* in contexts similar to those associated by other authors with the three-note form of the *Praller* (see Ex. 6.15), but with Bach the three-note ornament always has a particular notation distinct from the chevron, so that the latter is invariably in Bach a four-note ornament. Few composers adopted Bach's notational distinction (i.e. the chevron for the four-note *Praller* with tied upper auxiliary, and three small notes for the three-note *Schneller*—as in Ex. 6.15), but some theorists adopt either the term *Schneller*, a term apparently invented by Bach, the term 'inverted mordent', or some other term (such as *pincé reversé* which may be translated as 'inverted mordent'), to distinguish between the three- and four-note versions of the *Praller*, both of which were commonly notated by a single symbol, usually the chevron or *tr* symbol. The confusion is increased in the late eighteenth and early nineteenth centuries since the term 'mordent' is then sometimes used to refer to the three-note form of *Praller* (the eighteenth-century mordent proper disappeared from general use in the nineteenth century). Hummel, for instance, referred to the 'Mordente or transient shake' for the three-note form of *Praller* and, both paradoxically and unusually, used the eighteenth-century mordent symbol to indicate this ornament (⌇ or ⌇).[34] In general, however, the chevron symbol was used in the nineteenth century to mean the three-note form of *Praller*, and the four-note form, although mentioned in some treatises, disappeared from common use.

Ex. 6.15. C. P. E. Bach, H.245 (Wq.55/3)/ii

---

[33] Regarding the *Schneller* see Bach, *Versuch*, trans. Mitchell, 142–3, Türk, *Klavierschule*, trans. Haggh, 243–4.

[34] *Instructions*, III, 8. Similarly, in Fétis and Moscheles, *Méthode des méthodes de piano*, p. vi and Adam, *Méthode de piano*, 54, the short trill is referred to as a 'mordant', although unlike Hummel these authors indicate the 'mordant' by a chevron symbol.

Two forms of the *Praller* can therefore be distinguished in eighteenth-century treatises, a four-note form usually notated by the chevron or *tr* symbols, and a three-note form for which there was no generally recognized symbol or terminology to distinguish it from the four-note form. For the purpose of further discussion specifically in connection with Haydn's keyboard music the term *Praller* is used in this dual sense, while the term *Schneller* is employed only where the three-note ornament notated by three small notes is concerned.

In the treatises referred to above, the main-note trill is conspicuous by its absence. There seems, in fact, to be a resistance to the inclusion of this trill type within the North German codification of ornaments. Nevertheless, in making a distinction between trills which have a legato connection to a preceding note which is a step higher and those which do not, these writers are, in effect, describing the main contextual associations of the main-note trill and the upper-auxiliary trill. Marpurg comes the closest to admitting the main-note trill into his codification, when, in the passage quoted in full above, he describes how the tied note of the *tremblement lié*, the *Angeschlossene Triller* of Bach and Türk, may be omitted. There is surely an element of ideology involved in Marpurg's description of the main-note trill as an 'imperfect trill', but he does none the less admit that 'in certain cases [it] is a better usage than the normal and perfect trill'. Clearly, in the *Angeschlossene Triller* and the *Praller*, where the process of elision described by Marpurg is a possibility, the trill may begin with a tied upper auxiliary or with the main note. Some authors preferred (or in C. P. E. Bach's case, insisted on) the former; other authors allowed, or preferred, at least in certain cases, the latter. If the main-note trill is allowed in North German writings only, as it were, by default, in practice it is a valid alternative to beginning a trill with a tied upper auxiliary in those contexts associated with the *Angeschlossene Triller* and the *Praller*. The distinction between the two in theory is often far clearer than the difference in performance.

HAYDN'S NOTATION: CHRONOLOGICAL SURVEY

As is the case with other aspects of ornamentation, Haydn's notation of the trill, or rather of trill types, is not uniform throughout his career, but varies from loosely generic indications to a more specific use of specialized keyboard symbols. The specialized symbols which Haydn employed to notate various trill types for a decade or more from *c*.1766 are not an isolated phenomenon, but form part of a fundamental change in attitude at this period to the notation of ornaments, found in particular in the keyboard sonatas, Hob. XVI: 44–6, 18–20, and 21–6. This trend in the notation of trill types has, as mentioned in Chapter 5, important parallels in new methods of notating appoggiaturas and other ornaments adopted by Haydn in the mid-1760s, and is perhaps made particularly conspicuous by the concomitant change in style at this time. With regard to trill types, a marked contrast may be observed between the specific notation in this period and the generic use of the *tr* symbol in earlier works. In the latter, little or no attempt is made to distinguish between the various types of trill, and the *tr* symbol also serves to indicate other ornaments apart from trill types (concerning the contexts in which the *tr* symbol probably indicates a *Doppelschlag*, see Chapter 8). After the extensive experimentation in orthography in the late 1760s and 1770s, a marked simplification in the notation of ornaments, which has been commented on by Somfai,[35] is apparent from *c*.1780. In this later manner of notation the *tr* symbol is again the preferred indication for a variety of trill types although certain forms of trill, in particular the *Triller von unten*, are distinguished orthographically, although not altogether consistently. The characteristic simplification in the notation of trills in the keyboard music of the 1780s and 1790s is again paralleled by other changes in orthography which will be discussed in Chapters 8 and 9.

Table 6.1 shows the symbols employed to indicate various types of trills in the autograph manuscripts of Haydn's keyboard works. These manuscripts span the period from 1756 to 1795 and demonstrate a very clear evolution in orthography, from simple generic notation to a complex specialization of symbols and a return to relatively simple notation after 1780. Haydn's early works (before *c*.1766) are not well represented numerically, but the simple notation of Hob. XVIII: 1 and XIV: 4, where only the *tr* symbol is found, appears to be representative of those early compositions which do not survive in autograph manuscripts. A symbol for the *Triller von unten* found in Hob. XVI: 6 also occurs occasionally in non-autograph sources, but its use is so

---

[35] 'How to Read and Understand Haydn's Notation in its Chronologically Changing Concepts', in E. Badura-Skoda (ed.), *Haydn Kongress, Wien, 1982*, 23–35.

TABLE 6.1 *Trill symbols in Haydn's keyboard music, 1756–1795*

Autograph MS	Date	Trill symbols used
Hob. XVIII: 1	1756	*tr*
Hob. XVI: 6	*c.*1760	*tr* *tr*~ ♪♪ *tr*
Hob. XIV: 4	1764	*tr*
Hob. XVII: 1	1765	*tr* ∿
Hob. XIV: 5	*c.*1765/6	*tr*
Hob. XVI: 18	*c.*1766	*tr* ∿
Hob. XVI: 45	1766	*tr* *tr*~ *tr* ♪♪*tr* ∿∿ ∿
Hob. XVI: 19	1767	*tr* ∿∿ ∿
Hob. XVI: 20	1771	*tr* ∿∿ ∿
Hob. XVI: 20/ii*		*tr* ♪♪*tr* ♪♪∿∿ ♪♪∿ ∿ ∿
Hob. XVI: 21	1773	*tr* ∿ ∿
Hob. XVI: 22	1773	*tr* ∿ ∿
Hob. XVI: 23	1773	*tr* ♪♪∿ ∿∿ ∿ ∿
Hob. XVI: 26	1773	*tr* ∿
Hob. XVI: 29	1774	*tr* ∿
Hob. XV: 5	1784	*tr*
Hob. XV: 7	1785	*tr* *tr*~ ♪♪*tr*~
Hob. XV: 9	1785	*tr* *tr*~ ♪♪*tr* ∿
Hob. XVI: 49	1790	*tr* ∿ ∿(∿?)
Hob. XVII: 6	1793	*tr* ♪♪*tr*
Hob. XVI: 52	1794	*tr* *tr*~
Hob. XV: 31	1795	— — —

* not extant in autograph.
— indicates no trill symbol.

sporadic that the *tr* symbol must still be regarded as encompassing the *Triller von unten* in its semantic field. The hybrid symbol (*trw*) also found in Hob. XVI: 6, indicates that a *Nachschlag* is to be played at the end of the trill and appears to be an anticipation of the French–North German symbol (*w*) used in certain works in the 1770s; the *Nachschlag* is, however, more commonly notated in large notes, either semiquavers or demisemiquavers, or by small notes, but is indeed a general feature throughout Haydn's music whether notated specifically, by whatever means, or not. The increasing specialization in the use of trill symbols appears to have begun *c.*1765/6, when in Hob. XVII: 1 and XVI: 18 the chevron symbol often identified the *Praller* as distinct from other trill types; there is no indication of this trend, however, in the undated fragmentary autograph of Hob. XIV: 5, which is assumed to date from *c.*1765/6. The Sonata, Hob. XVI: 45 (dated autograph 1766) shows a remarkable change in Haydn's manner of notating ornaments, since not only are six different trill symbols used, but, as discussed in Chapter 7, this work is the first of Haydn's compositions to employ unambiguously the real notation of appoggiaturas. In this autograph particularly long trills, such as those lasting throughout tied notes, are identified by precise symbols and the *Triller von unten* by the symbol ♪ familiar from earlier works, as well as by the hybrid symbol *tr*. The *Praller* is indicated in specific contexts by the chevron symbol as opposed to the *tr* symbol which still, although to a lesser extent than in earlier works, retains its multi-faceted nature. In the autograph manuscripts of 1771 to 1774 the *Praller* is, in certain contexts, recognizably distinct from other trill types by the differentiation between chevron and *tr* symbols. In addition, Haydn's earlier symbols for the *Triller von unten* are replaced, for some time, by the standard North German symbol *cm* as the normal indication of this trill type in the composer's keyboard music. The process by which Haydn eventually adopted this symbol can be traced in the second movement of Hob. XVI: 20,[36] where the *Triller von unten* is used frequently but is variously notated: the earlier combination of lower appoggiatura and *tr* is replaced by the combination of lower appoggiatura and chevron and in turn by the tautologous compound ♪. The latter cannot be ascribed to the proverbial

---

[36] The primary source for the second movement of Hob. XVI: 20 is the 1st edn. of Artaria, since this movement is not extant in the autograph manuscript.

engraver's or copyist's error since it also occurs in the later autograph of Hob. XVI: 23; it represents, however, a transitory hybrid between the earlier indication and the standard North German symbol.

One of the most striking features of these works is that the specific notation is in general uncharacteristic of Viennese keyboard music. The notation of trills together with other features of orthography and style referred to below points clearly to the influence of C. P. E. Bach's music and/or his *Versuch* on Haydn from *c.*1766. It may have been at this time that Haydn's acquired Marpurg's *Anleitung zum Clavierspielen*, since a specialized symbol for the trill with *Nachschlag* (∿) is used in Hob. XVI: 23 (1773): this symbol is not mentioned by Bach in his *Versuch*, but is advocated by Marpurg.

Haydn does not, however, retain the North German manner of notation in his later works; while some vestiges of this style of notation remain in the sonatas published by Artaria as op. 30 (Hob. XVI: 35–9, 20), although with notably less consistency than in the earlier autograph sources, in general from the 1780s only two symbols for the various trill types occur, namely the *tr* symbol and the symbol for the *Triller von unten* found in earlier works by Haydn. The *tr* symbol must therefore be regarded as representing in Haydn's late works a variety of trill types, including, as will be pointed out below, the *Triller von unten* which is not always specifically identified by its own symbol. The chevron symbol becomes increasingly rare in these later works, but when it does occur in reliable, authentic sources it distinguishes the *Praller* from other trill types.

A progressively noticeable stylistic feature of Haydn's keyboard music from the 1780s is not only the simplification in the notation of trills but also the relative paucity of any indication for this ornament by comparison with earlier works: in a number of movements and even whole works from the late 1780s and the 1790s no trills whatsoever are indicated, and in those works where trills do occur they are strikingly few in number. The trend towards the use of fewer *Spielmanieren* is apparent in much keyboard music from the end of the eighteenth century and has been attributed by some authors to the influence of the fortepiano, which gradually from the 1770s ousted the harpsichord as the main keyboard instrument. However, since ornaments function stylistically and since it is dubious to associate stylistic change in Haydn's *œuvre* with his adoption of the fortepiano after 1780, it is perhaps wiser to regard the reduction in the number and variety of ornaments used in the late works as a result of internal stylistic change, which affected all genres in which Haydn wrote, rather than as a response in a single genre to a particular instrument. It is, of course, impossible to distinguish clearly cause and effect in this regard, but it is of relevance to the present discussion that the characteristic melodic-harmonic formulas associated with trills in the earlier works of Haydn become increasingly rare or almost totally absent in late works: it is the virtual abandoning of these galant cadential formulas, an element of stylistic change rather than a response to changes in keyboard technology, which leads more than any other factor to the numeric decrease in the occurrence of trills in the late keyboard works. In these late works, despite this numeric decrease and the generic manner of the notation of trills, the variety of trill types necessary in performance remains considerable.

NOTATION AND CONTEXT

More so than is the case with certain other ornaments, where a fairly direct correlation often exists between a symbol or symbols and one or more forms of the basic ornament type, the notation of the trill is generally imprecise and needs to be interpreted with some flexibility. Quite apart from matters of detail such as the speed of the trill, which by its very nature is a matter of personal taste and cannot be notated, the variety of symbols employed by Haydn, even when exercising his greatest precision, is insufficient to notate methodically all the various trill types. Thus, although a variety of symbols is employed by Haydn in the autograph manuscripts of the late 1760s and early 1770s, every type of trill is not necessarily always distinguished by a specific symbol, nor do the symbols which are employed occur with absolute consistency, so that one symbol may have more than one function. In works of this period surviving only in non-autograph sources, Haydn's specific, although by no means completely rational, notation is often corrupted in the process of transmission, justifying a further degree of flexibility on the part of the performer. In pre-1766 compositions and to a lesser extent in post-1780 works the notation of trills should be regarded not as a definite prescription of a specific ornament but as an invitation to the performer to select, often from a wide variety of possibilities, a trill type suited to the context. There is frequently a need, especially in relation to long cadential trills, to regard the *tr* symbol as an invitation to improvise a cadential formula rather than as a prescription for one particular ornament. There may in fact be more than one acceptable solution to any given situation, and context remains the best guide. The contexts appropriate to the various trill types can be determined by the information provided by theorists, as discussed above, and by an examination of those works which employ the greatest specialization in relation to trill symbols: there is, in this regard, a remarkably close agreement between North German theory and Haydn's most specific notation.

A fundamental distinction must be made in performance between adjoining trills and other types of common trill. The *locus classicus* of the adjoining trill is in the many cadential harmonic formulas, particularly associated in Haydn's keyboard music with the works written before the 1780s, in which the upper auxiliary is held and usually functions as the appoggiatura in $\frac{6-5}{4-3}$ or similar progressions on the dominant. Examples 6.16*a–d* illustrates some of the most common of these formulas in various metrical guises. The appoggiatura before the trill itself may be written as a small note or a large note,[37] but in

---

[37] Certain orthographic conventions can sometimes be discerned in relation to whether the appoggiatura is written as a large note or as a small note; for instance, in 3/4 metre when a $\frac{6-4}{5-3}$ progression occurs on the first two beats of the bar the notation is almost invariably $\frac{3}{4}$ 𝅘𝅥 𝅘𝅥 , but when it occurs on the second and third beats the notation $\frac{3}{4}$ 𝅘𝅥 𝅘𝅥 is preferred. Haydn is, however, by no means always consistent, and incidental factors often determine which method of notation is employed. In Ex. 4.4 the upper auxiliary preparation of the trill is written as a small note in bar 2, while in bar 10 where a melodic and harmonic variant of the main theme occurs it is notated by a large crotchet. In general it is true of Haydn's music that when a small note precedes a trill it should be sustained in the manner of a long appoggiatura, and that when no small note is present before a trill the repercussions of the trill itself should begin immediately without sustaining the upper auxiliary as a long appoggiatura. (This is very much in agreement with the policy stated by C. P. E. Bach and other theorists mentioned above.) The exceptions to this general practice are few, but when they occur are of two types. First, an obvious exception is when the small note is a lower auxiliary in which case a *Triller von unten* is intended and the initial note should not be sustained in the manner of a long appoggiatura. Very occasionally an upper auxiliary precedes a trill where, because of its context, a long appoggiatura preparation seems extremely unlikely. One such instance is discussed below in relation to Ex. 6.20*d*: in this instance the upper auxiliary is, unusually, present, not to indicate a long appoggiatura, but to clarify the pitch of the upper auxiliary which would otherwise be unclear. Secondly, very rarely trills may require a long appoggiatura although none is indicated. Christa Landon has pointed out two such instances in the sonatas Hob. XVI: 8 and 9, possibly among the earliest of Haydn's solo sonatas (see C. Landon, *Haydn: Sämtliche Klaviersonaten*, vol. ia, 2, 8). In bar 6 of the 1st movement of both works cadential formulas, very similar to that illustrated in Ex. 4.2, occur, but without the appoggiaturas which characterize such formulas. It is very likely that in these two instances the upper auxiliary should be held for a quaver, as suggested by Christa Landon.

both cases there is an implied legato articulation between the appoggiatura and the trilled main note which is placed on a metrically weak
beat. The performance of the trill in these cadences, where the main
note bearing the trill is preceded by an appoggiatura, whether notated
by a small note or a large note, is unproblematic. In all such instances
an adjoining trill is required and the repetition of the upper auxiliary
at the commencement of the trill (as for instance) is
inappropriate since such repetition is not compatible with the necessary legato articulation. Two realizations of the adjoining trill are
possible: or . The decision to include or
exclude the tied upper auxiliary is a matter of taste. In fast tempos its
inclusion is often not feasible, or, if feasible, scarcely audible, but at
more moderate tempos the inclusion of the *lié* effect can provide a
particularly expressive option in performance. It is particularly suited
to many of the formulas illustrated in Ex. 6.16 since the bass articulates the beat over which the tied note is audible and provides an
expressive rhythmic subtlety. The inclusion of a *Nachschlag* at the end
of the trills in these cadence figures (and generally where the trilled
note is followed by a stepwise ascent or descent) was considered *de
rigueur*, and, indeed, Haydn sometimes specifically requires a
Nachschlag in these contexts by using more specific notation (cf. Ex.
4.2, bar 6 and 2.13, bar 3). When the less precise *tr* symbol is used, as
in Ex. 6.16, a *Nachschlag* may, nevertheless, generally be considered
appropriate to these contexts. Türk commented that 'Especially for a
cadential trill . . . one would forego a termination [*Nachschlag*] only
reluctantly.'[38]

When a similar melodic context occurs (i.e. conjunct motion, with
the note bearing the trill on a relatively unaccented beat) but the
upper note preceding the trill is not an appoggiatura, a legato interpretation may be appropriate. In bar 1 of Ex. 6.17*a*, for instance, the
bass changes from tonic to dominant between the third and fourth
beats of the bar, but the articulation in the right hand is in all proba-
bility meant to be legato, prompting an interpretation of the trill
which begins with the main note, or with a tied upper auxiliary (the
first violin part has the same notes as the right hand of the keyboard
part and here a slur joins the notes *g″* and *f″*). It must be remembered,
however, that not every conjunct melodic progression is necessarily

---

[38] *Klavierschule*, trans. Haggh, 256.

Ex. 6.16(*a*) Hob. XVI: 8/ii, (*b*) Hob. XVI: 8/ii, (*c*) Hob. XVI: 14/i, (*d*) Hob.
XVI: 14/ii

legato: bar 3 of Ex. 6.17*a*, where *f″* is actually part of an appoggiatura
chord, but is separated from its note of resolution by a quaver rest, is
a cautionary reminder. In Ex. 6.17*b*, bar 42, the selection of the trill
type is dependent on the decision about the articulation of the
passage. If one plays the conjunct motion of the right-hand melody
legato, a trill beginning with a main note or a tied upper auxiliary is
entirely appropriate. However, a different articulation, for instance
slurring the first two notes of the right-hand part with a slight separation between the second and third notes, might well lead one to
choose an upper-auxiliary start to the trill on the third beat. The
decision here and in many such cases is dependent on the articulation
selected by the performer, when it is not explicitly marked by the
composer. Trills which occur in the context of conjunct motion
should often be realized as adjoining trills, but this is not necessarily
always the only, or, indeed, the most appropriate realization.

When a trill is approached from a note a step above but the trill is
on a metrically strong beat there is often little reason for regarding the
connection between the two notes as being legato, and thus employing either a main-note trill or a tied upper auxiliary. Ex. 6.18*a* is a case
in point: the trill is approached from the note above but is placed on
the strong first beat of the bar. In the absence of articulation markings to the contrary, one might well assume, as discussed in Chapter

Ex. 6.17(*a*) Hob. XIV: 11/i, (*b*) Hob. XVII: 1

2, a 'normal' pattern of articulation with a *silence d'articulation* between the third beat of bar 1 and the first beat of bar 2: repetition of the note *a'* as the upper auxiliary of the trill guarantees this articulation. The selection of this manner of articulation and the resultant placement of the dissonant upper auxiliary on the beat combine to emphasize the natural accentuation of the passage. The same is true of the passage quoted in Ex. 6.18*b*, where, in addition, the note that precedes the trill is marked staccato, making an adjoining trill impossible, suggesting the possibility of a dissonant upper-auxiliary start to the trill. There are many occasions in which the choice of articulation and the resulting choice of trill type in such contexts will remain a matter of subjective taste. The editorial fingering in C. Landon's edition of the Sonata, Hob. XVI: 23 is suggestive of legato articulation and a main-note trill in bar 19 of the second movement (see Ex. 8.18): the repetition of the note *e'* and the resultant *silence d'articulation* can, however, justifiably be seen as an effective way of articulating (especially on a harpsichord) the accentuation of the passage (i.e. with a secondary stress on the third and sixth quavers).

THE PRALLER

Until *c.*1766 the *Praller* can be identified in Haydn's music only by reference to contexts associated with this ornament in eighteenth-

Ex. 6.18(*a*) Hob. XVI: 21/ii, (*b*) Hob. XVI: 39/i

century theory; Haydn's notation for the *Praller* before this date is the same as his notation for other trill types, that is the symbol *tr*. In the Sonata, Hob. XVI: 45, however, Haydn begins to differentiate the *Praller* from other forms of the trill by using the chevron symbol. In this particular sonata the chevron is confined to one context only, the *locus classicus* of the ornament, over the second note of a descending second interval (see Ex. 6.19*a*). Haydn's usage here conforms closely to that advocated by C. P. E. Bach in that the descending seconds occurring at the end of an *Einschnitt* are ornamented by a *Praller* and notated by a chevron. The *Praller* is, of course, an essential ornament in earlier works by Haydn, usually in the other characteristic context associated with the ornament (see Ex. 6.19*b* and cf. Ex. 6.11–13), but is notated by the generic *tr* symbol. Somewhat curiously, when this latter context occurs in Hob. XVI: 45 the symbol used for the ornament is also the *tr* symbol despite the fact that, as mentioned in connection with Ex. 6.19*a*, the chevron is used elsewhere in this work to indicate the *Praller*.[39] It is extremely unlikely, however, that the nota-

[39] An extended chevron symbol (∿∿) is used in Hob. XVI: 45/i to indicate a continuous trill on a tied note and has the same meaning as the symbol *tr*∿ used elsewhere in Haydn's music. In Feder's edn. of this sonata the symbol ∿∿ is also used in the second movement, ornamenting the second note of a descending second interval. Given the context it is unlikely that an extended trill rather than a *Praller* is intended, but there is in any case a problem of palaeography concerning Feder's reading. The writing is a little unclear and it is difficult to identify precisely the number of 'turns' in the chevron. Feder's decision must be regarded as marginal and even if correct of no functional significance in this instance. C. Landon's edn. reads ∿∿ where Feder has ∿∿ .

Ex. 6.19(a) Hob. XVI: 45/ii, (b) Hob. XVI: 9/i, (c) Hob. XVI: 21/i, (d) Hob. XVI: 21/ii, (e) Hob. XVI: 21/i, (f) Hob. XVI: 31/ii

tional distinction between these two contexts implies any difference in performance.[40]

In the autograph manuscripts of the 1770s the chevron symbol is used in both of the characteristic contexts associated with the *Praller* (see Ex. 6.19*c* and *d*). The specialized use of the chevron to identify the *Praller* in the autograph manuscripts from 1766 to 1776 may sometimes be of value in the reading of other ornament signs in Haydn's keyboard works of this period: for instance, it is not unreasonable to believe that the chevron in bar 22 of Hob. xvi: 21/i indicates a *Praller*, while the *tr* symbol in bar 32 indicates a different trill form, probably in this case a longer trill with *Nachschlag* (both trills ornament the second note of a descending second interval but the important difference is that in bar 22 the chevron symbol coincides with the end of an *Einschnitt*, while in bar 32 the trill functions as part of the progression leading to the first beat of bar 33; cf. Ex. 6.19*c* and *e*).

However, even in the autograph manuscripts from the period 1766 to 1776 (which is undoubtedly the period of Haydn's greatest precision in the notation of ornaments) the graphic distinction between the chevron and the *tr* symbol cannot always be relied upon to distinguish the *Praller* from other trill forms: an exception to Haydn's very careful notation at this time is the Sonata, Hob. xvi: 26, the autograph manuscript of which displays signs of a very hasty redaction. In the first movement of this sonata the characteristic contexts associated with the *Praller* are usually carefully notated, but there are instances in which the chevron and *tr* symbols seem to be used indiscriminately.[41] Nor can the notational distinction between chevron and *tr* symbols be relied upon completely in works from this period which survive only in non-autograph sources. The *Praller* is very probably the required ornament in bar 2 of Hob. xvi: 46/i, dating from *c.*1767 (see Ex. 8.21), but the ornament is notated variously by the symbols *tr* and ∿ in the non-autograph sources. Similarly in mod-

---

[40] This notational distinction is at variance with 18th-cent. theory and with Haydn's previous and subsequent notational practices, where both contexts are associated with the same symbol, either *tr* or chevron.

[41] The haste in which the autograph manuscript was written is apparent not only in the calligraphy and inconsistent notation but also, perhaps, in the fact that the second movement of the sonata is an arrangement of the Menuet from Symphony No. 47 (1772). Since Hob. xvi: 26 is the last sonata in a set of six (the surviving autographs of other sonatas in the set are meticulous fair copies) it is a fair assumption that Haydn was under some pressure to finish Hob. xvi: 26 in order to complete the set.

ern editions of the third movement of Hob. XVI: 21 the chevron and *tr* symbols appear to be used interchangeably, but in fact the fragmentary autograph is consistent and the inconsistencies derive from the use of secondary sources for that section of the movement for which no autograph is extant.

In the set of sonatas Hob. XVI: 27–32 the distinction between chevron and *tr* symbol is often, if not always, functional, but increasingly from the mid-1770s the notational distinction between *Praller* and other trill forms apparent in earlier works becomes haphazard. In the Sonata, Hob. XVI: 29, for instance, the *tr* and chevron symbols are used interchangeably in bars 19–20 of the first movement, but in the parallel passage from bars 77–8 the chevron symbol is used consistently: in neither case is the symbol used a particularly reliable indication of idiomatic ornamentation. The third movement of this same sonata is even more inconsistent in the occurrence of these two symbols: in similar contexts the *tr* symbol is found in bars 2, 8, 22, 47, 49, 53, 65, 71, 73, 75, and 79 but the chevron is used in bars 4, 36, and 67. Much of the inconsistency may well derive from inaccuracies in the process of transmission, but it is also true that Haydn seems at this time to have begun to simplify his notation of ornaments and to abandon some of the notational conventions typical of North Germany and of his own autograph manuscripts from the period 1765 to *c.*1773 (the inconsistency referred to in Hob. XVI: 29/i derives from the extant autograph fragment dating from 1774). It may be, as suggested by Somfai,[42] that Haydn's simplification of notation was due to the fact he was writing keyboard music increasingly for publication: it is also possible that the inaccuracy of many manuscript copies and printed editions as regards performance indications discouraged Haydn from continuing to employ the wide variety of symbols in favour of a simpler generic notation less susceptible to corruption.[43] In Haydn's later music the chevron symbol becomes increasingly rare and the *Praller* must be identified very often by context alone. Contexts associated with the *Praller* are still sometimes notated with a chevron symbol (as in Hob. XVI: 49/ii, bar 50), but the more common indication in such contexts is now the *tr* symbol (as in Hob. XVI: 52/i, bar 19). As in the music dating from before 1766, in

[42] 'Notation', 25 ff.

[43] At least until 1781 Haydn still required a distinction to be made between the symbols ∞, ⌒ ⌄ , and *tr*, as is clear from his letter to Artaria dated 20 July 1781 (quoted in Ch. 8). Increasingly, however, the distinction between *tr* and ⌄ is not reflected in Haydn's music.

the late keyboard music context must be regarded as the most reliable guide to the identification of the *Praller*.

In performing the *Praller* the performer is, as has been mentioned in connection with theoretical discussion of the ornament, faced with a number of choices: in making these choices the notation is of no help. In the legato context usually associated with the ornament, in particular a legato descending second, a four-note *Praller* with a tied upper auxiliary, or a three-note *Praller*, beginning on the main note, may be used. The choice between these two forms of *Praller* is purely subjective and there can rarely be said to be a correct or incorrect interpretation. In some instances, such as that illustrated in Ex. 6.19c, a tied upper auxiliary is very effective since the rhythmic support in the bass makes the delay in the release of the upper note clearly audible. A characteristic occurrence in Haydn's works of the late 1760s and 1770s is the pattern illustrated in bar 70 of Ex. 4.4, where the delay is made explicit by the actual writing-out of the tied upper note: in this instance the further prolongation of the upper auxiliary would be pointless and the *Praller* should begin immediately on the last semiquaver of the beat with the main note.[44] In other instances, in particular where there is no rhythmic support in the bass to make a tied upper auxiliary audible, the *Praller* is also probably best played as a three-note ornament, beginning on the main note (see Ex. 6.19f).

The semiquaver patterns illustrated in Ex. 6.19b and d are also commonly associated with the three-note *Praller* (cf. Ex. 6.11, 6.13, and 6.14) and in many other semiquaver patterns, such as those illustrated in Ex. 6.20a and b, although the note bearing the *Praller* is not joined legato to a preceding note a step higher, a three-note realization beginning on the main note is none the less advisable and is sanctioned by eighteenth-century writers (cf. Türk's illustration (d) in Ex. 6.12).[45] It is also possible that the use of the three-note *Praller* should

---

[44] Türk clearly has a dislike of this unusually long prolongation of the upper auxiliary before the *Praller* (see *Klavierschule*, trans. Haggh, 262), but this usage seems to have been a particularly favourite device of Haydn's: other examples are to be found in Hob. XVI: 44/ii, XVI: 21/ii, XVI: 22/iii, and XVI: 24/i.

[45] It is worth noting that many of the contexts associated with the *Praller* are also found ornamented by short appoggiaturas. Agricola comments in his treatise that the short appoggiatura may be used as an alternative to the *Praller* when a fast tempo makes the latter difficult (see Agricola, *Anleitung zur Singkunst* (Berlin, 1757), 104, and P. Badura-Skoda's discussion of the 'Execution of the tr Sign as a Short Upper Appoggiatura' in 'Mozart's Trills', in Todd and Williams (eds.), *Perspectives on Mozart Performance*, 23–4). This licence cannot, however, be said to be applicable to Haydn's music, since the composer frequently

be extended to other contexts, not specifically associated with this form of the ornament in North German theory, in which the *Praller* is not preceded by a note a second higher. In Ex. 6.20*c*, for instance, because of the relatively fast tempo, a three-note ornament might be considered less cumbersome than a four-note ornament beginning with the upper auxiliary and certainly Clementi's *Introduction* of 1801 would support a more flexible practice in this regard: this source illustrates only three-note ornaments under the headings 'Short shake' and 'Transient of passing shakes', including one illustration, similar to Ex. 6.20*b*, where the three-note ornament occurs on the first note of a descending second interval (see Ex. 6.29).

Ex. 6.20(*a*) Hob. XVI: 3/ii, (*b*) Hob. XVI: 35/ii, (*c*) Hob. XVI: 37/i, (*d*) Hob. XVII: 3

(*a*)

(*b*)

(*c*)

uses the two characteristic ornamentations of the same pattern of notes apparently as a means of variation, which would be destroyed if the performer reduced the notational diversity of such passages to uniformity for no better reason than technical ease (see e.g. Ex. 6.20*b*; for further exx. see Hob. XVI: 27/ii, 32/i, 35/ii, 37/i, and xv: 5/ii).

Ex. 6.20 *cont.*

However, Paul Badura-Skoda's claim that the *Praller* in Haydn's music should always be realized as a three-note ornament cannot be accepted.[46] In the first place, the trills in bars 245–6 of Hob. XVII: 3 provide a strong argument against such a generalization (see Ex. 6.20*d*). Although the *tr* symbol rather than a chevron is employed here, the ornament must be a short trill, either a three-note *Praller* beginning on the main note or a four-note *Praller* beginning on the upper auxiliary, because of the relatively short note values involved. In this case Haydn, unusually, places a small note before the *tr* symbol to clarify the pitch of the upper auxiliaries (i.e. e♭ and d♭, in each case a diminished octave above the bass). In so doing, Haydn also makes it quite clear that he intended an upper-auxiliary start to the trills, that is in each case a four-note rather than a three-note *Praller*. Secondly, Badura-Skoda's evidence from Haydn's music concerns a unique instance which he then promotes as a generally applicable realization. Specifically, he points to a passage from Hob. XVI: 39/i (see Ex. 6.21*a*) in which Haydn, in unambiguous notation, decorates an appoggiatura with a three-note *Schneller*. However, a further examination of the context in which the *Schneller* occurs would seem to call for a rather more diversified treatment than Badura-Skoda allows.

The cadential formula associated with the *Schneller* in Ex. 6.21*a* is found consistently in Haydn's music: it is virtually omnipresent in Haydn's early music and although less frequent in later music, particularly from the 1780s, continues to recur. The harmonic progression involved is usually a non-final cadence (half-close or interrupted cadence), in which the second chord of the progression is decorated by a single or double suspension, which is itself ornamented by a trill

[46] 'Beiträge zu Haydns Ornamentik', *Musica*, 36 (Sept.–Oct. 1982): 409–18, esp. 412–13 (some of the numerous textual errors in this article are corrected in *Musica*, 36 (Nov.–Dec. 1982): 575).

Ex. 6.21(*a*) Hob. XVI: 39/i, (*b*) Hob. XVI: 2/i, (*c*) Hob. XVI: 6/i, (*d*) Hob.
XVI: 2/ii, (*e*) Hob. XVI: 38/i, (*f*) Hob. XVI: 47/iii, (*g*) Hob. XVII: 5, (*h*) Hob.
XVI: 24/ii

or other ornament (see Ex. 6.21*b–h*). There is disagreement in mid-
eighteenth-century theory concerning how a note which is itself an
appoggiatura should be ornamented: this matter is discussed further
in Chapter 7, but for present purposes it is necessary to note Quantz's
comment that 'Often two appoggiaturas are also found before a note,
the first marked with a small note, but the second by a note reckoned
as part of the beat; . . . Here the little note is again tipped briefly, and
reckoned in the time of the previous note in the upbeat.'[47]

[47] *Versuch*, trans. Reilly, 94.

Ex. 6.21 *cont.*

C. P. E. Bach and other North German writers maintain a contradictory view: for instance, Bach states that 'Descending appoggiaturas
written in large notation may be decorated by another appoggiatura,
long or short'.[48] By extension, the statement of Quantz provides
some theoretical evidence for the opinion of F. Neumann that when
a trill ornaments an appoggiatura the upper auxiliary of the trill
should anticipate the beat.[49] Similarly, by advocating the *Schneller* in
bar 19 of Hob. XVI: 39/i as a model for the interpretation of short
trills in Haydn's music, Badura-Skoda is also dismissing the possibility that a four-note *Praller* may be used in ornamenting a note which
is itself an appoggiatura. In this particular cadential context, however,
the appoggiatura is ornamented by Haydn in a wide variety of ways.
In parallel passages in Hob. XVI: 2/i the appoggiatura is ornamented
by another appoggiatura and by a trill (see Ex. 6.21*b*); in Ex. 6.21*c–h*
the same context is ornamented by a double trill; a *Doppelschlag*; an
inverted *Doppelschlag*; a four-note figure (in effect a measured
Doppelschlag), the first note of which is an appoggiatura; a trill followed by a *Nachschlag*; and, most elaborately, in the slow movement
of Hob. XVI: 24 the appoggiatura written in large notation is ornamented by another appoggiatura and a trill. A further, particularly
rich, illustration of the ornamentation employed by Haydn in this

---

[48] *Versuch*, trans. Mitchell, 97.
[49] Concerning Neumann's 'grace-note trill' see *Ornamentation in Mozart*, 129–33, esp.
131.

harmonic context is provided by the second movement of Hob. XVI:
30 (see Ex. 5.5).

Given this diversity, it seems to me ill-advised to restrict the trills
which occur in conjunction with this diversely ornamented cadence
to one interpretation (the *Schneller*, as Badura-Skoda would have it,
or the 'grace-note trill' according to Neumann). Since at least some
of the ornamentations of the appoggiatura in this context given in Ex.
6.21 can be said with reasonable certainty to involve the addition, on
the beat, of an upper auxiliary note to the appoggiatura or appoggiatura chord (for instance, another appoggiatura in the case of Ex.
6.21*f* and the first note of the *Doppelschlag* in the case of Ex. 6.19*d*)
Quantz's ruling in this regard cannot be seen as binding in Haydn's
music. It should also be pointed out that the notation of a *Schneller* in
association with this context (as in Ex. 6.21*a*) is a rarity in Haydn's
music (I know of no similar occurrence of the notation in this context). It is unwise to advocate the exception as the rule. Although the
Schneller might perhaps be used somewhat more frequently than its
clearly notated occurrences would suggest, it should not be assumed
that it is the norm, the required ornament, where the chevron or *tr*
symbols occur. Like the *Doppelschlag*, the four-note *Praller* seems to
me to be entirely at home in this cadential context and the sharp
rhythmic accent it imparts is both idiomatic and apposite given the
metrical placement of the ornament in these contexts on a strong
beat.

In the eighteenth century both four-note and three-note forms of
Praller were used. In legato contexts the four-note form requires a
tied upper auxiliary and is virtually interchangeable with the three-
note form. The three-note form was also undoubtedly extended to
contexts other than where a legato connection to the preceding note
is possible, and, indeed, in the nineteenth century is the only form of
Praller in general use. In Haydn's music, however, the four-note
Praller, beginning with an articulated upper auxiliary remains, in my
view, an essential ornament, specifically required by Haydn in Hob.
XVII: 3 (Ex. 6.20*d*) and, for reasons of articulation and accentuation,
an idiomatic usage in the cadential context discussed in connection
with Ex. 6.21.[50] Beyond the primary consideration of articulation

---

[50] Koch's *Lexikon* of 1802 continues to illustrate both three- and four-note ornaments
(s.v. 'Prall-Triller'). Paul Badura-Skoda's dismissal of the four-note ornament extends not
only to Haydn's music, but also to Mozart's. In a recent essay on ornamentation in Mozart
he writes that he 'could find no evidence for it [the *Praller* beginning on the upper auxiliary]

and accentuation, technical feasibility is undoubtedly a factor which influences the choice of three- or four-note *Praller*, but this criterion can be misused: it can easily lead to the dubious situation where technical frailty or sloth becomes the only justification for the interpretation.

MAIN CADENTIAL TRILLS AND THE *TRILLER VON UNTEN*

Marpurg's comment that the trill is a 'series of . . . descending appoggiaturas' has been cited frequently as the basis for understanding this ornament's function.[51] In the twentieth century Schenker has been the strongest advocate of this belief, finding therein the 'psychological basis for the trill'.[52] Other authors, notably F. Neumann, have decried the comment as simplistic.[53] Nevertheless, the trill does play an important harmonic role, particularly when it occurs at the most emphatic cadences in a movement. Most modern authors agree that such prominent cadential trills begins on the upper auxiliary,[54] although Neumann also frequently advocates a main-note trill even in this context.[55] In the discussion below it is suggested that the upper-auxiliary trill is indeed a common occurrence at structurally important cadences, but that alternatives are frequently to be found, not, as Neumann would have it, in the main-note trill, but in the *Triller von unten* and in a number of other prefix formulas strongly associated with the cadential trill.

Characteristically the cadential trill occurs at structurally important points in the course of a movement and is accompanied by a marked decrease in the pulse of the prevalent harmonic rhythm. Typically the trill ornaments the supertonic note, is harmonized by a dominant or dominant substitute and may therefore in the manner of Marpurg be interpreted as a repeated 6–5 progression on the dominant (or a $\begin{smallmatrix}6-5\\4-3\end{smallmatrix}$

which might in any way apply to Mozart' (P. Badura-Skoda, 'Mozart's Trills', 2 n. 3). This view, with which I cannot agree, seems to me to be at least in part due to the author's overreliance on relatively late theoretical sources, especially Clementi's *Introduction* of 1801.

[51] 'Eine Reihe in der grössten Geschwindigkeit hintereinander wiederhohlter fallenden Vorschläge' (*Anleitung*, 53).

[52] 'Ein Beitrag zur Ornamentik' (Vienna: Universal, 1903), trans. H. Siegel as 'A Contribution to the Study of Ornamentation', *Music Forum*, 4 (1976), 71–2.

[53] Neumann, *Ornamentation in Mozart*, 104.

[54] See e.g. P. and E. Badura-Skoda, *Interpreting Mozart*, 117–19; P. Badura-Skoda, 'Mozart's Trills', 5; and Rosenblum, *Performance Practices*, 241–4.

[55] *Ornamentation in Mozart*, 124.

progression, implied or real). When the trill on the supertonic is approached from below by the tonic or a combination of tonic and supertonic (see Ex. 6.22*a* and *b*), giving rise to the standard patterns and ,[56] a standard cadential trill beginning with the upper auxiliary would seem to be appropriate. When, however, the trill is approached from above and preceded by the supertonic note itself, there is much evidence to suggest that the *Triller von unten* is either required or an idiomatic alternative to the upper-auxiliary trill. In this latter context the *Triller von unten* is often specifically notated in one way or another (see Ex. 6.23*a* and *b* (in bar 47)) but, as pointed out above, the occurrence of specific notation for the *Triller von unten* is sporadic in Haydn's music and it is likely that, for instance, in bar 18 of Ex. 6.23*b* (cf. bar 47), and elsewhere when the symbol *tr* occurs in this context, a *Triller von unten* should be understood.

Ex. 6.22(*a*) Hob. XVI: 13/iii, (*b*) Hob. XVII: D1/i

Cadential patterns with a tonic–supertonic–tonic outline ( ) and a dominant-supertonic–tonic outline ( ) are harmonically interchangeable: the most frequently used bass formula is the mediant–subdominant–dominant–tonic pattern (see Ex. 6.24*a–c*), although other bass patterns with comparable implied harmonies also

[56] The occurrence of the tonic or tonic and supertonic notes before the cadential trill is such a common formula that it may virtually be considered as a distinct trill type, the upbeat acting as a prefix to trill. Cf. Ex. 6.24*b* and *d*.

Ex. 6.23(*a*) Hob. XVI: 13/iii, (*b*) Hob. XVI: 6/i

occur. In this context the trill itself is most frequently indicated simply by the *tr* symbol, but it is valid to regard this as a merely conventional notation which may be realized in a number of ways. Evidence for a certain latitude in the realization of these formulae is to be found in eighteenth-century theory and in analogies with procedures in concertos (see below), but the most direct evidence is the variety of ways in which Haydn ornaments these conventional outlines. The somewhat static tonic–supertonic–tonic or dominant–supertonic–tonic formulas are frequently, although not consistently, embellished by Haydn, giving rise to a varied repertoire of trill types which it can be argued are appropriate either when specifically notated or when only the conventional melodic outlines appear. In Hob. XVI: 2/i the conventional outline in bar 47 is ornamented in the parallel passage by the addition of the passing-note *c″* to the upper auxiliary of the trill (cf. Ex. 6.24*a* and *b*). The dominant–supertonic–tonic formula of Ex. 6.24*c* is sometimes found with an embellishment comprised of a two–note prefix (tonic and supertonic) before the beat (Ex. 6.24*d*), which has the same shape as the *Triller von unten* but with the first two notes notated and performed pre-beat. These cadential outlines also occur with a *Triller von unten* specified in some way in connection with the supertonic trill (Ex. 6.24*e* and *f*). It is arguable that these alternative realizations of the conventional cadential outlines should be used interchangeably (perhaps varied in repeats) and that the basic outline of Ex. 6.24*a* and *c* are merely conventional representations

Ex. 6.24(*a*) Hob. XVI: 2/i, (*b*) Hob. XVI: 2/i, (*c*) Hob. XVI: 2/i, (*d*) Hob. XIV: 5/i, (*e*) Hob. XVI: 21/i, (*f*) Hob. XVIII: 3/ii

(*a*)

(*b*)

(*c*)

(*d*)

(*e*)

(*f*)

which require a wider latitude in interpretation than other ornamental formulas in Haydn's music.

The most emphatic supertonic trills occur, of course, in concerto movements, especially after a cadenza but also underlining other structurally important events. The most frequent approach to the supertonic trill is from the tonic note, either contiguous to the trill (Ex. 6.25*a*), or a seventh above the trill (Ex. 6.25*b*): less frequently, the trill is approached by the interval of a fourth. The trill in such instances is frequently indicated conventionally only by the *tr* symbol, but this context is, in fact, strongly associated with the *Triller von unten*. Sometimes the *Triller von unten* is specified by the notation, but it is always a distinct possibility whether notated specifically or not. This is clear from the comments in eighteenth-century treatises which associate the *Triller von unten* with long notes (supertonic cadential trills are always on notes which are relatively long in comparison with the prevailing note values) and especially after cadenzas and *fermata*s. It is of interest in this regard that the extant cadenzas for Haydn concertos printed in *JHW* XV/2 usually end with a *Triller von unten* whether the supertonic trill in the score is indicated by a *tr* symbol or a specific symbol for the *Triller von unten*.[57]

Ex. 6.25(*a*) Hob. XVIII: 3/i, (*b*) Hob. XVIII: 11/i

The cadential formulas typical of concertos are also found in Haydn's keyboard sonatas and trios. The strongest analogy with the cadential formulas of concertos is provided by the slow movements of some early sonatas where cadences are marked by *fermata*s and improvised cadenzas are required. In Ex. 6.26*a* and *b* the trill on the

---

[57] Similar cadential formulas associated with the cadenza occur in Mozart's concertos and it is interesting in this regard that frequently those of Mozart's concertos which survive without cadenzas end with conventional formulas and the *tr* symbol, whereas most of the extant cadenzas end with either a *Triller von unten*, or a trill with a pre-beat prefix similar to those found in Haydn's music. Cf. e.g. K.449/i and K.467/i.

supertonic is notated by the *tr* symbol but, given its function as ending a cadenza, a *Triller von unten* might often be employed in place of
an ordinary upper-auxiliary trill. The trill type chosen in this context
will depend on the approach to the trill at the end of the improvised
cadenza, but many conventional cadenza endings lead naturally to a
Triller von unten, or one of the more elaborate trill prefixes illustrated
above. The *tr* symbol is merely a generic indication which invites a
more elaborate realization than is otherwise the norm. It is relevant
in this regard that in the Adagio from Hob. XVI: 39, where Haydn
supplies a written-out cadenza, the following trill is a *Triller von unten*
(Ex. 6.26*c*).

Cadences characteristic of cadenza endings also occur in later
sonatas and trios although they are not preceded by an improvised
cadenza. Particularly in the keyboard trios of the 1780s and 1790s
important cadences often owe much to common conventions of
concerto movements: first, the harmonic under-pinning is similar

Ex. 6.26(*a*) Hob. XVI: 6/iii, (*b*) Hob. XVI: 19/ii, (*c*) Hob. XVI: 39/ii

Ex. 6.27(*a*) Hob. XVI: 37/i, (*b*) Hob. XVI: 41/i, (*c*) Hob. XV: 8/i, (*d*) Hob.
XVI: 39/ii, (*e*) Hob. XVI: 41/i, (*f*) Hob. XV: 5/i

(often a prolonged $^{6-4}_{5-3}$ progression on the dominant); secondly, the melodic approach to the cadential trills resembles the penultimate bar of cadenzas; and thirdly, the trills of the trios last for an unusually long time in relation to the predominant note values, thus emphasizing the structural importance of the cadence in much the same way as a long trill at the end of a cadenza acts as a structural up-beat to the final ritornello. The supertonic trills approached by a descending fourth (or compound fourth), or a descending seventh are sometimes indicated only by the *tr* symbol (Ex. 6.27*a* and *b*), but in similar passages more specific notation indicates a variety of more elaborate possibilities. The *Triller von unten* is frequently prescribed and is wholly idiomatic in this context (see Ex. 6.27*c*). Equally characteristic are a number of pre-beat prefixes before the trill, which resemble in outline the *Triller von unten* and the *Triller von oben*. In Ex. 6.27*d* and *e* the descending fourth approaches to the supertonic trills are filled in by four passing notes. This is such a common formula that it virtually constitutes an independent trill type, the four passing-notes resembling the prefix of the *Triller von oben* but occurring before the beat. Arguably, it may be introduced freely as an embellishment at structurally important cadences where the supertonic trill is approached from a (long) dominant note a fourth higher.[58] Another hybrid trill type is also idiomatic at these cadences, that is, a *Triller von unten* pattern, but with the prefix played before the beat, as in Ex. 6.27*f*.

Prominent cadential trills can therefore be seen as taking a number of different forms. The performer may well be justified in trusting in the context rather than the literal meaning of the notation when selecting a trill type, especially in view of the association of these cadences with the cadenza formulas of concertos, and with improvised rather than strictly notated performance. The *tr* symbol may in this context be interpreted rather freely, and may encompass in its repertoire of possible realizations a number of hybrid trill formulas.

---

[58] The *Triller von oben* (Ex. 6.8) does not occur in Haydn's music, but formulas such as those illustrated in Ex. 6.27*d* and *e* are analogous, although the prefix occurs pre-beat. Türk illustrates a similar formula (Ex. 6.9*c*), commenting on 'the not unusual arrangement of note values . . . in place of the more correct realization' (Türk, *Klavierschule*, trans. Haggh, 261).

MAIN-NOTE TRILLS

Theory

It has long since been established that the main-note trill was not an invention of the nineteenth century. Neumann has provided much information that suggests its currency in the seventeenth and eighteenth centuries.[59] It should be clear from the discussion of Notation and Context, above, that in Haydn's music the main-note trill is also an important ornament. The adjoining trill, and very often the *Praller*, may legitimately be realized with a main-note start, although a tied upper auxiliary is often a valid alternative. Because of the frequency with which the contexts associated with the adjoining trill and the three-note *Praller* occur, trills which begin with the main note are indeed among the most common of trill types in Haydn's music, especially in the early keyboard works where they are associated with stereotypical galant cadence formulas. To this extent the realization of many, perhaps even the majority, of trills in Haydn's music should not be the subject of great dispute. What remains controversial, however, is the extent to which some scholars, particularly Neumann, advocate the main-note trill in contexts other than those associated with the adjoining trill and three-note *Praller*.

Neumann has dealt with a wide chronological and stylistic range of music, using, for the most part, similar logic in dealing with different styles. Although most scholars now recognize the importance of Neumann's arguments and consequently the part played by the main-note trill in specific styles, aspects of Neumann's research remain open to question, partly, I would suggest, because of difficulties in Neumann's evaluation of theoretical sources, but mostly, it must be admitted, because the evidence is inconclusive. In addressing the question of the wider use of the main-note trill in Haydn's music the controversies of modern research concerning the Baroque trill are of little relevance. It is advisable, considering the fundamental stylistic change in the mid-eighteenth century, which is particularly striking in keyboard music, to allow for the possibility of discontinuity in performance practice. Therefore, only those treatises dealing with performance practice which date from the second half of the eighteenth century may, even in the most general sense, be consid-

---

[59] Neumann, *Ornamentation in Baroque and Post-Baroque Music*, 241–411.

ered relevant to the present discussion. Of the mid-eighteenth-century theoretical sources which might be seen from this general perspective to be of relevance to what is usually referred to as 'galant' and 'classical' music, two authors, Quantz and Tartini, are frequently cited as evidence for the centrality of the main-note trill in performance,[60] but the evidence is ambiguous and the relationship to the keyboard music of Haydn is problematic.

Tartini's treatise on violin-playing gives realizations of the upper-auxiliary trill only, but in a letter offering advice on practising the trill Tartini's illustration is of a trill beginning on the main note.[61] In Quantz's *Versuch*, a trill beginning on the main note is illustrated in table VII, fig. 1, but in his subsequent description of the trill Quantz's wording seems to contradict the illustration, or at least creates a certain ambiguity which suggests caution: 'Each shake begins with the appoggiatura that precedes its note, and as explained in the previous chapter, the appoggiatura may be taken from above or below.'[62] Dolmetsch observed the ambiguity in Quantz's *Versuch* and concluded that the illustration of the main-note trill was an abstract representation intended to demonstrate the purely mechanical practice of the trill.[63] On the other hand Beyschlag thought that the upper-auxiliary trill in Tartini was purely a conventional representation and that the main-note trill represented Tartini's intentions.[64] It is problematic to argue for the general use of the main-note trill based on these references, since there are no clear contextual settings for this ornament to establish where and how often it was used. It is also important to consider how widely one should apply the 'main-note trills' of Tartini and Quantz (if, indeed, main-note trills are intended by the authors). The Italian school of violin-playing, of which Tartini is representative, had enormous influence in the earlier part of the eighteenth century and continued to exercise an influence on violin tutors into the nineteenth century. However, there is a great difference between these violin tutors and treatises on keyboard-playing,

---

[60] See esp. ibid. 345–86; and A. Beyschlag, *Die Ornamentik der Musik* (Leipzig, 1908; repr. Wiesbaden: Sandig, 1970), 145 ff.

[61] *Traité des agréments del la musique*, ed. E. R. Jacobi (Celle: Moeck, 1961), 74–83; the letter to Signora Maddalena Lombardini, dated 5 Mar. 1760, is reproduced in the appendix to Jacobi's edn. (ibid. 130–9, esp. 137). See also Neumann, *Ornamentation in Baroque and Post-Baroque Music*, 347–50.

[62] *Versuch*, trans. Reilly, 103.

[63] *The Interpretation of the Music of the Seventeenth and Eighteenth Centuries* (London: Novello, 1915), 181.

[64] *Ornamentik*, 145.

especially in connection with ornamentation and notation. This raises an important question concerning the advisability of transferring performance practice between genres. Late eighteenth- and early nineteenth-century flute treatises are likewise often strongly influenced by Quantz's *magnum opus*, but there is also a substantial difference between these treatises and sources dealing with keyboard music. Again, even if Quantz played all trills beginning on the main note (and this is by no means certain), we should not assume that what might be applicable to Quantz's flute works is relevant to Haydn's keyboard music.[65]

Somewhat less ambiguous information on the main-note trill is provided by a number of treatises and instruction books dating from the second half of the eighteenth century. Rosenblum has observed that 'during the last quarter of the [eighteenth] century more and more tutors and ornament tables included trills starting on the main note'.[66] Although these sources have been widely cited by modern authors as providing evidence for the general use of the main-note trill, their evidence seems to me to have been, at best, overinterpreted. It is frequently seen as significant that in the treatises of, for instance, Manfredini and Albrechtsberger, the only trill type illustrated is the main-note trill.[67] However, the main-note trills occur, in these and many other treatises from the second half of the eighteenth century, in connection with the ornamentation of the second note of a descending second interval (see Ex. 6.28).[68] The use of a main-note trill in this context is not unusual, is of no special signifi-

---

[65] On this point see E. Reilly, *Quantz and his Versuch: Three Studies* (American Musicological Society: Studies and Documents, 5; New York, Galaxy, 1971), 104 ff. It is also of interest that several contemporary reviews challenge Quantz's views on ornamentation (see Quantz, *Versuch*, trans. Reilly, pp. xxxi–xxxiii and esp. Reilly, *Quantz and his Versuch*, 40–92).

[66] *Performance Practices*, 242.

[67] Manfredini, *Regole armoniche*, 27; Albrechtsberger, 'Anfangsgründe zur Klavierkunst' Wgm (XIV 1952); id., 'Fundamento per il Clavicembalo di Giorgio Albrechtsberger' Wgm (VII 14372). Neumann comments that Albrechtsberger 'shows the trill only in its main-note form' (Neumann, *Ornamentation in Mozart*, 110). P. and E. Badura-Skoda also attach significance to this point: 'Note that it [the main-note trill] is given as a rule, not as an exception!' (P. and E. Badura-Skoda, *Interpreting Mozart*, 110). Similarly, Rosenblum highlights the fact that 'Manfredini's only trill example begins its oscillations on the main note' (Rosenblum, *Performance Practices*, 242).

[68] The comments made here concerning Manfredini, Albrechtsberger, and Tromlitz also apply to other authors frequently cited by scholars as advocates of the main-note trill. Gervasoni's illustrations (cited in Neumann, *Ornamentation in Mozart*, 109) are directly derived from Manfredini. Neither do the illustrations of Pleyel (ibid. 106), Bisch (ibid. 110), etc. represent particularly radical departures from mainstream theory.

Ex. 6.28(*a*) Albrechtsberger, *Anfangsgründe*, (*b*) Manfredini, *Regole armoniche*, p. 27

cance, and has no implications beyond this specific context. At most, the illustrations represent the author's preference in this context for a main-note trill as opposed to an adjoining trill with a tied upper auxiliary, but it should not even be assumed that the latter ceased to be a common option: some authors apparently prefer a performance with a tied upper auxiliary (as in Galeazzi's illustration of a *Trillo imperfetto*), while others offer a choice of realizations in this regard (as in Clementi's *Introduction*—see Ex. 6.29). Illustrations of main-note trills of this sort are perfectly compatible with mainstream mid-eighteenth-century theory and do not represent a new departure in performance practice. It is misleading therefore to cite these examples as evidence for a more general use of the main-note trill.

Tromlitz's *Unterricht* is also cited in modern literature for his apparent endorsement of the main-note trill. One illustration in this work gives the main-note trill in isolation in a similar manner to Quantz (on whose *Versuch* Tromlitz relies heavily). This is in itself unhelpful in determining the precise usage of the main-note trill advocated by Tromlitz. The author's concern with melodic outline might seem to favour a liberal use of the main-note trill. With the upper-auxiliary trill, according to Tromlitz, 'the sequence of the melody [is] interrupted, the real melody [is] made unrecognizable'.[69] It should be pointed out, however, that virtually the whole of Tromlitz's chapter on the trill is concerned with the performance of the trill in a single context, namely the conjunct descending pattern which naturally

[69] *Ausführlicher und gründlicher Unterricht, die Flöte zu spielen* (Leipzig, 1791), 267; trans. A. Powell as *The Virtuoso Flute-Player* (Cambridge: CUP, 1991), 241.

requires a main-note trill or adjoining trill.[70] His undoubted preference for a main-note trill, as opposed to an adjoining trill with tied
upper auxiliary, is not in itself remarkable. The trend that the illustrations of Tromlitz, Manfredini, Albrechtsberger, and others seem to
me to represent is not one whereby the main-note trill generally
replaces the upper-auxiliary trill (i.e. a fundamental change in performance practice), but rather a stylistic trend whereby in various
galant styles the ubiquity of the adjoining trill in cadential formulas is
reflected in treatises on performance practice to the extent that some
authors mention only this context. The prominence of a particular
context associated with galant cadential cliches may be largely
responsible for the emphasis on the main-note trill in certain treatises
in the second half of the eighteenth century. The emphasis may be
new, but the occurrence of the main-note trill as the product of
elision (i.e. the omission of a tied upper auxiliary in the context of a
adjoining trill) is not. Treatises which illustrate the main-note trill in
a single context cannot be used as evidence for the interpretation of
trills in other contexts.

Significantly new attitudes to the performance of the trill are characteristic, not of mid-eighteenth-century sources, but of sources dating from the end of the eighteenth century and from the nineteenth
century, and may be associated with contemporary stylistic changes.
Hüllmandel states that 'the Shake begins indiscriminately with either
of the two Shaken Notes, or sometimes by a note under those of the
Shake'.[71] The 'modern' taste is more emphatically stated by
Kalkbrenner:

It [the Shake] should commence and end on the note which bears its sign,
as the harmony is thus more satisfactory. Occasionally, composers desire, for
some particular reason that it should commence on the note above or
below it; in this case they must take care to indicate their intentions by small
notes.[72]

Spohr makes an almost identical statement in his *Violinschule* and
attributes the introduction of the main-note trill to Hummel. In this

[70] Apart from this context Tromlitz admits the possibility of a main-note trill in only one
other context—at the beginning of a melody: 'But if the melody begins with a trill, either
at the beginning [of the piece] or in the course of it, it can take an appoggiatura, though a
very short one; . . .—however, it can also be made without an appoggiatura' (Tromlitz,
Unterricht, trans. Powell, 240).

[71] *Principles of Music, Chiefly Calculated for the Piano Forte or Harpsichord* (London, 1796),
16.

[72] *A New Method of Studying the Piano-Forte* (London, [1837]), 30.

claim Spohr is obviously in error but what is significant is that, writing in 1832, he should regard the main-note trill as relatively new.[73] Hummel's comments in his *Instructions* are particularly revealing:

With regard to the shake, we have hitherto followed the practice of the ancient masters, and begun it always with the subsidiary note above; a custom to all appearance founded upon the earliest rules laid down for the voice in singing, and which were subsequently adopted for instruments. But, as each instrument has its own pecularities as to touch and position of the hand, so likewise has the piano-forte, and no reason exists that the same rules which were given for the management of the voice, must also serve for the piano-forte, without admitting of alteration or improvement.[74]

He continues by stating his new rule and gives his reasons for its adoption:

Two principal reasons determine me to lay down the rule, 'that, in general, *every shake* [emphasis original] should begin *with the note itself*, over which it stands, and not with the *subsidiary note* above, unless the contrary be expressly indicated:'
a) because the note shaken, after which a sort of close generally follows, ought to be more strongly impressed upon the ear, than the subsidiary note
. . .
b) because, on the piano-forte, the succession of notes differs in some respects from that usual on other instruments; and, on account of the position of the hands and the consequent arrangement of the fingers, it generally is more convenient for the player to begin with the principal note[75]

Hummel adds a caveat in the same manner as Kalkbrenner and Spohr:

If the composer desires that it [the Shake] should commence with the note *above* or *below* he must indicate this by an additional small sized note, above or below.[76]

Nineteenth-century illustrations of main-note trills could be multiplied here, but it is perhaps more important to consider the implications of these illustrations. It could be argued that since theory often lags behind practice by many years then the nineteenth-century illustrations could be applicable to music written in the eighteenth century, or at least in the later years of the eighteenth century. This generalization can, however, be fallacious, in particular in connection

[73] *Violinschule* (Vienna, [1832]), trans. J. Bishop as *Celebrated Violin School* (London, [1843]), 142.
[74] Hummel, *Instructions*, pt. III, p. 2.   [75] Ibid. 3.   [76] Ibid.

with performance practice. C. P. E. Bach's *Versuch* may be considered
quite avant-garde by comparison with the treatises of Quantz and
Türk, each of which contain many elements of retrospection; Spohr,
Czerny, and Clementi gave instructions based on their own music or
that of their near contemporaries. Hummel is perhaps the most interesting figure from this point of view. A pupil of Mozart, and regarded
by Czerny as being relatively old-fashioned as a pianist, he is none the
less accredited by Spohr with introducing the main-note trill.
Frederick Neumann attaches some importance to Hummel's tutelage
when he wishes to associate Hummel's main-note trill with Mozart,
but when considering the question of stylistically apposite cadenzas
and embellishments for Mozart's concertos he accuses Hummel of
sinning 'against Mozart's spirit',[77] thus endeavouring both to con-
sume and conserve his Hummellian cake. Granted that Hummel was
a pupil of Mozart and may indeed have been relatively conservative
as a pianist in comparison to Beethoven or Czerny, nevertheless, stylistically his compositions are far removed from those of his teacher;
the performance practices associated with these compositions as represented by Hummel's *Instructions* cannot therefore, without independent evidence, be assumed to be of relevance to Mozart's music.
There is a noticeable change in compositional style in the works of
the generation following Haydn and Mozart. It can be no accident
that new attitudes in performance practices, including the increasing
dominance of the main-note trill, arise in treatises contemporary with
the compositions of this new generation of composers. In keyboard
music many of the new trends in composition and performance practice are centred on London and Paris where new schools of pianism,
modern trends in piano manufacture, and writings on performance
practice represent a striking departure from eighteenth-century
norms. Although it is not verifiable, the increasing use of the main-
note trill seems to me to be associated with the 'new' advocacy of
legato as the main touch in keyboard performance and with an
emphasis on smooth melodic contours, which would often be dis-
rupted by upper-auxiliary trills. With regard to the former, Clementi
is, as pointed out in Chapter 2, a seminal figure who adopted the new
style of articulation relatively late in his career; it is interesting to
speculate on the possible relationship between the new manner of
articulation and the occurrence in Clementi's *Introduction* of some
main-note trills.

[77] *Ornamentation in Mozart*, 248.

Clementi's illustrations of the shake, the turned shake, the continued shake, and the prepared shake are consistent with general eighteenth-century attitudes (see Ex. 6.29). The transient or passing
shakes and the second of his illustrations of the 'Short shake beginning by the note itself' occur in those contexts commonly associated
with the three-note *Praller* in the treatises of Marpurg and others.
Clementi's first illustration of the 'Short shake beginning by the note
itself', in which a three-note *Praller*, beginning with the main note,
ornaments the first note of a descending second interval, is representative of the general expansion of contexts associated with the three-
note *Praller*, as witnessed above in the writings of Türk and others.
Thus, while Clementi's short and transient shakes are always three-
note ornaments beginning with the main note, the longer trills
labelled the shake, the turned shake, and the continued shake, are
upper-auxiliary trills. The most interesting of Clementi's realizations
are those given for the last two illustrations, which are, significantly,
labelled 'The shake LEGATO with the preceding note'. The first of
these is, of course, absolutely conventional, equivalent to Türk's
adjoining trill: the second is, however, a significant departure by
comparison with North German theory. This last realization is particularly revealing in the association which is made between the
main-note trill and legato articulation, not only in the context of
descending seconds but, uncharacteristic of eighteenth-century treatises, in the context of ascending seconds. It is, of course, possible that
this departure from the norms of eighteenth-century treatises, illustrated by Clementi in 1801, gained currency in the 1790s or earlier.
It is perhaps more realistic to regard this new context for the main-
note trill in Clementi's *Introduction* as an anticipation of nineteenth-
century practices, in the same way that Clementi's advocacy of legato
articulation is characteristic of a later generation of performers.

Modern Literature

Although the literature dealing specifically with performance practices in Haydn's keyboard music is relatively slight, modern writers
dealing with performance practices in Mozart, or with Classical performance practices in general, advocate the use of the main-note trill
in specific contexts, apart from those associated with the adjoining
trill and the *Praller*, where, for musical reasons, an upper-auxiliary trill
is seen as inappropriate. Neumann and Badura-Skoda give detailed

Ex. 6.29. Clementi, *Introduction*, p. 11

N.B. The GENERAL mark for the shake is this **tr** and composers trust CHIEFLY to the taste and judgement of the performer, whether it shall be long, short, transient, or turned.

listings of such contexts in connection with Mozart's music and, using similar reasoning, Rosenblum has provided a concise statement of those contexts in the music of 'Haydn, Mozart and their contemporaries' in which trills 'might have been played with their oscillations beginning on the main note'.[78] These contexts may be summarized, after Rosenblum, as follows:

i Trills approached by descending stepwise motion, with or sometimes without a written slur, but particularly if a legato line or clarity of the line is desired.

ii Some trills approached by ascending stepwise motion, with or without a slur, particularly where it is important to maintain clarity of the line (including trills at the ends of rising scales).

iii Some extended trills in noncadential settings where the purpose is melodic coloration of a note.

iv Trills on dissonant notes, in order to retain the significance and color of the dissonance.

v Trills in the bass, especially extended ones, if the harmonic function of the bass note would be weakened by an upper-note start.

vi Sometimes in chains of trills.

vii Where an upper-note start might prove less appropriate for other musical reasons (e.g., that it produces objectionable fifths or octaves; perhaps at the start of a piece . . . or after a rest, . . .) or might prove technically awkward.[79]

It must be admitted that, apart from the first context listed, contemporary documentation for these assertions is lacking or is ambiguous; equally it should be admitted that the lack of evidence cannot be regarded as proof of the inadmissibility of such reasoning. However, it seems to me quite dubious to regard these general rules as holding equal force in different music, irrespective of question of style: what is most striking about the contexts listed by Rosenblum as appropriate for the main-note trill in the music of Haydn, Mozart, and their contemporaries is their similarity to discussions of the same topic by earlier authors writing on ornamentation in J. S. Bach's music. Few of these authors are dogmatic in their assertions and all have the admirable aim of a flexible approach to performance practice, yet the underlying assumption, whether stated or not, that there are natural musical laws behind these assertions is very questionable. Many of

---

[78] *Performance Practices*, 245; see also Neumann, *Ornamentation in Mozart*, 117–28; P. Badura-Skoda, 'Mozart's Trills', 6–17.

[79] *Performance Practices*, 245–9.

Neumann's controversial interpretations of ornamentation are aimed
at a performance which is 'natural', *musikalisch schön*, Rosenblum's
rough equivalent being the preservation of 'clarity of line'. It is clear
that ornamentation is not simply a matter of applying rigidly the realizations found in ornament tables. It is, however, problematic to
regard the guidelines for the use of the main-note trill of Rosenblum,
Neumann, *et al.*, where it is seemingly the aim to highlight stepwise
part-writing,[80] as being universally applicable in a wide chronological range of styles. Even near contemporaries, such as Haydn and
Mozart, show significant differences in their characteristic ornamental practices and it certainly seems to me self-evident that what is
musikalisch schön on a seventeenth- or eighteenth-century harpsichord
is not necessarily so on a Broadwood piano.

Although virtually all of Rosenblum's contexts for the use of the
main-note trill can be supported by compelling internal evidence in
the works of individual composers, they will be more or less applicable depending on questions of style and chronology. Thus, the
second context mentioned by Rosenblum is applicable in different
ways to a number of different categories of composer. The general
use of main-note trills in the context of 'ascending stepwise motion
. . . to maintain clarity of the line' is supported by Clementi's
Introduction, but Clementi's instruction in this regard is, unlike
Rosenblum's, confined to legato ascending contexts. Yet even with
the qualification 'legato', Clementi's advice may, as I have suggested
above, be more appropriate as a general rule for composers in the
generation following Haydn and Mozart. Without Clementi's qualification 'legato', Rosenblum's rule might be regarded as being generally applicable only in the nineteenth century. On the other hand
Rosenblum's inclusion of the phrase 'including trills at the ends of rising scales' in her rubric will have a strong resonance with performers
of Mozart's music, in particular the piano concertos, where trills 'at
the end of rising scales' are something of a trademark of this composer. If, as may well be the case, the use of trills at the end of rising
scales is a stylistic innovation of Mozart, it is perfectly understandable
that eighteenth-century writers on performance practice did not find
it necessary to qualify there general advocacy of the upper-auxiliary
trill by reference to this context. For Mozart's music it is therefore
entirely plausible that main-note trills should be used at the end of

---

[80] It is ironic that Schenker, who as an analyst was so concerned with voice-leading, has
no recourse to this logic when writing about performance practices.

rising scales, but Rosenblum's wider advocacy of main-note trills in
ascending stepwise contexts, irrespective of articulation, should hold
no particular force in Mozart's music. In Haydn's music Rosenblum's
second context for the use of main-note trills is, I would suggest, misleading and in any case is largely irrelevant. Trills at the end of rising
scales are not characteristic of Haydn and, more generally, trills in the
context of ascending stepwise movement are a rarity. When they do
occur, as in the early work (certainly before 1766) Hob. XVII: D1/i,
bars 9–10, legato articulation should not be assumed, and the relevance of Clementi's *Introduction* to such a work seems far-fetched.

If, for whatever reason, an upper-auxiliary trill appears to be
incongruous, an alternative other than the main-note trill may be
possible and is very often more likely for text-critical or other
reasons, apart from the subjective concern with what is *musikalisch
schön*. Extended trills in the bass (Rosenblum's fifth context) occur in
the works of many composers and there is frequently good internal
evidence for regarding a main-note trill as more appropriate than an
upper-auxiliary trill.[81] They occur relatively infrequently in Haydn's
music, but in a number of works preserved in autograph manuscripts
(e.g. in bars 105–10 of Hob. XVI: 23/i, and bars 89–91 of the
Variations in F minor, Hob. XVII: 6), such trills are clearly indicated
as starting with the note below the main note, i.e. as a *Triller von
unten*. In works by composers who do not generally employ a specific
symbol for a *Triller von unten*, or in works surviving in secondary
sources which are careless as regards the notation of ornaments, a
Triller von unten is often a valid and also musically appropriate alternative to the upper-auxiliary trill, often preferable to a main-note
trill. In a wider context, the *tr* symbol may often be used generically
by composer, scribe, or engraver to represent 'an ornament', often a
Doppelschlag, so that while a literal interpretation as an upper-
auxiliary trill may well be inappropriate, a main-note trill is once
again by no means the only alternative.

With regard to other contexts for which Rosenblum advises a
main-note trill it must be admitted that the evidence is too inconclusive to allow any dogmatic claims, either for or against the practice. For chains of trills, for instance, Rosenblum frequently
recommends main-note trills, but advisedly, given the contradictory
available evidence, admits that a mixed practice must have existed:

---

[81] See e.g. W. Emery, Bach's *Ornaments* (London: Novello, 1953), 42.

Türk illustrates upper-auxiliary trills with *Nachschläge* for a succession
of trills in a diatonic ascending passage, while Hummel advises main-
note trills without *Nachschläge* in a similar context.[82] Most modern
writers advocate main-note trills in the context of a chromatic
ascending melodic line (such as, famously, in Mozart's Rondo in A
minor, K.511, bars 134–5 and Haydn's F minor Variations, Hob.
XVII: 6, bars 83–7),[83] but Louis Adam's *Méthode de piano* of 1805 gives
an exercise for practising a succession of trills on each note of a chromatic ascending scale in which an upper-auxiliary start to each trill is
illustrated.[84] In this case the absence of evidence in eighteenth-century theory for the use of a main-note trill in a chromatic ascending
succession of trills may well be due to the relative rarity of this context before the end of the eighteenth century. It would be unwise
therefore to dismiss the use of the main-note trill in this context based
on an absence of evidence. Equally, the main-note trill should not be
regarded as a panacea for the undoubted problems of arriving at convincing interpretations of trill chains. Bars 83–7 and 93–7 of Haydn's
F minor Variations lend themselves to a wide variety of interpretations (varied combinations of trills with and without *Nachschläge*,
main-note trills, adjoining trills with tied upper auxiliaries, upper-
auxiliary trills, and even the occasional *Triller von unten*). In the
absence of compelling evidence on the interpretation of such
passages, but given the undoubted problems with using only upper-
auxiliary trills, what is called for is inspired experimentation by
performers and not a slavish adherence to a single solution.

Further research on the orthographic conventions of composers,
scribes, and engravers and on the relationship between performance
practice and compositional style may well reveal in more detail the
role of the main-note trill in eighteenth-century keyboard music. As
far as Haydn is concerned there is no notational evidence (and no
convincing documentary evidence which can be directly related to
Haydn) to support a widespread use of the main-note trill, apart from
the all-important contexts associated with the adjoining trill and the
Praller. The situation may well be different with regard to other composers or to genres other than keyboard music, nor can the main-

---

[82] See Türk, *Klavierschule*, trans. Haggh, 252; the relevant passage from Hummel's treatise is quoted in P. Badura-Skoda, 'Mozart's Trills', 14.

[83] See e.g., Rosenblum, *Performance Practices*, 248; P. Badura-Skoda, 'Mozart's Trills', 5;
Neumann, *Ornamentation in Mozart*, 123–4.

[84] Pp. 54–5.

note trill be ruled out as an exceptional usage in other contexts. However, compelling evidence for the widespread use of the main-note trill in multiple contexts does not emerge until the nineteenth century and may be seen as the result of new styles of composition, new schools of pianism, and new keyboard instruments which differ radically from those Haydn would have known. Haydn employs a wide variety of trill types: an understanding of their manifold possibilities in performance, including a flexibility in the interpretation of non-specific notation, obviates the need for a panacea to problems of ornament interpretation which is frequently sought in the overuse of the main-note trill.

Haydn, Musical Clocks, and Performance Practice

Two dated musical clocks signed by Niemecz and containing music by Haydn survive from 1792 and 1793; another clock containing music by Haydn, unsigned though possibly also made by Niemecz, was traditionally dated 1772 but is now thought to be of later manu-facture, possibly dating from *c*.1796.[85] Many of the pieces reproduced on these clocks also survive in autograph manuscripts and other reli-able sources, providing a unique and potentially valuable insight into Haydn's performance practice.[86] Concerning the autograph manu-scripts and the surviving clocks Robbins Landon commented that 'they provide a unique record—indeed, almost a gramophone record — of Haydn's intentions. The realizations of the trills, "half mor-dents" and other ornaments, not to mention questions of phrasing, tempo and the like, are all, if not solved, at least presented to us in as authentic a form as we shall ever have.'[87] The fact that Pater Niemecz, the Esterházy librarian and maker of at least two of these clocks, collaborated closely with Haydn enhances the hope of 'authentic solutions' to problems of performance practice in Haydn. This potentially valuable material has been made accessible for study in *JHW* XXI, which presents a careful edition of the musical sources, reproducing the manuscript variants and a transcription of the texts as they appear on the surviving instruments. These sources must, how-ever, be examined in the same way as other information on perfor-mance practice, rather than being accepted at face value as the

[85] *JHW* XXI. *Stücke für das Laufwerk (Flötenuhrstücke)* (Munich: Henle, 1984), pp. ix, 57–60.

[86] Ibid. 53–7.

[87] 'Editorial', *EM* 10/3 (1982): 298–9.

panacea for problems of performance practice in Haydn's music. It is clear from Haydn's instructions to Niemecz on some of the autograph manuscripts that the composer was, at least on some occasions, directly involved in the production of the mechanical organs; the autograph manuscript of Hob. XIX: 16, for instance, contains instructions in Haydn's hand appended to the composition as a footnote.[88] It would be mistaken to regard all the texts, as they appear on the clocks, as the product of close collaboration. Indeed the extent of the collaboration has, perhaps, been overstated by enthusiasts of these clocks: it is certainly true that, until the publication of *JHW* XXI, inaccurate statements concerning the sources of Haydn's pieces for musical clocks went unchallenged.

The very authorship of at least fifteen pieces preserved on the three clocks must be seriously doubted. These pieces, many of them dubious arrangements or adaptations, are known only from the performance on the musical clocks but are either not preserved in any written source or only in a manuscript of questionable authenticity. While Ord-Hume believes that 'there can be no question that all the music upon the three instruments is from the pen of Haydn',[89] the editors of *JHW* XXI more realistically regard the attribution of these pieces as questionable, and their transcriptions of the same are relegated to an *Anhang*.[90] If the attribution of these pieces is in question, the performances cannot reliably be used as evidence for authentic Haydn performance practice.

Other pieces for musical clock, perhaps sixteen or seventeen in all, are undoubtedly authentic compositions or authentic arrangements by Haydn, and the preserved performances on musical clocks are worthy of attention. The value of these performances as evidence of authentic performance practice must, however, be questioned. The errors that occur in the normal process of written transmission and affect the interpretation of any source must also be considered in connection with the sources of mechanical organ pieces. As in the case of other genres, the autograph manuscript is the most reliable source and Haydn's precision in the notation of details of performance practice may, in general, be trusted to give an accurate reflection of the composer's intentions. The same is not necessarily true of secondary

[88] See facsimile repro. in *JHW* XXI, frontispiece; see also ibid. 22–4, 76.
[89] *Joseph Haydn and the Mechanical Organ* (Cardiff: University College Cardiff Press, 1982), 75.
[90] *JHW* XXI, pp. x, 79 ff.

sources, in this case the manuscript sources in the hand of Niemecz or Elssler, or the variant readings in autograph manuscripts not in Haydn's hand, which may represent the notational conventions of the scribe rather than those of the composer. One instance, cited below in Chapter 8, of the common scribal corruption of Haydn's typical *Doppelschlag* symbol to the *tr* symbol can be documented in Niemecz's variants in the autograph manuscript of Hob. XIX: 17. Of greater concern is the additional potential for error or deliberate emendation in the extra stage of transmission which arises only in connection with the musical clock pieces, i.e. the transmission of written text into recorded sound. The 'realization' of the written source may or may not be an accurate reflection of Haydn's intentions.[91] The version of these pieces recorded on the musical clocks frequently varies considerably from the written source in matters where there can be no question concerning the literal meaning of the notation. It is therefore dangerous to rely on the recorded sound for the interpretation of those aspects of notation (ornament signs for instance) which are less explicit than, for instance, the notation of pitch. Niemecz's variants, in particular of accompaniment figuration as in Hob. XIX: 17, may be the product of collaboration with Haydn, that is approved revision, or they may be the product of Niemecz's own creativity. When, in the performance of Hob. XIX: 18 on the 1792 clock, the first repeat sign in the autograph manuscript is ignored, it would be extremely foolish to base any argument concerning repeat conventions on this omission, since the reason for the omission is more likely to be connected with technical problems than with artistic intent. The reliability of the realizations of ornament symbols should also be regarded somewhat sceptically rather than being revered as authentic solutions to problems of ornamentation. In some instances the realizations of ornament symbols are so eccentric, corresponding to no known norm, that they cannot be regarded seriously as valid interpretations. Two illustrations may suffice to illustrate this point. Hob. XIX: 19 survives in the performance on the 1792 clock, but in no manuscript source. The piece is, however, an arrangement, probably not authentic, of the Haydn song Hob. XXVIa: 13 (*JHW* XXIX/1, p. 17). The ornament in bar 2 of the musical clock version is a strange compound of *Vorschlag* and *geschnellter*

[91] Somfai regards the evidence of the musical clocks as 'crucial . . . as far as the contemporary understanding — i.e. not necessarily Haydn's own reading!— . . . is concerned' (Somfai, 'Notation', 27).

Doppelschlag; if this is meant to be a realization of the ornamentation in the original song, it can be regarded only as misinterpretation (see Ex. 6.30). In Hob. xix: 14 the chevron symbol occurs in bar 19 of the manuscript source (in Elssler's hand). A standard interpretation of the symbol would be as a three- or four-note *Praller*. The realization of the ornament on the undated and the 1793 musical clocks as a mordent cannot be regarded as a valid interpretation of the source, since a mordent in Haydn's notation is indicated, as discussed in Chapter 8, either by two small notes, the standard mordent symbol, or by the Haydnesque symbol ∿ (see Ex. 6.31).

Ex. 6.30. Hob. xix: 19 (after *JHW*): version from the 1792 instrument

Ex. 6.31 Hob. xix: 14 (after *JHW*): (*a*) version from the undated instrument; (*b*) version from the 1793 instrument; (*c*) Elssler MS copy

   Another and perhaps the major objection to regarding the realizations as authentic solutions is concerned with the question of the relationship between genre and ornamentation. The problem is conveniently illustrated by comparing Hob. xix: 9, an authentic piece based on the Minuet from the String Quartet, Op. 54 No. 2, with the original string quartet version. One of the most striking aspects of the ornamentation in the musical clocks is the frequent use of continuous trills, usually beginning on the main note. It is important to realize that continuous trills are not a prominent feature of Haydn's ornamentation in other genres and no continuous trills are to be found in the Minuet of the String Quartet, Op. 54 No. 2.[92] Double trills beginning on the main notes are also common in the pieces for musical clock, but are certainly not characteristic of Haydn's keyboard music. If one wishes to apply the realizations found in the musical clock pieces to Haydn's works in other genres the distinctive nature of the ornamentation in the former is immediately apparent. In the 1780s and 1790s Haydn's instrumental music contains increasingly fewer ornaments, a stark contrast to the proliferation of ornaments in the musical clock pieces. The impression is unavoidable that the ornamentation of the mechanical organ pieces is *sui generis*, in the context of Haydn's practices of the 1790s a striking aberration.

---

[92] The transcriptions of XIX: 9 in *JHW* also illustrate the inconsistency in the realizations of ornaments on the various mechanical organs. The *Vorschlag* in bar 4 of the string-quartet version is realized as a main-note trill on the undated clock and as an upper-auxiliary trill on the 1792 clock. The emendation of the *Vorschlag* to a trill is in this instance authentic, but the inconsistency in the realization of the trill is at best unhelpful. A cursory glance at the transcriptions in *JHW* XXI will indicate far more problematic inconsistencies in the realizations of ornaments on individual clocks and, when a piece survives on more than one clock, between one clock and another. The inconsistencies extend far beyond the legitimate artistic choice which might be exercised in interpreting Haydn's notation. It is ironic that Neumann, in striving to free Haydn's ornamentation for the 'instant authenticity' of 'traditional rules', substitutes what might be termed a 'mechanical authenticity' based on an insufficiently critical approach to the realizations of the musical clocks (see Neumann, 'More on Haydn's Ornaments and the Evidence of the Musical Clocks', in *New Essays on Performance Practice* (Studies in Music, 108; Ann Arbor: UMI, 1989), 105–19).

7

Appoggiaturas:
Notation and Interpretation

◊

INTRODUCTION

Writing in *The New Grove*, Robert Donington commented as follows
on the duration of appoggiaturas in Classical music:

In Haydn, Mozart and even Beethoven the rules of Quantz and C. P. E.
Bach still apply in almost all respects, and the appoggiaturas shown by these
composers must be interpreted almost entirely in the light of the Baroque
conventions, rather than by their literal appearance.[1]

These rules, examined in some detail below, are usually formulated
as a number of stereotyped conventions: namely, that an appoggiatura
before a binary main note receives half the length of the main note,
an appoggiatura before a dotted note receives two-thirds of the overall value, while appoggiaturas before main notes which are 'tied' or
followed by a rest take the whole value of the main note, and the
resolution (i.e. the main note), falls in the place of the second of the
tied notes or on the rest.[2]

Such conventions feature in many modern prescriptions for the
realization of appoggiaturas in Classical music,[3] but their widespread
application cannot withstand close scrutiny. Notational habits vary
from one composer to another, and within the output of one composer important changes in orthography may also be identified; consequently the relevance of conventional interpretations must be

---

[1] S.v. 'Ornamentation, II Appoggiaturas'.
[2] These conventions are illustrated in Ex. 7.1. Frederick Neumann's term 'overlong' will
be used in referring to the last two of these conventions.
[3] See e.g. Donington, *Interpretation of Early Music*, 201–5, 212–14. A notable early exception to this approach is found in Schenker, *Ornamentik*, trans. Siegel.

assessed in the light of changing orthography. Two important general tendencies towards greater precision in the notation of appoggiaturas can be identified in the eighteenth century; these either necessitate a modification of the conventions used in determining the duration of appoggiaturas or completely dispense with these conventions.

The first of these tendencies is seen in the increasingly prevalent advocacy, in the theoretical writings from the second half of the eighteenth century, of 'real' notation, whereby the value of a small note used to represent an appoggiatura is indicative of its true value in performance. This manner of notating appoggiaturas is primarily associated with the theoretical writings of the North Germans, C. P. E. Bach, Marpurg, and Agricola in the 1750s, and later with those writers influenced by North German theory, most influentially, perhaps, Türk.[4] It is true that real notation was not universally adopted and that those composers who did adopt real notation did not employ it at all stages of their careers: it is also important to realize that real notation is associated mostly, although not exclusively, with keyboard music and that some Baroque conventions may, for example, be applicable to a composer's vocal music when in other genres real notation is employed. In modern commentaries on the subject of ornamentation, real notation has, with some notable exceptions, received little attention.[5] A common viewpoint is expressed in Howard Ferguson's statement that the value of the appoggiatura is 'not necessarily the one shown [by the small notes]' and in Paul Badura-Skoda's similar comment: 'Ihre Länge ist von der Notierung her nicht immer eindeutig determiniert.'[6] While these statements may be accepted as the literal truth concerning eighteenth-century music in general, and even concerning the totality of Haydn's music, it is nevertheless possible to identify considerable bodies of music in which real notation is employed by the composer and in which the literal value of the small notes is a much surer guide to interpretation than conventional realizations. Real notation is not confined to North Germany and it will be seen to have considerable relevance to

[4] C. P. E. Bach, *Versuch*, trans. Mitchell, 87; Marpurg, *Principes*, 59; Agricola, *Anleitung*, 61; Türk, *Klavierschule*, trans. Haggh, 202.

[5] See esp. Schenker's important discussion of appoggiaturas (*Ornamentik*, trans. Siegel, 54–63). Notwithstanding the originality of Schenker's account, some of his arguments must now be viewed as being fundamentally flawed, primarily because of the poor sources on which these arguments appear to be based.

[6] Ferguson, *Keyboard Interpretation* (London: OUP, 1975), 121; Badura-Skoda, '*Ornamentik*', 409.

the interpretation of appoggiaturas in Haydn's music, as indeed it has in the music of Mozart.

The second tendency towards precision in the notation of appoggiaturas is seen in the practice of writing these ornaments, not as small notes, but as large notes with specific time values within the metre of the music. This practice, unlike real notation, is not confined to the second half of the eighteenth century but is also relevant to a discussion of appoggiaturas in, for instance, the music of J. S. Bach.[7] Many theorists of the second half of the eighteenth century suggest that 'normal'-sized notes should be used to clarify the composer's intention on occasions, but few actually go as far as Türk in suggesting that 'Perhaps music would be even better served if all long appoggiaturas were indicated by notes of usual size in the values they should have, as some composers are already doing.'[8] No eighteenth-century composer actually notated all appoggiaturas in large notes, but it is equally true that a great number of composers wrote many appoggiaturas in this manner and that this practice has important implications for the manner in which one decides the duration of those appoggiaturas notated by small notes. There were in the eighteenth century no general practices determining which appoggiaturas should be notated by large notes and which by small notes; Renaissance concepts of dissonance, which were the logic behind the use of small notes, are no longer relevant and notational conventions depend essentially on the orthographic habits of each individual composer rather than on an accepted theoretical concept. In deciding on the applicability of any one convention governing the duration of appoggiaturas, the orthography of the composer under consideration is of prime importance. Frederick Neumann has, for instance, suggested that conventions which demand an 'overlong' realization of appoggiaturas notated by small notes are not relevant to J. S. Bach's music since, according to Neumann, long appoggiaturas of this type are notated in Bach's music by large notes.[9] It will be suggested that some of the conventional realizations of appoggiaturas are of limited or no relevance to Haydn's music, since Haydn had, from an early date, more precise methods of communicating his intentions; both of the above-

---

[7] See Neumann, *Ornamentation in Baroque and Post-Baroque Music*, 124–63, esp. 157.

[8] *Klavierschule*, trans. Haggh, 195. Advice to notate ornaments with large notes is typical of early nineteenth-century treatises. See e.g. Spohr, *Violin School*, 158 and Hummel, *Instructions*, pt. III, 1.

[9] See n. 7, above.

mentioned general tendencies towards precision in the notation of appoggiaturas will be found of relevance to Haydn's music, with consequent implications for the applicability of conventional realizations.

Rules governing the duration of appoggiaturas will obviously be potentially of greatest importance in music where appoggiaturas are normally notated by small notes, the denominations of which are constant (usually quavers or semiquavers), regardless of the actual performance values of the appoggiaturas. For instance, Quantz wrote that 'It is of little importance whether they [i.e. small notes] have one or two crooks.'[10] In Quantz's music the notation of appoggiaturas is obviously conventional. Conversely, C. P. E. Bach commented that 'Today, we could not do without the notation of their [i.e. appoggiaturas'] real values'[11] and in Bach's music, apart from some early works, the notation can be taken as a surer guide to the intended duration of appoggiaturas in performance than conventional rules which are largely redundant in this context. To some extent it is true that each composer created his own conventions regarding the notation of appoggiaturas and any discussion of interpretation must give due consideration to the individual notational practices of each composer. Conventional realizations may be found to be applicable, but rarely will they apply in the same way to different composers or indeed throughout the whole output of any one composer.

In an important article Georg Feder examined certain aspects of Haydn's orthography with a view to clarifying details of chronology;[12] of relevance to a discussion of the performance of appoggiaturas in Haydn's music is Feder's observation that in the extant autograph manuscripts written before 1762 Haydn uses small notes of quaver value to notate appoggiaturas. Feder also observed that in the autograph manuscripts written after 1762 values other than the small

---

[10] *Versuch*, trans. Reilly, 91.

[11] *Versuch*, trans. Mitchell, 87, quoted in full in Ch. 5. Türk makes the same point more forcibly: 'Many copyists and probably even some composers still have the bad habit of notating all appoggiaturas alike, without regard for the following longer or shorter note, for example, by notating them as eighths or sixteenths, even though these little notes should sometimes be notated as quarters or eighths. . . . If long appoggiaturas are nevertheless notated by small notes, then the required duration of each appoggiatura can and should be notated exactly. . . . If this is not done, then correct distribution of the note values cannot always be expected, even by more advanced students.' (Türk, *Klavierschule*, trans. Haggh, 202.)

[12] 'Zur Datierung Haydnscher Werke', in J. Schmidt-Görg (ed.), *Anthony von Hoboken: Festschrift zum 75. Geburtstag* (Mainz: Schott, 1962), 50–4.

quaver note are employed (Feder's *Halbwertnotierung*). This article makes no reference to performance practice but the information about the notation of appoggiaturas has implications for the means by which one should decide on the performance values of appoggiaturas in Haydn's music. When the value of the small notes which indicate appoggiaturas is constant it is obvious that the composer is relying on some performance conventions for the realization of the notation. For some time after 1762, although occasionally values other than the quaver are found, it is clear that conventions of some sort are still applicable and that the notational value of the small notes is not functional. However, as pointed out in Chapter 5, from *c.*1765/6 Haydn's notation, of other ornaments as well as appoggiaturas, changes significantly; and as regards appoggiaturas it is clear that real notation in the manner of C. P. E. Bach is employed, with obvious implications for the performer's method of deducing the composer's intentions. The following discussion of appoggiaturas in Haydn's keyboard music is therefore divided into two sections: the first considers the relevance of conventional realizations in the music written until *c.*1765/6, while the second considers Haydn's use of real notation from this date and the rather different approach to interpretation which this necessitates. Throughout both sections the evidence of theoretical writings is a prime resource, but this evidence must be assessed and modified in relation to Haydn's own notational conventions.

APPOGGIATURAS IN HAYDN'S KEYBOARD MUSIC TO
*C.*1765/6: THEORY AND PRACTICE

Theory

Ex. 7.1 shows the rules governing the length of appoggiaturas (as given by Quantz) which are most frequently cited in the eighteenth century and in modern textbooks.[13] These rules received their clearest formulation in North German treatises of the mid-eighteenth century. They are undoubtedly based on existent North German practices, but, at least in part, had a wider validity; the rules regarding the duration of appoggiaturas before binary notes and dotted

---

[13] Further illustrations of these conventional interpretations of appoggiaturas are to be found in Bach, *Versuch*, trans. Mitchell, 90–1; L. Mozart, *Violinschule*, trans. Knocker, 167–70; Agricola, *Anleitung*, 61–3; Koch, *Lexikon*, s.v. 'Vorschlag'.

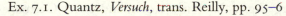

Ex. 7.1. Quantz, *Versuch*, trans. Reilly, pp. 95–6

notes are found in Tartini's treatise and obviously have some relevance to Baroque violin music.[14] Similarly, although they are formalized into stereotypes only in German treatises, the 'overlong' realizations of appoggiaturas are also probably derived from Italian practices: Geminiani, for instance, explains that the appoggiatura 'should be made pretty long, giving it more than half the Length or Time of the Note it belongs to'.[15] It is probably because these rules are presented with such uniformity in these North German sources that they have dominated modern writings on appoggiaturas to such a large extent. This apparent unanimity is, however, misleading and the universal application of these rules across boundaries of geography, chronology, and style has been questioned in recent research.[16] Considering that the 'Baroque' conventions were formalized only in mid-eighteenth-century treatises it is perhaps logical to assume their potential relevance to compositions written in various mid-century galant styles. However, even before considering internal evidence (discussed below specifically in connection with the early works of Haydn) it is clear that the theoretical evidence argues against the relevance of some of these rules, and against a rigid adherence even to those conventions which are undoubtedly of some relevance.

[14] *Traité*, ed. Jacobi, 65–73.
[15] *The Art of Playing on the Violin* (London, 1751), 7. Geminiani's description of the appoggiatura is repeated verbatim in Hoyle, *Complete Dictionary of Music*, s.v. 'Appoggiatura'.
[16] See e.g. Neumann, *Ornamentation in Baroque and Post-Baroque Music*, 47–199; Kirkpatrick, 'C. P. E. Bach's *Versuch* Reconsidered', 388–9; Gilbert, pref. to *The Sonatas of Scarlatti*, i (Paris: Heugel, 1984).

C. P. E. Bach, Marpurg, Agricola, Türk, Koch, and other German theorists, in addition to describing the long appoggiatura (*veränderliche Vorschlag* in Bach's terminology), devote considerable attention to the short appoggiatura (*unveränderliche Vorschlag*) which 'is played so rapidly that the following note loses scarcely any of its length'.[17] Bach makes the point that these short appoggiaturas often occur before short notes, but he and other theorists list a large number of other contexts in which they occur.[18] These contexts mostly involve short appoggiaturas before binary notes, but short appoggiaturas are also illustrated as occurring before dotted notes and before tied notes.[19] It is clear therfore that the durations for appoggiaturas suggested by Ex. 7.1 do not apply in contexts in which a short appoggiatura is more suitable.

With regard to the rule that an appoggiatura before a dotted note takes two-thirds the value of that note (illustrated in Ex. 7.1*b*), it is worth noting that alternatives to this duration are found in some sources. Galeazzi, for instance, recommends that the appoggiatura in this context takes one-third of the main note's value,[20] while Clementi gives examples of the appoggiatura taking both one-third and two-thirds the value of the main note, appending the advice 'as taste best directs in the passage'.[21] Türk, while giving the more usual rule for the duration of appoggiaturas before dotted notes, also lists a number of exceptions where the appoggiatura should be played for 'only a third of its [i.e. the dotted note's] value'[22] or where the appoggiatura 'must only be played short'.[23] Marpurg, while agreeing with other North German theorists in most respects, gives no rule for the duration of an appoggiatura before dotted notes in his *Principes du clavecin*.[24] These references suggest perhaps that a more flexible approach to the duration of long appoggiaturas before dotted notes may be appropriate: it should also be remembered, as mentioned above, that an appoggiatura before a dotted note may be a short appoggiatura, requiring a much shorter performance than the rule for the long appoggiatura in this context suggests.

The conventions regarding the overlong realizations of appoggiat-

---

[17] C. P. E. Bach, *Versuch*, trans. Mitchell, 91.

[18] Ibid. 91–5; Türk, *Klavierschule*, trans. Haggh, 211–21; Agricola, *Anleitung*, 66–72; Koch, *Lexikon*, s.v. 'Vorschlag'.

[19] See e.g. Bach, *Versuch*, trans. Mitchell, p. 92, fig. 76e and f; Türk, *Klavierschule*, trans. Haggh, 212.

[20] *Elementi*, quoted in Neumann, *Ornamentation in Mozart*, 8.   [21] *Introduction*, 10.

[22] *Klavierschule*, trans. Haggh, 203.   [23] Ibid. 219–20.

[24] This omission may be no mere oversight, but a purposeful reflection of French taste.

uras feature consistently only in the writings of North German theorists, and in these sources the illustrations are almost invariably
accompanied by important cautionary comments. Indeed, it is clear
that Bach, Marpurg, Türk, and others disapproved of the ambiguous
nature of the conventions. We may assume, because they are mentioned by theorists, that these conventions had a certain currency in
the eighteenth century and were used by some composers, but it
would be mistaken to assume they apply in every instance to the
works of every composer.

The first overlong rule, which concerns appoggiaturas occurring
before tied notes (see Ex. 7.1c), is usually illustrated in the context of
6/8 or 6/4 metre: Quantz and Koch mention this rule only in connection with compound metres, while Türk comments that realizations of this type 'occur very frequently in 6/8, 6/4, 9/8, 12/8, etc.
metre'.[25] The link with compound metres, together with Quantz's
specific association of the rule with gigues,[26] suggests perhaps that
this particular convention is of greatest relevance to Baroque dance
forms; it is in any case quite evident that instances in which this convention might be applied are far more abundant in Baroque dance
forms than in compound-metre movements by galant and Classical
composers. In the music of J. C. Bach, Haydn, and Mozart long
appoggiaturas in compound metres are almost exclusively written
in large notes and the relevance of the convention is consequently
at best marginal; typically one finds, for instance, the notation
♩ ♩ ♩ and not ♩ ♩ ♩ . Marpurg, in his *Principes du clavecin*,
contrasts these two methods of representing the same execution and
comments as follows:

But it is even better to use two ordinary notes & to write the *port de voix* as
it should be performed, at least in the contexts where the small notes can
be ambiguous.[27]

Generally, in galant and Classical keyboard music, the only appoggiaturas that are regularly notated by small notes in compound metres
occur before short main notes, where the overlong convention

[25] Quantz, *Versuch*, trans. Reilly, 95–6; Koch, *Lexikon*, s.v. 'Vorschlag'; Türk,
Klavierschule, trans. Haggh, 204.

[26] *Versuch*, trans. Reilly, 95.

[27] 'Mais il vaut encore mieux se servir de deux notes ordinaires & d'écrire le port de voix
tel qu'il doit être exécuté, du-moins dans des rencontres où les notes postiches peuvent
embarasser.' (Marpurg, *Principes*, 59.)

cannot apply; occasionally appoggiaturas a quaver in length are indicated by small notes,[28] but longer appoggiaturas are generally written in large notes.

This particular overlong convention is also illustrated by Bach, L. Mozart, Agricola, and Türk in 2/4 or 4/4 metre, but again because of the paucity of contexts in galant and Classical music in which the rule might conceivably be applied in these metres it seems also that in simple metres the practice of writing long appoggiatura patterns in large notes replaced the convention in general practice from *c.*1750. When on occasions small notes appear before tied notes, it cannot be assumed that an overlong realization necessarily applies and it will be argued, at least in connection with Haydn's music, that a short appoggiatura is more appropriate in these instances.

Regarding the second overlong convention (illustrated in Ex. 7.1*d*), C. P. E. Bach commented concerning the appoggiaturas in these patterns that 'Their notation is not the most correct, since in performance the rests are filled in. Dotted or longer notes should be written instead.'[29] Marpurg, L. Mozart, and Türk also advise against using this ambiguous notation, advocating, like Bach, the use of longer notes to replace the rests, or writing the appoggiatura unambiguously in large notes.[30] Even in those treatises which illustrate this overlong convention, it is clear that it does not apply on every occasion an appoggiatura occurs before a note which is followed by a rest. In the illustration from L. Mozart's *Versuch* (Ex. 7.2), the appoggiaturas occur in a context (i.e. before notes which are followed by rests) where an overlong realization is possible, but the figured bass makes it clear in this instance that the appoggiaturas are played as quavers and resolve before the rests, contradicting the rule given by the author elsewhere.[31] In describing the performance of appoggiaturas occurring before notes which are followed by rests, Koch significantly comments that 'in this case the *Vorschlag mostly* [emphasis added] lasts as long as the note itself, and only at the beginning of the rest will the main note be sounded'.[32] Türk's comments on this convention are also worth quoting *in extenso* in this regard:

---

[28] See Ex. 7.21. 　　　　　　　　　　　　　　[29] *Versuch*, trans. Mitchell, 90.

[30] L. Mozart, *Versuch*, trans. Knocker, 170; Marpurg, *Principes*, 59; Türk, *Klavierschule*, trans. Haggh, 204–5.

[31] L. Mozart, *Versuch*, trans. Knocker, cf. 167 and 170. Further exceptions to this rule are given in Türk, *Klavierschule*, trans. Haggh, 220.

[32] 'In diesem Falle dauert mehrentheils der Vorschlag so lange als die Note selbst, und die Hauptnote wird erst bey dem Eintritte der Pause angeschleift' (*Lexikon*, s.v. 'Vorschlag').

Ex. 7.2. L. Mozart, *Versuch*, trans. Knocker, p. 167

For appoggiaturas before notes which are followed by rests, some music teachers would follow the rule of the preceding paragraph. Nevertheless, they restrict themselves in doing so to passages of a gentle character. Consequently the appoggiatura would receive the complete value of the main note and this note would then fall during the value of the rest. . . . Somewhat more precision in the notation is also called for in this case. For if the appoggiatura is actually to receive the indicated value, a dot should be used rather than a rest or an even more certain way would be to notate the required durations in regular notes. . . . If, however, the appoggiatura is to receive only one-half of the value of its main note, then the notation in *c* [i.e. ♩♩ or ♩♩𝄾] would remove all doubt.[33]

Of interest here is Türk's comment that some and not all teachers advocate this convention, together with his inclusion of a restrictive caveat concerning passages of a gentle character. Türk, together with other theorists, suggests a more rational notation to replace this convention; interestingly, the final sentence of the above quoted passage is a tacit admission that the notation ♩♩𝄾 may mean ♩♩𝄾 and not ♩♩ .

　Two points emerge from the theoretical descriptions of this convention: first, in music where the convention is found to be relevant there will none the less be instances where it should not be applied, so that when appoggiaturas occur before notes which are followed by rests they should not on every occasion be realized as overlong appoggiaturas; secondly, in view of the widespread reservations about the convention, it must be considered that composers as well as theorists may have disapproved of its use. Consequently, although contexts in which the rule might be applied occur frequently in the works of many composers, it cannot be assumed that overlong interpretations are intended. Internal evidence suggests a wider range of possible interpretations.

[33] *Klavierschule*, trans. Haggh, 204–5. Similarly, Agricola comments that 'Certainly, this rule is not without exception' and he also associates the overlong convention with melodies of a 'flattering' character (*schmeichelnden Gesänge*) (*Anleitung*, 61).

Practice: Notational Practices before c.1765

Appoggiaturas before Binary Notes

An appoggiatura notated by a small note before a binary main note in Haydn's music can be assumed in the majority of cases to take half the value of that main note. This is not only the most obvious solution musically and one that features prominently in eighteenth-century theory, but it is also evident in almost any work, that Haydn frequently writes similar patterns both in large notes and using small notes, with in each case the ratio 1 : 1 between appoggiatura and main note being the composer's intent. Instances in the same movement in which these two types of notation are interchanged are frequently found (cf. bars 2 and 10 of Hob. xvi: 18/ii given in Ex. 4.4);[34] with regard to the common formulas ♪♩♩ and ♩♩♩, the choice of notation often appears to be a matter of caprice, with both notations serving to represent the same rhythm.

The following discussion concerning the duration of appoggiaturas before binary notes will deal with instances in which an even division between appoggiatura and main note may not be the only solution, and will consider particularly contexts in which the value of the appoggiatura might more suitably be assumed to be less than half the duration of the main note. The disproportionate emphasis given to these instances here is purely a consequence of the fact that contexts suggestive of a shorter realization of the appoggiatura are not always easily recognized, whereas the longer duration (i.e. half the duration of the main note) is always an obvious possibility and requires little comment.

As mentioned above, North German theorists distinguish between the variable long appoggiatura and the invariable short appoggiatura: this theoretical distinction, although valid, contains a lacuna which becomes apparent in practice. The shortest theoretical value for the long appoggiatura is usually given as half the value of a binary note (one-third the value of a dotted note is sometimes mentioned), while the short appoggiatura is described as being as fast as possible.[35] In between these two theoretical categories there exists in practice a variety of possible durations for the appoggiatura. Ratios of, for

---

[34] See *JHW*, XI/1, pp. viii–ix and cf. bars 4 and 20 of Hob. v: 8/ii in this vol. A compelling instance is also found in Hob. xvi: 45/i—see Ex. 7.22*b*.

[35] Bach, *Versuch*, trans. Mitchell, 91; Türk, *Klavierschule*, trans. Haggh, 199, 211.

instance, 1 : 3 and 1 : 2 between appoggiatura and main note cannot, especially in slow tempos, be considered to represent a performance of the appoggiatura which is 'as fast as possible', yet they are nevertheless shorter than the normal rules given for the duration of the long appoggiatura. It might be suggested therefore that the short appoggiatura of North German theorists be performed with durations which range from the 'as fast as possible' variety to the lower limits of the long appoggiatura. Türk, although maintaining the distinction between the long and short appoggiatura, comments on the ambiguity inherent in this distinction,[36] but perhaps the clearest statement regarding the ambiguity was made by Heinrich Schenker, who summarized the problem as follows: 'The long appoggiatura should be regarded as the outermost boundary of the short appoggiatura, so that the broad territory of the latter ends where that of the former begins.'[37]

The contexts in which the short appoggiatura is appropriate are listed in particular detail in the writings of C. P. E. Bach and Türk.[38] The most characteristic contexts may be summarized as follows:

1. Before short notes;
2. When appoggiaturas fill in the interval of a third;
3. Before triplets;
4. When the small note is more than a second from the main note, i.e. 'arpeggio' notes;
5. An appoggiatura before the second note of a melody which ascends a second and then returns (♪);
6. Before repeated notes;
7. Before syncopated notes;
8. When the appoggiatura is a chromatic note;
9. When an appoggiatura occurs at the beginning of a phrase or subphrase;
10. Before interval skips (*springenden Noten*);
11. Before staccato notes;
12. Before a caesura;
13. An appoggiatura (small note) before another appoggiatura (large note);
14. Before dotted notes in a rapid tempo;

---

[36] *Klavierschule*, trans. Haggh, 219.   [37] *Ornamentik*, trans. Siegel, 68.
[38] See esp. Bach, *Versuch*, trans. Mitchell, 91–4; Türk, *Klavierschule*, trans. Haggh, 211–21; Agricola, *Anleitung*, 66–78.

15. Before duple figures;
16. When the appoggiatura forms an octave with the bass.

In Haydn's keyboard music before *c*.1765 there is no notational distinction between long and short appoggiaturas. Sometimes, however, the short appoggiatura will not be merely a legitimate alternative to the long appoggiatura but decidedly preferable. In Ex. 7.3*a* the appoggiaturas occur before repeated notes (context 6, above) and are, additionally, chromatic notes (context 8, above); while a realization of the appoggiaturas as demisemiquavers is not impossible, the association of this context with the short appoggiatura is particularly strong and a realization of the appoggiaturas as shorter than demisemiquavers is apposite. Haydn occasionally specifies a short interpretation in this context by writing the appoggiaturas in large notes (as in Ex. 7.3*b*). In a similar passage given in Ex. 7.3*c* (see contexts 6 and 8, above) Haydn's distinction between the notation of the appoggiaturas before the repeated *c'''* and *a''* on one hand, and the notation of the appoggiaturas *c♯''* before the repeated *d''* may, with justification, be regarded as a functional rather than a purely arbitrary distinction, especially since the contrast in notation is retained on subsequent repetitions of the passage. Consequently, the appoggiaturas *b♮'* and *g♯'* may be regarded as short appoggiaturas and played approximately as demisemiquavers, in a similar manner to Ex. 7.3*b*. A short appoggiatura is also an obvious choice in connection with Ex. 7.3*d*, where the appoggiaturas occur between *springenden Noten* and where three of the five appoggiaturas are chromatic notes (contexts 8 and 10 above); the illustrations of this context found in Türk and Koch are strikingly similar (cf. Ex. 7.3*e* and *f*). Long appoggiaturas are of course not possible in many instances where small notes occur before notes of short duration (as in bar 28 of Ex. 6.18*b*), and elsewhere in the various contexts given above, even if long appoggiaturas are possible, short appoggiaturas may provide an equally valid or preferable interpretation.[39]

Appoggiaturas before Dotted Notes

The convention whereby an appoggiatura before a dotted note takes two-thirds the value of the main note is of little relevance to Haydn's early keyboard music. This statement is not a matter of subjective interpretation but rather a simple observation concerning Haydn's

[39] See e.g. Hob. XVI: 47/iii, bars 34–5, 43; XVI: 2/i, bar 15; XVII: D1/ii, bar 1.

Ex. 7.3(*a*) Hob. xv: 2/iii, (*b*) Hob. xvi: 12/iii, (*c*) Hob. xviii: 3/i, (*d*) Hob. xvi: 2/i, (*e*) Türk, *Klavierschule*, trans. Haggh, p. 212, (*f*) Koch, *Lexikon*, s.v. 'Vorschlag'

orthography: in his early music Haydn rarely writes appoggiaturas notated as small notes before dotted main notes and thus the possibility of applying the convention seldom arises. This does not, of course, mean that appoggiaturas in the ratio 2 : 1 to their main notes do not occur in Haydn's early music, but that Haydn largely dispensed with the conventional notation of such appoggiaturas by writing them in large notation: thus, while the notations ♩♩ , ♩♫ and ♫♫ are common, the patterns ♪♩. , ♪♩ ♪ , and ♪♩. are very infrequently found. Robbins Landon made a similar observation in relation to Haydn's symphonies, stating that Haydn wrote out 'in actual notes all the appoggiature in which the grace note [*sic*] would have taken two-thirds the value of the main note'.[40] Problems of interpreting long appoggiaturas of this type do not, therefore, in general arise and the few instances discussed below are exceptional.

Among the keyboard sonatas and trios appoggiaturas notated by small notes occur occasionally before dotted minims: a few examples of this uncharacteristic notation are found in Hob. XVI: 12/ii, XVI: 3/i, XV: 34/ii, and possibly in XVI: Es3/ii. The occurrences of this notation in Hob. XVI: 12/ii and XV: 34/ii are in connection with cadential formulas which are discussed in detail below. The notation in bar 14 of XVI: Es3/ii occurs also in the context of such cadential formulas, but there is in this case some doubt whether the notation $\frac{3}{4}$♪♩. , as found in Christa Landon's edition, is correct; in the sources the dot is lacking and while C. Landon's emendation makes mathematical sense, Georg Feder's addition of an editorial crotchet rest after the minim (instead of a dot) is probably more correct in view of Haydn's normal notation of this cadential formula. In Hob. XVI: 3/i the conventional realization of the appoggiatura as a minim does not arise, since the small note indicates the lower auxiliary before a trill and is Haydn's normal indication of a *Triller von unten* (see Chapter 6).

Small notes before dotted crotchets do not appear to occur at all in the early keyboard sonatas and are very rare in Haydn's early compositions in other genres. Ex. 7.4 cites one of these uncharacteristic occurrences, from Hob. XV: 37/ii, where the conventional realization as a crotchet is perfectly acceptable: it can, however, hardly be

---

[40] *Symphonies*, 139.

Ex. 7.4. Hob. xv: 37/ii

said to be obligatory since the notation is itself so exceptional. An alternative realization as a quaver is equally justifiable.

Dotted quavers are also rarely preceded by appoggiaturas in the early keyboard sonatas,[41] although this notation is found to a limited extent in other genres before *c*.1765. In these instances a realization of the appoggiatura as a quaver is certainly a possibility but it cannot be regarded as essential. In Ex. 7.5, for instance, while a quaver is perhaps the most likely choice, a short appoggiatura (see context 14, above) or possibly a semiquaver is also possible.

Ex. 7.5. Hob. xv: C1/i

Heinrich Schenker's suggestion that except in a few cases 'Haydn, Mozart, and Beethoven actually notated only short appoggiaturas as embellishments'[42] (i.e. by small notes as opposed to writing them in large notes with specific values) is too general an observation to be taken seriously and is in fact demonstrably inaccurate in certain regards. However, it was certainly Haydn's normal practice in his early instrumental music to write out in large notes those appoggiaturas which are long and in the ratio 2 : 1 to the main notes. Since Haydn did not adopt in his characteristic early notation the

---

[41] One instance is found in Hob. xvi: 47/i (E minor version): although the sources and chronology of this work are problematic, it is discussed below in connection with the real notation of appoggiaturas.

[42] *Ornamentik*, trans. Siegel, 69.

conventional notation for appoggiaturas in the ratio 2 : 1 to the main notes, it is perhaps unwise to utilize exclusively the conventional realization in the rare instances when appoggiaturas occur before dotted notes.

Overlong Conventions: (1) Appoggiaturas before tied notes
The various overlong interpretations of appoggiaturas found in North German writings are of questionable relevance to Haydn's keyboard music; in particular, the rule which requires that appoggiaturas before tied notes take the whole value of the main note, with the resolution falling on the second of the tied notes, can be seen to have little practical application. The most obvious place for this convention to apply is in movements with compound ternary time signatures. Such movements are rare in Haydn's early keyboard music, but in movements such as Hob. XVI: 47/i (E minor version) and in works in other genres, where 6/8 metre in particular is somewhat more common (Hob. V: 2/i, V: 6/i, V: 13/i, for instance), long appoggiaturas are mostly written in large notes and instances in which this overlong convention might be applied simply do not occur: thus, while dotted-crotchet appoggiaturas occur, they are indicated unambiguously in large notes and not by the formula ♪♩.

In movements with simple time signatures appoggiaturas do occur on occasions before tied notes, but for a number of reasons it is unlikely that an overlong realization is intended. First, since the convention does not apply in compound ternary movements where it might most naturally be expected to be employed, it cannot be assumed to apply automatically to movements in simple time signatures on the occasions where appoggiaturas occur before tied notes. Secondly, and more importantly, the contexts in which these appoggiaturas and tied notes occur strongly suggest interpretations other than the overlong realization. The most usual context is when a *Vorschlag* approaches the main note by leap (see Ex. 7.6): in this instance to play the main note only in the place of the second of the tied notes would completely alter the rhythmic character of the passages. The obvious interpretation is to play such 'arpeggio' notes as short appoggiaturas (see context 4, above); in addition the *Vorschlag* in Ex. 7.6 should be considered short because it forms an octave with the bass (see context 16 above). While the duration of such *Vorschläge* might here be extended from 'as short as possible' to as long as a quaver, overlong realizations would make little sense.

Ex. 7.6. Hob. XVIII: 3/i

When an appoggiatura, as opposed to an arpeggio note, occasion-ally appears before a tied note (as in Ex. 7.7) it is also difficult to believe that an overlong interpretation is intended: here the appog-giatura *c″* in bar 84 is most likely intended as a short appoggiatura, perhaps no longer than a semiquaver, since it forms a consonance with the bass (see context 16, above); to prolong the *c″* until the second beat would make little sense harmonically. In contrast, the crotchet appoggiatura in bar 86, forming a 7–6 suspension over a moving bass, is clearly written in large notes as a long appoggiatura. It is significant that here where a long appoggiatura is required the notation [image] is not employed. The contrast in function between the appoggiatura *c″* in bar 84 and the appoggiatura *d″* in bar 86 is reflected in the different notation and it is very difficult to believe that the notation in bar 84 should be read as a crotchet. In summary, there are good grounds for believing that this overlong convention is replaced in Haydn's keyboard music by the use of 'nor-mal' large notes (as advocated by Marpurg and others) and that when, as happens infrequently, a small note occurs before a tied note, a short appoggiatura is intended. Although the duration of the short appog-giatura may be flexible to some extent, it should not in general (for the various reasons outlined above) exceed half the value of the first of the tied notes.

Overlong Conventions: (2) Appoggiaturas before main notes which are followed by rests

The second overlong convention, which requires that an appog-giatura occurring before a main note followed by a rest takes the whole value of the main note, is potentially of far greater relevance to Haydn's music: contexts in which it can be used, in particular various typical galant cadence figures, occur frequently, and the

Ex. 7.7. Hob. XVIII: 3/i

overlong realization is often advocated in these contexts, notably in the performance suggestions found in Christa Landon's edition of the keyboard sonatas. There is, however, strong evidence to suggest that, if the convention cannot be dismissed in connection with Haydn's music, it is in many instances only one of a number of possible realizations; one, moreover, which is perhaps overused in these contexts. When an appoggiatura ornaments the final chord of a characteristic galant cadential formula, it is found notated in one of three different ways. First, in 3/4 metre the rhythm ♩♩ is sometimes unambiguously written in large notes. Secondly, the rhythm ♩♩♪ is frequently found, particularly when the appoggiatura is itself ornamented by another appoggiatura, a *Doppelschlag*, or a trill (in movements with duple time signatures one finds the corresponding notations ♩♪ or ♩♪). Thirdly, problems of interpretation arise when the ubiquitous and ambiguous notation ♩♪♪ occurs, for which the conventional interpretation ♩♩ is frequently offered.

These ornamented resolutions of cadences are characteristically accompanied by the common tonic–dominant–tonic arpeggiated bass patterns (as in Exx. 7.8 and 7.12 in 3/4, and 7.9 in 2/4 metre). It is perhaps because of this typical bass-line that the overlong convention is so commonly employed in this context. Writing about

Haydn's symphonies, for instance, Robbins Landon has commented that 'it is hard to conceive that Haydn ended dozens of pieces with this passing six-four chord, but such must have been the case unless passages written ♩♩𝄿 were altered to ♩♩. (i.e. ♩ ♩)'.[43] Christa Landon's frequent advocacy of this overlong convention would also seem to be motivated by the avoidance of a passing 6–4 chord, or, more accurately in the context of Haydn's predominantly two-part writing in the early keyboard music, an implied 6–4 ending at cadence figures.[44] This type of reasoning is not, however, a valid basis for interpreting the duration of appoggiaturas in these contexts. The aural effect if an appoggiatura is interpreted as a crotchet is not $^{4-6}_{(4)}$, but that of a simple 4–3 suspension over an arpeggiated tonic chord. This is even more apparent when root, third, and fifth of the tonic chord are arpeggiated (as in Exx. 7.8 and 7.9): notwithstanding the rhythmically active bass, the appoggiatura is heard as a 4–3 suspension and not as a succession of three or four different harmonies. Even

Ex. 7.8. Hob. XV: 40/ii

Ex. 7.9. Hob. XVI: 2/i

---

[43] H. C. R. Landon, *Symphonies*, 143.

[44] One of the more interesting exceptions in which Christa Landon does not consistently advocate the overlong resolution of appoggiaturas occurs in Hob. XVI: 14/i, where, for the notation ♪♩𝄿 Landon suggests a quaver interpretation in bars 8, 44, 74, and 82, while in bars 4, 40, and 78 a crotchet is advocated. Landon does not give a reason for these different interpretations of the same notation in similar contexts, and while variety might seem appropriate here, there is no reason why these interpretations should hold any particular force.

when the cadence involves a double suspension (and this is not the norm in the early keyboard works) the effect is $^{6-5}_{4-3}$ and not $^{6-6}_{4-4}$.

Haydn certainly had no reservations about resolving an appoggiatura against the fifth of an arpeggiated chord in the bass, as can be seen from the many instances in which the duration of the appoggiatura is notated unambiguously in large notes (see for instance Exx. 7.8, 7.9 (bar 109), and 7.12).[45] Particularly interesting is Ex. 7.9, from Hob. XVI: 2/i, where Haydn varied the length of the appoggiatura, at harmonically parallel points in the same movement, above an arpeggiated bass chord. Considering that Haydn wrote in large notes a variety of durations for appoggiaturas in these cadence figures, it is unwise to admit only the overlong realization where the ambiguous notation using small notes is found in the same context: internal evidence often suggests a variety of alternatives to this overlong interpretation. When the bass-line, moving conjunctly, leads from the cadence to a new phrase, the overlong interpretation of the appoggiatura in the cadence is in fact extremely unlikely. In Exx. 7.10 and 7.11, for instance, an interpretation of the appoggiaturas as minims gives unsatisfactory consecutives (consecutive fifths in Ex. 7.10 and particularly suspect consecutive octaves in Ex. 7.11).[46] Quite apart from the dubious consecutive intervals produced by an overlong realization, Haydn's intention is suggested by a comparison with similar contexts where the duration of the appoggiatura is specified unambiguously in large notes (see Exx. 7.12 and 7.13). Thus, potential consecutives are avoided in Ex. 7.13 by the use of a crotchet appoggiatura and a further comparison between Exx. 7.10 and 7.12, both of which have the same melodic line and harmonic pattern so common in the early works of Haydn, is particularly suggestive of a crotchet value for the appoggiaturas in Ex. 7.10. Concerning Ex.

---

[45] See also Hob. XV: C1/i, bar 6 and XV: 37/ii, bar 8.

[46] It is a matter of some controversy whether the avoidance of consecutive intervals in itself justifies an interpretation: conflicting views are found in Neumann, *Ornamentation in Baroque and Post-Baroque Music*, 13–15 and Donington, *AM* 17 (1970): 253–5. While some of Neumann's inferences from consecutive intervals are questionable, it is none the less clear that an interpretation which creates obvious consecutives should be avoided. Several treatises discuss the necessity to preserve good part-writing in the realization of ornaments; see e.g. Bach, *Versuch*, trans. Mitchell, 95, L. Mozart, *Violinschule*, trans. Knocker, 172, and Türk, *Klavierschule*, trans. Haggh, 219–21. In instances such as those cited in Ex. 7.10–7.11 the consecutives that arise from an interpretation of the appoggiaturas as minims are of such an obvious nature that the argument cannot be overlooked. However, in neither of these examples is the argument concerning consecutive intervals the sole basis for the interpretation.

Ex. 7.10. Hob. xv: 40/ii

Ex. 7.11. Hob. xvi: 1/iii

Ex. 7.12. Hob. xvi: 5/ii

Ex. 7.13. Hob. xvi: 5/ii

7.11, further reasons for a shorter interpretation than that implied by the overlong convention will be discussed below.

There are also a number of very clear instances in which, although the ambiguous notation ♪♩𝄽 is used, it is undeniable that an overlong realization of the appoggiatura was not intended by Haydn. In the Trio, Hob. xv: f1/ii (Ex. 7.14) the notation in the keyboard part at bar 36 is ambiguous, but the violin part in the same bar clearly indicates that the duration of the appoggiatura should be a crotchet and not a minim. Given this evidence it would be perverse to insist upon

Ex. 7.14. Hob. xv: f1/ii

a minim value for the appoggiaturas in bar 48 and also at the other
cadence points in the movement:[47] in bar 48 a minim appoggiatura
is, of course, a valid interpretation, but no more so than a crotchet.

In Haydn's early keyboard music there is a particular type of galant
movement involving widespread use of syncopation which characteristically occurs as the trio section of a minuet and trio and occasionally elsewhere (as in the variation movement Hob. xv: C1/iii, see
Ex. 7.15). This type of movement contains the usual cadential formulas found in minuets and trios, but it is notable that the cadences
consistently seem to require shorter appoggiaturas than those suggested by the overlong realization. In Ex. 7.15 the duration of the
appoggiaturas at the cadences in bars 124, 128, and 132, is consistently
a quaver (the same is true of the cadences at bars 136, 140, and 144 in
the second half of this variation). Although the syncopation in Hob.
xvi: 2/iii (Ex. 7.16) is less continuous, the appoggiaturas in the
cadences at bar 34 (and again at bar 50) are also quavers. In Hob. xv:
34/ii (Ex. 7.17), which is in many ways very similar to Hob. xv:
C1/iii, the appoggiaturas in bars 34 and 47 are again written unambiguously, but on this occasion as crotchets. In the cadence at bar 56
the appoggiaturas, notated as small notes, occur before dotted minims, a rather unusual occurrence in Haydn's early music, and while
the conventional realization of these appoggiaturas would be as minims, crotchet durations are also a distinct possibility, given the parallel cadences in this movement.

---

[47] In *JHW*, XI,/1, pp. viii–ix the editors make a similar point in connection with the
String Trio, Hob. v: 4/ii, bar 8.

Ex. 7.15. Hob. xv: C1/iii

Ex. 7.16. Hob. XVI: 2/iii

In Exx. 7.11 and 18, although the notation of appoggiaturas is ambiguous, the patterns of syncopation clearly identify these movements with the types illustrated in Exx. 7.15–17, and the overlong minim realization advocated by Christa Landon for bars 38 and 54 of Ex. 7.18 is perhaps the least likely of a number of possible durations: the analogy between bars 38 and 54 of Ex. 7.18 and bar 124 of Ex. 7.15 suggests a quaver value for the appoggiaturas in the former. Bar 35 in Ex. 7.11 might well be played with a crotchet appoggiatura as in bars 34 and 47 of Ex. 7.17, although a quaver duration for the appoggiatura is not impossible (both these values, as well as being appropriate to this syncopated type of movement, avoid, as mentioned above, the consecutive octaves resulting from an overlong realization).

In Hob. XVI: 10/ii (Ex. 7.19), the conventional overlong realization of the appoggiatura in bar 44 (as advocated by Christa Landon in her edition of the sonata) is, perhaps, especially suspect. The German theorists who illustrate overlong realizations do so in connection with the appoggiatura usurping the value of the main note: none of these theorists suggest that the appoggiatura takes the value of the main note and one of two following rests. In Hob. XVI: 10/ii, therefore, quaver and crotchet realizations of the appoggiatura are possible, but no basis exists for the interpretation of the appoggiatura as a minim.

Ex. 7.17. Hob. xv: 34/ii

Ex. 7.18. Hob. XVI: 12/ii

Ex. 7.19. Hob. XVI: 10/ii

In notating these cadential formulas Haydn specified various durations for the appoggiaturas, ranging from a quaver to a minim, by writing the appoggiaturas in large notes. When more ambiguous notation is employed we cannot be entirely certain of Haydn's intention, but it is clear from the examples cited that overlong realizations cannot always have been desired: other realizations, in particular quaver and crotchet appoggiaturas in 3/4 metre and quaver appoggiaturas in 2/4 or 4/4 metre, are often more appropriate. Flexibility in this matter and, at the very least, the avoidance of an overuse of the overlong convention, is desirable, as Haydn's use of real notation in later works also suggests.

It may, in summary, be advanced as an argument that in Haydn's keyboard music before *c*.1765 the conventional realizations of appoggiaturas illustrated in Ex. 7.1*b* and *c* are, at best, of marginal relevance and that the realization of Ex. 7.1*d* is but one of a number of possibilities in this particular context, one, moreover, which is in many instances the least likely. Appoggiaturas before binary notes, overwhelmingly the most common occurrence, frequently require the conventional realization with a duration of half the main note, but may be performed with a range of shorter values. Haydn's notational practices in even his earliest keyboard works confirm the trend towards a more rational notation of appoggiaturas which is apparent in theoretical writings of the 1750s, although no direct link can be established between Haydn and North German theory before the mid-1760s.

REAL NOTATION: THE KEYBOARD MUSIC FROM c.1765

The concept of real notation, whereby small notes are notated in the specific values required by the composer in performance, was established in eighteenth-century theory in the 1750s. It is not clear who 'invented' the practice,[48] but C. P. E. Bach was certainly one of the first advocates who employed the practice in his own music. Bach's 'Prussian' Sonatas (1742 or 1743) certainly rely on some conventional realizations of appoggiaturas, but already in the 'Württemberg' Sonatas (1744) the composer's notation is far more specific, if not quite as refined as in later works. When Bach advocated in the *Versuch* (1753) that all variable (*veränderliche*) appoggiaturas be notated by small notes with their real values, he was promoting an idea which he had utilized for many years in his own music. It is clear from Türk's advocacy of real notation near the end of the eighteenth century, that precision in the notation of appoggiaturas was not universally employed. However, real notation did gain a certain currency in the second half of the eighteenth century. For much music of this period, in particular keyboard music, the composer's notation should be taken as a quite literal indication of the intended meaning, not withstanding certain anomalies and cautionary comments discussed below.[49]

---

[48] Schenker's suggestion that J. S. Bach notated appoggiaturas at their real values appears to be based on suspect sources of Bach's music. It is clear from autograph manuscripts that this is not the case. See Schenker, *Ornamentik*, trans. Siegel, 55.

[49] Neumann's discussion of long appoggiaturas in Mozart's music highlights the general reliability of the durations of small notes in Mozart's notation (Neumann, *Ornamentation in Mozart*, 31–6), although it is clear that Mozart does not use real notation in his juvenilia. Interestingly, it is in the juvenilia of J. C. Bach, written when the young composer was studying with C. P. E. Bach, that the composer's notation of ornaments is most specific.

A dramatic change in style is apparent in Haydn's keyboard works in the second half of the 1760s and has been well documented in A. Peter Brown's description of what he terms 'Six Progressive Sonatas'.[50] As notable as the stylistic change in these works is Haydn's experimentation with notation, which continues into his works of the 1770s. As suggested in Chapter 5, Haydn's experimentation with notation and performance practice was very likely motivated by his reading at this time of C. P. E. Bach's *Versuch* and it is therefore not surprising that the 'real' notation of appoggiaturas, an important innovation in the *Versuch*, should be of relevance to the compositions in Haydn's new keyboard style. Haydn was certainly employing this manner of notation by 1766, as is clear from the dated autograph of the Sonata in E flat, Hob. XVI: 45, but precisely when he first adopted real notation is difficult to establish. Until 1762 appoggiaturas were, as established by Feder, notated uniformly in Haydn's autographs by small quaver notes: although in a number of pre-1766 works values other than the quaver are used to notate appoggiaturas, it is by no means clear that these values express the intended duration in performance.[51] Problems of chronology and the paucity of autograph manuscripts for the period 1762–5 make it impossible to locate precisely the date from which Haydn employed real notation, but in two works, the Capriccio in G major, Hob. XVII: 1, which definitely dates from 1765 and the Sonata in E minor, Hob. XVI: 47, which is dated by Brown as *c.*1765 and by Christa Landon as pre-1766,[52] there are suggestions that Haydn may have been experimenting with a more specific manner of notating appoggiaturas, even if it is impossible for various reasons to say that the notation always specifically represents the composer's intended realization.

The Capriccio in G survives in an autograph manuscript, and while only a handful of appoggiaturas are notated by small notes, the various values of these small notes (♪ before ♩ and ♩, ♪ before ♩

[50] *Keyboard Music*, 293–300.

[51] A number of writers associate Feder's remarks on *Halbwertnotierung* with C. P. E. Bach's description of real notation and suggest *c.*1762 as the date of Haydn's study of Bach's *Versuch*; see Somfai, 'Notation', 25, Brown, *Keyboard Music*, 219; Rosenblum, *Performance Practices*, 217, 451 n. 2. This is, however, a false association; the variety of values for the small notes in Haydn's real notation after 1766 (see Table 7.1) extends far beyond *Halbwertnotierung. c.*1765–6 is, as pointed out below, the probable date for Haydn's adoption of real notation and also a more likely date than 1762 for Haydn's reading of Bach's *Versuch*.

[52] Brown, *Keyboard Music*, 123; Christa Landon, of *Haydn: Sämtliche Klaviersonaten*, vol. 1b, pp. XVI, 114.

and ♩ before ♪) inspire confidence in the precision of the notation. The appoggiaturas notated by small notes in bars 50–4 and in bar 84 suggest unproblematic interpretations, i.e. the conventional half of the duration of the main notes. In bars 4 and 98 (see Ex. 7.20*a*), how-ever, the literal appearance of the notation prompts an interpretation of the appoggiaturas which is shorter than the conventional half of the main note. When these passages are repeated elsewhere in the work, the semiquaver notation of appoggiaturas is consistent: how-ever, on two occasions a quaver small note is used in similar although not identical passages (bars 38 and 117, Ex. 7.20*b*). In later works one could confidently regard the differing notations as representative of different performance intentions, but some doubts may be enter-tained with regard to this early work. It is noteworthy, for instance, that in notating the inverted *Doppelschlag* in small notes at bar 311 and elsewhere, quavers are used, but it is characteristic of Haydn's nota-tion from *c*.1766 that semiquavers or demisemiquavers are used for groups of small notes which indicate an ornament involving more than one note. In general, the notation in the Capriccio is credible as regards the performance values of appoggiaturas, but in Ex. 7.20, while the notation is highly suggestive, other interpretations cannot be ruled out. It is interesting none the less that in this example the quaver indication is the exception and the semiquaver the norm for this particular context throughout the Capriccio.[53] If a performer is inclined to 'regularize' the inconsistency, then a consistent use of semiquaver rather than quaver appoggiaturas seems plausible, although it is arguable that the contrasting notation indicates an intended distinction in the performance values of these appoggiat-uras.

Rather special problems are presented by the Sonata in E minor, Hob. xvi: 47. It is now generally accepted that the most probably authentic version of this sonata is that containing an Adagio in E minor, an Allegro in E major, and a Finale: Tempo di menuet, also in E major, the latter found in the *Dorsch Anthology* in the Gesellschaft der Musikfreunde and first commented on by Jens Peter Larsen.[54] It

---

[53] The semiquaver duration for the appoggiaturas in Ex. 7.20*a* is also credible because of the association of this context with the short appoggiatura (see context 5, above). The longer quaver appoggiatura of bar 37 (7.20*b*) may well be due to the melodic variation in which the appoggiatura is prepared on the previous beat.

[54] J. P. Larsen, 'Eine bisher unbeachtete Quelle zu Haydns frühen Klavierwerken', in D. Weise (ed.), *Festschrift Joseph Schmidt-Görg zum 60. Geburtstag* (Bonn: Beethovenhaus, 1957), 188–95.

Ex. 7.20. Hob. XVII: 1

(*a*)

(*b*)

is presented in this form in the modern editions of Feder and Landon, although the latter also contains the more suspect F minor version. The F minor version was published in 1788 by Artaria and in this version the Adagio and Allegro are in F minor and F major respectively and are preceded by a dubious F major movement which resembles in texture a two-part invention. Another source, in Kroměřiž, presents the Adagio and Allegro followed by the G major Capriccio, Hob. XVII: 1.[55] Given such source problems, it is impossible to say if real notation was employed in the original redaction of the work, especially since the notation of appoggiaturas varies from one source to another; there are, nevertheless, certain suggestive details in the notation. Ex. 7.21, based on Feder's text, shows bars 13–14 together with the immediate elaboration of this passage in bars 16–17. The durations of appoggiaturas suggested by the notation in bars 13 and 14 make musical sense and the distinction between quaver and semiquaver appoggiaturas is maintained in the ornamented repeat (bars 16–17), where the semiquaver is written as a large note, absorbed into the ornamental chromatic inflexion. However, in the Artaria edition this passage has a quaver appoggiatura in bar 14 and semiquaver appoggiaturas in bar 16, both, for musical reasons, unlikely. It is clear that even if the first redaction of this work employed real notation, the corruption of this notation in the ensuing chaos of transmission means that the notation as we know it, cannot be regarded as an

[55] See Brown, *Keyboard Music*, 71–2.

Ex. 7.21. Hob. XVI: 47/i

infallible guide to Haydn's intentions. However, despite the apparent carelessness of scribes and engravers it is possible to see in the general distinction between quaver and semiquaver small notes in this sonata, as it is in the Capriccio, the genesis of Haydn's precise use of real notation from 1766.[56]

The Keyboard Sonatas 1766 to c.1771

Haydn's most extensive use of real notation is found in the keyboard music written between 1766 and *c*.1771. In these works more appoggiaturas are notated by means of small notes than in subsequent compositions and the small notes also express a wider range of durations

[56] The association of Hob. XVI: 47 and the Capriccio in the Kroměříž source, although probably not indicative of the original cycle of movements for these problematic works, is interesting in other regards. Both of these works seem to require short-octave tuning of the keyboard instrument to enable the performance of certain chords involving large stretches. As mentioned in Ch. 1, there are undoubted problems concerning the disposition of the short octave, but it does seem as if both these works were written for the same instrument and possibly at the same time, i.e. in 1765 (the date of the Capriccio autograph). Another work which uses a short-octave tuning, the variation set Hob. XVII: 2, is also customarily dated *c*.1765 (see S. Gerlach, ed., *Haydn: Klavierstücke, Klaviervariationen* (2nd edn., Munich: Henle, 1981), 16, and Brown, *Keyboard Music*, 131). Stylistically Hob. XVI: 47 and the Capriccio also seem united in their anticipation of the works written between 1766 and 1771 and are labelled by A. Peter Brown as the 'Earliest Manifestations of the New Style' (Brown, *Keyboard Music*, 289–93). These factors combined seem to indicate 1765 as the likely date of composition of Hob. XVI: 47 and suggest that in these two works we find the genesis, not only of the style, but also of the orthographic habits characteristic of Haydn's works after 1766.

(unlike later works, where, as will be illustrated, most long appoggiaturas tend to be written in large notes with specific durations notated as part of the metrical scheme). Thus, for instance, in the sonatas Hob. XVI: 18, 19, 20, 44, 45 and 46 small notes of the following values occur: ♪, ♪, ♪, ♩, ♩. There can be no doubt, despite the qualification made below, that these values represent the intended duration of appoggiaturas. It is quite a common feature in mid-eighteenth-century publications of keyboard music that two or even three values of small note are employed without a direct relationship between the written values and the durations in performance being intended: in these instances the value of the small note is related mathematically to the value of the main note and remains constant, usually half the value of a binary note and one-third the value of a dotted note.[57] This practice differs significantly from the real notation of appoggiaturas as practised by C. P. E. Bach and Haydn, in that with these composers the value of the small notes is not in a constant relationship to the values of the large notes they precede. Thus, a semiquaver small note in the real notation of Haydn may appear before a quaver, dotted quaver, crotchet, dotted crotchet, or minim main note. Table 7.1 summarizes the various values of small notes and the values of the main notes before which each occurs for the sonatas Hob. XVI: 18, 19, 20, 44, 45, 46.

The notation is real in the sense that the denomination of the small note used in any given context is variable and is not merely a fixed fraction of the value of the main note. The durations of the appoggiaturas thus notated are in fact very varied, considerably more so than the few stereotyped durations prescribed in conventional realizations. The value prescribed for the appoggiatura is frequently half the duration of the binary main note (as are, for instance, the crotchet, semiquaver, and minim appoggiaturas in Ex. 7.22).[58] In Ex. 7.22*a* the literal reading of the notation is confirmed by the written-out appoggiaturas in the right hand of bar 4: similarly, the unambiguous notation in bar 80 of Ex. 7.22*b* confirms that the appoggiatura in bar 22 should indeed be a semiquaver. In many instances, however, the denomination of the small note explicitly requires a realization of the

---

[57] This type of notation is characteristic of most of J. C. Bach's instrumental music. See also the discussion of the notation of Caldara and Sammartini in Neumann, *Ornamentation*, 164.

[58] See also Ex. 4.4, where the crotchet value indicated for the appoggiatura in bar 2 is confirmed by analogy with bar 10.

TABLE 7.1 *The notation of appoggiaturas in Hob.* XVI: *18–20, 44–6*

Hob. no.	Values of main notes before which the following small notes occur:				
	♬	♪	♪	♩	♩
XVI: 18		♬♪♪	♩	♩♩.	
XVI: 45		♪	♩	♩.♩	♩.
XVI: 19	♬♪	♪♩♩.	♩	♩	
XVI: 20		♬♪♩	♩♩♪	♩♩♪	
XVI: 44		♬♪	♩.		
XVI: 46		♬♪♪♩♩♪♩	♩♩♪.♩	♩♩.	𝅝

Ex. 7.22(*a*) Hob. XVI: 25/ii, (*b*) Hob. XVI: 45/i, (*c*) Hob. XVI: 46/i

(*a*)

(*b*)

(*c*)

appoggiatura which is shorter than half the value of the main note. The opening of Hob. XVI: 46/i (cited as Ex. 8.21) is an interesting case in point. Although the appoggiatura *f″* in bar 1 is written as a semi-quaver, Howard Ferguson, in his edition of the work, suggests a crotchet duration, presumably by analogy with the appoggiaturas in bar 2 and in observance of the overlong convention. However, since the approach to the appoggiatura in bar 1 is quite different to that in bar 2, the difference in notation is justifiable musically. A literal read-ing of the appoggiatura in bar 1 as a semiquaver also avoids the three-fold repetition of the same rhythm.

Before dotted main notes the appoggiatura may be two-thirds of the value of the note of resolution (Ex. 7.23*a*), but a common dura-tion for such appoggiaturas is one-third of the main note's value (see Ex. 7.23*b*). In Ex. 7.23*c* and, from a later work, Ex. 7.23*d*, an inter-pretation of the appoggiaturas as longer than the prescribed one-third value causes problems harmonically, especially in Ex. 7.23*d* where very obvious consecutive fifths would result. Appoggiaturas which are noticeably shorter than one-third the value of a dotted main note are also used by Haydn, as in the Lombardic style appoggiaturas illus-trated in Ex. 4.5 (bar 6, 3rd beat and bar 7, 1st beat).

Ex. 7.23(*a*) Hob. XVI: 45/iii, (*b*) Hob. XVI: 46/ii, (*c*) Hob. XVI: 18/ii, (*d*) Hob. XVII: 4

The overlong conventions discussed in relation to Haydn's early music have no relevance to the keyboard music from 1766. C. P. E. Bach illustrates these conventions in his *Versuch* using real notation to rationalize to some extent the ambiguity inherent in the notation, although retaining a rejoinder that the notation is 'not the most correct'. He illustrates this combination of real notation and Baroque convention as in Ex. 7.24*a*. Interestingly, in his instruction on the performance of recitative in the famous 'Applausus' letter, Haydn does employ, in the manner of C. P. E. Bach, a mixture of real notation and convention: 'I suggest that the two boys [soloists] in particular have a clear pronunciation, singing slowly in recitatives so that one can understand every syllable; and likewise they should follow the method of singing the recitation whereby, for example

must be sung

and not

. The penultimate note "g" drops out entirely, and this applies to all similar cases. I rely on the skill of the tenor, who will explain such things to the boys.'[59] The conventional notation associated with recitatives remained current longer than the conventional notation of appoggiaturas in instrumental music. It is especially striking therefore that in this letter Haydn, while retaining the convention, none the less notates the appoggiatura in its real value. It seems to me quite significant that in Haydn's keyboard music one never finds the overlong conventions notated in the manner of Bach (Ex. 7.24*a*). The circumstances in which overlong realizations might be applied occur frequently in Haydn's music after 1766 (i.e. appoggiaturas before main notes which are either tied or are followed by rests), but the value of the small notes makes it clear that overlong realizations of these appoggiaturas are not intended. In the majority of instances in which an appoggiatura occurs before a tied main note the small note is a semiquaver as discussed above in connection with Hob. XVI: 46/i (Ex. 8.21). Longer appoggiaturas are sometimes used before tied notes but, as

[59] *CCLN*, 10.

in Ex. 7.23*c*, overlong realizations are not intended. When an appoggiatura occurs before a note which is followed by a rest, the real notation also clarifies that the appoggiatura does not take the whole value of the main note. Such is the case in Ex. 7.24*b* where a quaver appoggiatura is indicated: elsewhere in this movement where longer appoggiaturas are intended they are written as crotchets. A similar instance is found in the Trio, Hob. xv: 7/i, where again a quaver and not an overlong crotchet is intended: in this instance a comparison of the autograph manuscript and the Artaria edition (Ex. 7.24*c* and *d*) clarifies the composer's intention, even if this were not pellucidly clear from the notation in the autograph manuscript. Haydn also uses longer appoggiaturas at such cadences, as in the autograph of Hob. xvi: 45/ii, where, again using real notation, he specifies a crotchet appoggiatura in bar 28 and a minim in bar 73 (Ex. 7.24*e*). Considering the precision with which Haydn prescribes a variety of durations for appoggiaturas at these cadences (quavers in Ex. 7.24*b* and *c*, crotchets and minims in Ex. 7.24*e*), it seems to me to be, at best, ill-advised to invoke the overlong convention as justification for a minim appoggiatura in, for instance, bar 28 of Ex. 7.24*e*. To do so is to reduce variety to uniformity in the name of a 1750s convention which was superseded by Haydn's more precise notation of the 1760s.[60]

Although real notation in general indicates the intended value of appoggiaturas accurately, there are certain anomalies which necessitate some flexibility in the interpretation of the notation. The first ambiguity concerns Haydn's use of semiquaver and demisemiquaver small notes. From Table 7.1 it can be seen that Haydn uses demisemiquaver small notes in the Sonata, Hob. xvi: 19 but not in the Sonatas, Hob. xvi: 18, 20, or 44–6, where the shortest value of small note is a semiquaver. It cannot, however, be assumed that the shortest appoggiaturas in these sonatas are semiquavers, or indeed that demisemiquaver appoggiaturas occur in Hob. xvi: 19 only when demisemiquaver small notes are written. It is clear from an examination of Haydn's autograph manuscripts that demisemiquaver small

---

[60] Regarding the cadential formulas in Hob. xvii: 3 Paul Badura-Skoda comments that 'In manchen Werken kann also ein notierter Achtelvorschlag durchaus die Länge einer halben Note einnehmen' (Badura-Skoda, '*Ornamentik*', 409). This conventional reading produces a uniformity in performance of appoggiaturas, while on the other hand the notation suggests contrast. The source for Badura-Skoda's ex. is not clear, but where he gives quaver appoggiaturas, other sources, credibly, have crotchets (see *Klavierstücke*, ed. Gerlach, 28 ff.). The contrast between the crotchets appoggiaturas in the cadences of variations I, II, and III and the minim appoggiaturas in variations VI, X, XI, and XII seems to me to be intentional.

Ex. 7.24(*a*) C. P. E. Bach, *Versuch*, trans. Mitchell, pp. 90–1, (*b*) Hob. XVI:
45/ii, (*c*) Hob. XV: 7/i, after autograph; (*d*) Hob. XV: 7/i, after Artaria edition, (*e*) Hob. XVI: 45/ii

notes are used for single appoggiaturas in very few works and that the
semiquaver is normally the shortest value of small note employed; consequently the semiquaver value may serve not only to indicate appoggiaturas which are precisely a semiquaver in duration, but also a range
of values shorter than a semiquaver.[61] Very often this ambiguity is
unproblematic and it is clear from the context what is intended. Such
is the case, for instance, with the appoggiatura on the second beat of
bar 19 in Ex. 7.24c; clearly the appoggiatura cannot be a semiquaver
and should be played as a demisemiquaver. There are, however,
instances in which a semiquaver small note before a quaver main note
is problematic since either a semiquaver or a shorter duration, in the
short–long Lombardic rhythm, may be intended by the same notation.

Haydn's real notation does not therefore consistently make a distinction between variable long appoggiaturas a semiquaver in length
and invariable short appoggiaturas played as fast as possible. Whether
there is in practice any substantial difference between these two
interpretations depends on tempo: if a semiquaver small note occurs
before a minim or another relatively long note at a very fast tempo
there is unlikely to be a great deal of difference between an interpretation as a variable or invariable appoggiatura, but at moderate and
slower tempos a difference is distinguishable. Thus, for instance, the
appoggiaturas in Ex. 4.5 may be interpreted as semiquavers or
as being shorter than a semiquaver, in a Lombardic rhythm
(♫ and ♪.), as advocated in her edition by Christa Landon. In
deciding whether a semiquaver small note should be an invariable
short or a variable long appoggiatura, the extensive discussions of this
topic in North German treatises, particularly those of Bach and Türk,
are again relevant.[62] Türk's introductory comments to the chapter
entitled 'Concerning Invariable Appoggiaturas' summarize the problems of recognizing short appoggiaturas and are particularly relevant
to Haydn's keyboard music:

because of the negligent manner of notation of some composers, in which
the form of the small note is not always a certain indication of whether the
appoggiatura is long or short, it is our particular concern here to show the
cases in which an appoggiatura must be short or belong to the second
class.[63]

---

[61] Demisemiquavers are used consistently only for ornaments consisting of more than one
note (*Doppelschlag*, arpeggios, etc.) when they are notated by small notes.

[62] Türk, *Klavierschule*, trans. Haggh, 211–21. See also Bach, *Versuch*, trans. Mitchell, 91–3.

[63] *Klavierschule*, trans. Haggh, 211.

Türk's 'second class' concerns 'uncertain or doubtful' instances in which he 'properly leave[s] it up to each person to choose whichever side he will'.[64] The comments made above concerning the short appoggiatura in Haydn's early music are also of some relevance here, but in the post-1766 music the ambiguity arises in connection with the semiquaver small note while in the earlier compositions this extends to the quaver small note. In general in the post-1766 compositions the best formulation that can be offered is to regard the semiquaver as the upper limit of possible durations for the semiquaver small note, remembering that a shorter duration is always possible, particularly in the contexts associated with the short appoggiatura in eighteenth-century treatises.

There are occasional hints in the notation of particular passages which help to distinguish short from long appoggiaturas. The Sonata, Hob. XVI: 19 is one of those works in which Haydn intermittently used demisemiquaver small notes, but given the inconsistency in the parallel passages from the first movement quoted in Ex. 7.25, Christa Landon suggests, quite plausibly, that the appoggiaturas be played shorter than a semiquaver: it is, however, equally possible to interpret the notation of bars 33, 34, and 93 quite literally (i.e. a semiquaver appoggiatura in bars 33 and 93, a demisemiquaver in bar 34) possibly emending only the semiquaver of bar 94 in the parallel passage to a demisemiquaver. In Ex. 7.26*a* the contrast between the notation of the last three quaver beats of bar 25 and the notation used in the immediate repetition of this figure is suggestive of a corresponding contrast in the performance of these figures: a short–long (demisemiquaver–dotted semiquaver) interpretation in bar 25 provides such a contrast. An opposite view may well be appropriate for Ex. 7.26*b* where, although two types of notation are used for *Vorschläge*, an interpretation of the *Vorschlag g″* as a demisemiquaver, assimilating the Lombardic rhythm of the last beat, is a valid response to the notation.

A second reason for flexibility in the interpretation of appoggiaturas after 1766 is related to problems of source material and text-criticism. While it is clear from autograph manuscripts that Haydn employed real notation from 1766, scribes and engravers were not always as meticulous in their notation of appoggiaturas. Artaria published op. 53 (Hob. XVI: 18, 19, and a sonata, formerly Hob. XVI: 17, now known to be by Schwanenberger) and op. 54 (Hob. XVI: 44–6)) *c*.1788, some twenty-two years after the earliest of the sonatas

---

[64] Ibid. 213.

Ex. 7.25. Hob. XVI: 19/i

was composed. Three autograph manuscripts survive to compare with this edition and reveal that the engraving is highly inaccurate; in particular, the majority of appoggiaturas are not printed correctly. In this instance the inaccuracy of the engraver does not jeopardize the accurate recovery of the composer's intentions since the works concerned survive in more authoritative sources. Although op. 53 and 54

Ex. 7.26(*a*) Hob. XVI: 46/i, (*b*) Hob. XVI: 27/i

may be extreme examples, and other Artaria editions, in addition to the English editions of Haydn's later trios, are demonstrably more reliable, the possibility of inaccuracy in works surviving in non-autograph sources must be considered. The modern text-critical process has purged Haydn's works of many dubious readings. Nevertheless, a large number of works have been edited from texts which, although the best available, cannot be relied upon completely, especially with regard to fine details of notation which are of great importance to the performer.

The Sonata, Hob. XVI: 43 survives in various manuscript copies and the first edition of Birchall;[65] none of these sources is authentic and the editor is frequently obliged to choose, from among variant readings, one option which can often be supported by little more than informed intuition. Consequently, the editions of Landon and Feder differ on the minutiae of notation which affect interpretation. Ex. 7.27*a* is quoted after the text of Feder; of particular concern here is the appoggiatura in bar 13 which occurs in some sources as a crotchet small note and in others as a quaver. Feder's reading is based on his assessment of the sources and, given the rigorous critical policy of *JHW*, it represents a text based solely on the state of those sources. To the performer it may seem that a crotchet appoggiatura in bar 13 is unsatisfactory (the only variant with a textual foundation, i.e. a quaver, is scarcely more satisfactory) and it may well be preferable to play a short appoggiatura here, continuing the pattern of the

---

[65] See C. Landon, *Kritische Anmerkungen*, 47.

previous bar. Landon emends the sources in this manner, giving a semiquaver appoggiatura in bar 13 instead of the textually sound but musically inappropriate quaver or crotchet. In works based on in-authentic sources it is often necessary for the performer to emend in this manner, even if there is no textual basis for the emendation. It is, of course, a moot point whether the editor should indulge in such emendation, rather than providing a text of the work as represented in the extant sources. Modern editions of Hob. xvi: 40–2 are based on the first edition of Bossler, and while this may be an authentic edi-tion, it is nevertheless full of errors and careless placement of slurs, ties, and dynamics.[66] With regard to the notation of appoggiaturas there is no valid source for comparison to demonstrate the inaccuracy of the Bossler print, but one may suspect from the context that, for instance, the appoggiatura in bar 10 of Hob. xvi: 40/ii (Ex. 7.27*b*) should be a semiquaver (i.e. indicating a short appoggiatura) and not a quaver. The quaver small note in bar 6 of Hob. xvi: 44/ii may also be an error (Ex. 7.27*c*): the quaver reading is unexceptionable but since it is not based on an autograph source, the emendation of the appoggiatura to a crotchet is perfectly justifiable. Christa Landon draws attention to the parallel passage where the appoggiatura is written in large notes as a crotchet, and the evidence of this parallel reading must here be given consideration.

The Concerto, Hob. xviii: 11 provides further illustrations of instances in which one may be justified in adopting a more flexible approach to the notation of appoggiaturas than would be the case when dealing with works transmitted in autograph manuscripts or other reliable sources. This D major Concerto is one of Haydn's most popular works and survives in a large number of printed and manu-script sources, none of which can be proved to be authentic or can be relied upon as the sole basis for a modern edition.[67] Walter and Wackernagel have compiled a critical edition which presents the most reliable text of the work possible failing the discovery of new sources: there are, however, a number of details which, although acceptable on a text-critical basis, may require emendation in perfor-mance. In bars 26, 31, and 59 of the second movement of this work the lower appoggiaturas preceding trills may well be a corruption of Haydn's normal notation for a *Triller von unten* (see Ch. 6), so that in

---

[66] See ead., pref. to *Haydn: Sämtliche Klaviersonaten*, vol. iii, p. xviii and *Kritische Anmerkungen*, 83–7.

[67] See *JHW* XV/2, Vorwort, pp. vi–viii and *Kritischer Bericht*, 185–96.

Ex. 7.27(*a*) Hob. XVI: 43/i, (*b*) Hob. XVI: 40/ii, (*c*) Hob. XVI: 44/ii, (*d*) Hob. XVIII: 11/iii

performance the lower auxiliary may be incorporated into the trill and not necessarily treated as a long appoggiatura, whether a quaver or a crotchet, as the sources suggest.[68] In bar 49 from the third movement of this work (see Ex. 7.27*d*) the appoggiatura *d#″* should almost certainly be performed, not as a quaver, but as a short appoggiatura, played as fast as possible and probably crushed with the main note.

The main problem with real notation is therefore not the interpretation of the composer's notation but the fact that it requires an

---

[68] This is in fact quite a common error in sources, as can be seen from Ex. 6.26*c*, where a *Triller von unten*, as a cadential trill following a *fermata*, is almost certainly intended, despite the notation of the lower auxiliary as a crotchet in some sources.

accuracy in the transmission of the text which scribes and engravers did not always provide in the way that, for instance, Georg Winter did for C. P. E. Bach's works. By this statement it is not intended to imply that the notation of appoggiaturas can be dismissed as generally inaccurate and of little relevance in determining the values of appoggiaturas. As mentioned above, Haydn's most extensive use of real notation was from the mid-1760s to the mid-1770s and, fortunately, the works written in this period survive in generally reliable manuscript copies and first editions, as well as in a larger than usual number of autograph manuscripts. Later works, in particular the sonatas from Hob. XVI: 49 and almost all the trios from Hob. XV: 5 to XV: 31, survive in authentic editions and/or other reliable sources: in addition, as will be discussed below, the accuracy of the notation is somewhat less crucial to interpretation in these later works than is the case in the works of *c.*1765 to *c.*1775. The literal value of the small notes can therefore be said to be the most reliable guide to the duration of appoggiaturas in Haydn's music from 1765/6, but flexibility is required in the interpretation of this notation in the following circumstances:

1. In nearly all works, the semiquaver small note is ambiguous in nature and can be interpreted as either a long or short appoggiatura.

2. In a number of works which survive in poor sources (e.g. Hob. XVI: 40–2, 43, 44; XVIII: 11), because of corruption in the process of transmission, the small notes should not be regarded as always representing the real values of appoggiaturas.

3. In works which survive in authoritative sources, even autograph manuscripts, where real notation is employed, there may nevertheless be occasional lapses in the precision of the notation.[69]

The Keyboard Music from c.1775

Haydn's notation of ornaments in the late 1760s and early 1770s is characterized by widespread use of real notation and by a large variety of symbols indicating *Doppelschläge*, trills and other *Spielmanieren*.

---

[69] Although Haydn's autograph manuscript is always the most important source, it will be apparent that there are different types of autograph manuscript: thus, a hastily written autograph may contain occasional errors, whereas Haydn's 'fair-copy' autographs are meticulous.

This is followed in the works of the late 1770s, 1780s, and 1790s by a radical simplification in notation. As regards the notation of appoggiaturas this takes the form of an ever-increasing tendency to write long appoggiaturas in large notes, with small notes used only occasionally to represent crotchet and quaver appoggiaturas and mostly being employed to indicate appoggiaturas which are a semiquaver or shorter in duration. Minim small notes occur in only a few works, even in the 1760s, and are always written as large notes in the works from the 1770s. Crotchet small notes continue to occur in quite late works, but with considerably less frequency, and are mainly employed in 3/4 metre, on the first beats and in formulas involving trills. In general, however, crotchet appoggiaturas, like minims, are written in large notes. Quavers and semiquavers (the latter indicating a range of values from the long semiquaver to the most rapid short appoggiatura) are the only values of small note that occur consistently in Haydn's later music.

Tables 7.2, 7.3, and 7.4 show the values of small note occurring in a selection of Haydn's later keyboard works.[70] The main differences among these tables are the use of crotchet small notes in Hob. XVI: 35–9 and the absence of the same in later works represented in Tables 7.3 and 7.4. A number of points about these tables require further comment: first, although crotchet small notes occur in four of the five sonatas represented in Table 7.2, their occurrence is very infrequent, indicating that by 1780 Haydn had already begun to notate most crotchet appoggiaturas with large notes. Crotchet small notes occur in only five of the fifteen separate movements of Hob. XVI: 35–9 and in a number of instances occur only once in the movement. Secondly, with regard to quaver and semiquaver small notes, although the contexts in which they occur in the 1780s and 1790s are similar, there is a marked decline in the frequency of their occurrence. No single small notes whatsoever occur in, for instance, Hob. XVI: 51/ii, XV: 24/ii and iii; in Hob. XVI: 52/i single semiquaver small notes occur only in bar 115 (the penultimate bar of the movement) and in XVI: 52/iii again only in one bar (bar 34).

---

[70] The information concerning Hob. XVI: 35–9 is based on the first edn. of Artaria, dated 1780 (Hob. XVI: 20, published with these sonatas, is not included here since it dates from 1771); that for Hob. XVI: 49 and 52 on autograph manuscripts (dating from 1790 and 1794 respectively); and the notation of Hob. XVI: 50, 51, and XV: 24–6 is derived from the first editions of Caulfield, Breitkopf & Härtel, and Longman & Broderip respectively.

TABLE 7.2 *The notation of appoggiaturas in Hob.* XVI: *35–9*

Hob. no.	Values of main notes before which the following small notes occur:				
	♪	♪	♪	♩	𝅗𝅥
XVI: 35	♪ ♪ ♩	♩.	♩		
XVI: 36	♪ ♪ ♪.	♩ ♩ ♩	𝅗𝅥		
XVI: 37	♪ ♪				
XVI: 38	♪ ♪ ♪	♩	♩ ♩.		
XVI: 39	♪ ♪ ♩.	♩	♩ ♩.		

TABLE 7.3 *The notation of appoggiaturas in Hob.* XVI: *49–52*

Hob. no.	Values of main notes before which the following small notes occur:				
	♪	♪	♪	♩	𝅗𝅥
XVI: 49	♪ ♪ ♪ ♩ ♪ ♪ ♩.				
XVI: 50	♪ ♪ ♪ ♩ ♩				
XVI: 51	♪ ♪. ♩ ♩ ♩				
XVI: 52	♪ ♪ ♪.. ♪ ♪..				

TABLE 7.4 *The notation of appoggiaturas in Hob.* XV: *24–6*

Hob. no.	Values of main notes before which the following small notes occur:				
	♪	♪	♪	♩	𝅗𝅥
XV: 24		♪	♩.	(𝅝)*	
XV: 25	♪	♪			
XV: 26		♪	♩ ♩ ♩		

* The semibreve is ornamented by a trill: the preceding small note should almost certainly be a semiquaver, indicating a *Triller von unten* rather than a long appoggiatura before a trill.

There is obviously a relationship between this phenomenon and the compositional style of Haydn's later works, but the present concern is the implication for interpretation. It is important to realize that the small note, however infrequently occurring, still represents real values. In many instances the intended value would be obvious solely because of the context, whatever the notation. Two of the most common usages in the later works involve the formula ♪♫♫ , where a semiquaver is the obvious intention, and the occurrence of a semi-quaver small note before, for instance, a semiquaver or demisemiqua-ver group, where a short appoggiatura is implicit;[71] but on other occasions a semiquaver or quaver small note is used to indicate a vari-ety of relationships between appoggiatura and main note—a quaver small note may, for instance, indicate that the appoggiatura is one-third, one-half, one-quarter, or one-sixth of the main note (see Tables 7.3 and 7.4). The problems of interpreting appoggiaturas in Haydn's late works are relatively slight, the main dilemma being the already mentioned ambiguity of the semiquaver small note. Although occa-sionally longer appoggiaturas do occur, in general only appoggiaturas ranging in performance from a quaver to the quickest of short appog-giaturas are notated by small notes: their notation and the limited number of contexts in which they occur facilitate their interpretation.

PRE-BEAT *VORSCHLÄGE*

C. P. E. Bach's categorical statement that ornaments written as small notes begin on the beat and take their value from the following note exerted an enormous influence on treatises on performance practice in the second half of the eighteenth century.[72] Eighteenth-century theory is, however, far from unanimous on the subject and the fre-quent references to pre-beat performance of *Vorschläge* have been highlighted in particular by Frederick Neumann.[73] Although many of the theoretical references are ambiguous, the conclusion is unavoidable that C. P. E. Bach's rule was not universally accepted in the eighteenth century and that the pre-beat performance of *Vorschläge* played some part in contemporary practices of ornamenta-tion. This is implicit even in C. P. E. Bach's own statement that 'This observation [the on-beat rule] grows in importance the more it is

[71] In these contexts where the intention is self-evident, Haydn is occasionally careless about notation. In the autograph fragment of Hob. xv: 5 the pattern ♪♫♫ is found on a number of occasions, although a small semiquaver usually replaces the quaver on repetition of the passage. Similarly, in the autograph of Hob. xvi: 49 a quaver small note appears before a demisemiquaver note group, although a short appoggiatura, usually represented by a semi-quaver small note, is the obvious intention.

[72] *Versuch*, trans. Mitchell, 84.

[73] *Ornamentation in Mozart*, 8–15. See also Rosenblum, *Performance Practices*, 222–4, 226–34.

neglected.'[74] In any general discussion of ornamentation in the second half of the eighteenth century, as in Rosenblum's book, it is therefore valid, based on theoretical evidence, to assume a mixed practice, with pre-beat as well as on-beat *Vorschläge* in use. However, it remains an extremely difficult task to establish the practices of individual composers. A mixed practice, representative of the era as a whole, may not be true of each composer. Just as C. P. E. Bach's *Versuch* does not represent universal practice, so too general practice, as derived from a composite view of eighteenth-century theory, may be valid for one composer but not for another. It must be admitted that it is difficult to establish clear, relevant evidence which testifies to the practices of individual composers. The composite view has been stated by Neumann and Rosenblum and need not be restated in full here. The following discussion is not intended to refute this view; but when dealing with the question of pre-beat *Vorschläge* in connection with the works of one composer, the composite gleanings of eighteenth-century theory may represent a compromise which expresses only a partial truth.

The contexts most consistently associated with pre-beat *Vorschläge* are those mentioned by Quantz and repeated intermittently in later books on performance practice. *Durchgehende Vorschläge* 'occur when several notes of the same value descend in leaps of thirds':[75] thus the *Vorschläge* in Ex. 7.28*a* may, according to Quantz, be performed as in Ex. 7.28*b* and not necessarily as in Ex. 7.28*c* or *d*. Quantz associates the *durchgehenden Vorschläge* with 'the French style of playing'.[76] He also identifies a second context in which *Vorschläge* should be performed pre-beat:

Often two appoggiaturas [*Vorschläge*] are also found before a note, the first marked with a small note, but the second by a note reckoned as part of the beat; they occur at caesuras. . . . Here the little note is again tipped briefly, and reckoned in the time of the previous note in the upbeat. Thus the notes in Fig. 9 are played as illustrated in Fig. 10 [Ex. 7.28*e*].[77]

With regard to the first of the two contexts mentioned by Quantz, it is instructive to examine Haydn's notational practices in passages involving ornamented descending thirds, since the same notation can, at least according to some theorists, stand for two very different rhythms. To ask whether *durchgehende Vorschläge* are relevant to a per-

---

[74] *Versuch*, trans. Mitchell, 84.   [75] *Versuch*, trans. Reilly, 93.   [76] Ibid. 94.
[77] Ibid.

Ex. 7.28. Quantz, *Versuch*, trans. Reilly, pp. 93–4

(a) (b)

(c) (d)

(e)

Ex. 7.29(*a*) Hob. XVI: 41/i, (*b*) Hob. XV: 11/i

(a)

(b)

formance of Haydn's music is to misstate the question. The main question that arises is not if Haydn uses *durchgehende Vorschläge*, since, of course, they are part of the ornamental fabric of any tonal style, but rather how Haydn notates these unaccented ornamental notes? Haydn is generally very specific in distinguishing between appoggiaturas (whether in Lombardic or equal-note rhythms) and *tierces coulées*, particularly when one or other pattern occurs as part of a main theme in a movement: frequently he writes each pattern clearly and unambiguously in large notes (see Ex. 7.29*a* and *b*). Problems of interpretation arise only when the ambiguous notation employing small notes replaces this more explicit manner of notation (as in Ex. 7.30*a* and *b*). This happens in a relatively small number of instances, but when it does occur it is not immediately apparent if an on-beat performance or *tierces coulées* is intended. There is, however, a consistent distinction between Haydn's use of *tierces coulées* and on-beat patterns (whether Lombardic or equal rhythms) which is immediately apparent when one rewrites the explicit notation in Ex. 7.29*a* and *b* using small notes (as indicated in square brackets in these examples). It is noticeable that in each case where Haydn writes *tierces coulées* unambiguously, a small note would be required before the bar line (or change of harmony) if the passage were rewritten:[78] the rhythm does not halt abruptly on the last beat of the bar, but an unaccented *Vorschlag* leads across the bar line to the next accented beat. The rewritten Lombardic rhythm of Ex. 7.29*b* is quite different, since it lacks the last small note, ending instead with a main note. This rewritten pattern could not be performed as *tierces coulées* without producing an uncharacteristic rhythmic hiatus on the last beat of the bar, as the movement, wanting a third, unaccented *Vorschlag* halts abruptly.[79] In all passages where Haydn writes *Vorschläge* as small notes in the context of descending thirds (as in Ex. 7.30) the pattern always corresponds to the rewritten version of Ex. 7.29*b*, that is, there is never a *Vorschlag* before the bar line, as characterizes the *tierces coulées* pattern.

Small notes are on the other hand used by Haydn to indicate *Nachschläge*. In Ex. 7.31*a* the *Nachschlag* following a trill is slurred to the preceding note, establishing that the ornament is played in the time of the previous note and is not therefore a *Schneller*; in Ex. 7.31*b* and *c* the *Nachschläge* (*e♮″ f″*, *b♭″* in 7.31*b* and *c″* in 7.31*c*) are placed before the bar lines clearly establishing that these notes are played in the time of the preceding notes and are not arpeggio notes played on the first beats of the following bars. By neither of these expedients

---

[78] This would be true in all cases not just in Ex. 7.29*a*. See also Hob. XVI: 21/ii, bars 3–4; XV: 8/i, bars 14–5; XV: 17/i, bars 58–9.

[79] P. and E. Badura-Skoda, (*Interpreting Mozart*, 81–2) make a similar observation, arguing against a *tierces coulées* performance of the opening of Mozart's Rondo K.485. For Neumann's uncharacteristically weak counter-argument see Neumann, *Ornamentation in Mozart*, 77–8.

Ex. 7.30(*a*) Hob. xv: 6/ii, (*b*) Hob. xvi: 50/i

(*a*)

(*b*)

Ex. 7.31(*a*) Hob. xv: 15/ii, (*b*) Hob. xv: 11/i, (*c*) Hob. xvi: 50/ii

(*a*)

(*b*)

(*c*)

(placement in relation to the bar line nor by the use of a slur to the preceding note) does Haydn suggest a pre-beat performance for a small note in the context of ornamented descending thirds.

The implication from Haydn's notational habits is that while the composer wrote on-beat patterns of ornamented descending thirds in two ways (either using small note or written explicitly in large notes), *tierces coulées* are only notated using the explicit values of large notes. Consequently, although one frequently finds the two manners of notating on-beat patterns interchanged in parallel passages, this is not true of *tierces coulées*. In Ex. 7.32*a*, for instance, the *Vorschläge*, written first as small notes, are notated as demisemiquavers in bar 19, possibly as a matter of convenience because of the number of accidentals involved in the transposition. It is also of interest that while in an early version of Hob. XVI: 50/ii Haydn uses ambiguous small notes to notate *Vorschläge*, in a later version he wrote appoggiaturas, and not *tierces coulées*, unambiguously in large notes (cf. Ex. 7.32*b* and *c*).[80]

Frederick Neumann has suggested that Quantz's dictum regarding the pre-beat performance of a *Vorschlag* before a written-out appoggiatura 'has the ring of timelessness'.[81] Yet, despite the undoubted relevance of this manner of performance to certain styles, it should not be imagined that any inherently musical law requires such a performance in all styles. It is not possible to dismiss Quantz's statement as being irrelevant to Haydn's keyboard music, but equally it must be remembered that Quantz was not writing specifically about keyboard music, that he specifically links this aspect of performance with the earlier French style (which would seem to be irrelevant in the context of a discussion of Haydn's keyboard music) and that there is some evidence to suggest that Haydn did not find the on-beat performance of a *Vorschlag* in this context necessarily inappropriate. The variety of ways in which Haydn ornaments the cadential figure of Ex. 6.21 has already been mentioned (see Ch. 6); some of these ornamented cadences can be said categorically to require the addition, on the beat, of an upper-auxiliary to an appoggiatura. Similarly, in Ex. 7.33*a* the 6–4 appoggiatura chord is ornamented by the addition of the auxil-

---

[80] Further examples of such parallel passages support on-beat performance of *Vorschläge*. Cf. bars 3 and 4 of Hob. XV: 6/i and bars 9 and 27 of XVI: 49/ii. Rosenblum argues concerning bar 47 of XVI: 50/i (Ex. 7.30*b*) that 'grace notes are appropriate before the staccato notes' (Rosenblum, *Performance Practices*, 233), a context associated with the short appoggiatura in North German theory. A comparison of this passage with Ex. 7.32*b* and *c* suggests that an appoggiatura rather than a grace note is appropriate.

[81] *Ornamentation in Mozart*, 42.

Ex. 7.32(*a*) Hob. XV: 12/ii, (*b*) Hob. XVI: 50/ii: after Artaria edition, (*c*) Hob. XVI: 50/ii: after Caulfield edition

iary notes *a′* and *f#′*. Although the passage quoted in Ex. 7.33*b* is somewhat different, clearly the ornamental resolution, on the last beat, of the appoggiatura *bb′* involves the placement of another appoggiatura *c″* before the *bb′*, but on the beat. The fact that in this case the on-beat placement of the *c″* creates a momentary consonance, an argument Neumann generally uses in favour of a pre-beat performance of the first of two *Vorschläge*, is apparently irrelevant. In other contexts Quantz's dictum may be appropriate, but clearly it is in no sense timeless or universal. When no notational evidence exists to point to a particular manner of performance in this context, the choice exists between a performance in the manner of Quantz or the manner of C. P. E. Bach; Exx. 6.21 and 7.33 would seem to suggest, however, that Haydn had no objection to the addition of an upper-auxiliary note, on the beat, to an appoggiatura.

While the contexts mentioned by Quantz are those with the clearest association with pre-beat performance, Frederick Neumann has argued for a wider use of the 'anticipated *Vorschlag*'. There is a very close identification between the contexts associated with the short appoggiatura by North German theorists (listed above) and those associated with pre-beat *Vorschläge* by Neumann and Rosenblum.[82] Neumann, for instance, advocates the use of pre-beat *Vorschläge* 'before triplets', 'before groups of even binary notes', 'before staccato notes', 'before repeated notes', and so on, all of which, according to North German theory, should be performed with short appoggiaturas. There is some theoretical evidence to support this wider application of the pre-beat *Vorschlag*, but the references are often shrouded in ambiguity, and in general lack the clear contextual codification associated with the short appoggiatura in North German theory. In Löhlein's *Clavier-Schule* the author states that 'the small notes that stand before quavers and semiquavers in a fast tempo are played short, so that the main note loses little or nothing'.[83] Rosenblum comments reasonably that Löhlein's statement 'implies a choice between short appoggiatura or grace-note realization for those small notes meant to be played quickly'.[84] Nevertheless, the fact remains that Löhlein gave a realization of 'grace-note' performance only in his *Anweisung zum Violinspielen* (and there only in the context of *tierces coulées*) and not in his *Clavier-Schule*. A clearer reference to pre-beat *Vorschläge* is found in Bach–Ricci *Méthode*, where it is stated that small notes take their value from the preceding or the following note.[85] No further information is, unfortunately, given concerning the contexts in which a *Vorschlag* might take its value from the preceding note; it may simply be a reference to *tierces coulées* or may imply a more liberal usage. The

[82] *Ornamentation in Mozart*, 42–75; Rosenblum, *Performance Practices*, 226–34.

[83] *Clavier-Schule oder kurze und gründliche Anweisung zur melodie und harmonie* (3rd edn., Leipzig, 1779), 14, quoted in Rosenblum, *Performance Practices*, 228 and Neumann, *Ornamentation in Baroque and Post-Baroque Music*, 195.

[84] *Performance Practices*, 228. This point was made previously by Neumann in *Ornamentation in Baroque and Post-Baroque Music*, 195.

Ex. 7.33(*a*) Hob. XVI: 21/ii, (*b*) Hob. XVI: 29/ii

most emphatic advocacy of pre-beat performance of ornaments is found in Milchmeyer's *Die wahre Art das Pianoforte zu spielen*. This source, which illustrates the anticipated performance of *Vorschläge* in a wide range of contexts, is the strongest evidence to support the interpretations of *Vorschläge* advocated by Neumann and Rosenblum, but its relevance to the works of Haydn is questionable.[86]

On the other hand North German treatises generally make no mention of pre-beat *Vorschläge*, or actually criticize this manner of performance. This attitude is confined neither geographically to North Germany nor temporally to the mid-eighteenth century: both Koch and Clementi provide clear realizations of short appoggiaturas on the beat in the early years of the nineteenth century.[87]

Internal evidence such as that advanced by Neumann and Rosenblum for a liberal use of grace notes is in general incapable of distinguishing contexts appropriate for a short appoggiatura and those suitable for pre-beat performance. While the opposite is also true (i.e. that internal evidence cannot establish the primacy of the short appoggiatura over grace notes) there are occasional notational clues which suggest caution in the use of grace notes in Haydn's keyboard music. Neumann advocates a pre-beat performance of a small note which ornaments the second note of a melodic figure which rises a

[85] 'La valeur des Petites-Notes . . . se prend sur la durée de la Note qui les précède, ou de celle qui les suit' (p. 5).

[86] J. P. Milchmeyer, *Die wahre Art das Pianoforte zu spielen* (Dresden, 1797), 38. Concerning Milchmeyer's treatise see Ch. 9.

[87] Koch, *Lexikon*, s.v 'Vorschlag'; Clementi, *Introduction*, 10.

second and then returns (); this is one of the many contexts
which Neumann associates with a grace-note performance, but in
which North German theorists advocate a short appoggiatura (see
context 5, above). In a common cadential formula Haydn (and
indeed Mozart) often interchanges figures which have this melodic
outline, some with and some without an anticipatory note (see Ex.
7.34*a* and *b*); in 7.34*b* the *Vorschlag* is not only performed on the beat
but is a long appoggiatura. In Ex. 7.34*a* the performance of the
Vorschlag must be different than in 7.34*b* because of the following
anticipatory note. The analogy between these two examples suggests,
however, that Haydn did not necessarily associate the melodic shape
with a pre-beat performance of the *Vorschlag* and therefore that
the notational distinction between 7.34*a* and *b* may reflect a difference in the length of the appoggiatura and not necessarily a difference
in metrical placement.

Essential to Neumann's advocacy of the grace note is the argument
that 'an accent seeks the beat, and the soft antecedent to an accent
seeks the rhythmic shade before the beat'.[88] Neumann points out,
quite correctly, that theorists disagree on whether a short *Vorschlag* or

Ex. 7.34. Hob. xv: 22/i

a main note should be accented, but his claim that advocacy by a
theorist of an unaccented *Vorschlag* and an accented main note necessarily implies a grace-note performance is unacceptable. Clearly C. P.
E. Bach's practice of accenting the *Vorschlag* was not universally
accepted and contrary statements are common enough in eighteenth-
century theory to suggest flexibility on this point. However, the
placement of an unaccented *Vorschlag* on the beat is not in any way
impossible or unmusical. Koch, for instance, advocates an accented

---

[88] *Ornamentation in Mozart*, 8–9.

main note but provides realizations in which the (unaccented) short appoggiatura is none the less placed on the beat.[89] In many instances, particularly in fast tempos, where the main note is accented there will be little difference between a performance of a *Vorschlag* on-beat or pre-beat: in fast tempos a short appoggiatura played as fast as possible, simultaneously or almost simultaneously (crushed) with the main note, will be virtually indistinguishable from a grace note. An unaccented short appoggiatura on the beat may also be indistinguishable from a grace note when there is no movement in another part to articulate the beat. The differences in practice are not infrequently far less clearly defined than in theory. Nevertheless the point should be allowed that the on-beat placement of an unaccented short appoggiatura is possible and is documented in eighteenth-century theory. A short appoggiatura may be accented or unaccented, a subjective matter which is rarely indicated by the notation, but this question is essentially different from the question regarding the metrical placement of a *Vorschlag*.

With regard to the question of pre-beat *Vorschläge* in Haydn's music, notational or internal musical evidence may be suggestive but cannot in any way be said to resolve what remains an open question. Nothwithstanding the difficulties of this subject, I am none the less convinced with regard to the two *loci classici* for the grace note mentioned by Quantz, that, first, Haydn's practice was to write *tierces coulées* in large notes and consequently that small notes used in the context of descending thirds require on-beat performance, either in a Lombardic or equal rhythm; and, secondly, that Haydn frequently ornaments an appoggiatura with the addition, on the beat, of an upper-auxiliary note, rather than with a grace note in the manner of Quantz. Occasionally Haydn's notation suggests that short appoggiaturas are intended in other contexts which Neumann associates with grace notes, but for which North German theorists recommend short appoggiaturas. However, since internal evidence is incapable of drawing clear distinctions between short appoggiatura and grace-note realizations, ultimately, one must trust in either the clear codification of the *veränderliche* and *unveränderliche Vorschlag* in North German theory or in the less clearly defined references to grace notes in a less homogeneous group of treatises. The relevance of the former with regard to the interpretation of Haydn's keyboard music

[89] *Lexikon*, s.v. 'Vorschlag'.

would seem to be beyond doubt. The tendencies towards the more rational representation of ornaments which are characteristic of North German treatises have important parallels in Haydn's notation and C. P. E. Bach's *Versuch* is especially relevant to Haydn's keyboard music from the mid-1760s. Quantz's notation and performance practice would, by comparison, appear to be old fashioned and irrelevant and other theoretical references to the grace note might be regarded as being more suitable to genres other than keyboard music, or to other composers.

8

Doppelschlag and Mordent

THE *DOPPELSCHLAG* OVER A NOTE

The *Doppelschlag* placed over a note is relatively unproblematic as regards performance, the general opinion being that it is played on the beat as fast as possible. C. P. E. Bach gives three realizations appropriate for different tempos (see Ex. 8.1*a*) which illustrate his instruction that the *Doppelschlag* is 'almost always performed rapidly'.[1] Undoubtedly there is latitude for expressive rhythmic nuance, particularly in slow movements,[2] but it is characteristic that part of the value of the main note should remain 'unfilled' except in the fastest tempos (Bach's *presto* realization) where this is impossible. While the performance of the ornament in this context is clear, there are in Haydn's keyboard music undoubted problems of recognition. Haydn's notation of the *Doppelschlag* is diverse and changes considerably in the course of his career. He notates the *Doppelschlag* over a note from an early date by the characteristically Haydnesque symbol ∾ (often referred to somewhat ambiguously as the 'Haydn ornament') and not by the conventional symbol ∾. The latter, which is first found authentically in the undated autograph fragment of the Sonata in B flat, Hob. XVI: 18 (*c*.1766), occurs in a dated autograph manuscript for the first time in the Sonata in C minor, Hob. XVI: 20 (1771).[3] This symbol became the composer's preferred method of notating the *Doppelschlag*, but throughout his career Haydn uses both signs, frequently interchangeably, to notate the *Doppelschlag* ornament. A letter from Haydn to Artaria, dated 20 July 1781, establishes quite clearly that the composer required both symbols in the engraving of his music, despite their apparent synonymity:

---

[1] *Versuch*, trans. Mitchell, 113.   [2] Ibid. 115.
[3] Georg Feder suggests that the earlier occurrences of the symbol ∾ in non-autograph sources are probably unauthentic. See Vorwort to *JHW* XVIII/1 (Munich: Henle, 1970), p. ix.

Ex. 8.1. C. P. E. Bach, *Versuch*, table V, figs. l, lxi, lxiii, lxix, and *addenda* to 1787 edn., pp. 67–8

Above all I ask you to engrave the musical signs as I have written them: for instance, you will find the following: **~, ∞, *tr*, ℘** [4]

Haydn employs a third method of notation for the *Doppelschlag* in his keyboard music from the early 1780s, namely three small notes (as in Ex. 8.3). In Haydn's late keyboard music this third method of notation is used with increasing frequency although the two *Doppelschlag* symbols still occur.

    Christa Landon has suggested that the normal *Doppelschlag* symbol was preferred by Haydn in connection with *Doppelschläge* after dot-

[4] *CCLN*, 30–1.

ted notes, but she concedes that it is scarcely possible to create a rule regarding Haydn's practice.[5] Ex. 8.2*b* demonstrates that in this context, as in others, Haydn used two *Doppelschlag* symbols interchangeably. Landon's statement, repeated by Rosenblum, that the sign ∾ is almost entirely replaced in the late works by ∞,[6] is also an exaggeration, since the former is frequently found in Haydn's late piano trios. This matter is however of little consequence as regards interpretation since the diversity of the notation does not imply different realizations of the *Doppelschlag*. The following examples, all based on autograph sources, are among many which could be chosen to demonstrate that the three methods of notation are used interchangeably to indicate a *Doppelschlag* and that no difference in performance is implied by the various notations. In Ex. 8.2*a* the same ornament is represented by 𝄐 and ∾ in the piano and violin parts

respectively, while ∞ and ∾ (Ex. 8.2*b*), and 𝄐 and ∞ (Ex. 8.27*b*) are

interchanged in directly parallel passages (𝄐 = ∾ ; ∞ = ∾ ; 𝄐 = ∞). The interchange of the various symbols for the *Doppelschlag* is also typical of works surviving in non-autograph sources. In the Fantasia in C major, Hob. XVII: 4, the *Doppelschlag* in the main theme of the movement is notated on its first occurrence in bar 2 by three small notes, but, with one exception, all further occurrences of the themes contain a *Doppelschlag* notated by the symbol ∾ : the exception occurs in bar 294 where, at the point of an enharmonic modulation, Haydn reverts to the use of three small notes to indicate the *Doppelschlag*, presumably to clarify the accidentals pertaining to the ornament (see Ex. 8.3).

The inverted *Doppelschlag*[7] is uncomplicated as regards notation since it is indicated from an early date in Haydn's music by the use of three small notes (𝄐). Bach's symbol for this ornament, ∾, is not found in any Haydn autograph and although this symbol is found in certain printed sources, in such instances it is a corruption of Haydn's

---

[5] Pref. to *Haydn: Sämtliche Klaviersonaten*, vol. i, p. xviii.

[6] Ibid.; Rosenblum, *Performance Practices*, 268.

[7] C. P. E. Bach categorized the 'inverted *Doppelschlag*' as a variety of 'slide' (*Schleifer*) but used an inverted *Doppelschlag* symbol (∾) to indicate the ornament. Haydn's notation of the ornament (𝄐) is referred to by Bach as 'an occasional practice'; see Bach, *Versuch*, trans. Mitchell, 137.

Ex. 8.2(*a*) Hob. XV: 5/iii, (*b*) Hob. XVI: 26/i

(*a*)

(*b*)

normal notation for the *Doppelschlag* and does not indicate an
inverted *Doppelschlag*.[8]

It is important to consider, for a number of reasons, that the
Doppelschlag may be intended where symbols other than the three

---

[8] The symbol ∽ is commonly found in many English editions of Haydn's music,
which do not distinguish between ∽ and ∞, hence both signs indicate the common
Doppelschlag; as, e.g. in the John Bland edn. of Hob. XVI: 49 (see Ex. 8.6). Occasionally some
of Artaria's engravers employ the symbol ∽, sometimes, perhaps, because the engraver is
copying from an English source: invariably it indicates a *Doppelschlag* and not an inverted
Doppelschlag.

Ex. 8.3. Hob. XVII: 4

described above are found. First, in Haydn's earliest keyboard music, before he had evolved his own characteristic method of notating ornaments, the specific symbols for the *Doppelschlag* are not in general used. While in some early works the notation ![symbol] may well indicate a *Doppelschlag*,[9] this manner of notation is conspicuously absent in Haydn's keyboard music. In the early keyboard music the *tr* symbol is the only ornament symbol occurring with any frequency and it may legitimately be regarded as a generic symbol which may

---

[9] The notation ![symbol] is regarded by North German theorists as being equivalent to the symbol ∾ (Türk, *Klavierschule*, trans. Haggh, 271–2; Marpurg, *Anleitung*, 53 and table VI, fig. 6). Neumann has, however, made a strong case for regarding the former notation as an 'Italian mordent design', a mordent with a pre-beat *Vorschlag* (see Neumann, *Ornamentation in Baroque and Post-Baroque Music*, 455 and *Ornamentation in Mozart*, 58–62). It is clear, however, that the interpretation advocated by Neumann is not applicable to all composers. While it does seem to be of relevance to Mozart, who distinguished clearly between the notation ![symbol] and ∾, J. C. Bach and Clementi probably regarded these different indications as being synonymous, both signs indicating a *Doppelschlag*, as is suggested by the numerous occasions on which they used them interchangeably in parallel passages. Haydn does not employ the notation ![symbol] in keyboard music: this may in itself be an indication that when this notation does occur in Haydn's non-keyboard music it represents a *Doppelschlag* and not an 'Italian' mordent, since C. P. E. Bach and other North German theorists mention that this notation is used to indicate a *Doppelschlag* in non-keyboard music, where the symbol for the *Doppelschlag* is not generally used (Bach, *Versuch*, trans. Mitchell, 115; Agricola, *Anleitung*, 115).

have alternative meanings to the conventional trill; in particular it
may indicate the *Doppelschlag*.[10] For instance, in Hob. xvi: 9/ii, bar 1
(see Ex. 8.4*a*) the *tr* symbols may be realized as *Doppelschläge*, as suggested by Christa Landon in her edition of the Haydn Sonatas, since
in later sonatas Haydn often indicates a *Doppelschlag* in such contexts
(cf. Hob. xvi: 27/ii, bar 1, Ex. 8.4*b*).

Ex. 8.4(*a*) Hob. xvi: 9/ii, (*b*) Hob. xvi: 27/ii

Secondly, in all of Haydn's music for which no autograph manuscript survives, a variety of symbols, which have distinct meanings
unrelated to the *Doppelschlag*, may appear in place of the *Doppelschlag*
symbols as a result of the corruption of Haydn's notation in the
process of transmission. Although many ornament signs were incorrectly represented by copyists and engravers, the *Doppelschlag*
symbol ∾ was especially likely to appear in a corrupt form, probably
because this symbol was unfamiliar to many copyists and because
engravers frequently lacked a specifically cast punch to engrave the
symbol. The extent of this corruption has previously been remarked

---

[10] C. P. E. Bach comments that the symbol for the *Doppelschlag* is little known apart from
keyboard music and 'is often indicated by the signs of the trill or even the mordent' (*Versuch*,
trans. Mitchell, 117). It should be added that the generic use of the *tr* symbol is apparent not
just in non-keyboard music, but in the keyboard music of both C. P. E. Bach and Haydn
before they evolved their respective systems of specialized signs for the various
Klaviermanieren, i.e. Bach's music of the 1730s and 1740s and Haydn's of the 1750s. See also
Türk, *Klavierschule*, trans. Haggh, 273–4.

upon[11] and a few examples may suffice here as illustrations of wide-spread practices. In the autograph manuscript of the musical clock piece Hob. XIX: 17 Haydn indicates *Doppelschläge* in two ways (cf. bars 6 and 7 of Ex. 8.5),[12] but it is indicative of scribal misrepresentation that Niemecz, in rewriting some passages at the end of the autograph manuscript, substituted a *tr* symbol for Haydn's *Doppelschlag* indication.[13]

Ex. 8.5. Hob. XIX: 17 (after *JHW*)

The situation regarding printed editions is more complex since many engravers were as likely to follow their own conventions (presumably sometimes dictated by the availability of specific punches) than to reproduce Haydn's notation correctly. The signs for the *Doppelschlag* are represented differently, not only by different publishers, but by different engravers working for the same publisher. Thus, the engraver of Artaria's op. 57 (plate no. 239, containing the Trios, Hob. XV: 11–13), who apparently had no suitable punch to engrave Haydn's *Doppelschlag* symbols, frequently engraves the sign ∾ 'freehand', using a graver, but occasionally a punch is used to engrave the sign ⌁ (where a *Doppelschlag* is the likely intent and is given in the Longman & Broderip edition); on other occasions the sign ⌁ is engraved in the Artaria edition, presumably the equivalent of

---

[11] See esp. K. Päsler, Vorwort to *Joseph Haydn Klavierwerke, Joseph Haydn Werke*, XIV/1–3 (Leipzig: Breitkopf & Härtel, 1918), xi–xii.

[12] See facsimile reprod. in Ord-Hume, *Mechanical Organ*, 83. Both Robbins Landon and Howard Ferguson draw attention to the realization of the ornaments in bars 6 and 7 of Ex. 8.5 on the beat in the performance on the extant musical clock; see H. C. R. Landon, *Symphonies*, 162 and H. Ferguson, *Interpretation*, 122–3.

[13] Numerous instances of such scribal corruption are documented in Christa Landon's *Kritische Anmerkungen* to *Haydn: Sämtliche Klaviersonaten*. See e.g. 37–9 concerning the notation in the sources of the Sonata, Hob. XVI: 46.

Haydn's ❧. In Artaria's op. 61 (plate no. 327, containing the Trio, Hob. XV: 14) a different engraver uses a punch to engrave the sign ∽ (= Haydn's ∾) and improvises the sign ∽⌐ (= Haydn's ❧) by adding a staccato *Strich* to the previous sign; later this same engraver adds the signs ∽ and ❧ using a graver, but intermittently reverts to the punches ∽ and ∽⌐. A great variety of signs, many of them improvised and few apparently specially cast, is used by engravers and it is not always clear which of Haydn's signs is intended.[14] Therefore, Haydn's sign ❧ is represented in contemporary editions and manuscript copies by ∾, *tr*, t, ⌁, ⌁⊢ , and by various approximations to these symbols; conversely, the symbol ❧ sometimes appears in Artaria's editions as the engraver's 'shorthand' for Haydn's *tr* symbol or as a misreading of Haydn's *tr* symbol (see e.g. Ex. 8.6).[15]

Modern Urtext editions have standardized ornamental signs, mostly according to Haydn's autograph usage, and many dubious readings in this regard have been purged by the modern text-critical process; yet it must be suspected that in some instances inauthentic ornament symbols have been preserved in the editions of works which survive only in inferior sources; in particular, it is possible that the signs ⌁ and *tr* appear where Haydn may have intended ∾ or ❧. The chevron sign in bar 4 of Hob. XVI: 44/ii (Ex. 8.7*a*) appears in the most authoritative sources for this sonata and consequently in modern editions of the work, but in this context a *Doppelschlag* is frequently the required ornament, as in bar 72 of Hob. XVI: 18/ii (Ex. 8.7*b*; see also Ex. 8.32).[16] While the modern scholarly edition should perhaps do no more than reflect the most authoritative sources, however inadequate these might sometimes be, the performer may, indeed should, make considered emendations of this sort without compunction.[17] However, careful independent evaluation of every

---

[14] E.g. in the Hummel edn. of the Sonatas, Hob. XVI: 27–32, the notation of ornaments is often problematic. Various signs for the *Doppelschlag* are employed, but the most frequent sign (∽) cannot derive from Haydn. A comparison between this edn. and the autograph fragment of Hob. XVI: 29 establishes that ∽ occurs where Haydn wrote ∾.

[15] See Päsler, Vorwort to *Joseph Haydn Klavierwerke*, pp. ix–x.

[16] Türk (*Klavierschule*, trans. Haggh, 273–4) counts this context among those where the performer 'can make use of the turn without hesitation in place of these other ornaments [trills and mordents]'. See also Bach, *Versuch*, trans. Mitchell, 117; and Agricola, *Anleitung*, 118.

[17] Although the Sonata in E flat, Hob. XVI: 45 survives in an autograph manuscript, similar figures are notated in parallel passages with the symbols *tr* and ❧ interchanged (for instance, cf. first movement, bars 42–4 and 94–6); Christa Landon plausibly suggests the emendation of *tr* to ❧. It should be pointed out, however, that this type of inconsistency

Ex. 8.6. Hob. XVI: 49/i: (*a*) ornamental variants in the Artaria edition; (*b*) ornamental variants in the Bland editions, (*c*) after autograph

(*Note:* the ornamentation is consistent between parallel passages (bars 33–6, 163–6) in the autograph MS.)

suspect reading is necessary and no generalizations can be made regarding notational misrepresentation in non-autograph sources. Different notation in parallel passages may well be indicative of scribal error, but to regard every instance of divergent notation as inconsistent and in need of emendation is not necessarily valid. Christa Landon suggests the emendation of *tr* to a *Doppelschlag* in bars 2 and 21 of Hob. XVI: 3/i, yet in the melodic sequences of bars 18–19, 42–3, 46–7, etc. the two symbols are notated consecutively as local

is rare in Haydn's autograph manuscripts, in particular those from the late 1760s onwards. Although signs which have the same meaning are frequently interchanged, the interchange of signs with different meanings is unusual in the autograph manuscripts.

Ex. 8.7(*a*) Hob. XVI: 44/ii, (*b*) Hob. XVI: 18/ii

variations with such consistency as to inspire confidence in the
sources (see Ex. 8.8). In this particular instance one suspects that
emendation is unnecessary.

Ex. 8.8. Hob. XVI: 3/i

THE *DOPPELSCHLAG* OVER THE SECOND NOTE OF A
DESCENDING SECOND

Throughout his career Haydn used either of the two *Doppelschlag*
symbols over the second note of a descending second. The interpre-

tation of the *Doppelschlag* symbols in this context is problematic. The conventional realization in this context is only possible if non-legato articulation is indicated or is at least feasible: such an instance occurs in the G major Capriccio, Hob. XVII: 1 (see Ex. 8.9), where in bars 19–22 the implicit non-legato articulation across the bar lines, which is made explicit in bars 19–20 by the staccato *Strich*, allows the normal interpretation of the *Doppelschlag*. There are, however, many instances when, either because of the presence of a slur or because the upper note of the descending second is an appoggiatura, legato articulation is required in this context and in such cases the repetition of the upper auxiliary of the *Doppelschlag* is, because of the articulation, impossible. Undoubtedly the presence of the *Doppelschlag* symbol in this context may, in some sources, be the result of corruption: this is clearly the case in the Artaria and Bland editions of Hob. XVI: 49, as is revealed by a comparison of these editions with the extant autograph (see Ex. 8.6). It is also clear, however, that the *Doppelschlag* symbols occur authentically over the second note of a legato descending second, as illustrated in Ex. 8.10, which is based on the autograph incipit in the *Entwurf-Katalog* (see also Ex. 8.14*a* and *b* which are similarly based on autograph sources). A realization of the *Doppelschlag* symbol in this context with the upper auxiliary tied cannot be discounted. This particular use of the *Doppelschlag* is described by C. P. E. Bach, Marpurg, Türk, and other North German theorists and is found in C. P. E. Bach's keyboard music (see Ex. 8.11).[18] This interpretation would, however, seem to be almost exclusively North German and even within this tradition it is something of an exceptional usage, the most frequent ornament associated with the context being the *prallende Doppelschlag* and *Praller*. Robbins Landon and Howard Ferguson suggest that in Haydn's music the *Doppelschlag* in this context should be realized as in Ex. 8.11*c*.[19]

These suggestions have the merit of being idiomatic, and while it is impossible to be certain about the precise rhythm of the ornament in this context, or if a tied upper auxiliary is requisite, a detail of notation in the autograph manuscript of the C minor Sonata strongly suggests that the melodic shape of this realization is appropriate. In bar 8 of Hob. XVI: 20/i (see Ex. 8.12) Haydn notates the ornament over

[18] See Bach, *Versuch*, trans. Mitchell, 114; Türk, *Klavierschule*, trans. Haggh, 272.
[19] See H. C. R. Landon, *Symphonies*, 162–3. Howard Ferguson offers a similar suggestion in *Interpretation*, 123 and Paul Badura-Skoda treats the *prallende* and *geschnellte Doppelschlag* briefly in 'Ornamentik', 416–17.

Ex. 8.9. Hob. XVII: 1

Ex. 8.10. Hob. XIV: 5

Ex. 8.11(*a*) Marpurg, *Principes du clavecin*, table VI, fig. 9, (*b*) C. P. E. Bach, H.136 (Wq.50/1)/iii

the second note of a descending second as a *prallender Doppelschlag*[20] and while this movement contains Haydn's sole use of this Bach sym-

---

[20] Haydn's notation in bar 8 is an inversion of C. P. E. Bach's symbol 𝄾. However, from the context as well as from the nature of the compound symbol, despite the inversion, the intention in bar 8 is perfectly clear. In bars 9 and 12 Haydn rectifies his orthographic error and the correct symbol appears. Concerning the interpretation of the ornaments in bars 9 and 12 see Ex. 8.31.

Ex. 8.12. Hob. XVI: 20/i

bol, it is perhaps enough to suggest that Haydn intended a realization similar to the *prallende Doppelschlag* when he wrote ∾ or ❧ in this context.

Somfai has suggested another interpretation of the *Doppelschlag* symbols when they occur over the second note of a descending second interval; that is, as a *Praller*.[21] This interpretation also has the merit of being idiomatic, since ornamenting the second note of a descending second interval is regarded by theorists as being one of the most usual uses of the *Praller*. In non-autograph Haydn sources the interpretation advocated by Somfai may be justified because of the possibility that the *Doppelschlag* symbols may be a corruption of the similar chevron. In Ex. 8.13, for instance, the text is based on the rather unreliable edition of Birchall, an edition which is particularly suspect as regards the notation of performance instructions,[22] and in this case it is difficult to place much trust in the different signs which occur in parallel passages. Considering that the notation in this instance can hardly be regarded as inviolable, the choice of a *Praller* in bars 4 and 80 is both justifiable and, because of the *vivace molto* tempo indication, more practicable. However, in autograph manuscripts Haydn sometimes carefully distinguished between his use of the *Doppelschlag* and chevron symbols in the context of a legato descending second, suggesting that when the symbols are differentiated in reliable sources different realizations are intended. In Hob. XVI: 21, which survives in a very precise autograph fair copy, the distinction between *Praller* and *Doppelschlag* cannot be a matter of caprice since it is maintained consistently throughout the movement: in bar 3 the intended ornament is obviously a *Praller*, but in bar 4 another ornament must be intended (as suggested in Ex. 8.14*a*). In the autograph of the first movement of Hob. XVI: 26/i *Doppelschlag* symbols are frequently used in ornamenting the resolution of long

[21] 'Notation', 30.   [22] See C. Landon, *Kritische Anmerkungen*, 80–3.

Ex. 8.13. Hob. XVI: 34/iii

appoggiaturas, but the chevron is also used in this context, although, notably, not in directly parallel passages (see Ex. 8.14*b*). Again the notational distinction is suggestive of different realizations: in bars 14, 18, and 19 a *prallender Doppelschlag* would seem to be appropriate, although a realization in the manner of Marpurg (as in Ex. 8.11*a*) cannot be discounted. In both *a* and *b* of Ex. 8.14 it is unwise to reduce the clear notational diversity to a uniform interpretation as a *Praller*.

THE MORDENT

Haydn's concern expressed in his letter of 20 July 1781 to Artaria that a distinction should be made between ∾ and ⌀ might appear illogical since both signs serve to indicate a *Doppelschlag*; however, his concern is justified in view of the fact that, although the two signs are synonymous with regard to the notation of *Doppelschläge*, the sign ⌀ also appears to have an independent function in indicating the mordent. This Haydnesque symbol and the conventional mordent symbol (⌀) are clearly very similar and in the Haydn autographs, although many signs are easily recognizable as ⌀, others are indistinct hybrids which could be either: seldom is a sign clearly recognizable as ⌀. Editorial policies in modern Urtext editions differ markedly as regards these signs: Georg Feder transcribes all hybrid signs as ⌀ and comments in his preface that although this sign in general means a *Doppelschlag*, in the appropriate musical context it may mean a mordent.[23] Christa Landon on the other hand attempts to differentiate between the two signs but points out that they can 'barely be distinguished in the sources'; Somfai has also pointed to instances in which a conventional mordent symbol may be distinguished in the Haydn autographs from the symbol ⌀.[24] Such instances undoubtedly exist

[23] Vorwort to *JHW* XVIII/1, x.
[24] C. Landon, pref. to *Haydn: Sämtliche Klaviersonaten*, vol. i, p. xviii; Somfai, 'Notation', 27, 34, n. 3.

Ex. 8.14(*a*) Hob. XVI: 21/i, (*b*) Hob. XVI: 26/i

(as in Hob. XVI: 21/i, Ex. 8.14*a*, where, based on the autograph manuscript, it is possible, *pace* Feder, to transcribe the ornament over the third note of bar 5 as ∿ rather than ∿) and in such instances Feder may appear to be abdicating editorial responsibility. However, in the overwhelming majority of cases the sign is either clearly ∿ (Hob. XVI: 6/iii, bar 14) or a hybrid which it would be unwise to identify as the mordent symbol ∿ purely on palaeographic grounds (e.g. in

Hob. XVI: 23/ii, bars 1, 2, and 13).[25] The advantages of such marginal
palaeographic distinctions can perhaps be overstressed and in many
instances are not the most reliable guide to interpretation, since symbols readily recognizable as ∾ may also be interpreted as a mordent.[26] It would seem that Haydn found the duality of this symbol
acceptable and only occasionally thought it necessary to specify—
either by a more careful differentiation between ∾ and ∿, or by the
use of another notation for the the mordent (see below)—one or
other interpretation of this symbol. This may or may not be associated with the Italian tradition of regarding the *Doppelschlag* as a variety of mordent,[27] but the duality of Haydn's ∾ symbol is evident
from the fact that Haydn rarely, even in autograph fair copies, distinguished ∾ from ∿. The Haydn letter of 20 July 1781 quoted above
is also informative in this regard; while Haydn was concerned that ∞
be distinguished from ∾ , he did not specify that the Artaria engravers
should distinguish between ∾ and ∿. Since the only symbol in this
letter which may indicate a mordent is ∾ , and since it is known that
this symbol may also indicate a *Doppelschlag*, the dual function of the
symbol is implicit in Haydn's instructions to Artaria.

Although it may on occasions be possible to distinguish ∾ from ∿
in the Haydn autographs, in non-autograph sources the duality of the
sign ∾ is clearly a reality. In the first movement of Hob. XVI: 32 (Ex.
8.15) the notation of the mordent found in bar 1 is subsequently
abbreviated in parallel passages by the sign ∾ ; the ornament of bar 2
is also usually interpreted as a mordent.[28] While the notation given
in this example is found consistently in the non-autograph sources
(no autograph is extant) and is not a matter of dispute, modern editions differ on the notation of this passage. Feder reproduces the sym-

---

[25] C. Landon suggests that the symbol ∾ appears at times to be a hasty abbreviation for
the symbol ∿ (pref. to *Haydn: Sämtliche Klaviersonaten*, vol. i, p. xviii).

[26] A distinct disadvantage of C. Landon's editorial approach to the problem is that the
performer is reliant on the marginal palaeographic decisions of the editor and is also unaware
when the symbol ∿ is reproduced as a result of musical rather than palaeographic decisions.

[27] Following the Italian tradition L. Mozart regards the *Doppelschlag* as a type of mordent
(see L. Mozart, *Violinschule*, trans. Knocker, 207–9; see also Neumann, *Ornamentation in
Baroque and Post-Baroque Music*, 452–5; 459–62). Robbins Landon's association of this Italian
tradition with Haydn's notation of the *Doppelschlag* and mordent (H. C. R. Landon,
Symphonies, 161–3) should be regarded with circumspection: the Italian tradition is essentially concerned with a practice of improvised embellishment rather than with the matters
of notation which are the central concern here.

[28] See C. Landon, pref. to *Haydn: Sämtliche Klaviersonaten*, vol. ii, p. xiv, and *Kritische
Anmerkungen*, 71.

bol as in the sources. Landon reproduces the symbols of bars 2, 9, 29, etc. as mordent signs, the decision to do so evidently being based on musical rather than palaeographic grounds. It should therefore be understood that the mordent symbols in Landon's edition are frequently not the result of palaeographical decisions but of musical interpretation, in effect a tacit admission that palaeographic distinctions do not define function and that mordents are best identified by musical context. In autograph sources it would also be wise to identify the mordent according to context rather than confining its use to those instances where a marginal palaeographic decision might appear to identify the sign ⬥ as distinct from the sign ⬥ .

Ex. 8.15. Hob. XVI: 32/i

We know of one instance in which Haydn categorically requires the mordent symbol ⬥ and not the more general indication ⬥ . In a letter dated 10 December 1785, Haydn complained to Artaria about the poor quality of engraving in his Trios, Hob. XV: 6–8, then in press:

And on this very page, in the second stave, you should put instead of the sign *tr*: the following: ⬥, for the first one, as the engraver has done it, means a trill, whilst mine is a half mordent [*Halb Mordent*]. If, therefore, the Herr

Engraver doesn't know signs of this sort, he should inform himself by studying the masters, and not follow his own stupid ideas.[29]

It is noteworthy that here Haydn specified the mordent symbol as a
correction of an unacceptable use of the trill symbol and one is
inclined to suspect that had the sign ∿ been engraved instead of *tr*,
the engraver would not have merited the same censure.[30] Generally,
however, when Haydn specifically required the mordent as opposed
to the *Doppelschlag*, he did not specify the former by making the sign
∿ distinguishable from ∿, but wrote the mordent in small notes, as
in Ex. 8.15. Another instance of this notation occurs in the piece for
musical clock, Hob. XIX: 16: in the autograph manuscript the fugue
subject is unornamented, but a footnote in Haydn's hand instructs the
maker of the instrument that a mordent should be added to the first
note of the subject each time it occurs.[31] Haydn writes the ornament
in small notes and his term for the ornament is 'Halb Mordent' (see
Ex. 8.16):[32] clearly this term in Haydn's usage, here and in the letter
of 10 December 1785, refers to the common single mordent of one

Ex. 8.16. Hob. XIX: 16 (*a–b*) (after *JHW*); (*c*) Hob. XV: 16/ii

[29] *CCLN*, 51–2.

[30] The symbol ∿ in the Artaria edn. of Hob. XV: 6 is somewhat exceptional. Symbols such
as ∿ ʼare used by some engravers (e.g. in Artaria op. 57 and the Hummel edn. of Hob. XVI:
27–32), but are very likely meant to represent Haydn's symbol ∿ rather that specifically ∿.

[31] Haydn's footnote reads 'NB so oft als das Thema komt, mus bey jedweder Halben
Notte folgender Halbe Mordent komen'. Haydn's notation of the ornament is given in Ex.
8.16. Facsimile reprod. in *JHW* XXI.

[32] It is clear from the Artaria edn. of Hob. XV: 6, where the corrected passage reads ∿,
not ∿, in the bar referred to in the letter of 10 Dec. 1785 (i.e. bar 15, second movement),
and from the autograph of Hob. XIX:16, that Haydn's term 'Halb Mordent' refers to the
mordent specifically, whereas the modern term 'Haydn ornament', if used at all, should refer
to the symbol ∿, one, but by no means the only function of which is to indicate the

repercussion. Haydn rarely uses a 'long' mordent, i.e. the mordent of more than one repercussion, but on the few occasions it does occur it is notated in small notes, as in Ex. 8.16*c*, and is not represented by a symbol.

Therefore, as is the case with his notation of *Doppelschläge*, Haydn employs various means of indicating the mordent; sometimes it is indicated unambiguously by two small notes and in a few instances the conventional mordent symbol is distinguishable, but in general the more ambiguous symbol ❧ (or a hybrid sign which could be either ❧ or ❧) is used to notate the mordent as well as the *Doppelschlag*.

As suggested above, context is the most reliable guide to the identification of mordents when Haydn's notation is ambiguous. In the theory and practice of seventeenth- and eighteenth-century music the context mostly associated with the mordent is in ornamenting the second note of an ascending second interval.[33] It is in such a context in Hob. xv: 6/ii that Haydn specifically required the mordent symbol referred to in the letter to Artaria of 10 December 1785 (see Ex. 8.17). The *Doppelschlag* is, however, also idiomatically used in ornamenting ascending intervals and indeed Haydn sometimes specifies the *Doppelschlag* in connection with ascending second intervals by writing the symbol ∾, as in Hob. xvi: 23/ii, bar 29 (see Ex. 8.18). The use of the symbol ❧ in this context may suggest a mordent as

Ex. 8.17. Hob. xv: 6/ii

mordent. Thus, C. Landon (pref. to *Haydn: Sämtliche Klaviersonaten*, vol. i, p. xviii) and C. Tolstoy ('The Identification and Interpretation of Sign Ornaments in Haydn's Instrumental Music', in Larsen *et al.* (ed.), *Haydn Studies*, 315) are mistaken in suggesting that the 'Halb Mordent' is synonymous with the generic symbol ❧, the 'Haydn ornament', rather than one possible interpretation of this symbol.

[33] See e.g. the ornament tables of D'Anglebert, F. Couperin, and Rameau; Marpurg, *Principes*, 64–6, and C. P. E. Bach, *Versuch*, trans. Mitchell, 128.

Ex. 8.18. Hob. XVI: 23/ii

opposed to a *Doppelschlag* when the symbols ∾ and ❧ appear to be differentiated in a particular movement, as in Hob. xv: 15/ii (see Ex. 8.19), but generally when the multi-purpose symbol ❧ is used a legitimate choice between mordent and *Doppelschlag* exists. In bar 19 of Ex. 8.18, for instance, both ornaments are suitable and perhaps even a judicious mixture of both is here appropriate. Similarly, in Hob. xvi: 6/iii, bar 14 (Ex. 8.20) the symbol ❧, which is clearly identifiable in the autograph manuscript, may certainly be interpreted as a *Doppelschlag*, as is implied by the editorial fingering in Landon's edition, but a mordent is equally justifiable in this context.

A special case must, however, be recognized in connection with the ornamentation of the second note of an ascending second interval when the first note is an appoggiatura. In this instance the most appropriate ornament on the second note is nearly always the mordent, the association being so strong that in French music this combination virtually assumed an independent identity, the *port de voix* (or *chute*) *et pincé*, which is listed in almost every French language

Ex. 8.19. Hob. XV: 15/ii

Ex. 8.20. Hob. XVI: 6/iii

treatise from Saint Lambert to Marpurg.[34] In German treatises the association of lower appoggiatura and mordent is equally strong until the end of the eighteenth century, and the use of the *Doppelschlag* in this context is exceptional: C. P. E. Bach writes that 'the turn may appear over a *fermata* preceded by an ascending appoggiatura. It is never found, however, over a final note approached in a like manner.'[35] The *Doppelschlag* might perhaps be an occasional option after an ascending appoggiatura, but the mordent was widely regarded as the most idiomatic ornament; certainly the ornament in bar 39 of Hob. XVI: 23/ii (see Ex. 8.18), which in the autograph is indicated by a symbol which might be ꙮ or ꙮ, should be interpreted as a mordent rather than a *Doppelschlag*.

Theorists mention various other contexts in which the mordent may be used;[36] of these, the use of a mordent in ornamenting a long note at the beginning of a phrase or of a composition can definitely be regarded as appropriate in Haydn's music. The mordent, indicated by two small notes, is specified in such a context in Exx.8.15 and

---

[34] See Saint Lambert, *Les Principes de clavecin* (Paris, 1702), trans. R. Harris-Warrick as *Principles of the Harpsichord* (Cambridge: CUP, 1984), 84–5; and the ornament tables mentioned in n. 33, above.

[35] *Versuch*, trans. Mitchell, 118.

[36] Ibid. 127–32.

8.16; and similar passages as in Ex. 8.21,[37] in which the symbol ∿ occurs, may be interpreted as a mordent. Neither, however, is the *Doppelschlag* entirely alien to this context.[38] In a number of contexts, therefore, both mordent and *Doppelschlag* are idiomatic: Haydn's notation in some instances is specific, unequivocally indicating either a *Doppelschlag* or a mordent, but when the symbol ∿ is used, the ambiguous nature of this symbol is often eminently appropriate to the two possibilities in performance rather than being inconsistent and problematic.

Ex. 8.21. Hob. XVI: 46/i

INTER-BEAT *DOPPELSCHLÄGE*

Type 1

The *Doppelschlag* after a dotted note followed by one or more unaccented ornamental notes (usually arpeggio or passing-note/s) is one of the most common of melodic formulas in Classical music. It most frequently occurs in the forms illustrated in Ex. 8.22 and appeared in Haydn's keyboard music *c*.1766; by the 1780s it was an omnipresent pattern in Haydn's melodic writing. The realizations of this ornamental formula in eighteenth-century treatises are relatively uniform and correspond to Bach's illustration in his *Versuch* (see Ex. 8.1*c*), although some slight variation in the rhythm of the three unaccented notes is found, as for instance in the realization of Türk, Agricola, Clementi, and J. C. F. Bach (Ex. 8.22*a–d*). It is, however, a general

---

[37] The autograph incipit in *EK* has the symbol ∿ , which C. Landon emends in her edition to ✶. See C. Landon, *Kritische Anmerkungen*, 38.

[38] See e.g. C. P. E. Bach, *Versuch*, trans. Mitchell, 113–14; and Türk, *Klavierschule*, trans. Haggh, 272–3.

concern that there is a *point d'ârret* on the first note of the pattern[39] and that the three unaccented notes of the *Doppelschlag per se* are played before the time the dot is reached.[40] The realization given in Ex. 8.22*e*, which is suggested in some modern textbooks as being suitable for fast tempos, should not be regarded as a norm since it dispenses with the characteristic *point d'ârret* on the first note.[41] Undoubtedly some modification of the rhythm may be inevitable in fast tempos but this particular rhythm is not advocated by eighteenth-century theorists and should be used exceptionally. When Haydn writes out this ornamental pattern using large notes the rhythm generally agrees with C. P. E. Bach's realization and with Bach's statement that 'two notes acquire dots' (see Ex. 8.22*f*), but discretion should be exercised regarding the second dot. In effect the decision must be made between single- and double-dotting the pattern; at faster tempos the latter is not always feasible and Clementi's realization (Ex. 8.22*c*), may be more appropriate. The first of Türk's realizations (Ex. 8.22*a*) agrees with that of Bach, but significantly, in a footnote he adds that in faster tempos a realization without the second dot (i.e. the same as Clementi's realization) is preferred.[42] Despite the fairly standard rhythmic pattern, the interpretation of this formula offers a number of expressive possibilities, the variable element being articulation; the whole pattern may be played legato, but the last, or first note of the pattern may not be encompassed in the legato slur. When, as is frequently the case, no articulation is notated, a variety of possibilities exists in performance and although legato is often appropriate, it is, as Somfai has pointed out, by no means obligatory.[43]

In Haydn's autograph manuscripts the signs ∾ and ⮍ are used interchangeably in notating inter-beat *Doppelschläge*, but both signs can be seen to have exactly the same meaning in this context (see Ex. 8.2*b*). The errors that occur frequently in the transmission of this notation are for the most part easily recognized and corrected. In both manuscript copies and printed editions, the placement of the *Doppelschlag* symbol is often inaccurate; for instance, although Haydn is careful in his placement of the *Doppelschlag* in the autograph of the

[39] 'Two tones acquire dots and the turn is placed between them' (Bach, *Versuch*, trans. Mitchell, 120).

[40] 'The last (fourth) tone of the turn should fall on the dot' (Türk, *Klavierschule*, trans. Haggh, 274).

[41] Such a realization is proposed in Paul and Eva Badura-Skoda, *Interpreting Mozart*, 105.

[42] *Klavierschule*, trans. Haggh, 274, 489 n. 61.   [43] 'Notation', 33–4.

Ex. 8.22. Inter-beat *Doppelschlag* realizations after (*a*) Türk, *Klavierschule*, trans. Haggh, p. 274; (*b*) Agricola, *Anleitung*, p. 119; (*c*) Clementi, *Introduction*, p. 10; (*d*) J. C. F. Bach, *Musikalische Nebenstunden* (1787); (*e*) some modern textbooks; (*f*) Haydn, Hob. xv: 12/i, bar 68

Sonata, Hob. XVI: 49, the Artaria print on two occasions places it over the semiquaver and not between the dotted-quaver and semi-quaver (see Ex. 8.6). In view of the frequency of this type of error it is, perhaps, valid to play the *Doppelschlag* in bar 2 of the Sonata, Hob. XVI: 13/i between the dotted-quaver and semiquaver, although all of the extant (non-autograph) manuscript sources place the ornament over the dotted-quaver (see Ex. 8.23). In his autograph manuscripts Haydn is meticulous in his placement of *Doppelschlag* symbols and in a letter to Artaria, dated 10 December 1785, he admonishes the engravers specifically on this point:

On pages 6 and 8 most of the following signs ∾ are wrongly placed, for they ought not to be put directly over the note but over the neighbouring dot, in this way ⎢♩⎥ (page 6 bar 4). All the way through, the dots ought to be further away from the notes, so that the sign ∾ comes directly over the dot.[44]

[44] *CCLN*, 51.

Ex. 8.23. Hob. XVI: 13/i

Haydn's stipulation that the *Doppelschlag* be placed over the dot does not imply, as has been suggested,[45] that the *Doppelschlag* itself begins in the time of the dot, i.e. on the third part of the beat, since his concern is simply that the *Doppelschlag* be placed in an inter-beat position rather than 'directly over the note', as is clear was frequently done in error. Haydn's written-out realizations of this pattern (as in Ex. 8.22*f*) agree with the general practice that the three notes of the *Doppelschlag* are played before the repetition of the main note on the third quarter of the beat.

In the 1780s Haydn adopted a new notation for this ornamental pattern, which, in retrospect, may seem to derive from his concern about the placement of the *Doppelschlag* and the continuous errors of scribes and engravers in this regard. In place of a dot the new notation contains a repetition of the main note, but Haydn retains his three methods of indicating the *Doppelschlag per se*; that is, three small notes and the two distinct but interchangeable *Doppelschlag* symbols (see Ex. 8.24*a*). While this notation clarifies Haydn's intentions in some respects (notably, double- or single-dotting can be indicated specifically) and does seem to have been copied more accurately than the previous notation, it is also misleading in one important matter. According to eighteenth-century theory the *Doppelschlag* when written over a note, whether indicated by three small notes or by symbol, is played on the beat and the new notation appears to indicate that the *Doppelschlag* is played on the second beat, the repetition of the main note. C. P. E. Bach does not mention in his *Versuch* the manner of notation adopted by Haydn, but on the few occasions he makes use of it in his music, his modification of the notation clarifies this point, since the *Doppelschlag* sign is placed before the note repetition, as in Ex. 8.24*b*.

[45] Somfai, 'An Introduction to the Study of Haydn's Quartet Autographs (with Special Attention to Opus 77/G)', in Wolff (ed.), *The String Quartets of Haydn, Mozart, and Beethoven*, 32.

Ex. 8.24. Inter-beat *Doppelschläge*: (*a*) Haydn's notation; (*b*) C. P. E. Bach's occasional practice; (*c*) Somfai's interpretation; (*d*) Hob. xv: 17/ii

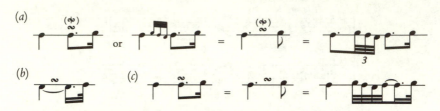

Despite Heinrich Schenker's clarification of Haydn's 'misleading' notation in this context,[46] recent commentaries by Somfai, which are amplified in Rosenblum, suggest that the notation of the 1780s is not simply a new manner of indicating a familiar ornamental pattern but is actually representative of a new realization of the pattern. Somfai believes that Haydn's new notation represents an ornament 'started on the beat, but preferably made quick enough to allow time for the dotted effect' (as in Ex. 8.24*c*).[47] However, Haydn uses the new notation in exactly the same contexts where he formerly wrote a *Doppelschlag* over the dot of a dotted rhythm, which suggests that the *Doppelschlag* in the new notation must be made to anticipate the main note repetition; that is, the repetition of the main note, which

[46] *Ornamentik*, trans. Siegel, 123–4.

[47] Somfai, 'Introduction', 32. For Rosenblum's gloss on this point see Rosenblum, *Performance Practices*, 271–4. Somfai again posed the question 'whether the *Doppelschlag* has to be started or to be finished on the weak note?' in E. Badura-Skoda (ed.), *Haydn Kongress, Wien, 1982* (see Somfai, 'Notation', 33).

replaces the dot, marks the point at which the *Doppelschlag* must be completed. Moreover, there are a number of works in which Haydn uses the new and old manners of notation interchangeably in parallel passages, as in bars 3 and 45 of Hob. xv: 17/ii (Ex. 8.24*d*), which would seem to indicate that the two notations are wholly equivalent. It is also relevant that the written-out realizations of the inter-beat *Doppelschlag* pattern in Haydn's music contain a *Doppelschlag* which anticipates the weak beat (as in Ex. 8.22*f*); the rhythm advocated by Somfai (Ex. 8.24*c*) is never written by Haydn. Rosenblum extends the use of Somfai's rhythmic interpretation of the inter-beat *Doppelschlag* and suggests that Haydn's earlier notation may be interpreted with the *Doppelschlag* occurring on, and not in anticipation of, the weak beat. She suggests that the notation in bar 1 of Hob. xvi: 36/i 'serves as a model for Somfai's realization' (see Ex. 8.25).[48] However, the notation of Hob. xvi: 36/i might well be taken as evidence of the contrary, i.e. that the *Doppelschlag* should anticipate the weak beat. In Hob. xvi: 36/i the first theme contains the pattern written as in Ex. 8.25*a*, but when the 'same' melody appears in E major in bars 12 ff., the ornamentation of the first beat is notated with the *Doppelschlag* symbol in the common inter-beat position (Ex. 8.25*b*). If one perceives both passages as directly analogous, as Rosenblum does, the notation in bar 12 being an abbreviation of that in bar 1, both ornaments could be played using Somfai-like realizations of the figure. It is, perhaps, more appropriate to regard the ornamentation in the respective bars as indicating a deliberate contrast, giving approximate realizations as suggested in Ex. 8.25.[49] The first theme is stated strongly in octaves and is characterized by staccato articulation and the accented *Doppelschlag*-like figure. On the other hand in bar 12 the melody in the relative major is legato and in a quasi-contrapuntal texture. Given the transformation, the different notation of the ornament in bar 12 is probably a considered variation and should arguably be played as the notation normally implies, with an unaccented inter-beat *Doppelschlag* being completed before the second quaver beat. The two ornamental patterns are consistent with the two different forms of the melody throughout the movement (the pattern of bars 12 ff. recurring in bars 34–6 and that of bar 1 in bars 7–8, 44, and 65), except for one instance (bar 37) where the ornamental pattern of bar

---

[48] *Performance Practices*, 271.

[49] It is of course quite common practice in Haydn's 'monothematic' sonata-form movements to have a varied version of the first theme in the dominant or relative major.

12 occurs in association with the texture of the first theme, bar 1 (Ex. 8.25*c*). This is an exception to the otherwise consistent practice of distinguishing the two notations and is probably not sufficient reason for adopting a single interpretation for the two otherwise differentiated notations.[50] It is debatable whether in bar 37 one should play an inter-beat *Doppelschlag* as written or emend this to agree with the ornamentation associated with this version of the theme on its other occurrences. Since, as I read this movement, the contrasting orna-

Ex. 8.25. Hob. XVI: 36/i

50 For an alternative viewpoint see P. Badura-Skoda, 'Ornamentik', 410–11.

mental patterns support contrasts in affect and texture, I am inclined to play the on-beat pattern of bar 1 in bar 37, reserving the inter-beat *Doppelschlag* pattern for the legato and contrapuntal textures of bars 12–14 and 34–6.

Somfai objects to the 'established stuffy legato style'[51] in which inter-beat *Doppelschlag* patterns are performed. The point about the articulation of the pattern is well made and there is a wealth of notational evidence to support a more varied approach to articulation, but, it must be said that there is no similar body of notational evidence to support Somfai's rhythmic interpretation. On the contrary, such notational evidence as exists (such as in Ex. 8.24*d*) suggests that Haydn's old and new manners of notating this ornamental pattern may indeed be synonymous.

Type 2

A second type of inter-beat *Doppelschlag* is illustrated in eighteenth-century treatises (see Ex. 8.1*b* and Ex. 8.26) and usually occurs after binary (i.e. undotted) notes. In many contemporary realizations of the ornament in this context the *Doppelschlag* begins at the mid-point of the ornamented note. Schenker's insistence that it should never begin after the mid-point seems to be untrue of Haydn's and Mozart's music, and perhaps too dogmatic for the music of C. P. E. Bach.[52] Although Bach's principal illustration in the *Versuch* shows the *Doppelschlag* beginning at the mid-point on the main note, another illustration demonstrates that the *Doppelschlag* can begin later to accommodate a moving bass-line, when 'the bass has two or more notes or a rest' (see Ex. 8.1*b*.ii–iv).[53] Similarly, while two of Türk's realizations have the *Doppelschlag* commencing at mid-point, another of his illustrations shows the *Doppelschlag* commencing on the last quarter of the main note's value, i.e. the last quaver of an ornamented minim (see Ex. 8.26).

Haydn begins to use this type of inter-beat *Doppelschlag* in his keyboard music of the 1770s and initially notates it in the same manner as C. P. E. Bach and Türk. In the 1780s, however, Haydn adopted a new notation (similar to the new notation of the other inter-beat *Doppelschlag* pattern which he adopted around the same time), in which the main note is divided in order to clarify the exact position

---

[51] 'Notation', 34.   [52] Schenker, *Ornamentik*, trans. Siegel, 109.
[53] C. P. E. Bach, *Versuch*, trans. Mitchell, 120–1.

Ex. 8.26. Türk, *Klavierschule*, trans. Haggh, p. 274

of the *Doppelschlag*. In the Sonata, Hob. XVI: 51 Haydn uses the old and new manners of notation interchangeably in the first movement, placing a *Doppelschlag* symbol between two minims in bar 104, but specifying the position of the ornament more precisely in the directly parallel passage of bar 37 (Ex. 8.27*a*). Characteristically, Haydn retains a diversity of symbols to notate the *Doppelschlag* itself, all the symbols being wholly equivalent (cf. bars 41 and 171 in Ex. 8.27*b*). This new notation would seem to indicate that in Haydn's music the *Doppelschlag* in this context begins on the last quarter of the main note, rather than at the mid-point, which seems to be the preferred realization in North German treatises.

A peculiarity of North German treatises is the inclusion of a *point d'ârret* (*Zeitraum*) at the end of the *Doppelschlag*, derived from a concern that the *Doppelschlag* should be played rapidly or snapped. It has been pointed out that in Mozart's music this type of inter-beat *Doppelschlag* consists of four equal notes beginning on the last quarter

Ex. 8.27(*a*) Hob. XVI: 51/i, (*b*) Hob. XVI: 49/i

(*a*)

(*b*)

of the main note, or, 'as late as possible'.[54] This point is well established since Mozart frequently wrote out the pattern in large notes,
as for instance in K.576/ii, bar 1. Haydn, like Mozart, seems to
prefer the *Doppelschlag* commencing after the mid-point of the main
note, but whether one should play this ornament in Haydn's music
as four equal notes, as in Mozart, or with a *Zeitraum* at the end of the
Doppelschlag is a moot point. It is undoubtedly less practicable to
include the *Zeitraum* if one commences the *Doppelschlag* near the end
of the main note, particularly in fast tempos, but when it is feasible,
the inclusion of a *Zeitraum* is often a valid and expressive option.

Schenker's interpretation of this type of inter-beat *Doppelschlag* is
both controversial and problematic. Assuming the presence of a
Zeitraum, he argues that the *Doppelschlag* should be anticipated, since
Haydn 'assigns a definite position and duration (a fourth of the total
value) to the last note of the turn':[55] thus, according to Schenker's
interpretation, the *Doppelschläge* in Ex. 8.27 should be played with the
last note of the ornament falling on the fourth quaver beat and not
with the *Doppelschlag* beginning on this quaver. The fact that some of
the examples quoted from Haydn's music by Schenker contain the
turn in this intermediary position seems to support his argument;
however, the textual basis for Schenker's examples is often dubious
and the evidence of Haydn's autograph manuscripts, with one exception, contradicts his assumptions. Haydn's Sonata, Hob. XVI: 52 is
particularly revealing in this regard, since in bar 97 of the first movement the autograph manuscript has the *Doppelschlag* placed clearly
over the semiquaver, but the Artaria edition has the ornament incorrectly placed between the dotted quaver and semiquaver (see Ex.
8.28*a*). The placement of the *Doppelschlag* in this context seems to
have been especially problematic: in the Longman & Broderip edition of the Trio, Hob. XV: 6/ii, the same dotted-quaver–semiquaver
rhythm appears, with the *Doppelschlag* placed in a variety of ways (see
Ex. 8.28*b*)—and the Artaria edition of the same work is scarcely more
consistent. In this instance no autograph readings are available for
comparison, and while the reading with the *Doppelschlag* placed
between two notes is in certain places the most authoritative reading
(and consequently appears in Urtext editions), it is likely that this is a
corruption, since the pattern as written by Haydn in other autographs

---

[54] P. and E. Badura-Skoda, *Interpreting Mozart*, 104.

[55] *Ornamentik*, trans. Siegel, 116. Beyschlag (*Ornamentik*, 192) suggests a similar interpretation.

is almost invariably as in the autograph reading given in Ex. 8.28*a* and the variant inter-beat placement is characteristic only of non-autograph sources. Schenker's example from Hob. XVI: 48/i,[56] illustrating 'Haydn's' use of the *Doppelschlag* in an intermediate position is also textually questionable; this example has the limited authority of *Haydn Verzeichnis* (in Elssler's hand), but the reading in the first editions of Breitkopf and John Bland is by no means indicative of anticipation (see Ex. 8.28*c*).

The only autograph evidence which indicates the anticipation of the *Doppelschlag* in this context occurs in the Trio, Hob. XV: 7, second

Ex. 8.28(*a*) Hob. XVI: 52/i, (*b*) Longman & Broderip edition of Hob. XV: 6/ii, (*c*) Hob. XVI: 48/i, (*d*) Hob. XV: 7/ii

[56] Schenker, *Ornamentik*, trans. Siegel, 117, ex. 60, 2.d.

movement (Ex. 8.28*d*). Since the source is authoritative it seems that anticipation is intended here; that is, the *Doppelschlag* should begin at the mid-point of the beat, or shortly after, and the pattern should end with a demisemiquaver *Zeitraum*. Apart from this instance, where it is notated unambiguously, the inclusion of a *Zeitraum* may be an appropriate expressive possibility elsewhere in Haydn's music, especially in slower tempos, and is, perhaps, also implied by the notation ⌂ , which occurs occasionally in Haydn's music. The evidence of Haydn's autographs suggests, however, that normally the inter-beat *Doppelschlag* in this context begin on the fourth quarter of the beat.

The 'late' performance of the *Doppelschlag* in this second inter-beat context is also attested by some interesting details of notation in relation to ornamented dotted notes. A comparison of parallel passages in Hob. xv: 30/i (see Ex. 8.29*a*) suggests that the *Doppelschlag* after the dotted minim should be played, not in anticipation of the third beat but on the last quaver beat. A similar realization is required in Hob. xvi: 26/i, bar 64 (Ex. 8.29*b*), as is clearly indicated by Haydn's careful placement in the autograph manuscript of the dot over the second crotchet beat of the alto voice with the *Doppelschlag* symbol following the dot:[57] again, the ornament is played after, and not in anticipation of the second beat. Examples of passages requiring this realization also occur in Hob. xvi: 31/i and xvi: 32/i.

Ex. 8.29(*a*) Hob. xv: 30/i, (*b*) Hob. xvi: 26/i

---

[57] Unfortunately, the precise spacing and alignment of Haydn's autographs is not reproduced in printed sources or in modern edns.

Apart from the suggested use of the *prallende Doppelschlag* discussed above, the particular type of *Doppelschlag* which establishes a link between Haydn and the North German tradition, and in this case more emphatically, is the *geschnellte Doppelschlag*. This ornament, which C. P. E. Bach claims in the *Versuch* 'is discussed in no other writings',[58] is notated by Bach as in Ex. 8.1*e*. Since this symbol for the *geschnellte Doppelschlag* is not commonly found except in Bach's music, in his *Versuch* and in treatises closely related to it (e.g. those of Marpurg, Agricola, and Türk), it is revealing that such a peculiarly North German invention is requisite in Haydn's music. As with the *prallende Doppelschlag*, only one instance is found of Haydn using Bach's own notation for the *geschnellte Doppelschlag*; this occurs in Hob. XVI: 24/i, dated 1773 (see Ex. 8.30*a*), but thereafter Haydn employs a more explicit notation (see Ex. 8.30*b* and *c*), which undoubtedly derives from Marpurg, an author with whom Haydn was familiar and who gives both notations of the *geschnellte Doppelschlag* as being synonymous.[59]

Haydn uses the *geschnellte Doppelschlag* over relatively long notes, over dotted quavers, in passages which may be assumed to be detached as regards articulation, and frequently in connection with arpeggio figures (Ex. 8.30*a–c*): in effect these are the characteristic usages of the ornament as described by C. P. E. Bach. In the keyboard Trios Hob. XV: 17/i, XV: 29/ii, and XV: 18/ii we find a specific use of the *geschnellte Doppelschlag* which seems to be characteristic of Haydn, namely, the use of the ornament as a means of variation. If the difference in the notation of the parallel passages in Ex. 8.30*c* were an isolated occurrence, one might suspect that the *Doppelschlag* in bar 37 was an abbreviation of the *geschnellte Doppelschlag* notation in bar 6. However, a similar procedure is found in the Trio, Hob. XV: 17/i, where the passage in bar 15 is ornamented by a *Doppelschlag*, while in bar 16, which repeats the music of bar 15, the *Doppelschlag* is altered to a *geschnellter Doppelschlag*: the notational distinction between *Doppelschlag* and *geschnellter Doppelschlag* is maintained in the parallel passage of bars 65–6. Similarly, in Hob. XV: 18/ii, when the main theme reappears at the end of the movement as a highly embellished

---

[58] *Versuch*, trans. Mitchell, 125.
[59] Marpurg, *Anleitung*, 53 and table VI, figs. 7 and 8.

Ex. 8.30(*a*) Hob. XVI: 24/i, (*b*) Hob. XVI: 49/i, (*c*) Hob. XV: 29/ii

reprise, the *Doppelschlag* ornament of bar 6 becomes a *geschnellter Doppelschlag* in bar 42.

The *geschnellte Doppelschlag* is not a frequently used ornament, either in C. P. E. Bach's music (where it is, for instance, much less common than the *prallende Doppelschlag*), or in Haydn's keyboard music (where it occurs only once in the autograph manuscripts and fewer than ten occasions in all). None the less, its use in these few instances, as well as being interesting musically, is irrefutable evidence of the influence C. P. E. Bach's performance practices exerted outside North Germany.

Since Haydn employed distinctive symbols for the *geschnellte Doppelschlag*, and although it might be used, for musical reasons, on occasions where other, less specific, symbols occur, it is, in general, not interchangeable with other *Doppelschlag* forms.[60] It has, however, been suggested by various scholars that the *geschnellte Doppelschlag*, or

[60] Neumann advocates a fairly liberal usage of the *geschnellte Doppelschlag* in Mozart's music notwithstanding the absence of notational evidence (see Neumann, *Ornamentation in Mozart*, 139–41).

a rhythmic variant of the *geschnellte Doppelschlag*, should be used in a number of passages in Haydn's music, although neither of the two ways which Haydn used to indicate this ornament is employed on these occasions. The first of these concerns the *prallende Doppelschlag* notation in Hob. XVI: 20/i, which has already been mentioned in connection with Ex. 8.12. It is clear that while in bar 8 the *prallende Doppelschlag* is the intended ornament, occurring as it does in a characteristic context, in bars 9 and 12, where the symbol ℀ occurs in connection with repeated notes and not descending second intervals, a *prallender Doppelschlag* cannot be played in the normal way (Ex. 8.31*a*). In the subsequent repetition of this passage the symbol ℀ is emended to ∾ in the Artaria edition, but since only 37 bars of the autograph are extant for the first movement of this sonata, we have no way of knowing if the emendation is Haydn's own or derives from the publisher. One possible interpretation of the ornaments in bars 9 and 12 is to play the notes of the *prallende Doppelschlag*, but obviously without the tied upper auxiliary, which is impossible without a suspended note (Ex. 8.31*b*). Christa Landon has, in her edition of the work, suggested the interpretation of Ex. 8.31*c*, that is, in effect, a *geschnellter Doppelschlag*. This interpretation assumes that Haydn confused Bach's notations for the *geschnellte Doppelschlag* and the *prallende Doppelschlag* and is, perhaps, given some credence by the obvious confusion in bars 8–9, and by the fact that this sonata, dated 1771, predates the occurrence of the *geschnellte Doppelschlag* proper in Hob. XVI: 24 (1773). In a brief section dealing with unconventional usages of the *prallende Doppelschlag*, Türk gives two realizations: one exhibits the normal shape and rhythm of the *prallende Doppelschlag* but without a tied upper-auxiliary note (i.e. no descending second is involved — as in Ex. 8.31*b*), and the other is a hybrid of Bach's *geschnellter Doppelschlag* and *prallender Doppelschlag* symbols, for which Türk offers the realization of Ex. 8.31*d*.[61] I tend to favour the realization of Ex. 8.31*b*, but it is difficult to come to any firm conclusions regarding the performance of the ornaments in this passage. This problematic notation does not, however, occur except in this one instance, and has no implications for the interpretation of other works.

This cannot be said of the interpretation of Ex. 8.32 suggested by Christa Landon, which, if correct, would have widespread implica-

---

[61] *Klavierschule*, trans. Haggh, 280.

Ex. 8.31(*a*) Hob. XVI: 20/i, (*b*) possible realization, (*c*) after C. Landon, (*d*) realization after Türk

tions for the interpretation of *Doppelschläge* in Haydn's music. Landon suggests that the *geschnellte Doppelschlag* is intended not only where Bach's or Marpurg's symbols for this ornament occur (as in Ex. 8.30), but where a note ornamented by a *Doppelschlag* is preceded by a short note (semiquaver) on the same pitch, which occurs widely in Haydn's keyboard music.[62] Specifically in connection with Hob. XVI: 18/i, she suggests the *geschnellte Doppelschlag*-like realization given in Ex. 8.32*b*. Somfai also sees this context as a 'special case': 'a normal-size 16th anticipation should probably be played very short—perhaps together with the turn . . .—like a genuine accented

Ex. 8.32(*a*) Hob. XVI: 18/i, (*b*) realization after C. Landon, (*c*) realization after Somfai

---

[62] Pref. to *Haydn: Sämtliche Klaviersonaten*, i. pp. xviii and 123.

five-notes [*sic*] turn' (Ex. 8.32*c*).[63] For a number of reasons this interpretation may be regarded as suspect. First, the realization as suggested by Landon and others is a hybrid ornament, in effect a
geschnellter Doppelschlag partially anticipated, the existence of which is
not supported by any theoretical evidence or by any written-out realizations in the works of Haydn or any other composer. Secondly, the
realization assumes legato articulation: indeed, both Landon and
Somfai add editorial slurs over the pattern. This seems unlikely, since
conventional articulation assumes a *silence d'articulation* over the bar
line. Thirdly, the use of the *Doppelschlag* in connection with dotted
rhythms is one of the most obvious and characteristic uses of the
Doppelschlag and occurs as such in the music of J. C. Bach, C. P. E.
Bach, Haydn, and Mozart and most Classical music (it is particularly
characteristic of Haydn's minuets and Tempo di Menuetto movements): the pattern is specifically cited by many theorists as a characteristic use of the conventional *Doppelschlag*.[64] Certainly, if such a
hybrid ornament existed, it would not have been notated in so conventional a manner as Ex. 8.32. Hob. XVI: 18 was written in 1766 at
a time when Haydn was adopting increasingly precise practices for
the notation of ornaments, but nowhere does Haydn's notation suggest that this pattern is a special case requiring an unconventional
realization.

The history of the interpretation advocated by Landon for dotted
figures ornamented by *Doppelschläge* begins only in the twentieth
century. A similar interpretation was first mooted by Schenker in his
original, at times brilliant, but often flawed *Ein Beitrag zur
Ornamentik*:[65] more recently these interpretations have gained currency in the writings of Somfai and Rosenblum. Not withstanding
its strong twentieth-century advocacy this interpretation lacks an
eighteenth-century pedigree.

---

[63] 'Notation', 31–2. Similar points are made in Rosenblum, *Performance Practices*, 267–8;
and Badura-Skoda, 'Ornamentik', 416–17.

[64] C. P. E. Bach, *Versuch*, trans. Mitchell, 117; Agricola, *Anleitung*, 118; Türk,
Klavierschule, trans. Haggh, 273–4.

[65] See *Ornamentik*, trans. Siegel, 122 where the 'displacement of the snapped turn
[*geschnellte Doppelschlag*]' is advocated in Hob. XVI: 28/ii, bars 1–2 and XVI: 49/iii, bar 28.

9

Arpeggio, Slide [*Schleifer*], and *Anschlag*

◊

THE ARPEGGIO

The attention given to the arpeggio in eighteenth-century treatises is minimal by comparison with the detail in which other ornaments are discussed. The reason for this may not be, as Neumann believes,[1] that theorists resorted to a few stereotyped comments and standard realizations because of the difficulty of describing and illustrating the actual performance of this ornament, but because the arpeggio in galant and Classical keyboard music is relatively unproblematic. The complex notational systems used in French keyboard music of the early part of the eighteenth century to distinguish between ascending and descending arpeggios and to indicate various types of arpeggios ornamented with passing notes are not relevant to Haydn's keyboard music, or, in general, to music and treatises on performance practice from the second half of the eighteenth century. Problems relating to the performance of passages written as a series of chords but marked 'arpeggio' (such as occur in J. S. Bach's Chromatic Fantasy in D minor, BWV.903, or in a number of C. P. E. Bach's *freien Fantasien*) are also irrelevant to a discussion of Haydn's keyboard music, since passages of this type do not occur: continuous arpeggios are, of course, found in Haydn's music but they are figurative and written with precise note values rather than being a function of improvisation. Arpeggios, as ornaments, in Haydn's music occur relatively infrequently, are almost always associated with the strongest beats in the bar, and, I would suggest, primarily serve the purpose of accentuation.

The descriptions of the arpeggio found in North German treatises can be seen to derive largely from earlier French performance

---

[1] *Ornamentation in Mozart*, 165 ff.

traditions, but, unlike other aspects of French–North German notation and performance, they are largely irrelevant to later Viennese
keyboard music. Marpurg's *Principes du clavecin* is, in particular,
indebted to this French tradition and lists a variety of arpeggio types
with specifically French notational symbols which are not found in
Viennese keyboard music.[2] C. P. E. Bach distinguishes by symbol
between ascending and descending arpeggios,[3] but this notational
practice too is absent from Haydn's music (indeed, within Bach's
own music the descending arpeggio is a rarity). Significantly,
although Türk repeats Bach's symbols for distinguishing between the
ascending and descending arpeggio, he comments that the 'breaking'
of arpeggios from top to bottom 'is seldom the case'.[4] Also derived
from the French tradition and repeated in North German treatises is
the use of the oblique stroke through a chord to indicate an arpeggio
with an acciaccatura. In Haydn's music, however, an altogether different notation for the acciaccatura is used. Moreover, the oblique
stroke is Haydn's normal indication of the simple arpeggio without
acciaccatura. Haydn does not use the modern symbol for the arpeggio, although it became increasingly popular towards the end of the
eighteenth century: this symbol, when it occurs in modern editions
of Haydn's music and in the musical examples in this book, is a tacit
emendation, the modern equivalent of Haydn's standard arpeggio
indication 𝄋 .

The notational practices concerning arpeggios which are illustrated
in treatises and instruction books and which have parallels in Haydn's
music are described in very few words, and are accompanied by a
number of standard realizations. Of the two realizations given in Ex.
9.1 from Marpurg's *Anleitung a* shows the standard notation for the
arpeggio commonly found in Haydn's music (both in autograph and
secondary sources), but Marpurg's alternative placement of the
oblique stroke to distinguish between the ascending and descending
forms of arpeggio is not applicable to Haydn.

Apart from the oblique stroke through the chord, Haydn's other
common manner of notating the arpeggio is by two or more small
notes. In later works this notation becomes increasingly prominent,
but it is important to note that Haydn does not use the two methods
of notation interchangeably. Often (as in Ex. 9.12a) right- and left-

---

[2] Pp. 69–71.   [3] *Versuch*, trans. Mitchell, 159–60.
[4] *Klavierschule*, trans. Haggh, 282.

Ex. 9.1. Marpurg, *Anleitung*, table v, (*a*) fig. 16 and (*b*) fig. 17

hand chords on the same beat are distinguished by different notations for the arpeggio which suggests a difference in the performance of the chords. Two writers, Türk and Clementi comment on this difference. In his *Klavierschule*, Türk lists five ways of indicating that a chord should be arpeggiated (see Ex. 9.2), the last two of which are those used by Haydn. When an arpeggio is indicated in the manner of Ex. 9.2*a*, *b*, *c* or *d*, the 'fingers must not be raised from the keys before the value of the notes . . . has been completed', but, according to Türk, when the notation of Ex. 9.2*e* is used 'the fingers must be immediately lifted from the keys. Only the tone shown as a main note . . . is held'.[5] Clementi makes the following comment on the arpeggio:

Ex. 9.2. Türk, *Klavierschule*, trans. Haggh, p. 282

This mark ⦚ prefixed to a chord 𝄞 signifies, that the notes must be

played SUCCESSIVELY, from the lowest; with more or less velocity, as the sentiment may require; keeping each note DOWN 'till the time of the chord be filled up.[6]

Significantly, however, in the section entitled 'APPOGGIATURAS, and other GRACES in small notes explained', Clementi illustrates an arpeggio written with small notes and adds a realization in which, as in Türk, only the top note is held (see Ex. 9.3). It seems likely that in distinguishing between arpeggios indicated by an oblique stroke and

---

[5] Ibid.; trans. slightly modified.   [6] *Introduction*, 9.

Ex. 9.3. Clementi, *Introduction*, p. 10

by small notes, Haydn had in mind the difference between held and released arpeggio notes.

One further notational feature mentioned by Türk may be associated with the arpeggio in Haydn's music. In the Trio, Hob. xv: 1 different note values are used in an arpeggiated chord with the likely intention that only the top note with its longer value is held (see Ex. 9.4). It seems to be the equivalent to writing arpeggios with small notes, i.e. not sustaining the whole chord but only the longer note(s), an interpretation which is also offered by Türk. Regarding the notation reproduced in Ex. 9.5 Türk comments as follows:

Ex. 9.4. Hob. xv: 1/i

Ex. 9.5. Türk, *Klavierschule*, trans. Haggh, p. 284

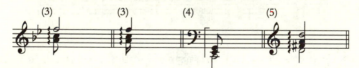

If only a single tone is to be held, then this is shown as in 3 and in 4. In example 3, the finger is allowed to remain on the note f and in 4 on the note c. The notation in 5 also requires that only the lowest and the highest tones be held and that the fingers are to be immediately released after playing the a and the f♯.[7]

This type of notation occurs very rarely in Haydn's music although it is not uncommon in the works of Mozart. It is noticeable that in Mozart, chords of this type are not usually accompanied by an arpeg-

---

[7] *Klavierschule*, trans. Haggh, 284.

gio sign, although a manner of performance other than that described
by Türk is difficult to imagine.[8] The chords in bars 16 and 17 of
Haydn's Trio, Hob. xv: 41/i should also, perhaps, be regarded in this
way (see Ex. 9.6). The contrast in the notation of bars 16–17 and
18–19 would initially seem to suggest a difference in performance,
but in the parallel passage small notes are used throughout bars 96–9
in notating the chords, suggesting that the chords in bars 16–17
should also be arpeggiated.[9]

Ex. 9.6. Hob. xv: 41/i

    The speed at which the arpeggios should be played remains a
matter of personal taste. There are no notational clues regarding such
specifics of performance and there is no reason to believe that
Haydn's adoption of more than one way of indicating an arpeggio has
any implication as regards the speed at which the arpeggios should be
performed. Theorists also leave this matter to the discretion of the
performer, making only general comments such as that quoted above
from Clementi's *Introduction*. Türk, who writes at greater length than
his contemporaries concerning the arpeggio, offers similar advice to
that of Clementi:

    [8] This form of notation is e.g. found in Mozart's piano concertos K.449 and K.451 (see
Vorwort to *NMA* V:15/iv, p. xi).
    [9] A similar interpretation might be posited for the opening chord of Hob. xvi: 13/i, sus-
taining the lower e′ of the chord while releasing the upper notes after striking them.

Whether the chord is broken faster or slower depends on the character
of the composition. Most of the time it is broken rather quickly. . . . In
compositions of a very lively character the keys are almost struck
simultaneously.[10]

It would seem sensible that in slow, expressive movements (e.g. Ex.
9.10) arpeggios be played slower than in faster movements: similarly,
the emphatic arpeggios on relatively long note values often found at
the beginning and ending of fast movements (e.g. Ex. 9.9*a* and *c*)
might well be played more deliberately than arpeggios associated
with shorter note values, or notes marked staccato (e.g. Ex. 9.12*a*; in
this particular instance the staccato markings and the *Allegro* tempo
would seem to suggest that the notes of the arpeggios be struck
'almost simultaneously').

   Arpeggio markings of any type are quite rare in Haydn's early keyboard music. This is a consequence, not of lack of precision in notation, but of the predominance of two-part texture in Haydn's style
until *c*.1766. When chords with four or more notes occur, it is usually for the purpose of emphasis, often at the beginning and/or ending of each half of a binary movement, at structurally important
cadences, or to accent particular details. These chords are very often
arpeggiated in one way or another. The most extensive use of arpeggios among the early keyboard works occurs in the autograph
manuscript of the Sonata, Hob. XVI: 6. Here, characteristically, the
arpeggios occur on strong beats, as in Ex. 9.7*a,* where the strong third
beat is emphasized by the addition of an arpeggio,[11] and in Ex. 9.7*b*
where the final arpeggiated chord occurs at the climax in each half of
the binary movement. The minuet is particularly noteworthy in this
regard, since arpeggios occur on the first beats of selected bars and
clearly articulate the beginnings of phrases and subphrases (Ex. 9.7*c*).
There are some instances in the early works where chords occur in
contexts associated with arpeggios in these examples, but where symbols indicating the arpeggiation of these chords are lacking. In such
instances (as in Ex. 9.8) it would seem appropriate to arpeggiate the
chords. Occasionally movements with generally fuller textures occur
in Haydn's early works. A particularly striking example is the Adagio
from the Sonata, Hob. XVI: 6, a movement strongly associated with

---

[10] *Klavierschule*, trans. Haggh, 282.
[11] See also Hob. XV: 1/i, bars 20–1, where the tied crotchet notes which articulate each
segment in a sequence are emphasized in a like manner by arpeggios.

Ex. 9.7(*a*) Hob. XVI: 6/i, (*b*) Hob. XVI: 6/iv, (*c*) Hob. XVI: 6/ii

(*a*)

(*b*)

(*c*)

the earlier Viennese tradition of cantilena slow movements,[12] in which it would seem natural (at least in a performance on a harpsichord) to arpeggiate some of the repeated left hand chords, although no indication for such a performance is present.

  In the keyboard works written after *c.*1766 Haydn makes use of the arpeggio in a somewhat more liberal manner, but in general the context and function associated with the ornament seems to be similar to that found even in Haydn's earliest works. In Hob. XV: 8/i and XV: 12/i (Ex. 9.9*a* and *b*) arpeggios function dynamically and are associated with a thickening of the prevalent texture to achieve the *p* to *f* contrast, while in Ex. 9.9*c* the obviously climactic ending of the first movement is similarly achieved through a thicker texture and, in this instance, arpeggios in both right and left hands. Similarly, in bar 3 of Hob. XV: 5/i the arpeggio in the right hand is associated with the *fz* marking in the autograph, and, indeed, if the work is performed on

  [12] See Brown, *Keyboard Music*, 198–200.

Ex. 9.8. Hob. xvi: 9/i

Ex. 9.9(*a*) Hob. xv: 8/i, (*b*) Hob. xv: 12/i, (*c*) Hob. xv: 13/i

(*a*)

(*b*)

(*c*)

a harpsichord the arpeggio is the primary means of effecting this
accent.

Somfai has commented on Haydn's awareness of acoustical considerations in his London works and has singled out the way in which
Haydn often begins a string quartet with a ' "noise killer", a simple
and loud opening, which allows the actual musical substance to start
in any manner'.[13] Somfai further observed that this tendency is to be

---

[13] 'The London Revision of Haydn's Instrumental Style', *PRMA* 100 (1973–4): 167.

found in some 'pre-London' works, particularly the instrumental music of the 1780s. Nowhere is the tendency more apparent than in the keyboard trios from the 1780s and 1790s written for London publishers. The Trios, Hob. xv: 11, 12, 14, 17, and 18 all open with clear statements of the tonic chord containing as many as eight notes, at a dynamic level which is either explicitly marked, or can be assumed to be, *forte*, and with a clearly indicated arpeggio in the right hand, or in both right and left hands (see e.g. the opening of Hob. xv: 18/i, quoted in Ex. 2.21*a*). Similar openings are found in the trios which immediately precede these works (in particular Hob. xv: 8 and 9, dating from 1785) and occasionally among Haydn's later trios (e.g. Hob. xv: 24) in which the arpeggio indication is lacking, but where an added arpeggiation by the performer would seem entirely appropriate to the style.

The arpeggiation of chords not specifically marked as arpeggios is to some extent problematic in Haydn's music. In harpsichord music before *c.*1750 a more or less free use of arpeggiation is not only feasible but an essential technique in harpsichord playing. In Haydn's early keyboard music, predominantly intended for performance on a harpsichord, a similar freedom might be assumed, but in reality the appropriate circumstances seldom arise, except as mentioned above when the prevailing two- or three-part texture is expanded for the purposes of emphasis. In later works with more varied textures it would seem excessively purist in manner to insist that arpeggios should be used only when indicated by the composer, but it is none the less probably advisable to restrict the use of the arpeggio to those instances in which it is indicated and to similar contexts which, for whatever reason (perhaps carelessness on the part of the composer, scribe, or engraver) lack such an indication. Keyboard music from the 1780s was increasingly performed on the fortepiano and there is a general tendency in this music (Mozart's as well as Haydn's) to use the arpeggio, and indeed other *Spielmanieren*, sparingly; the composer's notation of arpeggios may not always be complete but, in a time of changing attitudes to ornamentation, it may be regarded as defining the contexts and approximately the frequency of arpeggiated chords. In this regard it is impossible to say whether the limited use of arpeggios is a consequence of an evolving fortepiano idiom or of the general changes in compositional style in the 1780s; most probably it is the interaction of both elements which rendered the improvisatory arpeggiation of chords, as described earlier in the century, *démodé.* Increasingly in the 1780s arpeggios and other ornaments become part of the function of composition.

Haydn's notation of arpeggios, although not necessarily complete, is in general very precise and should arguably be interpreted quite strictly by the performer. He appears to differentiate between chords which should be arpeggiated by the right hand only (the most frequent occurrence, as in Ex. 9.9*b*) and by both hands (Ex. 9.9*c*). He further distinguishes between instances where the whole chord is sustained (Ex. 9.9*c*), where in right-hand arpeggios only the top note is sustained (Ex. 9.9*b*), or, as in Hob. XVI: 46/ii (Ex. 9.10) where the top two notes of the right-hand chord are sustained; these non-*tenuto* right-hand arpeggios may be accompanied by left-hand chords which are either arpeggiated in a *tenuto* manner or not arpeggiated at all (cf. Exx. 9.10 and 9.9*b*). These distinctions seem to be intentional and deserve serious attention from the performer, but there are occasions when the performer must exercise discretion in the completion of Haydn's notation.

Ex. 9.10. Hob. XVI: 46/ii

One of the most striking and problematic instances of (possibly) incomplete notation of arpeggios occurs in the first movement of the Sonata, Hob. XVI: 52. In the autograph manuscript of the first movement only one chord (the left-hand chord in bar 1, first beat) contains an oblique stroke. During the course of the movement the music of bar 1 appears in various guises, three times in the exposition and four times in the recapitulation; none, apart from the first occurrence, has any arpeggio indication. In the first edition of Artaria there is, however, a proliferation of arpeggio markings, including indications of arpeggios for both right and left hands in connection with a number of chords in bar 1 and its recurrences, and also in unrelated passages (see Ex. 9.11, which is based on the autograph manuscript but with the additional arpeggio markings from the Artaria edition

Ex. 9.11. Hob. xvi: 52/i

indicated in square brackets). There are twelve arpeggio indications in the first seventeen bars alone of the Artaria edition, by comparison with the single arpeggio marking of the autograph manuscript. Arpeggio indications are also numerous in the recapitulation according to the Artaria text, although these are not consistent with its markings in the exposition. Although the Artaria print was the first to appear it is not a reliable source and was most probably prepared without Haydn's permission or at least without his active participation.[14] On the other hand, the first London edition of Longman, Clementi & Co. was prepared from the autograph manuscript, as is testified by the instructions to the engraver, in English, which are visible on the autograph manuscript. This London edition follows the text of the autograph in meticulous detail and, as in the autograph, only one arpeggio indication is to be found in the first movement. The performer may well feel inclined to 'complete' Haydn's notation

[14] Landon, pref. to *Haydn: Sämtliche Klaviersonaten*, vol. iii, p. xx and *Kritische Anmerkungen*, 98.

with regard to the arpeggio markings, but it is clear that the Artaria edition should not be used as the basis for this task. This edition may well represent an envisaged eighteenth-century performance by a hypothetical performer but such a performance would not appear to be in accordance with Haydn's practices. The modern edition in *JHW* XVIII/3 is a diplomatic transcription of the autograph with only one arpeggio indication in the first movement: if the performer wishes to supplement this single marking, the discreet use of arpeggiated left hand chords on the first beats of bars 9 and 17 and parallel passages (as suggested by Christa Landon in her edition of the Haydn sonatas) would seem to be appropriate. Further supplementary arpeggios run an increasing risk of straying from Haydn's practices as we know them from contemporaneous works, in particular the late piano trios.

Acciaccaturas are indicated in Haydn's music by small notes and not by an oblique stroke, as in French keyboard music and as advocated by some treatises from the second half of the eighteenth century. Treatises from the sixteenth to the eighteenth century describe the usual manner of performance, in which consonant notes are sustained, but the dissonant note released immediately after being struck.[15] Haydn notates arpeggios with acciaccaturas in two ways. In one way, perhaps the most frequent occurrence, small notes are used to indicate both the acciaccatura and the consonant arpeggio notes, and in this manner it seems Haydn intended that the small notes, whether consonant or dissonant, should be released immediately. It is usual in Haydn's music that the acciaccaturas notated in this manner are confined to the right-hand chord, while the accompanying left-hand chord may either be arpeggiated simply, without an acciaccatura (bar 1 of Ex. 9.12*a*), or is not arpeggiated (Ex. 9.12*b*).

In another manner of notation Haydn indicates an acciaccatura by a single small note placed before a chord which bears an arpeggio marking (see Ex. 9.13*a*). This notation would appear to imply a *tenuto* for the consonant notes of the chord. The small note when combined with an arpeggio marking in this manner does not indicate a long appoggiatura struck against the bass, even when, as in Ex. 9.13*b*, the small note is (misleadingly) written as a crotchet. Here the dissonant note *f*♯' is clearly an acciaccatura, played fleetingly as part of the arpeggio and not sustained as a long appoggiatura. Its appearance as a

---

[15] See Williams, *Accompaniment*, i. 40–4.

Ex. 9.12(a) Hob. xv: 27/i, (b) Hob. xvi: 36/i

crotchet (rather than as a quaver or semiquaver) is undoubtedly due to an engraver's error. Occasionally when Haydn requires a particularly slow and *tenuto* performance of an arpeggio he writes the notes out methodically with specific note values, as in Ex. 9.13c. This arpeggiated chord also contains an acciaccatura (the *g#″*) which, unlike the consonant notes of the chord, is not sustained. This very precisely notated performance could serve as a model for the performance of the notation of, for instance, Ex. 9.13a.

Frederick Neumann has advanced the opinion that compound appoggiaturas, among them the arpeggio, should often be interpreted as pre-beat ornaments.[16] This view will be contested again in the

[16] *Ornamentation in Mozart*, 97 ff., 165 ff.; id., 'Bemerkungen über Haydns Ornamentik', in E. Badura-Skoda (ed.), *Haydn Kongress, Wien, 1982*, 35–42, trans. in *New Essays*, 93–104; id., 'More on Haydn's Ornaments and the Evidence of the Musical Clocks', in *New Essays*, 105–19, esp. 107–9.

Ex. 9.13(*a*) Hob. XVI: 48/i, (*b*) Hob. XV: 22/ii, (*c*) Hob. XV: 28/iii

(*a*)

following pages in connection with the *Schleifer*, but since his arguments also concern arpeggios, the following comments are relevant here.

The basis of Neumann's argument is:

1. an unambiguous realization found in Milchmeyer's *Die wahre Art das Pianoforte zu spielen* (Dresden, 1797) in which arpeggios anticipate the beat;

2. an emphasis on melodic outline which is, supposedly, 'distorted' when arpeggios (or other compound ornaments) occur on the beat;

3. the placement of *f* or *fz* dynamic markings which, according to Neumann, emphasize the melody note and not the arpeggio notes.

The writings of Milchmeyer are mentioned by Neumann without any attempt to provide a context against which to assess their relevance. Milchmeyer would appear to represent 'new' trends in performance practice associated with a younger generation of piano virtuosi centred in London and Paris. He spent eighteen years living in Lyons and Paris and can hardly be said to be strongly connected with the Viennese keyboard tradition.[17] His writings are perhaps most notable for their strong advocacy of developments in piano construction and increasing use of the various pedal mechanisms; in the latter regard he praised Steibelt as an innovator (a view not widely held).[18] His illustration of arpeggios (see Ex. 9.14) is unrepresentative of eighteenth- and early nineteenth-century treatises and can scarcely be regarded as proof of a widespread use of pre-beat performance when evaluated against the innumerable treatises which recommend 'on-the-beat' performance of the ornament (all of the latter are dismissed cursorily by Neumann).

Ex. 9.14. Milchmeyer, *Die wahre Art das Pianoforte zu spielen*, p. 38

Regarding Neumann's other reasons for recommending pre-beat performance of the arpeggio, Somfai has already commented succinctly on this approach in his reply to Neumann's paper on Haydn in *Kongress Wien*:

One last remark on the question of accentuation of 2- and 3-note graces (Neumann, Ex. 3–4), and of what is "natural", *musikalisch schön*. Naturally, I believe that one should play these graces with on-the-beat accent—giving the *f♯* to the whole 3-note group—, as an important component of the character, not because C. P. E. Bach suggests it but because a dissonance, a rhythmic impetus is important, maybe more important than the supposed melodic contour.[19]

---

[17] See the anonymous review of Milchmeyer's *Die wahre Art das Pianoforte zu spielen* (Dresden, 1797) in *AMz* 1 (1798–9): 135–7, in which the author asks the pertinent rhetorical question 'aber kennet denn Hr. Milchmayer [*sic*] die Meisterstücke von Mozart und Clementi nicht?'. It is also interesting that in the subscription list for Milchmeyer's book, there are 131 Dresden subscribers and only 37 Viennese subscribers.

[18] Concerning Milchmeyer's comments on pedalling see Rowland, 'Early Piano Pedalling: 1750–1850'; and id., 'Early Pianoforte Pedalling: The Evidence of the Earliest Printed Markings', *EM* 13/1 (1985): 5–17.

[19] *Haydn Kongress, Wien, 1982*, 42. The Neumann examples to which Somfai refers appear on p. 37 of the same publication.

The characteristic contexts in which arpeggios occur in Haydn's music (as outlined above) lend credence to Somfai's point of view. These contexts are primarily associated with accentuation which is achieved by denser texture, in the later works by dynamic emphasis, and by the presence of the ornament itself. In other words, the arpeggiation of chords serves accentual and rhythmic rather than purely or even primarily melodic purposes.

The example which Neumann cites from Haydn's Sonata in E flat, Hob. XVI: 38 is particularly interesting, but it seem to me to support the practice of playing arpeggios indicated by small notes on the beat, and not, as Neumann advocates, pre-beat. Neumann cites the passage from Hob. XVI: 38 given in Ex. 9.15a 'where of three arpeggios over the ascending Bb major triad the first, starting the measure, is written in little notes; the second and third show anticipation in regular notes. That the first has to be equally anticipated is a matter of elementary musical logic. The identical design recurs in measure 66.'[20] It is, however, a twisted logic that assumes that Haydn's consistent notational distinction between arpeggios notated in small notes and pre-beat patterns written in large notes should be ignored. The fact that the notational distinction is reproduced in the parallel passage at bar 66 supports the view that the differentiation is purposeful and suggests two different manners of performance (on-beat for arpeggios indicated by small notes and pre-beat for the written-out arpeggios). In effect Neumann's logic proposes that Haydn's entirely consistent notational distinction should be read inconsistently, producing uniform pre-beat performance.

It is of relevance to the interpretation of this example that bar 18 of this movement (not shown by Neumann in his example) ends with a crotchet rest. Frequently an advantage of notating an ornament in small notes is the avoidance of a cumbersome rhythmic notation, but clearly this is not true in this instance, where had Haydn required a pre-beat performance of the first arpeggio he could have written it precisely as he did for the second and third arpeggios. Similar passages in Hob. XVI: 41/i, bars 20–2 (Ex. 9.15b) and XVI: 51/i, bars 1–2 (Ex. 9.15c), make interesting comparisons with XVI: 38. In Hob. XVI: 41 where Haydn required consistent pre-beat performance of arpeggios he notated the passage without ambiguity. In Hob. XVI: 51/i, bars 1–2 on the other hand, while the melodic and harmonic framework is similar to XVI: 41/i, bars 20–3, the arpeggios are notated differently,

[20] 'More on Haydn's Ornaments', 107.

Ex. 9.15(*a*) Hob. XVI: 38/i, (*b*) Hob. XVI: 41/i, (*c*) Hob. XVI: 51/i

indicating, I would argue, on-beat performance. In Hob. XVI: 51/i it would also have been an easy matter to indicate pre-beat perfor-mance in large note with precise rhythmic values if this were the intention. In both Hob. XVI: 51 and XVI: 41 Haydn is again absolutely consistent in his notation of parallel passages (bars 116–18 in Hob. XVI: 41/i and bars 5–6, 44–5, 48–9, 80–1, 84–5 in Hob. XVI: 51/i). Nowhere is a pre-beat pattern such as that in Ex. 9.15*b* notated in a parallel passage by the use of small notes. The only 'logic' which explains Haydn's consistent notation is that arpeggios indicated by small notes imply a different performance than those written before the beat with large notes, that the small notes indicate (as the vast majority of eighteenth-century writers tell us they did) on-beat per-formance and that when Haydn required a pre-beat performance he notated this unambiguously.

Haydn's notation is, of course, neither always complete, consistent, or precise, but when, as in his notation of arpeggios, he is consistent, our interpretations cannot ignore this. Neumann's logic assumes an attitude of unconcern on the part of the composer which is at variance with the sources.

THE SLIDE (*SCHLEIFER*)

Treatises from the second half of the eighteenth century illustrate two forms of slide, the Lombardic and the dotted or dactylic. The former would seem to be the prevalent form and is associated particularly with earlier galant styles. In Haydn's music it is in fact the most obvious indicator of Italianate galant influences, occurring far more frequently than that other hallmark of the Italian galant, the Alberti bass. The Lombardic slide is always performed quickly, and realizations in treatises are uniform in their rhythmic presentation of the ornament

Ex. 9.16(*a*) Koch, *Lexikon*, s.v. 'Vorschlag', (*b*) C. P. E. Bach, *Versuch*, table VI, fig. lxxxviii, (*c*) C. P. E. Bach, *Versuch*, table VI, fig. xciii

(see Ex. 9.16*a* and *b*):[21] it is precisely this type of slide which is so prominent in Haydn's early music.

Haydn most frequently writes the Lombardic slide in precise note values, nearly always those illustrated in contemporary treatises, rather than using small notes. A characteristic example from his early works is given in Ex. 9.17*a*, from which it may be noted that, like the arpeggio, the Lombardic slide is principally associated with the main beats of the bar, a fact commented on by Türk.[22] An exceptional instance of a slide occurring in association with a weak beat is found in the Sonata, Hob. XVI: 4/i, where, interestingly, a parallel passage suggests a triplet rhythm for the slide which is initially notated by small notes (see Ex. 9.17*b*). As seen here, Haydn also (if less frequently) uses the other common method of notating a slide, namely two small notes, but although the possibility that this duality in notation may imply a distinction in performance cannot be ruled out, the respective manners of notation are not employed in a consistent way which would suggest that Haydn associated a different realization with each. There are no instances of seemingly purposeful alternation or contrast of notational patterns as is the case with Haydn's consistently contrasted methods of notating pre-beat arpeggios written in large notes and (on-beat) arpeggios written in small notes. The possible alternatives to the Lombardic slide when the notation of, for instance, Ex. 9.17*d* is used, are the dactylic and the anapaestic slides, which are discussed below. Frequently though, when small notes are used to indicate a slide, the impression is gained (it can, of course, be no more than that) that a simple calligraphic convenience is responsible for the choice of notation. Ex. 9.17*c* from Hob. XVI: 2/i is suggestive in this regard. In bar 10 the initial statement of the principal theme ends with a cadence on the tonic; the 'transition' section which follows is dominated melodically by repetitions of the slide pattern mostly written out in Lombardic rhythm, but with two patterns (bars 11 and 16) notated with small notes. There seems to be no musical reason (melodic, rhythmic or least of all accentual) why the slides in bars 11 and 16 should differ from the Lombardic slides, and indeed even Neumannesque melodic logic might well be advanced as a (subjective) reason for preferring the Lombardic slide throughout. The most obvious and simple explanation for the inconsistency

[21] See also Türk, *Klavierschule*, trans. Haggh, 240; Marpurg, *Principes*, 62–3; id., *Anleitung*, 52.

[22] *Klavierschule*, trans. Haggh, 240.

Ex. 9.17(*a*) Hob. xv: 38/iii, (*b*) Hob. xvi: 4/i, (*c*) Hob. xvi: 2/i, (*d*) Hob. xvi: 46/i

(d)

in notation is that, because the slides in bars 11 and 16 occur before minims, small notes are used to avoid the more cumbersome notation. This suggestion is supported by the passage in the 'development' which leads to the restatement of the principal theme and in which the music of bars 16 ff. recurs, but with bar 16 compressed into one beat. Here, in a parallel passage although not an exact repetition, the slide is written out with a Lombardic rhythm. Haydn in general seems to use small notes to indicate a slide which ornaments long note values, especially tied notes, when by so doing he avoids unnecessarily complex rhythms (see Ex. 9.17d).[23]

The dactylic slide, in which the first note of the ornament may be prolonged in a number of ways, is characteristic of North German treatises, and, although also mentioned by Clementi (see Ex. 9.3), it is, in general, far less common than the Lombardic slide. C. P. E. Bach uses the dactylic slide in his compositions as well as in the *Versuch*, but because he uses 'real' notation it is always easily distinguishable from the Lombardic slide. The dactylic slide may find expression in quite a wide variety of rhythms, the most common of which are illustrated in Ex. 9.16c. There is an absolute absence of evidence in Haydn's music for the performance of slide patterns notated as in Ex. 9.17d in a dactylic rhythm, and it would seem likely that, if used at all, the dactylic slide was not a prominent feature: in Haydn's early keyboard music, in particular, the Lombardic slide is so often expressly notated in precise rhythms that this must be regarded as the predominant form. It is also suggestive that after c.1766 when Haydn adopted the practice of notating appoggiaturas at their real values, the slide continues to be written as either semiquaver or demisemiquaver small notes (when not expressed as a metrically precise Lombardic rhythm), and not in real values with the dotted initial note normally associated with the dactylic slide. Patterns similar to some of the

---

[23] See also Hob. XV: 1/ii, bar 9 and XV: C1/iii, bar 14 where, similarly, the use of small notes in notating slides avoids complex rhythmic notation.

realizations of the dactylic slide illustrated in Ex. 9.16 are found in
Haydn's music, but these are written in 'large' notes and not in the
manner advocated in North German theory. Türk's concluding
comment concerning the dactylic slide may be significant in this
regard: 'It seems to me that composers would do better if they would
notate the values of this very irregular ornament with notes of
customary size, at least in doubtful cases'.[24] If the dactyl has a significance in Haydn's music it is probable that it should be confined to
those movements which, to quote Türk, are of 'an agreeable or tender character in rather slow tempo'.[25]

Notwithstanding the relevance of the anapaestic (pre-beat) slide to
various styles of Baroque music,[26] its use in galant and Classical music
is open to serious doubt. There is little support for it use in treatises
from the second half of the eighteenth century[27] and the internal evidence which has been cited in support of its relevance is scant indeed.
The main basis of Neumann's advocacy of the anapaestic slide in
Haydn and Mozart is accentuation and, linked to this, certain
dynamic markings.[28] Neumann cites Koch's comment that, regarding the illustration in Ex. 9.16a, the main note (i.e. *d"*) is accented.[29]
Neumann insists that 'This virtually forms an anapest since an accent
seeks the beat', but he omits Koch's realization which is unambiguously a Lombardic slide beginning on the beat.[30] The question of
accentuation is surely unproblematic as regards the Lombardic slide,
since the first note is relatively accented by virtue of its placement on
the beat but the main note also 'naturally', because of the rhythm of
the Lombardic slide, receives an agogic accent. The effect is of an
accented 'beat', the accent being inherent in the mere presence of the
ornament, although in Haydn's later keyboard music this may be supplemented by a *f* or *fz* marking. The latter, as Somfai points out,
should not be understood as referring to a particular note but rather
to the ornament or to the particular beat.[31]

[24] *Klavierschule*, trans. Haggh, 243.   [25] Ibid. 241.

[26] See Neumann, *Ornamentation in Baroque and Post-Baroque Music*, 203–38.

[27] Two exceptions from the treatises of Ricci [–J. C. Bach] and Petri are given by
Neumann in *Ornamentation in Mozart*, 97.

[28] *Ornamentation in Mozart*, 97–103; and id., 'Ornamentik', 36–7.

[29] 'Wenn vor einer Hauptnote mehr Vorschlagsnoten stehen, werden sie mit gleicher
Geschwindigkeit an die Hauptnote angeschleift, die auch in diesem Falle den Accent
bekommt' (Koch, *Lexikon*, s.v. 'Vorschlag').

[30] *Ornamentation in Mozart*, 98.

[31] *Haydn Kongress, Wien, 1982*, 42. It is worth noting in connection with Ex. 9.17b that
even when the slide uncharacteristically occurs on a weak beat it apparently begins on the beat.

The slide, like the arpeggio, appears to serve primarily accentual and rhythmic purposes, but it is noticeable that the stylistic associations of the two ornaments are quite different with regard to Haydn's music. While, as has been pointed out above, the arpeggio is rare in Haydn's early keyboard works, where two and three-part textures are the norm, it is in these works that the slide is common. The slide continues to occur in Haydn's music after *c*.1766, but becomes quite a rarity in comparison both to its previous prominent usage and to the increasing instance of arpeggios. It is difficult to avoid the impression that the popularity of the slide waned together with the particular galant style of Haydn's keyboard music before *c*.1766 and that the functions of the slide are to some extent fulfilled by the arpeggio in Haydn's later music. The chronological association of each ornament is obviously of interest to the performer when considering the question of appropriate improvised embellishments for Haydn's music.

THE *ANSCHLAG* (COMPOUND APPOGGIATURA)

Marpurg states in his *Principes* that the ornament most commonly referred to as the *Anschlag* was (in the 1750s) a 'new' ornament, the name and use of which was not widely known.[32] This may not in fact be entirely true since Quantz, writing in 1752, implied that the ornament was widely used by singers,[33] but as regards instrumental music, and in particular keyboard music, the *Anschlag* is strongly associated with North German treatises and compositions. C. P. E. Bach is sometimes cited as the first composer to apply the term *Anschlag* to the ornament,[34] a term which gained general acceptance, not withstanding various comments that the term *Doppelvorschlag*, as used by Marpurg,[35] is a more accurate description of the ornament.

There can be no question as regards the placement of the *Anschlag* in relation to the beat. The name *Anschlag* itself emphasizes the on-beat nature of the ornament and the realizations found in treatises from the second half of the eighteenth century are unanimous in this regard (see Ex. 9.18). C. P. E. Bach gives two melodic patterns in his illustration of the *Anschlag* (Ex. 9.18*a*) but the first of these is rather

---

[32] Pp. 61.   [33] *Versuch*, trans. Reilly, 159.

[34] Marpurg, *Anleitung*, 51. See also Türk, *Klavierschule*, trans. Haggh, 475 n. 8.

[35] Marpurg, *Die Kunst das Clavier zu spielen* (Berlin, 1750), 26; *Principes*, 61–2; *Anleitung*, 51; Türk, *Klavierschule*, trans. Haggh, 235.

Ex. 9.18(*a*) C. P. E. Bach, *Versuch*, table VI, figs. lxxx, lxxxi, (*b*) C. P. E. Bach, *Versuch*, table VI, fig. lxxxvi, (*c*) Türk, *Klavierschule*, trans. Haggh, p. 237, (*d*) C. P. E. Bach, *Versuch* (1787 edn.), p. 77

flattering expression
[schmeichelhafter Ausdruck]

uncommon even in his own music; it does not occur in the keyboard music of Haydn and will therefore not be considered further. In the second and more common type, two appoggiaturas 'the tone below and then the tone above are prefixed to it [the main note]':[36] this form of *Anschlag* is considered by theorists to be 'generally' more appropriate to slow or moderate tempos. Türk comments as follows on the function of the ornament:

Since the double appoggiatura strongly emphasizes the note before which it is played and for that reason makes it an important note, it follows that this ornament should never be used on other than an emphasized or a main beat and never for an unimportant (passing) note, assuming that the intention is not to go contrary to the feeling for the meter.[37]

Some theorists also give dotted or dactylic realizations of the *Anschlag*, similar to those discussed in connection with the slide (see Ex. 9.18*b* and *c*). The dactylic *Anschlag* is primarily associated with the treatises of C. P. E. Bach and of Türk, who echoes Bach's thought closely. Marpurg also gives the dactylic pattern but he comments that

[36] C. P. E. Bach, *Versuch*, trans. Mitchell, 132.   [37] *Klavierschule*, trans. Haggh, 237.

this rhythmic interpretation is 'better written in ordinary notes'.[38] Quantz, Koch, and Clementi, who otherwise discuss or illustrate the *Anschlag*, do not mention the dactylic rhythm in connection with the ornament. Again, as is true of the dactylic realization of the slide, real notation is used by Bach and Türk in the representation of the dactylic *Anschlag*. The fact that Haydn always uses two semiquavers or demisemiquavers, and not a dotted initial note, in notating the *Anschlag* probably indicates that the *Anschlag* with dactylic rhythm is not appropriate for his music. It is also noteworthy that in one instance in Haydn's keyboard music where an *Anschlag* is written in large notes, the rhythm is Lombardic rather than dactylic (see Ex. 9.19*a*). Bach comments that the dactylic *Anschlag* 'never appears in rapid movements but is well used in affettuoso passages'.[39] It may not be culpable to use the dactylic *Anschlag* occasionally in 'affettuoso' passages in Haydn's music, but it is probably fair to say that Haydn never specifically requires this rhythmic interpretation. On the other hand a realization of the *Anschlag* added to the 1787 edition of Bach's *Versuch* may be regarded as a particularly expressive way of executing the ornament (Ex. 9.18*d*) and since it is an 'improvised' interpretation without any special indication (unlike the dactylic *Anschlag*) it may be used rather more freely than the dactylic pattern.

Haydn seems to notate the *Anschlag* for the first time in the 1770s, and throughout his keyboard music it occurs on no more than a handful of occasions. It is used in slow or moderate tempos (on one occasion it occurs in a movement marked Allegro moderato) and is associated with strong beats; most often it ornaments a main note which is itself an appoggiatura (Ex. 9.19*b* and *c*). It was pointed out in Chapter 6 that the *Anschlag* is used in Hob. XVI: 30/ii in the same way as a short appoggiatura, a *Praller*, an inverted *Doppelschlag*, and a *Doppelschlag*, in ornamenting main notes which are in fact appoggiaturas (see Ex. 5.5). This raises the possibility that the *Anschlag* might be used by the performer somewhat more frequently than the instance of its notated occurrences would suggest, as an improvised ornament contributing to the process of variation, especially in repeats. The Tempo di Menuet from Hob. XVI: 30 provides a striking model for such a practice. The *Anschlag* must, however, be regarded as occupying a relatively minor place in Haydn's ornamental practices as we know them from his notation. Quantz's comments on the *Anschlag* are in this regard worth recalling:

---

[38] *Anleitung*, 51; *Principes*, 62.   [39] *Versuch*, trans. Mitchell, 135.

Ex. 9.19(*a*) Hob. XVI: 38/i, (*b*) Hob. XV: 18/ii, (*c*) Hob. XVI: 30/i

Although the *Anschlag* expresses a tender, sighing, and pleasing sentiment in singing and playing, I do not advise that it be used too lavishly; it is better to introduce it infrequently, since one quickly remembers that which is very pleasing to the ear, while something in excess, no matter how beautiful it may be, may eventually engender distaste.[40]

As is clear from the realization given in Ex. 9.18*a* and from specific comments in treatises, the performance of the *Anschlag* involves placing the accent on the main note and not the two appoggiaturas of the *Anschlag*, yet it is absolutely clear that an on-beat performance of the ornament is intended. Neumann's notion that accentuation of this type necessarily implies a pre-beat interpretation (because an accent 'seeks the beat'), is therefore emphatically countered. The accentuation of the slide and the *Anschlag* is related to touch, as well as being to some extent inherent in the Lombardic rhythm, but is not reliant on a pre-beat performance.

[40] *Versuch*, trans. Reilly, 159.

10

Epilogue:
Beyond the Notation

◊

The emphasis in much of this book, particularly in those chapters dealing with articulation and ornamentation, has been, unashamedly, on the evidence of the notation. Haydn's notation is a series of codes, some of which may be read by the contemporary performer with relative ease, while others involve a more complex process of decoding, mediated by indirect knowledge gleaned from sources other than the composer. In Haydn's notation the pitches which make up a melody and the harmonies which accompany them are generally prescribed without ambiguity, allowing a fairly literal reading of the notation in this regard and, in the interpretative chain suggested by Fig. 10.1, creating a direct link between the composer and the interpretation via the notation. At its most precise Haydn's notation can at various times, although not consistently, be equally unambiguous in prescribing aspects of 'performance practice': when in an autograph manuscript Haydn writes out in unambiguous pitch and rhythmic notation the realization of an ornament (an appoggiatura, for instance) the interpretation of this ornament need not be determined by reference to performance-practice conventions which Quantz or any other theorist discusses in relation to the appoggiatura. At the other extreme, the interpretation of Haydn's tempo indications must always be informed by numerous factors. (Do the sources agree on the tempo designation and time signature? Do eighteenth-century theorists agree on what the tempo indication means in relation to other tempo indications? What do later metronome markings suggest? Are these relevant? What seems to work in relation to the rhythmic profile of the movement?)

In between the extremes of a prescriptive notation which links the

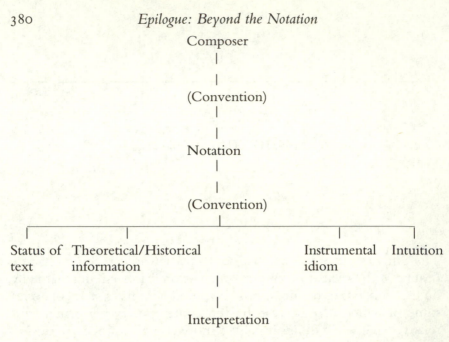

Fig. 10.1

composer and the interpretation directly and vague notation which is interpreted in the light of the factors listed in Fig. 10.1 (and perhaps others) lie a myriad of possible readings. Our reading of Haydn's notation is constantly shifting, from note to note, beat to beat, and symbol to symbol, between literal and modified meanings. Indeed, for the notation of any given beat of music in a piece, literal and modified meanings operate simultaneously. Thus we might accept literally the notation of pitch and duration, modify precise instruction regarding articulation because of the instrument, and base an interpretation of an imprecise ornament symbol on a variety of factors (various historical factors might determine the reading, or intuition might overrule historical-theoretical information, and this reading might be further determined by the instrument being used).

If we view notation as the most tangible connection with the composer, then interpretation is an enhanced reading of the notation and the various factors which mediate between the notation and the performance produce an infinite variety of enhanced readings. Two facts seem to me to result from this view. First, the absolute notion of an 'authentic' performance is untenable and, secondly, the common perception of a rigid divide between 'early music' performances on eighteenth-century instruments and 'modern' performances on modern instruments is simplistic. Clearly it follows from these viewpoints that the remarkably complacent association of authenticity with performance on 'original' instruments is a nonsense.[1] An authentic performance would only be possible, even hypothetically, if the link between composer and performance, that is the notation, were, in all regards and on every occasion, unambiguous, which is clearly not the case. The performer of Haydn's keyboard music on an 'original' instrument mediates between ambiguous notation and performance in much the same way as the performer using a modern instrument, albeit with altogether different results.

The difficult problem of how and when one should use the sustaining mechanism of a piano (whether operated by a pedal, a knee-lever, or a hand-stop) illustrates the extent of the gap that can exist between notation and interpretation, and the broadly similar interpretative task faced by early-music and modern performers alike. Haydn indicated the use of a mechanism which raises the dampers in only one work, Hob. XVI: 50 (see Ex. 2.20c), where the open-pedal indication is a special effect occurring twice in the work in conjunction with the imaginative transformation of the articulation of the main theme of the first movement. The context in which this open-pedal marking occurs is unique in Haydn's music and it does not provide us with a model for the use of the pedal elsewhere. Since there is no passage in Haydn's music which is apparently unplayable without the use of a damper mechanism, one might conclude that the pedal is not necessary in Haydn's music and indeed comments by some nineteenth-century writers broadly support this view. Hummel, Czerny, and Kalkbrenner give the distinct impression that Mozart and Austrian pianists of his generation either did not use, or at least did not specifically require the use of, the pedal.[2] There seems to be a consensus that Austrian pianists in the late eighteenth century were conservative in their use of the pedal and innovations in the use

---

[1] On the problematic notion of 'authenticity' in performance see esp. R. Taruskin, 'The Pastness of the Present and the Presence of the Past', in N. Kenyon (ed.), *Authenticity and Early Music* (Oxford: OUP, 1988), 137–207; id., 'The Limits of Authenticity: A Discussion', *EM* 12/1 (Feb. 1984): 3–12; and L. Dreyfus, 'Early Music Defended against its Devotees: A Theory of Historical Performance in the Twentieth Century', *MQ* 69/3 (Summer 1983): 297–322.

[2] Hummel. *Instructions*, pt. III, p. 62; Czerny, *Pianoforte School*, iii. 63–4, 100; Kalkbrenner, *A Complete Course of Instruction for the Piano Forte*, 8.

of pedals are associated with composers such as Dussek, Cramer, Field, and Beethoven.

Yet this view, although compatible with Haydn's notation, is, in practice, accepted generally neither by fortepianists nor by performers on modern pianos. As justification for the use of damper mechanisms it might be argued that the statements of Hummel, Czerny, and Kalkbrenner are undoubtedly biased and demonstrably inaccurate in certain regards.[3] Furthermore it is clear that Haydn and Mozart were aware of the various mechanisms in eighteenth-century pianos for lifting the dampers and although neither composer prescribed their use, apart from the single instance of Hob. XVI: 50, it is plausible that they experimented with these mechanisms at least occasionally. In attempting to reconstruct how Haydn or Mozart might have used damper mechanisms, a fortepianist might well take account of the increasingly frequent pedal indications in printed music by other composers from the 1790s which provide information on how the later contemporaries of Haydn and Mozart used the pedal,[4] but of arguably greater importance is a knowledge of what is idiomatic on the various types of eighteenth-century piano. The ways in which one might use a hand-stop on a square piano are different to the potential for the use of a knee-lever on a Viennese fortepiano: the completely different acoustical characteristics of Broadwood or Erard pianos suggest rather different uses for the pedals on these instruments. The performer on 'original' instruments who chooses to experiment with the damper mechanisms on eighteenth-century instruments, may be aided by indirect sources of information, but is essentially attempting to reconstruct idiomatic uses of these devices virtually *ab initio* in a largely intuitive response to the capabilities of the instruments. This process may be intellectually credible and musically justifiable, but the results, no matter how convincing, can hardly be regarded as authentic.

Performers of Haydn's or Mozart's music on a modern piano rarely eschew the use of the pedal: it is generally regarded as essential to the technique and sound of the modern instrument, the 'soul of the instrument'. Most performer's would agree that pedalling in this music should be carefully judged: it should not, generally, blur details of articulation, or obscure phrasing, or be used to achieve a legato

---

[3] See Rowland, 'Early Pianoforte Pedalling: The Evidence of the Earliest Printed Markings', 16.

[4] Ibid. 5–17.

which is not otherwise attainable through the use of the fingers alone. Continuous legato pedalling such as may be appropriate in later piano music is often injurious to the music, but while many performers modify their use of the pedal in playing Haydn so that it is unobtrusive, few abandon the use of the pedal completely, since to do so seems alien to performance on the instrument. In practice most pianists achieve a compromise between what is idiomatic on the modern piano and characteristics of the music which seem to conflict with later pedal techniques.

Pedalling, whether on a fortepiano or a modern instrument, is determined more by what is idiomatic on the instrument than by the intentions of the composer. In many other ways inherited notions of what is idiomatic on an instrument play a large part in interpretation, sometimes to the extent that there is a conflict between nineteenth- or twentieth-century aesthetic views of what is beautiful in performance and the evidence of the notation. This is particularly apparent in attitudes to articulation. Nineteenth-century preferences for a predominantly legato touch, beginning perhaps with Clementi's advocacy of the 'highter beauties of the legato', have exerted an enormous influence on twentieth-century schools of pianism and the survival into the twentieth century of Czerny's practice of eliding slurs is a striking instance of conflict between changing aesthetics of performance and the composer's notation. In an interesting recent article Malcolm Bilson compared various recordings of the first movement of Mozart's Sonata, K.282 and observed that '*None* [of the performers] followed Mozart's clear and specific directives [on articulation]; all played a simple uninflected legato'.[5] Comparisons of performances of Haydn's keyboard music often elicit similar results. Bilson is quite rightly careful not to equate adherence to the composer's notation with correct or beautiful performance, but it is none the less clear that frequently in modern performance the highlighting of long continuous melodic lines is seen as aesthetically more pleasing than the more articulated style of performance indicated by the composer. This aesthetic may be connected with the heavier action and the acoustical properties of nineteenth- and twentieth-century pianos by comparison with their eighteenth-century counterparts, but again it would be simplistic to associate performances on 'original' instruments with adherence to a composer's articulation markings and performance on

[5] 'Execution and Expression in the Sonata in E flat, K.282', *EM* 20/2 (May 1992): 237.

modern instruments with continuous lines and a legato touch. Many fortepianists and writers on performance practice continue to espouse Czerny's attitude to slurs[6] and the way in which attitudes to articulation influence other performance decisions is highlighted in a recent article by Paul Badura-Skoda.

Concerning bars 33–4 of the second movement from Mozart's Concerto, K.467 (Ex. 10.1*a*) Badura-Skoda makes the following observation in advocating a main-note trill: 'A long trill should begin on the main note if the trill is preceded by the upper note in a legato context. . . . Probably only an unmusical person would play here a trill starting with the upper note.'[7] The first sentence is quite valid and I have discussed this context in some detail in connection with the 'adjoining trill' in Chapter 6. However, in Badura-Skoda's example the context is only legato if one extends Mozart's slur over the bar line. In other words, Badura-Skoda advocates a main-note trill and legato articulation which is contrary to Mozart's notation, while one of a number of possible realizations of the trill which observes Mozart's articulation is labelled an 'unmusical execution' (Ex. 10.1*b*). The seminal issue here is not the debate over which note a trill should begin on, but rather a matter of changing aesthetics. Badura-Skoda's interpretation with a main-note trill and legato articulation highlights a melodic line which descends from the dominant to the leading note before resolving on the tonic and the importance of this line seems to overrule Mozart's slur marking and dictates the realization of the trill. A plausible interpretation which articulates the change of harmony between bars 33 and 34 with a *silence d'articulation* and delays the arrival of the leading note (in the manner of a 4–3 suspension) is regarded, not merely as incorrect, but as an interpretation which would only be countenanced by an unmusical player.

There are many ways of playing this passage beautifully and a legato performance with each note merging with the preceding and succeeding notes in a carefully shaped melodic line is one such possibility, which has been demonstrated on innumerable recordings of distinction. Whether it is inherently unidiomatic on a modern piano to observe Haydn's or Mozart's slur marking exactly remains a moot point—it may be no more than fashion, albeit a fashion which has lasted since Beethoven and Czerny to regard this manner of execution as 'choppy'—but, it seems to me no less aesthetically pleasing

---

[6] R. Stowell, 'Leopold Mozart Revised', 138. [7] 'Mozart's Trills', 6.

Ex. 10.1. Mozart, Concerto in C, K467/ii

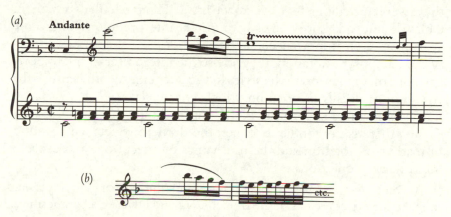

and a more interesting interpretative challenge to arrive at an interpretation which reconciles idiomatic and beautiful playing with the
composer's notation.

Careful study of the details of a composer's notation does not dimin-
ish in any way the interpretative task of the performer. It does not
relieve the performer of the responsibility of judgement and choice,
it does not mean that the uninterpreted text must be venerated, or
that a performance free from error and anachronism may be equated
with an interpretation. Least of all does it imply that, in a recently
much-quoted phrase, 'problems of interpretation will be resolved
into operational procedures'.[8] While for me an interpretation
involves an engagement with what might be labelled 'positivistic'
activities (for instance, editorial and source problems, understanding
precisely the meaning of signs, determining precisely where slurs
begin and end), this is not to say that such pursuits are an end in
themselves. Concern for the minutiae of textual transmission as an
ally to interpretation is not new, it is not (*pace* Taruskin) a product
of twentieth-century 'positivistic' and 'dehumanizing' tendencies,
nor is it historically a consequence of the early-music or authentic-
performance movement.

The reason D'Anglebert and François Couperin devoted immense
care to their notation of ornaments is not, one must assume, that
either composer was at heart a pedant, but because ornamentation is

---

[8] Quoted in Taruskin, 'Limits of Authenticity', 8.

of crucial import to their musical style, a means of expression which they were unwilling to leave to chance. Their detailed ornament tables do not today provide us with instant interpretations, but, quite apart from their importance as a starting-point for the understanding of the composer's notation, they advise the interpreter of the import-ance of ornamentation in the style. In the later eighteenth century the attention to details of notation which characterizes C. P. E. Bach's music is no mere superficial exercise in orthography and in Bach's *Versuch* there is no conflict between the numerous detailed accounts of matters of notation and the mechanics of execution, and broader interpretative questions.

What comprises good performance? The ability through singing or playing to make the ear conscious of the true content and affect of a composition. Any passage can be so radically changed by modifying its performance that it will be scarcely recognizable.

The subject matter of performance is the loudness and softness of tones, touch, the snap, legato and staccato execution, the vibrato, arpeggiation, the holding of tones, the retard and accelerando. Lack of these elements or inept use of them makes a poor performance.

Good performance, then, occurs when one hears all notes and their embell-ishments played in correct time with fitting volume produced by a touch which is related to the true content of a piece.[9]

For Bach the 'subject matter of performance' is minute attention to detail in execution (elsewhere he refers to such matters as 'details of beauty'),[10] through which the performer can reveal the 'true content and affect of a composition'. These details of beauty are, for Bach, in no sense incompatible with the quest for 'freedom of performance that rules out everything slavish and mechanical': they are no restric-tion to the performer who must 'Play from the soul, not like a trained bird!'[11]

Haydn has not left us a tome which testifies, as does Bach's *Versuch*, to the importance of the details of beauty which transmit the com-poser's message. Nevertheless, his occasional letters which rebuke engravers for corrupting his notation of ornaments, or his advice to the performers of his 'Applausus' Cantata which comments equally on the spirit of the work and on details of execution such as bowing and the duration of appoggiaturas in recitative, give much the same

---

[9] C. P. E. Bach, *Versuch*, trans. Mitchell, 148.   [10] *Versuch*, 150.   [11] Ibid.

impression as Bach's *Versuch*.[12] Similarly, the meticulous attention to details of notation in many of Haydn's autograph manuscripts speaks volubly for the importance of these details to Haydn's style. We should never make the error of assuming that the notation is the content of a composition, but the details of beauty which the composer chooses to notate are intrinsic to that composition.

In the twentieth-century performers have by and large sought to convey in their performances the intentions of the composer. The spirit behind this goal is not new; it is in effect a manifestation of the age-old obsession of composers and good performers with details of execution, the same spirit which motivated D'Anglebert's ornament table, C. P. E. Bach's *Versuch*, or Haydn's 'Applausus' letter. What is new in the twentieth century is not the obsession with detail in performance (positivism is to this extent innate in performance), but that in the twentieth century performers have concerned themselves to a far greater extent than ever before with the performance of 'old music'. The reformulation of the composer's concern for details of beauty as the twentieth-century performer's concern for the intentions of the composer signifies not a different attitude to performance, but a radical shift in repertoire performed. This reformulation was, in short, necessitated by the creation in the late nineteenth century and the twentieth century of a musical canon.

Much of what is today associated with the early-music movement grew up as a corollary to performance and scholarly traditions which developed earlier in the twentieth century, as witnessed in the interesting parallels which can be drawn between the careers of two of the most influential musicians of the twentieth century, Arturo Schnabel and Heinrich Schenker. In their respective spheres both were influential in the establishment of a musical canon (Schenker's work as a theorist concentrated on a Bach-to-Brahms repertoire and Schnabel performances were notable for his classical repertoire, departing from the virtuoso repertoire typical of his contemporaries); both Schenker and Schnabel were pioneers in establishing new standards in the editing of the old music of which they were champions (as in Schenker's pioneering edition of C. P. E. Bach and the editions of Beethoven's piano sonatas by both Schnabel and Schenker); and both were very much concerned with *Aufführungspraxis*, with the detail of the composers' notation—the intentions of the composer (as witnessed in

---

[12] *CCLN*, 9–11, 51–2.

Schenker's *Ein Beitrag zur Ornamentik* and in, for instance, Schnabel's attitude to Beethoven's pedal indications). No doubt many of the attitudes that we observe in the work of Schenker and Schnabel might today be characterized as positivistic, but this spirit of positivism is different from D'Anglebert's, C. P. E. Bach's, or Haydn's concern for text only in that it is directed at music which is not contemporary.

The twentieth-century practice of playing old music on 'original' instruments has taken longer in gaining widespread acceptance than, for instance, modern editorial practices, yet historically the enthusiasm for original instruments has its roots in the same performance and scholarly traditions which saw the creation of a musical canon, the first 'Urtext' editions, and the first tomes on *Aufführungspraxis*. We may empathize with Richard Taruskin's scepticism regarding what has been perceived as the characteristic underinterpretation of certain performers in the 1980s, where the unfortunate view is often implicit that 'the medium is the message', that 'the "right instrument", yielding the "right sound", holds an automatic key to the music';[13] nevertheless, the use of 'original' instruments remains a valid interpretation of the premiss which motivated Schnabel's performances of Beethoven or led to the first Urtext editions. They are of value not by virtue of their 'authentic sound', which supposedly flourishes in underinterpreted performances, but because they create different interpretative possibilities; the greater variety of eighteenth-century instruments by comparison with modern instruments creates the potential for a rich diversity of enhanced readings, different, not more authentic, than those available on modern instruments.

The idiomatic playing and beautiful sounds which good performers draw from their instruments, whether old or modern, are crucial adjuncts to interpretation, but the instruments, and their inherited traditions of technique are the mediums of transmission, they are not the message itself. We can only know the composer's message through the notation which encodes it. In the first instance this notation must be read accurately, but it also suggests interpretative possibilities beyond the literal meanings of the signs. A crucial function of interpretation is in translating the details of execution and the literal meanings of signs into affective gestures which relate to the content of the music. To read the sign *f* as indicating a *forte* dynamic and a

---

[13] 'Limits of Authenticity', 8.

fermata as indicating a prolonging of the duration of a note or rest is unproblematic, but in different pieces these signs convey different meanings beyond what they signify literally. In bars 62 to 124 of the Fantasia in C major, Hob. XVII: 4 (Ex. 10.2*a*) the *f*, *p*, and *cresc*. markings prescribe dynamic levels but they also tell us in some detail about the compositional intent. The crescendo from *p* to *f* between bar 62 and 69 signifies movement towards a goal, and the *forte–piano* contrast of 69–70 ff. signifies arrival. The *p* dynamic emphasizes a new theme, a thinner texture, and the establishing of G major as a (temporary) new tonic. At the end of this passage the return to C major is articulated in a similar manner with a *pianissimo–forte* contrast (bars 116–24). The tonal centres of G major and C major are each signalled by lead-ins in which dynamics mark movement towards a goal and the points of arrival. The stable G major tonality from bar 70 to 87 has a continuous *piano* dynamic, but from this point to the return of C major the abrupt changes of dynamics highlight Haydn's wonderfully adventurous modulation from G major to C major. The *f* markings of bars 88 and 106 emphasize the dramatic basic progression G major–B flat major–E major[7]–C major, that is, quite radical tertiary relationships. The immediate approach to B flat is from a D major chord, another tertiary relationship, and this is articulated as an abrupt change from *p*[*p*] to *f*. Likewise, the abrupt shift to a *piano* dynamic in bar 103 allows the *forte* E major of bar 106 ff. to sound emphatic, while by quitting the E major chord *pianissimo* (bar 116) the next *forte* indication, which marks the arrival of C major, articulates the E major–C major progression. These markings indicate more than contrasts in dynamics: they are intrinsic to the music, of structural significance, an analogue to the compositional ideas. They signify at different times movement towards a goal, points of arrival, interruptions and abrupt juxtapositions and in terms of Bach's description of a good performance they are related to the true content of the piece.

In bar 192 of this same work Haydn's instruction to hold the octave E until the sound fades provides another interesting example of how a detail of execution, the *fermata*, has a significance for the understanding of the passage beyond the literal meaning of the sign (Ex. 10.2*b*). The prolongation of the E to an unusually long duration is not an end in itself, a detail of execution applying only to the note to which it is attached: it heightens attention and expectation, focusing attention on the unconventional harmonic juxtaposition (E is heard as the dominant of A major and the resolution, F, is first heard

Ex. 10.2. Hob. XVII: 4

Ex. 10.2. *cont.*

(*b*)

as the flat submediant of A major). Two bars of silence in the right
hand above the F pedal prolong further the uncertainty until the
second theme of the movement enters unambiguously in B flat major
and the F pedal is reinterpreted as the dominant of B flat. Thus the
stasis signals to the listener in a quite wonderful way that a coup is
imminent, in this case the juxtaposition of A major and B flat major.
This example with its emphatic instruction regarding the length of
the *fermata* arguably provides us with a key to the interpretation of the
fermatas which are particularly characteristic of Haydn's late piano
trios. In Hob. XV: 24/i (Ex. 10.3) the *fermata* in bar 29 adds considerably to the harmonic surprise of bar 30, again by heightening expectation after the apparently stable closure on the dominant: it seems to
signal that something unusual is about to occur (in this instance a tertiary relationship) in much the same way as an orator might delay
before an important point to make it more emphatic.

Neither are ornaments merely decorative additions to the music
but an intrinsic part of the musical substance. They may function fig-
uratively as the building blocks of melody (as in the opening of Hob.
XVI: 49/ii), and as a repertoire of formulas which are manipulated as
variation. Equally, they effect accents and, in their association with
conventional cadential formulas, they mark phrase endings and signal
important structural events, in much the same way as punctuation
does in writing. The conventionality of the ornaments in the cadence

Ex. 10.3. Hob. xv: 24/i

figures of Ex. 6.21 signals almost as strongly as the harmony the end of a subphrase, the musical equivalent of a comma. On the other hand the ornaments associated with the cadences of Exx. 6.22–6.27 or Ex. 10.1 might be regarded as equivalent to a paragraph-ending.

It is not enough in performance that the dynamic markings or *fermatas* are observed, or that ornaments are played correctly (or in a manner which we assume to be correct): what they signify must be understood and conveyed to the audience. What we know of the ways Haydn and Mozart thought about music leads us to believe that they were very much concerned with the impact of their works on their listeners.[14] In the large eighteenth-century literature on performance, perhaps the most frequently invoked analogy is that between the performer and the orator. Frequently the analogy is used in describing technical aspects of performance (accentuation is explained by reference to the grammatical and rhetorical accents of the orator and phrasing is described in the terminology of punctuation), but the similarity of musical performance and oratory is never

---

[14] See M. E. Bonds, *Wordless Rhetoric: Musical Form and the Metaphor of the Oration* (Studies in the History of Music, 4; Cambridge, Mass.: Harvard University Press, 1991), 57–8. C. P. E. Bach's awareness of his audience is everywhere apparent in his writings on performance. 'Nature has wisely provided music with every kind of appeal so that all might share in its enjoyment. It thus becomes the duty of the performer to satisfy to the best of his ability every last kind of listener.' (C. P. E. Bach, *Versuch*, trans. Mitchell, 153.)

far from the surface when writers describe the more general aims of performance:

A musician cannot move others unless he too is moved. He must of necessity feel all of the affects that he hopes to arouse in his audience, for the revealing of his own humor will stimulate a like humor in the listener. In languishing, sad passages, the performer must languish and grow sad. Thus will the expression of the piece be more clearly perceived by the audience. . . . And so, constantly varying the passions, he will barely quiet one before he rouses another. Above all, he must discharge this office in a piece which is highly expressive by nature, whether it be by him or someone else. In the latter case he must make certain that he assumes the emotion which the composer intended in writing it.[15]

The performer must not only assume 'the emotion which the composer intended' but is required to 'stimulate a like humor in the listener'. To the eighteenth-century musician the art of performance is therefore the art of persuasion. In the all-important task of persuasion the details of execution which the composer notates assume a particular importance: the refinements of performance, be they ornaments, *fermatas*, or slurs, are inseparable from the message, since they are no less crucial than the notes and rhythms of the music in defining the affect or humour which the performer must convey.

Twentieth-century interpreters may choose to understand the 'necessity [to] feel all of the affects' of a work as an analytical process of understanding a composer's style, or understanding in formalistic terms the structure of a work. Similarly we may express the task of assuming the emotion which the composer intended as the quest for the intentions of the composer. What matters is that affects or the understanding of a composer's style, the emotions which the composer intended, or the intentions of the composer become the basis of advocacy and that in this process every aspect of the composer's notation is brought to bear on the task of interpretation.

---

[15] C. P. E. Bach, *Versuch*, trans. Mitchell, 152. The last sentence in this passage provides a compelling answer to Richard Taruskin's argument that 'the claim of self-evidence for the virtue of adhering to a composer's "intentions", is really nothing but a mystique' (Taruskin, 'Limits of Authenticity', 7).

BIBLIOGRAPHY

◊

I CONTEMPORARY THEORY, TUTORS, AND ORNAMENT TABLES

ADAM, LOUIS, *Méthode ou principe général du doigté pour le forte-piano* (Paris, 1798).

—— *Méthode de piano du conservatoire* (Paris, 1805; facsimile repr., Geneva: Minkoff, 1974).

AGRICOLA, J. F., *Anleitung zur Singkunst* (Berlin, 1757); ed. Erwin R. Jacobi (facsimile repr., Celle: Moeck, 1966).

D'ANGLEBERT, J. H., *Pièces de clavecin* (Paris, 1689; facsimile repr., New York: Broude Brothers, 1965).

AVISON, CHARLES, *An Essay on Musical Expression* (London, 1752).

BACH, C. P. E., *Versuch über die wahre Art das Clavier zu spielen*, 2 vols. (Berlin, 1753, 1762); ed. Lothar Hoffmann-Erbrecht (facsimile repr., Leipzig: Breitkopf & Härtel, 1957), English trans. William J. Mitchell as *Essay on the True Art of Playing Keyboard Instruments* (New York: Norton, 1949).

BACH, J. C. F., *Musikalische Nebenstunden* (Rinteln, 1787).

BRODERIP, R., *Plain and Easy Instructions for Young Performers on the Pianoforte or Harpsichord* (London [1788]).

—— *A Short Introduction to the Art of Playing the Harpsichord, Op. 6* (London [1790]).

BURNEY, C., *A General History of Music*, 4 vols. (London, 1776–89).

BUSBY, T., *A Complete Dictionary of Music* (London [1786]).

CAMIDGE, M., *Instructions for the Pianoforte or Harpsichord* (London [1799]).

CLEMENTI, M., *Introduction to the Art of Playing on the Pianoforte* (London, 1801); ed. Sandra Rosenblum (facsimile repr. New York: Da Capo Press, 1974).

COUPERIN, F., *Premier Livre de Pièces de Clavecin* (Paris, 1713).

—— *L'Art de toucher le clavecin* (Paris, 1716; 2nd edn. Paris, 1717); ed. and trans. A. Linde and M. Roberts (Leipzig: Breitkopf & Härtel, 1933).

CRAMER, J. B., *Instructions for the Piano Forte* (London [1812]).

CZERNY, C., *Vollständige theoretisch-praktische Pianoforte-Schule . . . Op. 500*, 3 vols. (Vienna, 1839), iv. *Die Kunst des Vortrags der älteren und neuern Klavierkompositionen* (Vienna, 1846).

CZERNY, C., *Complete Theoretical and Practical Piano Forte School . . . Op. 500*, 3 vols., trans. J. H. Hamilton (London, 1839); iv. *The Art of Playing the Ancient and Modern Piano Forte Works* (London [1846]).

—— *Über den richtigen Vortrag der sämtlichen Beethoven'schen Klavierwerke*, facsimile repr. of chapters 2 and 3 of *Die Kunst des Vortrags . . .*, ed. P. Badura-Skoda, (Vienna: Universal, 1963).

—— *On the Proper Performance of all Beethoven's Works for the Piano*, facsimile repr. of chapters 2 and 3 of *The Art of Playing . . .*, ed. P. Badura-Skoda (Vienna: Universal, 1970).

DALE, J., *Introduction to the Pianoforte, Harpsichord or Organ, Op. XII* (London [1797]).

DUSSEK, J. L., *Instructions on the Art of Playing the Pianoforte or Harpsichord* (London, 1799).

FÉTIS, F. J., and MOSCHELES, J., *Méthode des méthodes de piano* (Paris, 1840; facsimile repr., Geneva: Minkoff, 1973).

GALEAZZI, F., *Elementi teorico-pratici di musica*, 2 vols. (Rome, 1791, 1796).

GEMINIANI, F., *The Art of Playing on the Violin* (London, 1751); ed. D. Boyden (facsimile repr. (London: OUP [1952]).

—— *A Treatise of Good Taste in the Art of Musick* (London, 1749; facsimile repr., New York: Da Capo, 1969).

HECK, J. C., *The Art of Fingering* (London [c.1766]).

HILLER, J. A., *Anweisung zum musikalisch-zierlichen Gesange . . .* (Leipzig, 1780; facsimile repr., Leipzig: Peters, 1976).

HOOK, J., *Guida di Musica: Being a Complete Book of Instructions for Beginners on the Harpsichord or Pianoforte, Op. 37* (London [c.1785]).

HOYLE, J., *A Complete Dictionary of Music* (London, 1791; facsimile repr., Geneva: Minkoff, 1976).

HÜLLMANDEL, J. N., *Principles of Music, Chiefly Calculated for the Piano Forte or Harpsichord* (London, 1796).

HUMMEL, J. N., *Ausführliche theoretisch-praktische Anweisung zum Piano-Forte-Spiel*, 3 vols. (Vienna, 1828); trans. as *A Complete Theoretical and Practical Course of Instructions on the Art of Playing the Piano Forte* (London, 1829).

KALKBRENNER, F., *A Complete Course of Instruction for the Piano Forte* (London, 1835).

—— *A New Method of Studying the Piano-Forte* (London [1837]).

KOCH, H. C., *Versuch einer Anleitung zur Composition*, 3 vols. (Leipzig, 1782, 1787, 1793; facsimile repr., Hildesheim: Olms, 1969).

—— *Musikalisches Lexikon* (Frankfurt, 1802; facsimile repr., Hildesheim: Olms, 1964).

KOLLMANN, A. F., *An Essay on Musical Harmony* (London, 1796).

—— *An Essay on Practical Musical Composition* (London, 1799; facsimile repr., New York: Da Capo Press, 1973).

LACASSAGNE, J., *Traité general des elements du chant* (Paris, 1766).

LÖHLEIN, G. S., *Clavier-Schule, oder kurze und gründliche Anweisung zur melodie und harmonie* (Leipzig, 1765).

—— *Anweisung zum Violinspielen* (Leipzig, 1774).

MANCINI, G., *Riflessioni pratiche sul canto figurato* (3rd edn., Milan, 1777); trans. E. Foreman as *Practical Reflections on Figured Singing* (Champaign, Ill.: Pro Musica Press, 1967).

MANFREDINI, V., *Regole armoniche* (Venice, 1775; facsimile repr., New York: Broude Brothers, 1966).

MARPURG, F. W., *Die Kunst das Clavier zu spielen* (Berlin, 1750; 4th edn. Berlin, 1762; facsimile repr. of 4th edn., Hildesheim: Olms, 1969).

—— *Anleitung zum Clavierspielen* (Berlin, 1755; 2nd edn. Berlin, 1765; facsimile repr. of 2nd edn., Hildesheim: Olms, 1970).

—— *Principes du clavecin* (Berlin, 1756; facsimile repr., Geneva: Minkoff, 1974).

—— ed., *Kritische Briefe über die Tonkunst*, 3 vols. (Berlin [1759–64]).

—— *Historisch-kritische Beyträge zur Aufnahme der Musik*, 5 vols. (Berlin, 1754–8).

MATTHESON, J., *Der vollkommene Capellmeister* (Hamburg, 1739; facsimile repr., Kassel: Bärenreiter, 1954); trans. E. Harriss (Ann Arbor: UMI, 1981).

MILCHMEYER, J. P., *Die wahre Art das Pianoforte zu spielen* (Dresden, 1797).

MILLER, E., *Institutes of Music, or Easy Instructions for the Harpsichord* (London [1771]).

MOZART, L., *Versuch einer gründlichen Violinschule* (Augsburg, 1756); trans. E. Knocker as *A Treatise on the Fundamental Principles of Violin Playing* (Oxford: OUP, 1948).

PARKINSON, W., *A New Book of Instructions for Beginners on the Forte Piano or Harpsichord* (London, n.d.).

PASQUALI, N., *The Art of Fingering the Harpsichord* (Edinburgh, 1757).

PETRI, J. S., *Anleitung zur praktischen Musik* (Lauban, 1767; 2nd edn. Leipzig, 1782).

PLEYEL, I., *Méthode pour le pianoforte* (Paris, 1797; 3rd edn. enlarged as *Klavierschule*, Leipzig, 1804).

PRINTZ, W. C., *Phrynis Mitilenaeus* (Dresden, 1696).

QUANTZ, J. J., *Versuch einer Anweisung die Flöte traversiere zu spielen* (Berlin, 1752; 3rd edn. Breslau, 1789); ed. H.-P. Schmitz (facsimile repr. of 3rd edn., Kassel: Bärenreiter, 1953), trans. E. R. Reilly as *On Playing the Flute* (London: Faber & Faber, 1966).

RAMEAU, J.-P., *Premier livre de pièces de clavecin* (Paris, 1706).

—— *Pièces de clavecin* (Paris, 1724; facsimile repr., New York: Broude Brothers, 1967).

RELLSTAB, J. K. F., *Anleitung für Clavierspieler* (Berlin, 1790).

RICCI, P. [and BACH, J. C.], *Méthode ou recueil de connoissances [sic] élémentaires pour le forte-piano ou clavecin* (Paris, 1786; facsimile repr., Geneva: Minkoff, 1974).

ROUSSEAU, J.-J., *Dictionnaire de musique* (Paris, 1768; facsimile repr., Hildesheim: Olms, 1969).

SAINT LAMBERT, *Les Principes de clavecin* (Paris, 1702; trans. Rebecca Harris-Warrick as *Principles of the Harpsichord by Monsieur de Saint Lambert* (Cambridge: CUP, 1984).

SPOHR, L., *Violinschule* (Vienna [1832]); trans. J. Bishop as *Celebrated Violin School* (London [1843]).

STARKE, F., *Wiener Pianoforte-Schule*, 3 vols. (Vienna, 1819–21).

STEIBELT, D., *Méthode de piano* (Paris, 1809).

SULZER, J. G., *Allgemeine Theorie der Schönen Kunste*, 2 vols. (Leipzig, 1771, 1774; 2nd edn. enlarged 4 vols., Leipzig, 1792–4; facsimile repr. of 2nd edn., Hildesheim: Olms, 1967–70).

TANS'UR, W., *The Elements of Music Display'd* (London, 1772).

TARTINI, G., 'Regole per arrivare a saper ben sonare il violino'; French trans. P. Denis (Paris, 1771); facsimile repr. of Italian version and French, German, and English trans. in *Traité des agréments de la musique*, ed. E. R. Jacobi (Celle: Moeck, 1961).

TOSI, P., *Opinioni de' cantori antichi e moderni* (Bologna, 1723); facsimile repr. in Agricola, *Anleitung*, ed. E. R. Jacobi (Celle: Moeck, 1966); trans. J. Galliard as *Observations on the Florid Song* (London, 1742; repr. London: Stainer & Bell, 1987).

TROMLITZ, J. G., *Ausführlicher und gründlicher Unterricht, die Flöte zu spielen* (Leipzig, 1791; facsimile repr., Buren: Frits Knuf, 1985); trans. A. Powell as *The Virtuoso Flute-Player by Johann George Tromlitz* (Cambridge: CUP, 1991).

TÜRK, D. G., *Klavierschule, oder Anweisung zum Klavierspielen für Lehrer und Lernende* (Leipzig and Halle, 1789; 2nd edn. Leipzig and Halle, 1802); ed. E. R. Jacobi (facsimile repr. of 1st edn., Kassel: Bärenreiter, 1962); trans. R. Haggh (Lincoln, Nebr.: University of Nebraska Press, 1982).

WALTHER, J., *Musikalisches Lexicon* (Leipzig, 1732; facsimile repr., Kassel: Bärenreiter, 1953).

WOLF, E. W., 'Vorbericht', to *Eine Sonatine, Vier affectvolle Sonate und freien Fantasie anfangt und endiget* (Leipzig, 1785); trans. C. Hogwood, 'A Supplement to C. P. E. Bach's *Versuch*: E. W. Wolf's *Anleitung* of 1785', in S. Clark (ed.), *C. P. E. Bach Studies* (Oxford: Clarendon Press, 1988), 133–57.

WOLF, G. F., *Kurzer aber deutlicher Unterricht im Klavierspielen* (Göttingen, 1783).

II SECONDARY LITERATURE

ABERT, H., 'Joseph Haydns Klavierwerke', *ZfMw* 2 (July 1920): 553–73.

—— 'Joseph Haydns Klaviersonaten', *ZfMw* 3 (June–July 1921): 535–52.

ALBRECHT, H., ed., *Die Bedeutung der Zeichen Keil, Strich und Punkt bei Mozart* (Kassel: Bärenreiter, 1957).

ANDERSON, E., ed., *The Letters of Beethoven*, 3 vols. (London: Macmillan, 1961).

—— *The Letters of Mozart and his Family* (rev. 3rd edn., London: Macmillan, 1985).

ARNOLD, F. T., *The Art of Accompaniment from a Thorough-Bass as Practised in the XVIIth and XVIIIth Centuries* (London: OUP, 1931; repr., 2 vols., New York: Dover, 1965).

BADURA-SKODA, E., 'Performance Conventions in Beethoven's Early Works', in R. Winter and B. Carr (eds.), *Beethoven, Performers, and Critics: The International Beethoven Congress, Detroit, 1977* (Detroit: Wayne State University Press, 1980), 52–76.

—— 'Prolegomena to a History of the Viennese Fortepiano', *Israel Studies in Musicology*, 2 (1980): 77–99.

—— ed., *Joseph Haydn: Bericht über den Internationalen Joseph Haydn Kongress, Wien 1982* (Munich: Henle, 1986).

—— 'Zur Frühgeschichte des Hammerklaviers', in C.-H. Mahling (ed.), *Florilegium Musicologicum: Hellmut Federhofer zum 75. Geburtstag* (Mainzer Studien zur Musikwissenschaft, 21; Tutzing: Schneider, 1988), 37–44.

—— 'Komponierte J. S. Bach "Hammerklavier-Konzerte"?', *BJb* (1991): 159–71.

BADURA-SKODA, P., 'Beiträge zu Haydns Ornamentik', *Musica*, 36 (Sept.–Oct. 1982); 409–18 errata in *Musica*, 36 (Nov.–Dec. 1982): 575.

—— 'Mozart's Trills', in Todd and Williams (eds.), *Perspectives on Mozart Performance*, 1–26.

BADURA-SKODA, P. and E., *Mozart-Interpretation* (Vienna, 1957); trans. L. Black as *Interpreting Mozart on the Keyboard* (London: Barrie & Rockliff, 1962).

BAMBERGER, J., 'The Musical Significance of Beethoven's Fingerings in the Piano Sonatas', *Music Forum*, 4 (1976): 237–80.

BARNETT, D., 'Non-Uniform Slurring in 18th-Century Music: Accident or Design?' *HYb* 10 (1978): 179–99.

BARTHA, D., ed., *Joseph Haydn: Gesammelte Briefe und Aufzeichnungen* (Kassel: Bärenreiter, 1965).

BECKER-GLAUCH, I., 'Franz Joseph Haydn', *RISM*, series A, I/4: 140–279.

—— 'Die Cellostimme in Haydns Klaviertrio Hob. XV: 32', in E. Badura-Skoda (ed.), *Haydn Kongress, Wien, 1982*, 568–71.

BENTON, R., 'A Resumé of the Haydn–Pleyel "Trio Controversy" with Some Added Contributions', *H-St* 4/2 (May 1978): 114–16.

BEYSCHLAG, A. *Die Ornamentik der Musik* (Leipzig, 1908; repr., Wiesbaden: Sandig, 1970).

BILSON, M., 'Execution and Expression in the Sonata in E flat, K282', *EM* 20/2 (May 1992): 237–43.

BOALCH, D. H., *Makers of the Harpsichord and Clavichord: 1440–1840* (2nd edn., Oxford: OUP, 1974).

BONDS, M. E., *Wordless Rhetoric: Musical Form and the Metaphor of the Oration* (Studies in the History of Music, 4; Cambridge, Mass.: Harvard University Press, 1991).

BRENET, M., *Les Concerts en France sous l'ancien régime* (Paris, 1900; repr., New York: Da Capo, 1970).

BRODER, N., 'Mozart and the Clavier', *MQ* 27 (1941): 422–32.

BROWN, A. P., 'Problems of Authenticity in Two Haydn Keyboard Works (Hoboken XVI:47 and XIV:7)', *JAMS* 25/1 (Spring 1972): 85–97.

—— 'Notes on Some Eighteenth-Century Viennese Copyists', *JAMS* 34/2 (Summer 1981): 325–38.

—— 'Joseph Haydn and C. P. E. Bach: The Question of Influence', in Larsen, Serwer, and Webster (eds.), *Haydn Studies,* 158–64.

—— *Joseph Haydn's Keyboard Music: Sources and Style* (Bloomington, Ind.: Indiana University Press, 1986).

—— *Performing Haydn's 'The Creation': Reconstructing the Earliest Renditions* (Bloomington, Ind.: Indiana University Press, 1986).

—— and BERKENSTOCK, J. T., 'Joseph Haydn in Literature: A Bibliography', *H-St* 3/3–4 (July 1974): 173–352.

BROWN, H. M., and SADIE, S., eds., *Performance Practice: Music after 1600* (New Grove Handbooks in Music; London: Macmillan, 1989).

BROYLES, M., 'Organic Form and the Binary Repeat', *MQ* 66/3 (July 1980): 339–60.

BRUSATTI, O., ed., *Joseph Haydn. Klaviersonate in Es-Dur, Hob. XVI: 49, Vollständige Faksimile-Ausgabe* (Graz: Akademische Druck- und Verlagsanstalt, 1982).

CHURGIN, B., 'Francesco Galeazzi's Description (1796) of Sonata Form', *JAMS* 21/2 (Summer 1968): 181–99.

COLLINS, M., 'The Performance of Triplets in the 17th and 18th Centuries', *JAMS* 19/3 (Fall 1966): 281–328.

—— 'A Reconsideration of French Over-Dotting', *ML* 50/1 (Jan. 1969): 111–23.

—— 'In Defense of the French Trill', *JAMS* 26/3 (Fall 1973): 405–39.

CRUTCHFIELD, W., 'Voices', in Brown and Sadie (eds.), *Performance Practice: Music after 1600*, 292–319.

Dadelsen, G. von, ed., *Editionsrichtlinien musikalischer Denkmäler und Gesamtausgaben* (Kassel: Bärenreiter, 1967).

Dannreuther, E., *Musical Ornamentation*, 2 vols. (London: Novello [1897]).

Darbellay, E., 'C. P. E. Bach's Aesthetic as Reflected in his Notation', in S. Clark (ed.), *C. P. E. Bach Studies* (Oxford: Clarendon Press, 1988), 43–63.

Dart, T., *The Interpretation of Early Music* (London: Hutchinson, 1954).

Deutsch, O. E., *Mozart: A Documentary Biography* (rev. edn., London: Simon & Schuster, 1990).

Dolmetsch, A., *The Interpretation of the Music of the Seventeenth and Eighteenth Centuries* (London: Novello, 1915).

Donington, R., *The Interpretation of Early Music* (London: Faber & Faber, 1963; rev. edn., 1989).

—— *The Performer's Guide to Baroque Music* (London, 1973).

—— 'Ornamentation', in S. Sadie (ed.), *The New Grove Dictionary of Music and Musicians* (London: Macmillan, 1980).

Dreyfus, L., 'Early Music Defended against its Devotees: A Theory of Historical Performance in the Twentieth Century', *MQ* 69/3 (Summer 1983): 297–322.

Dunsby, J., 'The Formal Repeat', *JRMA* 112/2 (1987): 196–207.

Ehrlich, C., *The Piano: A History*, (rev. edn., Oxford: Clarendon Press, 1990).

Eibner, F., 'Die authentische Klavierfassung von Haydns Variationen über "Gott erhalte" ', *HYb* 7 (1970): 281–306.

—— and Jarecki, G., eds., *Joseph Haydn: Klavierstücke* (Vienna: Universal, 1975).

Emery, W., *Bach's Ornaments* (London: Novello, 1953).

Feder, G., 'Zur Datierung Haydnscher Werke', in J. Schmidt-Görg (ed.), *Anthony van Hoboken: Festschrift zum 75. Geburtstag* (Mainz: Schott, 1962), 50–4.

—— 'Probleme einer Neuordnung der Klaviersonaten Haydns', in A. A. Abert and W. Pfannkuch (eds.), *Festschrift Friedrich Blume zum 70. Geburtstag* (Kassel: Bärenreiter, 1963), 92–103.

—— 'Zwei Haydnzugeschriebene Klaviersonaten', in G. Reichert and M. Just (eds.), *Gesellschaft für Musikforschung: Bericht über den internationalen Musikwissenschaftlichen Kongress Kassel, 1962.* (Kassel: Bärenreiter, 1963), 181–4.

—— 'Die Überlieferung und Verbreitung der handschriftlichen Quellen zu Haydns Werken (Erste Folge)', *H-St* 1/1 (June 1965): 3–42, trans. E. Hartzell as 'Manuscript Sources of Haydn's Works and Their Distribution', *HYb* 4 (1968): 10–39.

—— and Larsen, J. P., 'Haydn-Ausgabe', in Dadelsen (ed.), *Editionsrichtlinien musikalischen Denkmäler und Gesamtausgabe*, 81–98.

FEDER, G., 'Wieviel Orgelkonzerte hat Haydn geschrieben?', *Mf* 23/4 (Oct.–Dec. 1970): 440–4.

—— 'Haydns frühe Klaviertrios: Eine Untersuchung zur Echtheit und Chronologie', *H-St* 2/4 (Dec. 1970): 289–316.

—— 'Die Eingriffe des Musikverlegers Hummel in Haydns Werken', in H. Hüschen (ed.), *Musicae Scientiae Collectanea: Festschrift Karl Gustav Fellerer zum siebzigsten am 7 Juli 1972* (Cologne: Volk, 1973), 88–101.

—— 'Bemerkungen zu Haydns Skizzen', *Beethoven-Jahrbuch* (1973–7): 69–86.

—— 'Haydns Korrekturen zum Klavierauszug der "Jahreszeiten" ', in T. Kohlhase and V. Scherliess (eds.), *Festschrift Georg von Dadelsen zum 60. Geburtstag* (Neuhausen: Hanssler, 1978), 101–12.

—— 'Über Haydns Skizzen zu nicht identifizierten werken', in D. Altenburg (ed.), *Ars Musica. Musica Scientia: Festschrift Heinrich Hüschen zum 65. Geburtstag* (Cologne: Gitarre & Laute Verlagsgesellschaft, 1980), 100–11.

—— 'Die Echtheitskritik in ihrer Bedeutung für die Haydn–Gesamtausgabe', in H. Bennwitz, G. Buschmeier, G. Feder, K. Hofmann, and W. Plath (eds.), *Opera incerta: Echtheitsfragen als Problem musikwissenschaftlicher Gesamtausgaben*, Kolloquium Mainz 1988. (Akademie der Wissenschaften und der Literatur; Stuttgart: Steiner, 1991), 71–106.

FERGUSON, H., *Keyboard Interpretation* (London: OUP, 1975).

FILLION, M., 'Eine bisher unbekannte Quelle für Haydns frühes Klaviertrio Hob. XV: C1', *H-St* 5/1 (Mar. 1982): 59–63.

—— 'Scoring and Genre in Haydn's Divertimenti Hob. XIV', in E. Badura-Skoda (ed.), *Haydn Kongress, Wien, 1982*, 435–44.

FINSCHER, L., *Studien zur Geschichte des Streichquartetts*, i. *Die Entstehung des klassischen Streichquartetts: Von den Vorformen zur Grundlegung durch Joseph Haydn* (Saarbrücker Studien zur Musikwissenschaft, 3; Kassel: Bärenreiter, 1974).

FORSCHNER, H., *Instrumentalmusik Joseph Haydns aus der Sicht Heinrich Christoph Kochs* (Beiträge zur Musikforschung, 13; Munich: Musikverlag Emil Katzbichler, 1984).

FOX, P., 'The Stylistic Anomalies of C. P. E. Bach's Nonconstancy', in S. Clark (ed.), *C. P. E. Bach Studies* (Oxford: Clarendon Press, 1988), 105–31.

FRANZ, G., 'Mozarts Klavierbauer Anton Walter', *MJb* 1 (1941): 211–17.

FRUEHWALD, S., *Authenticity Problems in Joseph Haydn's Early Instrumental Works: A Stylistic Investigation* (Monographs in Musicology, 8; New York: Pendragon, 1988).

FULLER, D., ed., *Armand-Louis Couperin: Selected Works for Keyboard*, 2 vols. (Recent Researches in the Music of the Pre-Classical, Classical, and Early Romantic Eras; Madison: A-R Editions, 1975).

GEIRINGER, K., *Haydn: A Creative Life in Music* (2nd edn., London: Allen & Unwin, 1964).

GERLACH, S., ed., *Haydn: Klavierstücke, Klaviervariationen* (2nd edn., Munich: Henle, 1981).

GERICKE, H., *Der Wiener Musikalienhandel 1700–1778* (Wiener Musikwissenschaftliche Beiträge, 5; Graz: Hermann Böhlaus, 1960).

GERSTENBERG, W., 'Authentische Tempi für Mozarts "Don Giovanni"?', *MJb* (1960–1): 58–61.

GILBERT, K., Preface to *The Sonatas of Scarlatti*, i (Paris: Heugel, 1984).

GOOD, E. M., *Giraffes, Black Dragons and Other Pianos: A Technological History from Cristofori to the Modern Concert Grand* (Stanford: Stanford University Press, 1982).

GOTWALS, V., *Haydn: Two Contemporary Portraits* (Madison: University of Wisconsin Press, 1968).

GRUNDMANN, H., 'Per il Clavicembalo o Piano-Forte', in S. Kross and H. Schmidt (eds.), *Colloquium Amicorum. Joseph Schmidt-Görg zum 70. Geburtstag* (Bonn: Beethovenhaus, 1967), 100–17.

HAAS, R., *Aufführungspraxis der Musik* (Handbuch der Musikwissenschaft, ed. E. Bücken; Potsdam: Akademische Verlagsgesellschaft Athenaion, 1934).

HARDING, R., *The Pianoforte: Its History Traced to the Great Exhibition of 1851* (Cambridge: CUP, 1933; repr., New York: Da Capo, 1973).

HASE, H. VON, *Joseph Haydn und Breitkoph & Härtel. Ein Rückblick bei der Veranstaltung der ersten vollständigen Gesamtausgabe seiner Werke* (Leipzig: Breitkopf & Härtel, 1909).

HATTING, C., 'Haydn oder Kayser?—Eine Echtheitsfrage', *Mf* 25/2 (Apr.–June 1972): 82–7.

HAYDN, *Joseph Haydn Werke* (Munich: Henle, 1958–).

HELM, E., *Thematic Catalogue of the Works of Carl Philipp Emanuel Bach* (New Haven: Yale University Press, 1989).

HESS, A. G., 'The Transition from Harpsichord to Piano', *GSJ* 6 (1953): 77–83.

HOBOKEN, A. VAN, *Joseph Haydn: Thematisch-bibliographisches Werkverzeichnis*, 3 vols. (Mainz: Schott, 1957–78).

HOGWOOD, C., 'A Supplement to C. P. E. Bach's *Versuch*: E. W. Wolf's *Anleitung* of 1785', in S. Clark (ed.), *C. P. E. Bach Studies* (Oxford: Clarendon Press, 1988), 133–57.

HOLLIS, H. R., *Pianos in the Smithsonian Institution* (Smithsonian Studies in History and Technology, 27; Washington: Smithsonian Institute Press, 1972).

—— *The Piano: A Pictorial Account of its Ancestry and Development* (London: David & Charles, 1975).

—— *The Musical Instruments of Joseph Haydn: An Introduction* (Smithsonian

Studies in History and Technology, 38; Washington: Smithsonian Institute Press, 1977).

HOULE, G., *Metre in Music, 1600–1800: Performance, Perception, and Notation* (Bloomington, Ind.: Indiana University Press, 1987).

HUBBARD, F., *Three Centuries of Harpsichord Making* (Cambridge, Mass.: Harvard University Press, 1965).

JACKSON, R., *Performance Practice, Medieval to Contemporary: A Bibliographic Guide* (New York: Garland, 1988).

JAMES, P., 'Haydn's Clavichord and a Sonata Manuscript', *MT* 71 (Apr. 1930): 314–16.

JENKINS, G., 'The Legato Touch and the "Ordinary" Manner of Keyboard Playing from 1750 to 1850', 2 vols., Ph.D. diss., Cambridge University, 1976.

JOHNSTONE, H. D. and FISKE, R. (eds.), *Music in Britain: The Eighteenth Century* (Blackwell History of Music in Britain; Oxford: Blackwell, 1990).

KELLER, H., *Phrasierung und Artikulation* (Kassel: Bärenreiter, 1955); trans. L. Gerdine (London: Barrie & Rockliff, 1966).

KENYON, N., ed., *Authenticity and Early Music* (Oxford: OUP, 1988).

KINSKY, G., 'Haydn und das Hammerklavier', *ZfMw* 13 (June–July 1931): 500–1.

KIRKPATRICK, R., 'C. P. E. Bach's *Versuch* Reconsidered', *EM* 4/4 (Oct. 1976): 384–92.

KLEINDIENST, S., 'Haydns Clavier-Werke: Kriterien der Instrumenten-wahl', in E. Badura-Skoda (ed.), *Haydn Kongress, Wien, 1982*, 53–64.

KOLISCH, R., 'Tempo and Character in Beethoven's Music', *MQ* 29/2 (Apr. 1943): 169–87, 29/3 (July 1943): 291–312; revised repr. *MQ* 77/1 (Spring 1993): 90–131, 77/2 (Summer 1993): 268–342, with an introd. by T. Levin, 'Integral Interpretation: Introductory Notes to Beethoven, Kolisch and the Question of the Metronome', *MQ* 77/1 (Spring 1993): 80–9.

KRONES, H., 'Carl Philipp Emanuel Bachs Präsenz im Wien des 18. Jahrhunderts', in *Konferenzbericht der XVI. Wissenschaftlichen Arbeitstagung, Michaelstein, 9. bis 12. Juni 1988: Studien zur Aufführungspraxis und Interpretation der Musik des 18. Jahrhunderts*, 39: 39–51.

LANDON, C., ed., *Joseph Haydn: Sämtliche Klaviersonaten*, 3 vols. (Vienna: Universal, 1964–6; 3rd edn., Vienna: Universal, 1972); *Kritische Anmerkungen* (Vienna: Universal, 1982).

LANDON, H. C. R., *The Symphonies of Joseph Haydn* (London: Universal & Rockliff, 1955; suppl., London: Barrie & Rockliff, 1961).

—— ed., *The Collected Correspondence and London Notebooks of Joseph Haydn* (London: Barrie & Rockliff, 1959).

—— *The Piano Trios of Joseph Haydn: Foreword to the First Critical Complete Edition* (Vienna: Doblinger, 1970).

—— *Haydn: Chronicle and Works*, 5 vols. (London: Thames & Hudson, 1976–80).

—— *Haydn: A Documentary Study* (London: Thames & Hudson, 1981).

—— 'Joseph Haydn: A Sketch to Piano Trio No. 30 (Hob. xv: 17)', *HYb* 13 (1982): 220–7.

—— 'Editorial', *EM* 10/3 (1982): 298–9.

—— and JONES, D. W., *Haydn: His Life and Music* (London: Thames & Hudson, 1988).

LARSEN, J. P., *Die Haydn-Überlieferung* (Copenhagen: Einar Munksgaard, 1939).

—— ed., *Drei Haydn Kataloge in Faksimile* (Copenhagen: Einar Munksgaard, 1941); revd. edn. as *Three Haydn Catalogues* (New York: Pendragon Press, 1979).

—— 'Eine bisher unbeachtete Quelle zu Haydns frühen Klavierwerken', in D. Weise (ed.), *Festschrift Joseph Schmidt-Görg zum 60. Geburtstag* (Bonn: Beethovenhaus, 1957), 188–95.

—— ed., *Joseph Haydn: Klaviersonate A-dur [Hob. : 26]. Faksimile* (Munich: Henle, 1958).

—— 'A Haydn Contract', *MT* 17 (Sept. 1976): 737–8.

—— *Handel, Haydn & the Viennese Classical Style* (Ann Arbor: UMI, 1988).

—— and FEDER, G., 'Haydn', in S. Sadie (ed.), *The New Grove Dictionary of Music and Musicians* (London: Macmillan, 1980); revd. edn. as *The New Grove Haydn* (London: Macmillan, 1982).

—— SERWER, H., and WEBSTER, J. (eds.), *Haydn Studies: Proceedings of the International Haydn Conference, Washington, 1975* (New York: Norton, 1981).

LATCHAM, M., 'The Check in Some Early Pianos and the Development of Piano Technique around the Turn of the 18th Century', *EM* 21/1 (Feb. 1993): 28–42.

LEE, D., 'Some Embellished Versions of Sonatas by Franz Benda', *MQ* 62/1 (Jan. 1976): 58–71.

LEVIN, R., 'Improvised Embellishment in Mozart's Keyboard Music', *EM* 20/2 (May 1992): 221–33.

—— 'Instrumental Ornamentation, Improvisation, and Cadenzas', in Brown and Sadie (eds.), *Performance Practice: Music after 1600* (London: Macmillan, 1989), 267–91.

LUITHLEN, V., 'Der Eisenstädter Walterflügel', *MJb* (1954): 206–8.

—— 'Haydn-Erinnerungen in der Sammlung alter Musikinstrumente des Kunsthistorischen Museums zu Wien', in J. Schmidt-Görg, *Anthony van Hoboken: Festschrift zum 75. Geburtstag* (Mainz: Schott, 1962), 100–14.

MACDONALD, H., 'To Repeat or Not to Repeat?', *PRMA* 111 (1984–5): 121–38.

MALLOCH, W., 'Carl Czerny's Metronome Marks for Haydn and Mozart Symphonies', *EM* 16/1 (Feb. 1988): 72–82.

—— 'The Minuets of Haydn and Mozart: Goblins or Elephants?', *EM* 21/3 (Aug. 1993): 437–44.

MARTY, J.-P., 'Mozart's Tempo Indications and the Problems of Interpretation', in Todd and Williams (eds.), *Perspectives on Mozart Performance*, 55–73.

MARX, H., 'Some Unknown Embellishments of Corelli's Violin Sonatas', *MQ* 61/1 (Jan. 1975): 65–76.

MAUNDER, R., 'Mozart's Keyboard Instruments', *EM* 20/2 (May 1992): 207–19.

MELKUS, E., 'Zur Auszierung der Da-Capo-Arien in Mozarts Werken', *MJb* (1968–70): 159–85.

MERTIN, J., 'Zu den Orgelinstrumenten Joseph Haydns', in E. Badura-Skoda (ed.), *Haydn Kongress, Wien, 1982*, 72–5.

MIES, P., 'Die Artikulationzeichen Strich und Punkt bei Wolfgang Amadeus Mozart', *Mf* 11 (1958): 428–55.

MÖRNER, C.-G. STELLAN, 'Haydiana aus Schweden um 1800', *H-St* 2/1 (Mar. 1969): 1–33.

MÜNSTER, R., 'Authentische Tempi zu den sechs letzten Sinfonien W. A. Mozarts?', *MJb* (1962–3): 185–99.

NEUMANN, F., 'Misconceptions about the French Trill in the 17th and 18th Centuries', *MQ* 50/2 (Apr. 1964): 188–206.

—— 'The French *Inégales*, Quantz, and Bach', *JAMS* 18/3 (Fall 1965): 313–58.

—— 'A New Look at Bach's Ornamentation', *ML* 46/1 (Jan. 1965): 4–15, 46/2 (April 1965): 126–33.

—— 'La Note pointée et la soi-disant "manière française"', *Revue de Musicologie*, 51 (1965): 66–92.

—— 'External Evidence and Uneven Notes', *MQ* 52/4 (Oct. 1966): 448–64.

—— 'The Use of Baroque Treatises on Musical Performance', *ML* 48/4 (Oct. 1967): 315–24.

—— 'Ornament and Structure', *MQ* 56/2 (Apr. 1970): 153–61.

—— *Ornamentation in Baroque and Post-Baroque Music: With Special Emphasis on J. S. Bach* (Princeton: Princeton University Press, 1978).

—— *Essays in Performance Practice* (Studies in Musicology, 58; Ann Arbor: UMI, 1982).

—— *Ornamentation and Improvisation in Mozart* (Princeton: Princeton University Press, 1986).

—— 'Bemerkungen über Haydns Ornamentik', in E. Badura-Skoda (ed.), *Haydn Kongress, Wien, 1982*, 35–42; trans. as 'Remarks on Haydn's Ornaments', in *New Essays on Performance Practice* (Ann Arbor: UMI, 1989), 93–104.

—— 'More on Haydn's Ornaments and the Evidence of the Musical Clocks', in *New Essays in Performance Practice* (Ann Arbor: UMI, 1989), 105–19.

—— 'Dots and Strokes in Mozart', *EM* 21/3 (Aug. 1993): 429–35.

NEWMAN, W. S., *The Sonata in the Classic Era* (Chapel Hill, NC: University of North Carolina Press, 1963).

—— *The Sonata since Beethoven* (Chapel Hill, NC: University of North Carolina Press, 1969).

—— 'Haydn as Ingenious Exploiter of the Keyboard', in E. Badura-Skoda (ed.), *Haydn Kongress, Wien, 1982*, 43–53.

—— *Beethoven on Beethoven: Playing His Piano Music His Way* (New York: Norton, 1988).

NOTTEBOHM, G., *Beethoveniana* (Leipzig: Peters, 1872).

ORD-HUME, A., *Joseph Haydn and the Mechanical Organ* (Cardiff: University College Cardiff Press, 1982).

PARRISH, K., 'The Early Piano and Its Influence on Keyboard Technique and Composition in the Eighteenth Century', Ph.D. diss., Harvard University, 1939).

—— 'Haydn and the Piano', *JAMS* 1/3 (Fall 1948): 27–34.

PÄSLER, K., ed., *Joseph Haydn: Klavierwerke, Joseph Haydns Werke*, XIV/1–3 (Leipzig: Breitkopf & Härtel, 1918).

PLANTINGA, L., *Clementi: His Life and Music* (London: OUP, 1977).

POLLACK, H., 'Some Thoughts on the "Clavier" in Haydn's Solo *Claviersonaten*', *Journal of Musicology*, 19/1 (Winter 1991): 74–91.

PRAEGER, F., 'On the Fallacy of the Repetition of Parts in the Classical Form', *Papers of the Musical Association*, 9 (1882–3): 1–16.

RADICE, M., 'Haydn and his Publishers: A Brief Survey of the Composer's Publishing Activities', *MR* 44/2 (May 1983): 87–94.

RATNER, L., *Classic Music: Expression, Form, and Style* (New York: Schirmer, 1980).

REILLY, E., *Quantz and his Versuch: Three Studies* (American Musicological Society, Studies and Documents, 5; New York: Galaxy, 1971).

RICE, J., 'The Tuscan Piano in the 1780s', *EM* 21/1 (Feb. 1993): 5–26.

RIPIN, E., ed., *Keyboard Instruments: Studies in Keyboard Organology, 1150–1800* (Edinburgh: Edinburgh University Press, 1971; 2nd edn., New York: Dover, 1977).

—— 'Haydn and the Keyboard Instruments of His Time', in Larsen, Serwer, and Webster (eds.), *Haydn Studies*, 302–8.

ROGERS, P. J., *Continuo Realization in Handel's Vocal Music* (Studies in Music, 104; Ann Arbor: UMI, 1989).

ROSEN, C., *The Classical Style: Haydn, Mozart, Beethoven* (London: Faber & Faber, 1971).

—— 'Influence: Plagiarism and Inspiration', *19th Century Music*, 4/2 (Fall 1980): 87–100.

ROSENBLUM, S., *Performance Practices in Classic Piano Music: Their Principles and Application* (Bloomington, Ind.: Indiana University Press, 1988).

ROTHSCHILD, F., *Musical Performance in the Time of Mozart and Beethoven* (Lost Tradition in Music, 2; London: Adam and Charles Black, 1961).

ROWLAND, D., 'Early Piano Pedalling: 1750–1850', Ph.D. diss., Cambridge University, 1986.

—— 'Early Pianoforte Pedalling: The Evidence of the Earliest Printed Markings', *EM* 13/1 (Feb. 1985): 5–17.

RÜCK, U., 'Mozarts Hammerflügel erbaute Anton Walter, Wien', *MJb* (1955): 246–62.

RUDOLF, M., 'Ein Beitrag zur Geschichte der Temponahme bei Mozart', *MJb* (1976–7): 202–24.

RUSSELL, R., *The Harpsichord and Clavichord* (London: Faber & Faber, 1959).

SADIE, S., *Mozart: Sonatas for Piano*, i (London: Associated Board of the Royal Schools of Music [1981]).

SASLAV, I., 'Tempos in the String Quartets of Joseph Haydn', D.M. diss., Indiana University, 1969.

SCHENKER, H., *Ein Beitrag zur Ornamentik* (Vienna: Universal, 1903); trans. H. Siegel as 'A Contribution to the Study of Ornamentation', *Music Forum*, 4 (1976): 1–139.

SCHMID, E. F., 'Joseph Haydn und die Flötenuhr', *ZfMw* 14 (Jan. 1932): 193–221.

—— 'Joseph Haydn und Carl Philipp Emanuel Bach', *ZfMw* 14 (Mar. 1932): 299–312.

—— 'Die Göttweiger Sonaten von Joseph Haydn', *ZfM* 104 (Apr. 1937): 429.

—— 'Franz Anton Hoffmeister und die "Göttweiger Sonaten" '. *ZfM* 104 (July–Oct. 1937): 760–70, 889–95, 992–1000, 1109–17.

—— 'Joseph Haydn und die vokale Zierpraxis seiner Zeit, dargestellt an einer Arie seines Tobias-Oratoriums', in B. Szabolcsi and D. Bartha (eds.), *Bericht über die Internationale Konferenz zum Andenken Joseph Haydns, Budapest, September 1959* (Budapest: Akadémiai Kiadó, 1961), 117–30.

SCHOTT, H., 'From Harpsichord to Pianoforte: A Chronology and Commentary', *EM* 13/i (Feb. 1985): 28–38.

SCHWARZ, V., 'Die Rolle des Cembalos in Österreich nach 1760', in id. (ed.), *Der junge Haydn: Bericht der Internationalen Arbeitstagung des Instituts für Aufführungspraxis der Hochschule für Musik und darstellende Kunst, Graz, 1970* (Beiträge zur Aufführungspraxis, 1; Graz: Akademische Druck- und Verlagsanstalt, 1972), 249–58.

—— 'Missverständnisse in der Haydn-Interpretation', *ÖMz* 31/1 (Jan. 1976): 25–35.

SERWER, H., 'C. P. E. Bach, J. C. F. Rellstab, and the Sonatas with Varied

Reprises', in S. Clark (ed.), *C. P. E. Bach Studies* (Oxford: Clarendon Press, 1988), 233–43.

SISMAN, E., 'Haydn's Hybrid Variations', in Larsen, Serwer, and Webster (eds.), *Haydn Studies* (New York: Norton, 1981), 509–15.

—— 'Haydn's Theater Symphonies', *JAMS* 43/2 (Summer 1990): 292–352.

—— *Haydn and the Classical Variation* (Studies in the History of Music, 5; Cambridge, Mass.: Harvard University Press, 1993).

SOMFAI, L., *Joseph Haydn: His Life in Contemporary Pictures* (London: Faber & Faber, 1969).

—— 'The London Revision of Haydn's Instrumental Style', *PRMA* 100 (1973–4): 159–74.

—— 'An Introduction to the Study of Haydn's Quartet Autographs (with Special Attention to Opus 77/G)', in C. Wolff (ed.), *The String Quartets of Haydn, Mozart, and Beethoven: Studies of the Autograph Manuscripts* (Isham Library Papers, 3; Cambridge, Mass.: Harvard University Press, 1980), 5–51; 'Response (Larsen) and Discussion', 52–61.

—— 'How to Read and Understand Haydn's Notation in its Chronologically Changing Concepts', in E. Badura-Skoda (ed.), *Haydn Kongress, Wien, 1982*, 23–35, 42.

STEGLICH, R., 'Eine Klaviersonate Johann Gottfried Schwanbergs (Schwanenberg[er]s) in der Joseph Haydn Gesamtausgabe', *ZfMw* 15 (Nov. 1932): 77–9.

—— 'Kadenzen in Haydns Klaviersonaten', *ZfM* 99 (Apr. 1932): 295–7.

STOWELL, R., *Violin Technique and Performance Practice in the Late Eighteenth and Early Nineteenth Centuries* (Cambridge: CUP, 1985).

—— 'Leopold Mozart Revised: Articulation in Violin Playing during the Second Half of the Eighteenth Century', in Todd and Williams (eds.), *Perspectives on Mozart Performance*, 126–57.

STRUNK, G., 'Notes on a Haydn Autograph', *MQ* 20/2 (Apr. 1934): 192–205.

TARUSKIN, R., 'The Limits of Authenticity: A Discussion', *EM* 12/1 (Feb. 1984): 3–12.

—— 'The Pastness of the Present and the Presence of the Past', in Kenyon (ed.), *Authenticity and Early Music*, 137–207.

TEMPERLEY, N., 'Haydn's Tempos in *The Creation*', *EM* 19/2 (May 1991): 235–45.

THAYER, A., *Thayer's Life of Beethoven*, ed. E. Forbes (rev. edn., Princeton: Princeton University Press, 1967).

TODD, R. L. and WILLIAMS, P. (eds.), *Perspectives on Mozart Performance* (Cambridge Studies in Performance Practice; Cambridge: CUP, 1991).

TOLSTOY, C., 'The Identification and Interpretation of Sign Ornaments in Haydn's Instrumental Music', in Larsen, Serwer, and Webster (eds.), *Haydn Studies*, 315–23.

TOVEY, D. F., *Essays and Lectures on Music*, ed. H. J. Foss (London: OUP, 1949).

TUNG, L., 'Indicators of Early Piano Writing in the Haydn Sonatas', in Larsen, Serwer, and Webster (eds.), *Haydn Studies*, 323–6.

TYSON, A., 'Haydn and Two Stolen Trios', *MR* 22/1 (Feb. 1961): 21–7.

—— 'New Light on a Haydn Trio (Hob. xv: 32)', *HYb* 1 (1962): 203–5.

UNVERRICHT, H., 'Haydn und Bossler', in N. Schiørring, H. Glahn, and C. Hatting (eds.), *Festkrift Jens Peter Larsen 14. VI. 1902–1972* (Copenhagen: Wilhelm Hansen Musik-Forlag, 1972), 285–300.

VINQUIST, M., and ZASLAW, N. (eds.), 'Bibliography of Performance Practices', *Current Musicology*, 8 (1969); suppls. 10 (1970); 12 (1972); 15 (1973).

WACKERNAGEL, B., *Joseph Haydns frühe Klaviersonaten: Ihre Beziehungen zur Klaviermusik um die Mitte des 18. Jahrhunderts* (Tutzing: Schneider, 1975).

WAINWRIGHT, D., *Broadwood by Appointment: A History* (London: Quiller Press, 1982).

WALTER, H. 'Haydns Klaviere', *H-St* 25/4 (Dec. 1970): 256–88.

—— 'Das Tasteninstrument beim jungen Haydn', in V. Schwarz (ed.), *Der junge Haydn: Bericht der Internationalen Arbeitstagung des Instituts für Aufführungspraxis der Hochschule für Musik und darstellende Kunst, Graz, 1970* (Beiträge zur Aufführungspraxis, 1; Graz: Akademische Druck- und Verlagsanstalt, 1972), 237–48.

—— 'Haydn's Keyboard Instruments', in Larsen, Serwer, and Webster (eds.), *Haydn Studies*, 213–16.

—— 'Haydn: Bibliographie 1973–1983', *H-St* 5/4 (1985): 205–93.

—— 'Haydns Klavierkonzerte aus textkritische Sicht', in E. Badura-Skoda (ed.), *Haydn Kongress, Wien, 1982*, 444–51.

WEBSTER, J., 'The Chronology of Haydn's String Quartets', *MQ* 61/1 (Jan. 1975): 17–46.

—— 'The Significance of Haydn's Quartet Autographs for Performance Practice', in C. Wolff (ed.), *The String Quartets of Haydn, Mozart, and Beethoven: Studies of the Autograph Manuscripts* (Isham Library Papers, 3; Cambridge, Mass.: Harvard University Press, 1980), 62–95; 'Discussion', 96–8.

—— *Haydn's 'Farewell' Symphony and the Idea of Classical Style: Through-Composition and Cyclic Integration in his Instrumental Music* (Cambridge Studies in Music Theory and Analysis; Cambridge: CUP, 1991).

WHITMORE, P., *Unpremeditated Art: The Cadenza in the Classical Keyboard Concerto* (Oxford Monographs on Music; Oxford: Clarendon Press, 1991).

WILLIAMS, P., *Figured Bass Accompaniment*, 2 vols. (Edinburgh: Edinburgh University Press, 1970).

WINTER, R., 'Keyboards', in Brown and Sadie (eds.), *Performance Practice: Music after 1600*, 346–73.

WOLLENBERG, S., 'A New Look at C. P. E. Bach's Musical Jokes', in S. Clark (ed.), *C. P. E. Bach Studies* (Oxford: Clarendon Press, 1988), 295–314.

WOTQUENNE, A., *Catalogue thématique des œuvres de Charles Philippe Emmanuel Bach* (Leipzig, 1905).

ZASLAW, N., 'Mozart's Tempo Conventions', in *Report of the Eleventh Congress of the International Musicological Society, Copenhagen 1972*, 2 vols. (Copenhagen: Hansen, 1974), ii. 720–33.

—— *Mozart's Symphonies: Context, Performance, Reception* (Oxford: Clarendon Press, 1989).

ZIMMERMAN, E., 'Das Mozart-Preisausschreiben der Gesellschaft für Musikforschung', in D. Weise (ed.), *Festschrift Joseph Schmidt-Görg zum 60. Geburtstag* (Bonn: Beethovenhaus, 1957), 400–8.

INDEX

◊

Italic numbers denote reference to music examples